Critical Essays on Thomas Hardy: The Novels

Critical Essays on Thomas Hardy: The Novels

Dale Kramer

with the assistance of
Nancy Marck

G. K. Hall & Co. • Boston, Massachusetts

First published 1990.
10 9 8 7 6 5 4 3 2 1

Critical essays on Thomas Hardy : the novels / [edited by] Dale Kramer
    with the assistance of Nancy Marck.
        p.   cm. — (Critical essays on British literature)
    ISBN 0-8161-8850-5 (alk. paper)
    1. Hardy, Thomas, 1840–1928—Criticism and interpretation.
I. Kramer, Dale, 1936–   . II. Marck, Nancy.   III. Series.
PR4754.C74   1990
823′.8—dc20
                                                                    90-30431
                                                                    CIP

The paper used in this publication meets the minimum requirements of American National
Standard for Information Sciences—Permanence of Paper for Printed Library Materials,
ANSI Z39.48-1984. ⊗™

Printed and bound in the United States of America

CRITICAL ESSAYS ON BRITISH LITERATURE

The Critical Essays on British Literature series provides a variety of approaches to both the classical writers of Britain and Ireland and the best contemporary authors. The formats of the volumes in the series vary with the thematic designs of individual editors, and with the amount and nature of existing reviews, criticism, and scholarship. In general, the series represents the best in published criticism, augmented, where appropriate, by original essays by recognized authorities. It is hoped that each volume will be unique in developing a new overall perspective on its particular subject.

Dale Kramer's book is devoted entirely to Thomas Hardy's novels. The editor's introductory historical survey is a masterful, thoughtful summary of the enormous body of scholarship accorded Hardy's work. Kramer's balanced selection of the best examples of recent Hardy criticism includes six essays representing various overall critical approaches to major segments of the Hardy canon, while the remaining two-thirds of the studies presented deal with individual major novels.

ZACK BOWEN

University of Miami

CONTENTS

INTRODUCTION
"Thomas Hardy" Then to Now

Criticism of Thomas Hardy's novels has tracked changes in the fashions of reading, even though he has never been a stable presence in literary history. His imagination created scenes and characters' dilemmas that undermined the unspoken code restricting the choice and handling of subject matter that operated through most of the nineteenth century and well beyond the First World War; to gain serial publication for several of his novels he had to rewrite scenes and alter characterizations, and his original intentions were not always revived for the book versions. Yet at a discernible if unconscious level Hardy subscribed to his culture's given "truths" governing gender roles and to the acculturated delighted anguish at the spectacle of innocent female suffering. Perhaps partly owing to this element of ultimate congruence between self and society, the manner and style of his writing seem on a first reading to be conventionally Victorian: stress on events, plots developed lineally, readers' reactions guided by a generous supply of allusions and even by direct authorial observations. But as the narrative in a novel continues, it becomes more and more apparent that straightforwardness is in the tone, not in the technique, and certainly not in the "message." In short, if an effort to convey stability (social, psychological, conceptual) underlies most nineteenth-century writing, then Hardy clearly represents a deviance, or an anticipation of the more obviously self-subversive writing of the twentieth century.

Hardy's reading of his own fiction insists upon ad hoc particularity rather than upon encompassing generalization. He notes, in the preface to the first edition of *Jude the Obscure,* that his works represent "a series of seemings, or personal impressions," not conclusions, and that he was not primarily concerned with "their consistency or their discordance" or with "their permanence or their transitoriness." Nor did he much like his works to be discussed as if they could somehow be understood according to catchwords and categories. It's true that as a concession to merchandising, he grouped them, for the Wessex Edition of his works, according to certain rubrics ("Novels of Character and Environment"; "Romances and Fantasies";

1

"Novels of Ingenuity"; and "Mixed Novels"). But his unease with such arrangements is revealed in his indecision whether to classify *A Pair of Blue Eyes* as a novel of character and environment or as a romance or fantasy, as well as whether the Wessex Edition would be a suitable occasion to reverse the title and subtitle of his second novel, to bring them into the order he had initially wanted. (The publisher advised against creating the new title *The Mellstock Quire: Under the Greenwood Tree.*)

Hardy's novels exceeded the concept of fiction his times would have constricted them with ("the times" is, of course, a euphemism for people and institutions); tracing the history of critical responses to them reflects changing interests and concerns of the critics, developments in methodology and terminology. But a consistency in the basic problems identified in Hardy's fiction and in critics' interpretations of them span the decades—for example, Philip Weinstein builds a good deal on the conflict between culture and nature, and notes that the self exists as an interplay of relations involving an individual and his or her social world.[1] Obviously, critics can disagree about basic issues, and definitions are not protected possessions of individuals. Nonetheless, with the dominance of theory in literary studies at present, it is an irony that the features that keep Hardy problematic and open—his intuitive, expressionistic psychology, his stylistic power, and the themes whose localized contexts evoke readers' personal knowledge and closest concerns— do not rely upon interpretive ingenuity, but instead enrich and measure his interpreters' methodologies.

The earliest reviewers of Hardy's novels noticed their internally discordant qualities, whose long-range effect has been to prevent settled readings. They were struck by the seemingly uncoordinated, coincidence-laden plots, and also by the rural settings where the sense of time was that of an idyll, by fantastic implausibilities mixed with poetic revelation of inner identities, and by the folklore of "Wessex" that resisted the importunities of modern existence. One of the most consistently magnetic areas in Hardy's work has been what he made of regional details, in other writers more a limitation upon their appeal than a major source of it. Perhaps the attractiveness of Hardy's use of place is apparent simplicity and rural foreignness offering the site for a markedly individual perception of alienation and instability on that level of society which made up most of the reading audience in the late nineteenth century.

A simple instance of this kind of discordance: Although the railroad plays a role in few of Hardy's novels, the narrator often refers to its presence just off-scene, as if ready to be inserted to destroy the tenor of rural isolation. Thus, agricultural rhythms of event bolster a sense of security, which is all the while being undermined by information about new machinery and processes that separate the workers from the activities that give meaning to their lives.

Apart from differences on local issues in the individual novels, and apart from emphases that have shifted as ways of reading fiction and as perspectives upon the Victorian period have changed, Hardy has been judged with remarkable consistency. From his first published novel, he was taken seriously as a writer of a level beyond those whose work may have sold more copies, and was discussed as a significant figure on the literary scene. Even the most cutting and unfriendly of the reviewers of *Desperate Remedies* recognizes "redeeming features" in the descriptive passages, which are seen to be remarkably evocative, and encourages the anonymous author of *Desperate Remedies* to write "far better ones [novels]."[2] By the time of *Far from the Madding Crowd* even critical reviewers realized they were dealing with substantial works calling for judgment not in relation to popular writers of the day, but in relation to recognized masters.

An indication of the cohesiveness of Hardy studies is that some current pieces on Hardy could have been used as starting or focus points insights by Hardy's contemporary critics. Thus, although Hardy criticism (like most criticism) reflects the most energetic critical forces of the times in which it has been produced, tracing the evolution of the "Thomas Hardy" that critical analysis purports to identify uncovers recurring points of contact. For instance, from his first novel Hardy was praised for his female characters more than for his male ones,[3] to the extent that Havelock Ellis in one of the first retrospective reviews of Hardy's career (going up to 1883) said that only John Loveday of *The Trumpet-Major* was a match for Hardy's many strong female characters.[4] Hardy's reaction was to write *The Mayor of Casterbridge*, about which there can be no question of the gender of the most dominant character—although according to Elaine Showalter even this novel shows the development of the feminine side of Henchard's nature.[5] But the next three novels after *The Mayor of Casterbridge* rest upon Hardy's remarkable empathy with female characters, not overlooking the harsh angularity of male treatment of females. And most critics still build their cases more on Eustacia than on Clym, and more on Sue than on Jude even though Jude is nearly as complex and problematic as Sue.

Hardy's evident response to Ellis is one of the instances in which he allowed criticism to guide his efforts with future novels without compromising his sense of artistic requirements. (A damaging instance was the turning away in 1875 from the topic that became *The Woodlanders* because he feared becoming "typed" as a novelist of rural scenes, delaying for nearly a decade his recognizing and sticking with his true mode.) But Hardy was not dependent upon his critics to know how to shape his work. He was able to allow suggestions to affect certain aspects of certain works, but the larger curves of his career were not to be altered by advice or opposition. The most obvious area of Hardy's independence is in the treatment of "morality" or of sensitive issues of human relations. With nearly all of his novels, one or more readers raised questions of propriety (for instance, the revelation in *Desperate Remedies* that Aeneas Manston is the son of the unmarried Miss Aldclyffe); and toward the end of his career as a novelist the majority of contemporary reviewers were evaluating the stories according to conventional moral and aesthetic standards. Such readers did not query *The Mayor of Casterbridge*, perhaps because the largest act of immorality, Henchard's monstrous selling of his wife and child, dwarfed lesser offenses that they ordinarily would have complained of (e.g., Susan's living with Newson for many years—but perhaps their silence reflects the fact that this irregular arrangement was within the lower classes and thus less offensive to genteel readers). But *The Wood-landers* made many readers distinctly uneasy, and some of them angry, particularly with its climactic portrayal of Grace's reacceptance of her truant husband.[6] For the second English edition of this novel Hardy made revisions clarifying that Grace was in for a bad time with Fitzpiers, suggesting that he may have seen the aesthetic merit of their complaints, which had been voiced on moral grounds. When Hardy finished the manuscript of *Tess of the d'Urbervilles* he evidently felt it appropriate to subtitle the book "*A Pure Woman Faithfully Presented*" and to add the line attributing to "the President of the Immortals" the motive for destroying Tess as a game of "sport." The moralists were outraged with these implicit criticisms of conventional positions. But Hardy held an agenda independent of reviewers' pressure that he conform. In contrast to his acceding to reviewers' objections about Fitzpiers, Hardy's subsequent revisions of *Tess of the d'Urbervilles* emphasized Tess's unusual personality and made Alec's more shallow and melodramatic. His revisions also stubbornly refused either to backtrack from declaring that Tess was a "pure" woman or to remove decisively indications in the text that Tess had *not* been raped.[7] Likewise, Hardy did not allow their attacks to affect his working out of *Jude the Obscure*. He took the course of implying that the plot was more a product of his characters than of his intentions—that is, that his characters simply did what they had to do, that his creating their situations had provided them with minds of their own.[8]

Despite Hardy's lifelong complaint of the impercipience and unfairness of critics, then, he held his own with them, and in fact, all in all he was not badly treated. He was thin-skinned, and resentful of criticism. But this does not mean his sensitivity ended his career as a novelist. He had better reasons to stop writing fiction so suddenly, despite his string of stories whose power he could measure by critics' outrage and whose advanced art by their misunderstandings. He had a more "literary" ambition than to be a writer only of novels. It would not be unreasonable to suggest that Hardy—having attained financial security with the great success of *Tess of the d'Urbervilles* and having that security enlarged with *Jude the Obscure*—simply seized opportunistically upon several of the denunciating critics' outbursts. As if to confirm his response to the *Quarterly Review*'s slashing attack on *Tess of the d'Urbervilles*—"A man must be a fool to deliberately stand up to be shot at"[9]—he retired from the fray he had invigorated with his controversial fiction, in order to devote the remainder of his life to poetry.

In addition to reviews, published commentary on Hardy's fiction during his productive career came in the form of "retrospectives," or summations of what he had accomplished to date. One of the first as well as the best known of these has already been cited, Havelock Ellis's respectful chiding in the *Westminster Review* in April 1883. Ellis emphasized that although he regretted it, he expected to see more novels in Hardy's future like *The Trumpet Major* and *Two on a Tower* rather than *Far from the Madding Crowd*, which he admired above all other Hardy novels to that time. Ellis, then, not only may be the spur for the creation of the masculine Henchard but probably also helped to turn Hardy away from the occasional or topical and the historical novels he had written following *The Return of the Native*, back to novels set squarely in "Wessex" and taking place in an indeterminate time setting that is not the present. The small cluster of J. M. Barrie's (1889), Edmund Gosse's (1890), and William Minto's (1891) retrospectives concentrate on the qualities of "Wessex" and of Hardy's women characters. Barrie, for instance, laments that Hardy had "thrown away skill on books [the non-Wessex novels] that have no value and little momentary interest" (a judgment made also by Edmund Gosse); but Barrie also distinguishes the realistic touch of rustic wisdom (" 'Why should death deprive life of four-pence?' ") from the scarcely believable (" 'Oh, and what d'ye think I found out, Mrs. Yeobright? The parson wears a suit of clothes under his surplice! I could see his black sleeve when he held up his arm.' ")[10]

Gosse makes much of his belief that all Hardy's readers are men, hinting that Hardy's female characters are inconstant even when " 'quite nice'," "and some of them are actually 'of a coming-on disposition'."[11] It's not clear whether Gosse thinks Hardy is exploiting wish fantasies about women or is presenting more realistic women than such writers as Walter Besant do. For William Minto, Hardy's "women have very complex characters," but while "there is not the faintest trace of pruriency in his short stories, any more than in his long," one or two of his tales are unfit "for reading in a mixed company. A more serious objection is that in these tales [*A Group of Noble Dames*] he occupies himself too exclusively with the weakness of the female heart."[12]

The earliest book-length studies—which began to appear as Hardy's fiction writing was nearing its end—take similar approaches to Hardy's popularity. They are essentially impressionistic, not in the disciplined manner of a Walter Pater, who founds his impressionism on a philosophy and an awareness of developments in science, but in their confident assessment of Hardy according to narrower interests. Memorable for acute if uncritical appreciativeness, the first book on Hardy, by the poet Lionel Johnson, considers Hardy in a general way in light of Greek tragedy and such contemporaries as Robert Louis Stevenson and George Eliot, giving a good deal of attention to the variety Hardy achieved through "Wessex" and its people; Lascelles Abercrombie categorizes Hardy's novels according to such arbitrary classes as "minor novels," "annexes," "dramatic form," and "epic form," and discusses their poetic approximations of moods and their sensitive portrayal of Wessex scenes; like Johnson and Abercrombie, Samuel Chew—perhaps the first academic to study Hardy at length—considers him in the contexts of tragedy, philosophical forebears, and ideas about divorce and love, providing a general literary agenda with the conclusion that Hardy is a Victorian novelist, not a modern.[13] The lengthy period from roughly 1895 to 1940 is a time of appreciative observation rather than analysis; there is some objection to Hardy's pessimism, an objection from which Hardy has never been free, indeed one that even the most au courant readers of today frequently voice as their initial or strongest reaction. But basically during this time Hardy's broadest concerns are being better understood—through Helen Garwood's study of Hardy from the perspective of Schopenhauer and Ruth Firor's book on folkways, as well as through, on a more special level, the perpetual production of travel and walking-tour books on Wessex/Dorset.[14] One of the more sensitive and sensible studies of these years is Joseph Warren Beach's *The Technique of Thomas Hardy*—although this is the work that elicited Hardy's disingenuous comment, "Upon reading it, I found he had made no reference to my technique as a poet. There isn't any technique about prose, is there? It just comes along of itself."[15]

The culmination of this stage of primary stocktaking was William R. Rutland's pioneering *Study of His Writings and Backgrounds,* which notices in a somewhat sketchy but far-ranging manner some of the Greek, biblical, and Victorian models to whom Hardy "went to school." Rutland's book remains a useful starting point for investigations of influences upon Hardy. Part of Rutland's approach, studying Hardy's intellectual development in light of English and Continental ideas of his time, was taken further ten years later by Harvey Curtis Webster in *On a Darkling Plain.*[16]

In more senses than as a pun, a new era in criticism of Hardy was inaugurated with the "Thomas Hardy Issue" of *Southern Review* (1940). The journal was founded by theorists and developers of the so-called New Criticism that was then developing in selected academic circles in the United States; indeed, R. P. Blackmur, John Crowe Ransom, and Allen Tate each wrote an essay for the issue.[17] Although none gave Hardy's verse a full or detailed treatment, the fact that these writers acknowledged their interest in it gave a powerful boost to his stock. Still, the ambiguity and indeterminacy of Hardy's prose were achieved through techniques other than—at once more subtle and stark than—those used by, for example, Henry James and James Joyce, and his prose was slow in gaining attention from practitioners of the New Criticism. (Possibly the first subsequent essay that shows New Critical tactics, with its insights and limitations, is by Robert W. Stallman in 1947.)[18] At least two essays in the "Thomas Hardy Issue" of the 1940 *Southern Review* scrutinized Hardy's ideas and fiction under more intensely evaluative criteria than previous methods of reading had conceived, and although the conclusion of one of them, Arthur Mizener's essay, is negative—owing to Mizener's judgment that Hardy is unable to maintain artistic distance[19]—they demonstrated that works which up to that time had undergone primarily impressionistic readings and subjective evaluations could stand up to rigorous analysis without wilting. Mizener's essay, together with Morton Dauwen Zabel's identification of the self-exploitative intentions underpinning Hardy's aesthetic, marks Hardy's entry into the canon alongside James, Thackeray, and Austen—although in the following three decades of James's ascendancy the idea that Hardy could stand comparison with him took some time for general acceptance. In refutation of the assumption of most previous enthusiasts that Hardy was a sort of "naïf" or instinctive genius who wrote better than he knew, Zabel argued that Hardy not only was fully aware of the dichotomous tendencies of his temperament (which were also characteristic of "post-rationalist Europe") but developed a means to convey the "central discordance" of his full vision without compromise, refusing either to resort to exhortation or to forgo the tactics that exploited his "natural lack of artistic sophistication."[20] Perhaps owing to the Second World War, no essays of comparable intensity soon followed Mizener's and Zabel's, although eventually such readers as Dorothy Van Ghent, with her interests in psychology and myth, expanded upon Zabel's attention to the energies that gave narrative shape to the essential incongruities of Hardy's world.[21]

Several of Hardy's obsessive concerns that seemed to conflict with his general placement with the realists attracted the notice during and shortly after the Second World War of Albert J. Guerard, who included Hardy as part of a triumvirate with Joseph Conrad and André Gide which traced the development of the modern novel from realism to something less easily categorized. Conceding that Hardy presents a more simple artistry than Conrad or Gide, Guerard more than any previous critic explored the psychology underlying many of the novels' central issues, going well beyond (while purportedly merely supplementing) such commentary as Lionel Johnson's "[Hardy's] interest in modern subtleties of emotion and of thought is an interest, which separates him, as a novelist, from the older novelists."[22] Probably more significant books and important articles stem from, develop, or independently follow upon Guerard's insights not expressed by him at great length, or enlarge upon topics Guerard had earlier opened, than is the case with any other book on Hardy. For example, Richard Beckman intelligently classifies a few categories of characters, similar to (but not aping) Guerard's grouping of Hardy's women;[23] in a similar fashion Frederick R. Karl develops a premise about Hardy's shaping the novel within the nineteenth-century milieu that is quite consonant with Guerard's, and amplifies it exhaustively in regard to one of the novels.[24] Another example: A common practice in recent years has been to trace Hardy's "anticipation" of intellectual positions that were articulated after he had written his novels.[25] Guerard thinks such anticipation not a remarkable feat, since "obviously" the "essential human data do not change radically, and every neurosis antedates its professional discovery"; for example, he notes that "Hardy, who probably had not read the few first theorists of this impulse, wrote one of the great studies of the subconscious impulse to self-destruction in *The Mayor of Casterbridge*"—two or three sentences that put into an ahistorical perspective Hardy's insights into suicidal impulse as tellingly as does an interesting recent study of Hardy's relationship to such theorists as Emile Durkheim.[26] (Guerard himself plays the game of anticipations, noting that Hardy anticipates Conrad and Gide in such techniques as "symbolic use of mischance and coincidence" and in his understanding of the spiritual isolation in modern times.)

Guerard's study is almost literally a turning point in Hardy criticism, despite his unquestioning acceptance of a judgment residual from previous generations of critics schooled in belles lettres, that the strain of craftsmanship caused Hardy to write convoluted and awkward prose. Although Guerard obviously is acknowledging that in substantive concerns Thomas Hardy was, from his first, unpublished novel (*The Poor Man and the Lady*), a reformer and even a revolutionist in terms of social behavior, he does not query the then-common assumption that in means of communication—one of the most social aspects of all human activity—Hardy was conventional and uninspired. Opinions about Hardy's stylistic crudeness have been so pervasive, indeed, that even today it is not unusual to find readers of Hardy who think of him as plodding, awkward, perhaps a bit obtuse, with a definite lack of effective style. Robert Heilman's devastating, detailed observations about *The Mayor of Casterbridge* are a thorough and sensible deterrent to anyone who would carry an enthusiasm for Hardy into a claim for sophisticated smoothness;[27] but critics and readers in sympathy with modern poetics and expressionist techniques may have the better tack for approaching Hardy's specialness. Guerard manifests a degree of this sympathy, even while conceding that Hardy had stylistic shortcomings. Guerard throws himself into his subject to a marked degree, so that at times his work approximates that of earlier clearly impressionistic readers. But in concentrating on the sources of Hardy's tone in personal (if indecipherable) upwellings, discussing interrelationships among the novels, and giving little space to strictly intellectual elements in his work, Guerard anticipates phenomenological and synchronistic analysis.

Hardy studies in more recent decades have immense bulk. He has attracted a great variety of commentators. *Thomas Hardy: An Annotated Bibliography of Writings about Him* already consists of two large volumes (1973, 1983), with a total of 7,687 items—and goes only through 1978, with the proportionately largest share appearing since World War II.[28] Many of these items comprise references to Hardy of a by-the-way sort in books or writings on other subjects; many of the early items are contemporary reviews of Hardy's novels and poems; many are dissertations that were never published, even in part; and a goodly share consists of contributions of topographical and dialectal information that is of interest to relatively few and only the most fanatical enthusiasts. Nonetheless, the number includes hundreds of full-length books and substantial monographs and articles. These are of mixed merit, naturally: Hardy, like Shakespeare and Dickens, attracts wayward commentators, and perhaps to an even greater degree than is the case with books and articles on Shakespeare and Dickens, many studies of Hardy rearrange well-known materials to supply the seemingly inexhaustible curiosity about the fairly easily grasped essentials of the novels and poems. But there are several general categories of Hardy studies, concentrated in the past few decades, that indicate "developments" in our understanding of his work, and certainly changes in cultural values and critical fashions. An overview of such studies also confirms that his contemporaries and ourselves were and are noticing, in rough generalization, the same focus of his imagination.

The obvious instance of this centripetality is tragedy. Hardy's frequently aggrandizing, portentous tone has remained acceptable to his readers despite an increased resistance all around to authors who behold their subjects with great seriousness, a skepticism perhaps fostered by our being in an age of anxiety about attachments personal and social. Ironically, Hardy's retention, even expansion, of his wide readership may be the product of his allegiance to personal values, however scornful he may be of conventional ones and skeptical of theological or absolute ones. His essential responsiveness to relationships (however unsatisfactory he may have been as a spouse) complements another side of his approach, what might be termed his "straight-ahead" assignment of values. Although Hardy deals with particulars and with the social level of his scenes and created beings, they are all counters in a grand economics of existence. His imagery comparing humans with gods, mythic figures, and classic heroes is not occasional metaphor but a means of "placing" his subjects.

Hardy's interest in and ability to write tragedies were recognized early in his career, and nearly every statement on Hardy has something to say about tragedy in his fiction. Early accounts took his success for granted, and even after Joseph Wood Krutch in 1929 called into question whether tragedy itself is achievable in modern times because man can no longer look upon himself as the center of a universe governed by meaningful laws,[29] commentary on Hardy's success in tragedy continued nearly unabated. That Hardy's work has continued to draw commentary on its quality as tragedy is owing to his persuasion that even though humanity might not be perceived as the center of the universe, the individual human perceives himself or herself as the center of *a* universe—his or her own. Hardy's detached sympathy for his sufferers, in combination with the intensity and the random inevitableness of their suffering, creates his works' characteristic impact. Whatever the explanation, one of the richest fields of critical inquiry from the 1950s to the present has been the authoritativeness of Hardy's tragic imagination. Most critics do not question Hardy's achievement, but attempt to explain his strategies and methods, and give details of local techniques. A good number concentrate on *The Mayor of Casterbridge*, with *The Return of the Native* a close rival. These are the novels in which Hardy most ostensibly conceives his subjects as needing tragic treatments, which may suggest that students looking for pertinent approaches to Hardy can benefit from following Hardy's own guidelines.[30] Most of these essays perform acts of analogy on Hardy's novels, seeing them in relation to intellectual influence or classical or mythic parallels; and such is the effort of one book specifically on Hardy as a tragic writer, although treating him in a larger context.[31] Other studies emphasize the relationship between *form* and the attainment of tragedy: My own book takes this tack, as does an essay by Jerome Hamilton Buckley, who relates tragedy to the generic form of the bildungsroman.[32] Present-day critical approaches resonate in various ways in the contexts of tragedy; James Kincaid considers Hardy along with other Victorian tragedians in the context of modern literary theory, which sees the necessity of "incoherence" if a work of art is to be taken seriously, and finds *Jude the Obscure* an instance that at once fails as tragedy and yet satisfactorily raises expectations of tragedy.[33] No full-fledged modernist or postmodernist approach to Hardy's tragedies has been (successfully) attempted; and that is probably the main desideratum in Hardy critical studies at present. In the meantime, the deviousness in Hardy's deployment of traditional values continues to engage critics; R. P. Draper nondeconstructively unpacks the interwoven and conflicting elements, the inconsistencies and contradictions that lie side by side in *The Mayor of Casterbridge.*[34]

The relationship between form and meaning that has agitated literary critics since the dawning of New Criticism (and before, if evoking less self-conscious language) has been discussed frequently by critics of Hardy. In the "modern" era, one of the earliest and still one of the most instructive is that by John Holloway in his landmark application of this rhetorical principle to Victorian literature, *The Victorian Sage,* in which Arnold, Carlyle, Newman, and George Eliot, among other prose writers, are analyzed for their stylistic enhancements of their driving ideas.[35] Among many deductions from form-and-meaning analogies, Holloway suggests that Hardy's plots and proleptic images illustrate the integration of nature and organic process in a universe of undeviating law. A more dramatic use of the form-and-meaning approach is by Dorothy Van Ghent, whose chapter on *Tess of the d'Urbervilles* in *The English Novel* extrapolates from the novel's use of stark symbolism to an analysis of Tess's fate in terms of myth. Going even further toward linking myth and symbolism with literary interpretations is Richard Carpenter; a more restrained, somewhat more traditionally oriented mythic study is Allan Brick's "Paradise and Consciousness in Hardy's *Tess,*" which as the title suggests correlates Hardy's novel with biblical and Milton parallels.[36]

Another concern of New Criticism was authorial voice, activated by Wayne Booth's *The Rhetoric of Fiction* in 1961, and thereafter reformulated by numerous critics, such as Roy Pascal.[37] Many writers on Hardy had long been taken with the nature of Hardy's presence in his novels, and still are; but while by now the question of narrative stance has invoked the law of diminishing returns in studies of Henry James and Joseph Conrad (and many others), Hardy remains available for inquiry. He demands an analyst more subtle than is required for other writers, whose methods do not include solecisms and deliberate violations of plausibility, at least not to the same discordant degree as Hardy's do. Probably the most nearly adequate reading of Hardy's voice is in David Lodge's *The Language of Fiction*, which considers the hermeneutic implications of the interactions of the various voices the narrator employs in *Tess of the d'Urbervilles*: that of the local historian, the dialectician, the writer of strained prose, the writer of perfect English, the writer as creator.[38] Voice is now a common topic in Hardy criticism; such recent critics as John Bayley elicit delicate connections between the creator and his created scenes and situations.[39] But probably the most productive period in terms of clarifications of central discriminations came shortly after Booth's book (which itself deals only incidentally with Hardy), with discussions of Hardy's ambiguity, a creation of the stance he chooses to give his narrator. Two basically positive analyses of Hardy's techniques are by Frederick P. W. McDowell and Robert C. Schweik; a less sympathetic study of Hardy's use of the narrator is by Bernard J. Paris.[40] Daniel R. Schwarz discusses the postulated attitudes of individual narrators.[41]

Supplementing these concerns about Hardy-as-artist in the 1960s and early 1970s was a more sophisticated interest in the manner in which Hardy was affected by his reading and by intellectual issues of his times. This was scarcely a "new" approach, of course: As already indicated, a book on Schopenhauer and Hardy came while the novelist was still alive; Rutland's book canvassed some classical influences upon Hardy; and Webster's *On a Darkling Plain*, various contemporary influences as well. But we are still in an early phase of this sort of critical study. The literary, historical, and intellectual allusions in the primary materials—the novels and poems themselves—have been well identified and exploited. But enticing questions remain to be examined. Fortunately, with several crucial, large-scale scholarly enterprises either under way or recently completed, the critic of Hardy now and in the future has more material to work with than commentators of previous generations had. In particular, there are his *Collected Letters* and the *Personal Notebooks*, the latter of which includes notes for *The Trumpet-Major* and Hardy's "Schools of Painting" notebook.[42] The most pertinent may be the *Literary Notes*, renamed *Literary Notebooks* in its more complete form (both edited by Lennart Björk), which consists of Hardy's jottings of ideas raised by his reading, and both short and lengthy excerpts from the reading itself.[43] Perhaps the principal demonstration of Björk's scholarship is its evidence of the determination of Hardy the autodidact to read widely and his tendency to take notes extensively on material that interested him. But while scholar-prepared materials allow critics to venture into projects impractical to consider without such guides, notebooks and letters are not essential to the practice of influence study. They simply make generally available materials that previously required extensive planning and traveling to consult. Certainly, scholars for long have gone to the notebooks themselves, and to those letters whose location they were aware of; and there have been fine studies of influence in recent years. David DeLaura's remains among the most valuable, one readers can peruse repeatedly for insight into Hardy's responses to (and exploitations of) not only Arnold and Pater but also *Robert Elsmere*.[44] Two books of distinction—but ones that deal primarily or exclusively with Hardy's poetry—are J. O. Bailey's *Thomas Hardy and the Cosmic Mind*, which discusses the similarity of some of Hardy's thinking to Ernst Haeckl's and Eduard Von Hartmann's, and Walter F. Wright's *The Shaping of "The Dynasts": A Study in Thomas Hardy*, whose name accurately indicates its coverage.[45] Michael Millgate's *Thomas Hardy: His Career as a Novelist* contains many suggestions of influence—local (Dorset history), literary (predecessors and contemporary novelists and poets), and intellectual.[46] Also deserving mention is Mary Jacobus's study of Hardy's awareness of both William Morris and Scandinavian myth.[47]

One critical method deserving isolated attention is phenomenology. This method of reading and interpretation is associated with one writer who, during the past two decades, has written often on Hardy's fiction, sometimes using Hardy to illustrate a point of theory, sometimes using theory to explicate a crux in Hardy's work. The critic is J. Hillis Miller, who in *The Form of Victorian Fiction* drew upon *A Pair of Blue Eyes* to demonstrate how multiple time frames are interwoven in a novel, and who devotes an entire book (*Thomas Hardy: Distance and Desire*) to a phenomenological reading,[48] dealing both with the narrator and with the shadow author, who appear to be reflected in characters simultaneously drawn to human contact and love and repelled by it when obtained. Although Miller is widely read in the academic world, and although phenomenology would appear to be particularly well suited to providing an orientation toward Hardy's individuality, few substantial or successful attempts have followed Miller's example in readings of Hardy. One competent critic has gone to the extent of naming his book after Miller's method, but Bruce Johnson's actual subject in *True Correspondence: A Phenomenology of Thomas Hardy's Novels* is the appearance of the pastoral in Hardy's fiction.[49] Miller himself, shortly after finishing *Distance and Desire*, shifted his theoretical approach to a more reflexive language-based analysis, and again applied that to Hardy, the most distinctive example (for this summary) being an essay on *Tess of the d'Urbervilles* founded in philosophical concepts of repetition.[50]

I could discuss several other ways of reading Hardy, for he is an author who attracts controversies that have no resolution. Limited space prevents a complete survey even of all the major categories of the massive amount of criticism of Hardy that precedes this volume. But there should be some mention of the dispute as to whether Hardy was an advocate of determinism (pessimism) or free will. He himself denied he was a pessimist, but did not seem to feel the need to settle the issue by declaring explicitly for free will. In recent years this controversy has been restirred by Roy Morrell (*The Will and the Way*), whose position is that Hardy gives his characters ample (or at least adequate) opportunity to mend their courses and avert the disasters that loom before them, and J. Hillis Miller, who reviewed Morrell's book negatively, saying that Hardy's characters lack free will and thus are not to blame for their fates.[51] Within this larger philosophical issue lies the question of Darwinism. Peter R. Morton gives a "A Neo-Darwinian Reading," arguing that Hardy kept up to date on Darwinism, and drew upon it for *Tess;* J. R. Ebbatson refutes Morton a year later, noting that Hardy allowed too much measure of happiness, however impermanent, and allowed effective human intervention in the struggles he depicted.[52]

Discussions of "pessimism" in Hardy have not favored a balanced perspective, although writers from Abercrombie to Webster to J. O. Bailey have given examples of how to perceive both freedom and restriction; and indeed the usual tack for students of Hardy has been to speak (or write) dogmatically from either one point of view or the other. This should have been a longtime truly dead horse in literary scholarship, but Hardy's ability to arouse readers seems to ensure that for as long as he is read readers will continue to flog it, arguing vehemently either that he sees no hope in human life or that he does indeed believe people can affect their own fates. Nevertheless, Hardy's insistence that he was not a philosopher and had written with no intention of illustrating consistent patterns gained a purchase by the early 1970s, at least as evidenced by several books that gave Hardy general reassessments rather than arguing narrow theses. Among the best of these studies are those by Jean R. Brooks, Ian Gregor, and John Bayley.[53] It will be interesting to see whether this acquiescence to Hardy's self-judgment holds.

Oddly, given the decades-long admiration for his skill and sympathy in portraying women's lot, feminist critics have been fairly slow in taking on Thomas Hardy, possibly because other authors have been seen to be more problematic or even antagonistic, thus in one sense in more need of analysis. But Hardy's attitudes toward women, and toward feminism, are quite complex, and merit far more substantial investigation than they have been given to date. In this area contemporary responses and modern meet uneasily, with some modern readers convinced that Hardy fully understands what women want and others equally convinced that such novels as *Tess of the d'Urbervilles* are male fantasies. It is appropriate that feminist critics with some sophisticated analytic tools have begun to study Hardy. Regrettably, some of the early feminist analysts of Hardy, such as Katharine Rogers, had not developed such tools at the time they worked with him. Likewise, Anne Z. Mickelson does not largely develop fresh feminist perspectives, but takes one of the most familiar in correlating women with nature and indicating how in novel after novel women (and thus nature) are defeated in the drive toward acculturation and in the triumph of convention in Hardy's settings.[54] One of the more traditional and sensible (qualities that don't necessarily go together, and in any case are, singly or in tandem, no guarantee of correctness) of today's critics, A. O. J. Cockshut, says that Hardy rejects the entire feminist argument.[55] It is true that Hardy rejected the idea of votes for women, concerned (he said) with risks to the family structure, but in letters and personal converse with feminists he gave the impression of supporting them, and the issue remains very much an open one. Lloyd Fernando's *New Women in the Late Victorian Novel* is more a book about a type of novel than a book oriented according to a feminist outlook; still, his study is a useful starting point in the study of the New Woman novel, a form with particular relevance for *Jude the Obscure*, and whose development in the late 1880s Hardy followed with care and interest. Moreover, feminist studies of Hardy are not entirely initiatory: Kathleen Blake has been writing on Hardy from the feminist perspective for a decade and more; Penny Boumelha's *Thomas Hardy and Women* deals also with New Woman novels in a brilliant combination of Marxist and feminist analysis; and Elaine Showalter discusses the feminine elements necessary to be brought out in Henchard before he is able to realize his true self.[56]

The past few years have seen major contributions to a fuller understanding of Hardy through detailed study of his writing practices, a matter on which his contemporaries seldom felt the need to comment, although that an interest was there is attested by such phenomena as the publication of a portion of the manuscript of *Tess of the d'Urbervilles* in the *Bookman*.[57] As early as the 1920s Mary Ellen Chase studied several versions of several novels to point out the alterations Hardy made between serialization and book publication; but because she ignored the manuscripts and did not realize there were a number of different book versions—in particular overlooking the centrality of the 1912 Wessex Edition, which amounted to Hardy's last revision—it was inevitable that her work, however interesting, would be superseded. Richard Little Purdy culminated several decades of bibliographical research with his *Thomas Hardy: A Bibliographical Study* (1954, 1968). Concentrating on collecting and verifying facts, and identifying different printings, Purdy's work has provided the foundation of much of the bibliographical study of Hardy that has followed. Carl Weber's useful studies of Hardy's publishers, editors, and readers preserve a massive amount of secondary information that might otherwise have been lost or overlooked;[58] moreover, Weber offered steady and enthusiastic encouragement to other people's work, a measure of a scholar's life that does not show up adequately in bibliographies or even in acknowledgment pages. Neither Purdy's nor Weber's interests lay in close and exhaustive examination of the texts and history of a single novel; two of the earlier instances of this sort of criticism were performed by Robert Slack and Otis Wheeler. Another was conducted by John Paterson, whose work, although criticized as too imaginative by such scholars as Dieter Riesner,[59] may have been partly the inspiration for the more substantial bibliographical, textual, and manuscript work on Hardy of the 1960s and 1970s.[60] A crucial issue in much textual study of Hardy is distinguishing between Thomas Hardy's hand and Emma's, a difficult job that has been attempted primarily by Weber (in a slight way), myself, and especially Alan Manford,[61] whose essay in this collection provides the first extensive and satisfactorily defined analysis of the couple's handwritings, and the most authoritative analysis to date of the degree and nature of Emma's role in her husband's creations.

Granted the rootedness of Hardy's works in the grit-hard lives of the agricultural workers of Dorset (generally thought to be among the lowest paid and hardest worked of all nonindustrial workers in England during the nineteenth century), it is not surprising that his first venture in fiction was *The Poor Man and the Lady*, nor that a fairly large structure of Hardy studies has been built up around the ideology of social revolution. Probably the best-known analysis from this perspective is Arnold Kettle's pronouncement about the "destruction of English peasantry" in 1951 and his subsequent partial retraction a decade and a half later ("my assessment of Tess [was] somewhat one-sided").[62] Other central statements in this matter are by Douglas Brown and William J. Hyde,[63] and in more recent years by Raymond and Merryn Williams.[64] The nondogmatic Laurence Lerner says that both tragedy and social history are valid, and noncontradictory, approaches. A Marxist essay by Roger Bromley is lamentably jargonistic, a characteristic shared by the most academically ambitious, ideologically oriented book on the subject, by George Wotton, which deserves to be read, although it too often fails to rise beyond its flattening, repetitious language.[65]

A significant, if not final, gauge of a writer is the placement he or she acquires in the overall scheme of reading and explanation. In recent years Thomas Hardy has become one of those writers whose work formulators of general theories build their theories to explain, or use to prove the validity of their theories. During Hardy's lifetime, Virginia Woolf contrasted him with such limited realists ("materialists") as Arnold Bennett, H. G. Wells, and John Galsworthy, and such "spiritual" writers as James Joyce,[66] but other critics influential during the early and mid-twentieth century had relatively little to say about Hardy. For instance, Percy Lubbock assumed there was nothing in Hardy's techniques that bore discussing when Lubbock's primary attention was upon Henry James's management of perspective; F. R. Leavis in effect left Hardy out of the literary pantheon, and E. M. Forster and Wayne Booth refer to him only in the briefest terms. For most of these writers, Hardy has been incidental to the main drift of their argument. They have had to acknowledge his existence, but, as often as not, they have placed him in the periphery of the development of fiction on such matters as stream of consciousness, the unity of form, representation, and perspective. In the past two decades, the dominant theory in the American literary academy has cast off its preceding intense concern with formal matter—that is, with the application of deliberate and consistent technique—and has concentrated on more basic issues such as language, the sign system, indeterminacy, and the (im)possibility of meaning itself. During this period, Hardy has gained a preeminence and esteem that would have baffled Henry James and enraged George Moore. Although he is one of the more recurrent critics, J. Hillis Miller is not the only one who has returned continually to this writer, once assumed to be crude and unsophisticated, as an exemplar of insight and expressiveness that address readers' aesthetic and moral values.

Obviously, no collection of essays on Hardy can hope to be more than partial. The essays I've chosen or solicited are intended to represent a range of critical approaches, as well as to cover major parts of Hardy's career in novels. Allowing for the natural regret that I would have liked to have more essays in this volume than was possible, owing to cost or availability of some essays, in addition to limitations on the size of the volume itself, I believe these essays are among the best pieces on Hardy, the most valuable interpretations as well as representative of future possibilities, of recent years. I am especially pleased that I am able to include chapters on Hardy from several general studies of fiction. These, I think, underscore the inescapability of Hardy's continuing and indeed increasing relevance for students of interpretation and of culture, perhaps particularly so when he is seen, as in the chapter from George Levine's book, as a divergence from the practice and concept of most other Victorian writers.

DALE KRAMER

University of Illinois at Urbana-Champaign

Notes

1. Philip M. Weinstein, *The Semantics of Desire: Changing Models of Identity from Dickens to Joyce* (Princeton: Princeton University Press, 1984), 8.

2. [Anonymous], review in *Spectator*, 22 April 1871, 482–83.

3. [Horace Moule], *Saturday Review*, 30 September 1871, 441. As an illustration of how women remain a core concern among Hardy students, see John Lucas, "Hardy's Women," in *The Literature of Change: Studies in the Nineteenth-Century Provincial Novel* (Sussex: Harvester Press, 1977), 11–91.

4. [Havelock Ellis], "Thomas Hardy's Novels," *Westminster Review* 119(1883): 334.

5. Elaine Showalter, "The Unmanning of the *Mayor of Casterbridge*," in *Critical Approaches to the Fiction of Thomas Hardy*, ed. Dale Kramer (London: Macmillan, 1979), 99–115.

6. [R. H. Hutton], *"The Woodlanders,"* *Spectator*, 26 March 1887, 419. Coventry Patmore complained about Hardy's use of *phenomenal* (*St. James's Gazette*, 2 April 1887, 9), one instance of which Hardy altered, one of which he left unchanged.

7. See the introduction by Juliet Grindle and Simon Gatrell to their critical edition of *Tess of the d'Urbervilles* (Oxford: Clarendon Press, 1983), 45–49.

8. Letter to Edmund Gosse in *The Collected Letters of Thomas Hardy*, Vol. 2, *1893–1901*, ed. Richard Little Purdy and Michael Millgate (Oxford: Clarendon Press, 1980), 93 (10 November 1895). A subsequent letter to Gosse undercuts the excuse that the book may instance automatic writing: Hardy points out that "the book is all contrasts—or was meant to be in its original conception . . .—e.g., Sue & her heathen gods set against Jude's reading the Greek Testament; Christminster academical, Christminster in the slums; Jude the saint, Jude the sinner; Sue the Pagan, Sue the saint; marriage, no marriage; &c. &c." (Vol. 2, 99 [20 November 1985]).

9. In *Life and Work of Thomas Hardy*, ed. Michael Millgate (Athens: University of Georgia Press, 1985), 259.

10. J. M. Barrie, "Thomas Hardy: The Historian of Wessex," *Contemporary Review* 56 (1889): 61–62; Edmund Gosse, "Thomas Hardy," *Speaker*, 13 September 1890 (quoted in *Thomas Hardy: The Critical Heritage*, ed. R. G. Cox [New York: Barnes & Noble, 1970], 168–69).

11. Gosse, "Thomas Hardy," *Speaker* (quoted in Cox, 169–70).

12. William Minto, "The Work of Thomas Hardy," *Bookman* 1 (December 1891) (quoted in Cox, 175–76).

13. Lionel Johnson, *The Art of Thomas Hardy* (London: Mathews & Lane, 1894); Lascelles Abercrombie, *Thomas Hardy: A Critical Study* (London: Secker, 1912); Samuel C. Chew, *Thomas Hardy: Poet and Novelist* (New York: Knopf, 1921, 1928).

14. Helen Garwood, *Thomas Hardy: An Illustration of the Philosophy of Schopenhauer* (Philadelphia: John C. Winston, 1911); and Ruth Firor, *Folkways in Thomas Hardy* (Philadelphia: University of Pennsylvania Press, 1931). Most of the travel books have no noticeable value; but Hardy cooperated with the makers of several of them, particularly with Hermann Lea, whose *Thomas Hardy's Wessex* (London: Macmillan, 1913) remains in print.

15. Joseph Warren Beach, *The Technique of Thomas Hardy* (1922); the passage from Hardy's conversation is quoted by Carl J. Weber, *Hardy of Wessex: His Life and Literary Career* (New York: Columbia University Press, 1940), 17.

16. William R. Rutland, *Thomas Hardy: A Study of His Writings and Their Background* (Oxford: Blackwell, 1938); Harvey Curtis Webster, *The Art and Thought of Thomas Hardy: On a Darkling Plain* (Chicago: University of Chicago Press, 1947).

17. "Thomas Hardy Issue," *Southern Review* 6 (1940): R. P. Blackmur, "The Shorter Poems of Thomas Hardy"; John Crowe Ransom, "Honey and Gall"; Allen Tate, "Hardy's Philosophic Metaphors."

18. Robert W. Stallman, "Hardy's Hour-Glass Novel," *Sewanee Review* 55(1947): 283–96.

19. Arthur Mizener, "*Jude the Obscure* as Tragedy," *Southern Review* 6(1940): 193–213; rev. as "The Novel of Doctrine in the Nineteenth Century: Hardy's *Jude the Obscure*," *The Sense of Life in the Modern Novel* (Boston: Houghton Mifflin, 1964), 55–77.

20. Morton Dauwen Zabel, "Hardy in Defense of His Art: The Aesthetic of Incongruity," *Southern Review* 6(1940): 125–49; rev. and repr. in *Craft and Character: Texts, Method, and Vocation in Modern Fiction* (New York: Viking, 1957), 70–96. The quoted passages are from pp. 72–74 of the book version.

21. Dorothy Van Ghent, "On *Tess of the d'Urbervilles*," in *The English Novel: Form and Function* (New York: Holt, Rinehart & Winston, 1953), 195–209.

22. Quoted by Albert J. Guerard, *Thomas Hardy: The Novels and Stories* (Cambridge, Mass.: Harvard University Press, 1949), 100.

23. Richard Beckman, "A Character Typology for Hardy's Novels," *ELH* 30(1963): 70–87.

24. Frederick R. Karl, "*The Mayor of Casterbridge*: A New Fiction Defined," *Modern Fiction Studies* 6(1960): 195–213.

25. For example, Rosemary Sumner, *Thomas Hardy: Psychological Novelist* (London: Macmillan, 1981).

26. Guerard, 101–2; Frank R. Giordano, Jr., "*I'd Have My Life Unbe*": Thomas Hardy's *Self-Destructive Characters* (University: University of Alabama Press, 1984).

27. Robert B. Heilman, "Hardy's *Mayor*: Notes on Style," *Nineteenth-Century Fiction* 18(1964): 307–29.

28. *Thomas Hardy: An Annotated Bibliography of Writings about Him*, vol. 1 (De Kalb: Northern Illinois University Press, 1973 [ed. Helmut E. Gerber and W. Eugene Davis]; second volume, 1983 [ed. W. Eugene Davis and Helmut E. Gerber]).

29. Joseph Wood Krutch, "The Tragic Fallacy," in *The Modern Temper* (1929; repr. New York: Harcourt, Brace & World, 1956), 79–97.

30. Only a few of these essays can be named here: D. A. Dike, "A Modern Oedipus: *The Mayor of Casterbridge*," *Essays in Criticism* 2(1952): 169–79; Julian Moynahan, "*The Mayor of Casterbridge* and the Old Testament's First Book of Samuel: A Study of Some Literary Relationships," *PMLA* 71(1956): 118–30; John Paterson, "*The Mayor of Casterbridge* as Tragedy," *Victorian Studies* 3(1959): 151–71; John Paterson, "The 'Poetics' of *The Return of the Native*," *Modern Fiction Studies* 6(1960): 214–22; John Paterson, "Hardy, Faulkner, and the Prosaics of Tragedy," *Centennial Review* 5(1961): 156–75; Robert Evans, "The Other Eustacia," *Novel* 1(1968): 251–59; James Hazen, "*Tess of the d'Urbervilles* and *Antigone*," *English Literature in Transition* 14(1971): 207–15; Duane D. Edwards, "*The Mayor of Casterbridge* and Aeschylean Tragedy," *Studies in the Novel* 4(1972): 608–18; Richard Benvenuto, "*The Return of the Native* as Tragedy," *Nineteenth-Century Fiction* 26(1971): 83–93; Lawrence J. Starzyk, "Hardy's *Mayor*: The Antitraditional Basis of Tragedy," *Studies in the Novel* 4(1972): 592–607. Among traditionally oriented essays on tragedy are Thomas Hinde, "Accident and Coincidence in *Tess of the d'Urbervilles*," in *The Genius of Thomas Hardy*, ed. Margaret Drabble (London: Weidenfeld, 1976), 74–79; and Juliet M. Grindle, "Compulsion and Choice in *The Mayor of Casterbridge*," in *The Novels of Thomas Hardy*, ed. Anne Smith (London: Vision Press, 1979), 91–106.

31. Jeannette King, *Tragedy in the Victorian Novel: Theory and Practice in the Novels of George Eliot, Thomas Hardy, and Henry James* (Cambridge: Cambridge University Press, 1978).

32. Dale Kramer, *Thomas Hardy: The Forms of Tragedy* (London: Macmillan; Detroit: Wayne State University Press, 1975); Jerome Hamilton Buckley, "The Obscurity of *Jude*," in *Season of Youth: The Bildungsroman from Dickens to Golding* (Cambridge, Mass.: Harvard University Press, 1974), 162–85.

32. James Kincaid, " 'Why Unblooms the Best Hope?': Victorian Narrative Forms and the Explanation of Calamity," *Victorian Newsletter*, no. 53 (Spring 1978): 1–4.

34. R. P. Draper, "*The Mayor of Casterbridge*," *Critical Quarterly* 25(1983): 57–70.

35. John Holloway, *The Victorian Sage: Studies in Argument* (London: Macmillan, 1953), 244–89, esp. 264–72.

36. Dorothy Van Ghent, *The English Novel: Form and Function* (New York: Holt, Rinehart & Winston, 1953), 195–209; Richard Carpenter, *Thomas Hardy* (New York: Twayne, 1964); Allan Brick, "Paradise and Consciousness in Hardy's *Tess*," *Nineteenth-Century Fiction* 17(1962): 115–34.

37. Wayne C. Booth, *The Rhetoric of Fiction*, 2d ed. (Chicago: University of Chicago Press, 1961, 1983); Roy Pascal, *The Dual Voice: Free Indirect Speech and Its Functioning in the Nineteenth-Century European Novel* (Manchester: Manchester University Press, 1977).

38. David Lodge, *The Language of Fiction: Essays in Criticism and Verbal Analysis of the English Novel* (London: Routledge & Kegan Paul, 1966), 164–88.

39. John Bayley, *An Essay on Hardy* (London: Cambridge University Press, 1978).

40. Frederick P. W. McDowell, "Hardy's 'Seemings or Personal Impressions': The Symbolic Use of Image and Contrast in *Jude the Obscure*," *Modern Fiction Studies* 6(1960): 233–50; Robert C. Schweik, "Moral Perspective in *Tess of the d'Urbervilles*," *College English* 24(1962): 14–18; Bernard J. Paris, " 'A Confusion of Many Standards': Conflicting Value Systems in *Tess of the d'Urbervilles*," *Nineteenth-Century Fiction* 24(1969): 57–79.

41. Daniel R. Schwarz, "The Narrator as Character in Hardy's Major Fiction," *Modern Fiction Studies* 18(1972): 155–72.

42. *The Collected Letters of Thomas Hardy*, ed. Richard Little Purdy and Michael Millgate (Oxford: Clarendon Press, 1978–1988); *The Personal Notebooks of Thomas Hardy*, ed. Richard H. Taylor (London: Macmillan, 1979).

43. *The Literary Notebooks of Thomas Hardy*, ed. Lennart A. Björk (Göteborg, Sweden: Acta Universitatis Gothoburgensis, 1974); a fuller edition is *The Literary Notebooks of Thomas Hardy*, ed. Lennart A. Björk (New York: New York University Press, 1985).

44. David J. DeLaura, " 'The Ache of Modernism' in Hardy's Later Novels," *ELH* 34(1967): 380–99.

45. J. O. Bailey, *Thomas Hardy and the Cosmic Mind* (Chapel Hill: University of North Carolina Press, 1966); Walter F. Wright, *The Shaping of "The Dynasts": A Study in Thomas Hardy* (Lincoln: University of Nebraska Press, 1967).

46. Michael Millgate, *Thomas Hardy: His Career as a Novelist* (New York: Random House, 1971).

47. Mary Jacobus, "Tree and Machine: *The Woodlanders*," in *Critical Approaches to the Fiction of Thomas Hardy*, ed. Dale Kramer (London: Macmillan, 1979), 116–34.

48. J. Hillis Miller, *The Form of Victorian Fiction* (Notre Dame, Ind.: University of Notre Dame Press, 1968); *Thomas Hardy: Distance and Desire* (Cambridge, Mass.: Harvard University Press, 1970).

49. Bruce Johnson, *True Correspondence: A Phenomenology of Thomas Hardy's Novels* (Tallahassee: University Presses of Florida, 1983).

50. J. Hillis Miller, "Fiction and Repetition: *Tess of the d'Urbervilles*," in *Forms of Modern British Fiction*, ed. Alan Warren Friedman (Austin: University of Texas Press, 1975), 32–71; rev. and repr. as *"Tess of the d'Urbervilles*: Fiction as Immanent Design," in *Fiction and Repetition: Seven English Novels* (Cambridge, Mass.: Harvard University Press, 1982).

51. Roy Morrell, *Thomas Hardy: The Will and the Way* (Kuala Lumpur: Oxford University Press, 1965); J. Hillis Miller, *Victorian Studies* 11(1967): 119–21.

52. Peter R. Morton, *"Tess of the d'Urbervilles*: A Neo-Darwinian Reading," *Southern Review* (Adelaide) 7(1974): 38–50; J. R. Ebbatson, "The Darwinian View of *Tess*: A Reply," *Southern Review* (Adelaide) 8(1975): 247–53.

53. Jean R. Brooks, *Thomas Hardy: The Poetic Structure* (London: Elek, 1971; Ithaca: Cornell University Press, 1971); Ian Gregor, *The Great Web: The Form of Hardy's Major Fiction* (London: Faber & Faber; Totowa, N.J.: Rowman & Littlefield, 1974); John Bayley, *An Essay on Hardy*.

54. Katharine Rogers, "Women in Thomas Hardy," *Centennial Review* 19(1975): 249–58; Anne Z. Mickelson, *Thomas Hardy's Women and Men: The Defeat of Nature* (Metuchen, N.J.: Scarecrow Press, 1976).

55. A. O. J. Cockshut, *Man and Woman: A Study of Love and the Novel, 1740–1940* (London: Collins, 1977), 128–29.

56. Lloyd Fernando, "Hardy: 'The Fiction of Sex and the New Woman'," in *New Women in the Late Victorian Novel* (University Park: Pennsylvania State University Press, 1977), 129–46; Kathleen Blake, "Sue Bridehead, 'The Woman of the Feminist Movement'," *Studies in English Literature, 1500–1900* 18(1978): 703–26 (repr. in *Love and the Woman Question in Victorian Literature: The Art of Self-Postponement* [Sussex: Harvester Press, 1983], 146–67; Penny Boumelha, *Thomas Hardy and Women: Sexual Ideology and Narrative Form* (Madison: University of Wisconsin Press, 1982); Elaine Showalter, "The Unmanning of the Mayor of Casterbridge."

57. *Bookman* 21(November 1901): 40.

58. Mary Ellen Chase, *Thomas Hardy from Serial to Novel* (Minneapolis: University of Minnesota Press, 1927); Richard Little Purdy, *Thomas Hardy: A Bibliographical Study* (Oxford: Oxford University Press, 1954 [repr. with some revisions, 1968]); among Weber's books bearing mention here are *Hardy in America: A Study of Thomas Hardy and His American Readers* (Waterville, Maine: Colby College Press, 1946) and *Hardy and the Lady from Madison Square* (Waterville, Maine: Colby College Press, 1952).

59. Robert C. Slack, "The Text of Hardy's *Jude the Obscure*," *Nineteenth-Century Fiction* 22(1957): 261–75; Otis B. Wheeler, "Four Versions of *The Return of the Native*," *Nineteenth-Century Fiction* 14(1959): 27–44; John Paterson, *The Making of "The Return of the Native"* (Berkeley and Los Angeles: University of California Press, 1960); Dieter Riesner, "Uber die

Genesis von Thomas Hardys *The Return of the Native*" ("On the Genesis of Thomas Hardy's *The Return of the Native*"), *Archiv* 200(1963): 53–59.

60. Examples of this work are Juliet Grindle, "A Critical Edition of Thomas Hardy's *Tess of the d'Urbervilles*" (D.Phil. thesis, Oxford University, 1974); Simon Gatrell, "A Critical Edition of Thomas Hardy's *Under the Greenwood Tree*" (D.Phil. thesis, Oxford University, 1973); Alan Manford, "A Critical Edition of Thomas Hardy's *A Pair of Blue Eyes*" (Ph.D. diss., University of Birmingham, 1980); my own critical edition of *The Woodlanders* (Oxford: Clarendon Press, 1981); and the edition of *Tess* prepared jointly by Grindle and Gatrell in 1983 (see n. 7). Stemming less directly from the interest in editing during the 1960s are the World's Classics Editions, published by Oxford University Press, of *The Well-Beloved* (ed. Tom Hetherington [1986]), *Jude the Obscure* (ed. Patricia Ingham [1985]), and *A Pair of Blue Eyes* (ed. Alan Manford [1985]); and Robert Schweik's Norton Critical Edition of *Far from the Madding Crowd* (New York: W. W. Norton, 1986).

61. Carl J. Weber, "The Manuscript of Hardy's *Two on a Tower*," *Papers of the Bibliographical Society of America* 40(1946): 1–21; Dale Kramer, "A Query Concerning the Handwriting in Hardy's Manuscripts," *Papers of the Bibliographical Society of America* 57(1963): 357–60; and Alan Manford, "Materials for an Edition of Thomas Hardy's *The Woodlanders*" (unpublished M.A. thesis, University of Birmingham, 1976).

62. Arnold Kettle, *"Tess of the d'Urbervilles,"* in *An Introduction to the English Novel*, Vol. 2, *Henry James to the Present* (London: Hutchinson, 1951; New York, Harper, 1960), 49–62; Kettle, introduction to *Tess of the d'Urbervilles* (New York: Harper & Row, 1966), xii n.

63. Douglas Brown, *Thomas Hardy* (London: Longmans, 1954); William J. Hyde, "Hardy's View of Realism: A Key to the Rustic Characters," *Victorian Studies* 2(1958): 451–59; also worth consulting is J. C. Maxwell, "The 'Sociological' Approach to *The Mayor of Casterbridge*," in *Imagined Worlds: Essays on Some English Novels and Novelists in Honour of John Butt*, ed. Maynard Mack and Ian Gregor (London: Methuen, 1968), 225–36.

64. Raymond Williams, "Thomas Hardy," *Critical Quarterly* 6(1964): 341–51; Raymond Williams, "Wessex and the Border," in *The Country and the City* (New York: Oxford University Press, 1973), 197–214; Merryn Williams, *Thomas Hardy and Rural England* (London: Macmillan; New York: Columbia University Press, 1972).

65. Laurence Lerner, Thomas Hardy's The Mayor of Casterbridge: *Tragedy or Social History?*" (London: Sussex University Press, 1975); Roger Bromley, "The Boundaries of Hegemony: Thomas Hardy and *The Mayor of Casterbridge*," in *Literature, Society and the Sociology of Literature* (proceedings of the conference held at the University of Essex, July 1976), ed. Francis Barker et al. (Colchester: University of Essex, 1977), 30–40; George Wotton, *Thomas Hardy: Towards a Materialist Criticism* (Dublin: Gill & Macmillan, 1985). A fuller review of Wotton, as well as comments on other books on Hardy's novels, is in my "Recent Studies in Thomas Hardy's Fiction, 1980–1986," *Dickens Studies Annual* 17(1988): 241–76.

66. Virginia Woolf, "Modern Fiction," in *The Common Reader* (New York: Harcourt, Brace, 1925), esp. 208–10, 213–15.

Overviews

Hardy and Marxism

John Goode*

For the purposes of this essay, I take *Marxism* to indicate an orientation rather than a specific doctrine. Most of the important issues raised by the term are continually debated and need to be so since Marxism is not merely or even primarily a theory but a program of action and must therefore be developed in relation to the historical change to which it is a response and a stimulus. I will therefore begin with a working definition that admittedly leaves many questions unanswered. First, Marxism entails historical materialism as the basis of its understanding of human society. Humanity is thus defined by its ability to reproduce its own means of existence, and all social formations are determined by (constrained and activated by) this basic characterization and its historical manifestations. The products of the social formations, material objects, and cultural events of ideological tendencies are therefore to be explained in relation to the productive forces and the social relations of production that together make up the identity of a concrete historical moment. There is no eternal social formation, and although there is a human nature it never appears in an abstract manner shorn of the historical variation that the material base determines.

Second, this historical variation is not meaningless. As productive forces and relations develop, they yield a surplus that at once leads to and intensifies a division of labor. This division tends to allot the surplus to the class that dominates the conditions of development. In crude terms, the main modern stages of this tendency are feudalism, which allots it to the class that controls the security of land (the overlords who conquer and/or defend it); capitalism, which allots it to the class that controls and finances the high level of technology necessary for the development of the industrial revolution; and socialism, which allots it to the class, the proletariat, that produces the surplus itself. The changes brought about by this reallocation of the surplus is neither gradual nor peaceful, since the dominant class never willingly hands over its power to its emergent successor. Thus Marxism has three related constitu-

*This essay was written specifically for this volume and is published here for the first time by permission of the author.

21

ents: It is materialist, but *historically* materialist, and history is dialectical—that is, it moves through the conflict of opposites to revolution.

Marxism is relevant to Hardy in two distinct, though related, ways. First, Hardy wrote about the world he saw in the late nineteenth and early twentieth centuries. Marxism was the most powerful way of seeing that world to grow up in this period—because it was the intellectual system that had the most influence in changing it. This is the historical relevance of Marxism. There is also a theoretical relevance, in that Marxism is a recognizable orientation within literary studies and is thus as appropriate or inept to the study of Hardy as it is to that of any other writer. The historical relevance is more specific, in that there are many writers to whom it would not apply. Chronologically, if one takes the history of Marxism to begin with the date of the first appearance of the first volume of *Capital* in 1867 and to reach its first great practical success with constitution of the USSR in 1923, it almost exactly coincides with the history of Hardy's literary career (his earliest poems are dated 1866; the last volume he saw through the press, *Human Shows, Far Phantasies*, was published in 1925). Second, there are other writers whose work falls within this same period to whom Marxism would not be so relevant, because if Marxism has any undeniable feature it is that it is preoccupied with the fate of the working class. And unlike, let us say, Henry James, whose literary career also begins in the 1860s and ends just before the Russian revolution, or Yeats, who started writing at the time of the first English translation of *Capital* and died a few months before the Stalin/Hitler pact, Hardy explicitly concerned himself in a large number of novels, stories, poems, and even, to some extent, *The Dynasts*, with sections of the working class in their specific social role as subordinate workers.

It is also equally clear, however, that this specific historical relevance to Hardy is problematic, for although Hardy wrote at the same time as the emergence of Marxism and although, like Marx, Engels, and Lenin, he was concerned with the condition of the working class, there is no evidence that he read Marx, read anything about Marxism, or had any ideas that can be shown to coincide with Marxism. On the contrary, if Hardy had a social vision at all it was probably subsumed in a larger metaphysical vision that owed more to the pessimistic Schopenhauer than to the (ultimately) optimistic Marx. When, at the lowest point of their social fate, Sue says to Jude that "there is something external to us that says 'You shan't!' " we can be almost certain that Hardy intended her to mean that there were forces in life itself conspiring to defeat their (restless) aspirations.[1] If there is a specific social doctrine at work in the novel, it probably has more to do with birth control than anything that could be related to Marxism. *The Dynasts*—on the face of it, at least—makes it even clearer that Hardy attributed human misery to the inept and uncaring universe. There is no sense that by uniting (to use the rhetoric of *The Communist Manifesto*), the workers of the world could throw off their chains. When, at the end of act 1, scene 2, of *The Dynasts*, the Shade of the Earth argues that "uncreation" would be better than the "tedious conjuring" that is history, the Spirit of the Years can only answer that "something hidden" urges matter to motion and that this history is as good as any. The Spirit of the Pities asks "why any" at all and is told that there is no answer. "I am but an accessory of its works," the Spirit of the Years says, "bounden witness of Its laws." The Immanent Will to which this refers never appears in the drama. In both senses of the word, it is unaccountable.[2] We shall have to come back to *The Dynasts*, whose ending is less clear than this opening position, but it is clear that this version of history is far removed from Marxism. However deterministic Marxism is, there is no doubt that, in Marx's own words, people make their own history. Nothing answerable or even voiced makes Hardy's history.

The pursuit of the specific historical relevance of Marxism to Hardy thus meets a very early resistance. We are left, weakly, with some idea that Marxism ought to be relevant in this sense, more relevant than to any other major nineteenth-century British author, but that it is only negatively so. Hardy deals with the working class, but never as a class, always as individuals experiencing "history" only as a meaningless manipulation thwarting their lives.

The more profitable way for the Marxist critic to proceed seems, therefore, to be through general theoretical relevance. Marxism is an intellectual position from which it is possible to investigate any historical social phenomenon, and Hardy, like any other writer, is a historical social phenomenon. This is indeed how most "Marxist" critics approach him.

Some remarkable criticism of Hardy has come from critics who are either explicitly Marxist or, like Raymond Williams, within terms of reference defined by Marxism. They are also highly various, but I can identify two major points that many of them have in common. First, there is what Terry Eagleton has termed Hardy's "recalcitrance."[3] Most of the great writers of the nineteenth century have to be demystified—there is always a level at which they are limited by the ideology of capitalism with which they work. Hardy is frequently seen to be different. Christopher Caudwell, whose few pages on Hardy in *Romance and Realism* remarkably forecast later interpretations, writes: "While all this was happening, the artist who as long as he lived in England could not be deceived by the ideology of capitalism's mercenary class was wrestling with the problems involved in that more profound motion of culture which had produced both the imperialising bourgeoisie, and its mercenary class."[4] This recalcitrance leads to a good ideal of critical self-identification. Raymond Williams's essay in *The English Novel from Dickens to Lawrence*, which is certainly one of the best criticisms of Hardy ever written, ends with the strong claim that Hardy is "our flesh and our grass."[5]

Now, as Charles Swann has pointed out,[6] there is a line that is crossed here between singling Hardy out and appropriating him into a socialist worldview that he palpably did not share. The concept of recalcitrance, though useful and important, is also in two ways distorting. First, Hardy is the isolated refuser of the dominant ideology only if one accepts the canonical versions of literary history taught in the institutions, within which, it is argued, Hardy cannot be contained. Hardy himself, however, feels that he belongs with a very strong radical literary tradition—Shelley, Browning, Swinburne, Meredith, and, in important ways, Pater. He is certainly very different from these writers but not as insulated from them as he seems to be, for example, from George Eliot and Arnold. More important, he is not the only figure in his own day to be unpacking the assumptions of dominant ideology—I think of Olive Schreiner and Mark Rutherford, as well as discursive writers such as J. A. Symonds and Havelock Ellis.

Moreover, this reading involves a conscious deformation of Hardy's project. Again Caudwell summarizes what others develop in different ways: "Blind unconscious bourgeois society is the antagonist of *Jude the Obscure* and also the real enemy of *The Dynasts.*" Arnold Kettle in his first essay on *Tess of the d'Urbervilles*, which (let me add) in its time was vitally important for keeping Hardy out of the hands of second-rate philosophers, argued that that novel was really about the decline of the peasantry.[7] As Williams commented—and Kettle accepted the point—this could hardly be true when there was no English peasantry to decline. But Kettle's later essay still wants to defer Hardy's texts to a symbolic level, and even Williams, as Swann points out, reduces Hardy to a concern with his own "border country." Sherman's book is a classic and sad case of a writer whose warmth for and understanding of Hardy does not prevent him from failing to analyze what is actually there.[8] Two later accounts of Hardy—Boumelha's and Wotton's—are explicitly committed to the idea that it is on an unconscious level of the text, manifest in its gaps and slippages, that a materialist account of Hardy can take place.[9]

I am certainly not dismissing these accounts. I am merely arguing that they leave a great deal to be done, both about Hardy's place and about his project, both of which, in my view, are susceptible of materialist analysis. There is also a danger that a great deal of Hardy has to be left out in order to make him fit. Eagleton, for example, is so unwilling to take on Hardy's pessimism that he even, at one point, praises Roy Morrell's petit bourgeois, Boy Scout moralizing of Hardy.[10] Williams ends by saying that Hardy *mourns* what he sees. Both critics in this way emasculate the writer of the angry bitter endings of *Tess of the d'Urbervilles* and *Jude the Obscure* or even the sardonic "happy" endings of *Far from the Madding Crowd* and *The Mayor of Casterbridge.* Hardy was a lot less innocent and a lot more devastating than such critiques allow for.

Swann calls attention to the distorting effect, encouraged to some extent by *The Life,*[11] of seeing Hardy's career begin with *The Poor Man and the Lady,* which is supposedly a socialist novel, and end with the furor over *Jude the Obscure.* This account of Hardy's career ignores the fact that Hardy not only went on writing for thirty years after *Jude the Obscure,* but even published a second version of one novel, *The Well-Beloved,* and carefully revised most of his novels in 1911–1912 for the Wessex Edition. It is also not very likely that the first novel would have been "socialist" in any sense that would be accepted by Hardy's "Marxist" critics. Effectively, Swann says that we should pay more attention to Hardy's dismantling of organic form, so that we are concerned not so much with suppressed or underlying political issues but, rather, with the literary politics of the deconstruction of the coherent subject and the supplanting of depth, by narrative, by linearity within time. Such an approach at least restores to Hardy a level of consciousness that he manifestly has. But I think we have to go further. If we consider the question of how Hardy historically relates to Marxism instead of asking how he fits a coherent theoretical orientation, I think we shall find a writer who more than any other English novelist engages with its major concerns.

Let me stress, however, that we are not concerned with historical impossibility. At least when he was writing novels, Hardy would have had very little idea of and probably not much interest in a political ideology that had almost no adherents in Britain and no visible role in world history. Nor should we expect Hardy to arrive by his own route at insights comparable to those we find in Marx. Marx was effective precisely because he saw what nobody else *could* see, the mechanics of capitalism. It is still rare and difficult to read and understand Marx, and nothing can act as a substitute for the understanding he demands. What we shall, rather, find in Hardy is a series of thrusts in his writing that takes him to the impasse Marxism moves through. Hardy, I shall argue, gets nearer than any other nineteenth-century English novelist to defining the need for Marxist analysis, and has to move away from that need when he most closely approaches it.

2

Hardy himself thought that his novelistic career started with a "socialistic, not to say revolutionary novel," *The Poor Man and the Lady,* "a sweeping dramatic satire of the squirearchy and nobility, London society, the vulgarity of the middle class, modern Christianity, church restoration, and political and domestic morals in general" (*Life* 61). It is certainly true that not only what seems to have remained of this rejected text, the story entitled "An Indiscretion in the Life of an Heiress" (1888), but also all of the novels of the first phase (up to 1876) that deal with modern life, are preoccupied with the destructive effects of social inequality. *A Pair of Blue Eyes* is a variant on the poor-man-and-lady theme. *Desperate Remedies* is about the exploitation of the social disadvantage of a young woman whose father is an impecunious tradesman. *The Hand of Ethelberta* charts the campaign of the daughter of a butler to conquer and enter the nobility. Class difference is both a spur and an inexorable barrier to the achievement of desire. Egbert Mayne, the hero of *An Indiscretion in the Life of an Heiress*, summarizes the sense of transgression that class imposes on love, as he watches his pupils go home after a visit from his Lady:

> Much as he loved her, his liking for the peasantry about him—his mother's
> ancestry—caused him sometimes a twinge of self reproach for thinking of
> her so exclusively. . . . He watched the rain spots thickening upon the
> faded frocks, worn out tippets, yellow straw hats and bonnets, and coarse
> pinafores of his unprotected little flock as they walked down the path and
> was thereby reminded of the hopelessness of his attachment, by perceiving
> how much more nearly akin was his lot to theirs than to hers.[12]

Egbert's recognition of his true social identity is purely negative; it is the
separation that matters, not the identification. The separation remains
constant—"the madness of hoping to call that finished creature wife" (93).
Moreover, it is shared by her as a fate in which she, too, is bound: "To be
woven and tied in with the world by blood, acquaintance, tradition, and
external habit, is to a woman to be utterly at the beck of that world's customs" (91). Egbert saves her from certain death, enlists enough of her love to
put "in abeyance" the fine-lady position of her existence, so that they speak
and act "simply as a young man and woman" (62), and even goes off for five
years "to try to rise to her level by years of sheer exertion" (72), all to no avail.
Only when she is forced with the direct prospect of marriage to Lord Bretton
does she run to Egbert, and even in elopement she stops to appease her
father, in whose arms she dies.

On the other hand, Egbert's awareness of the "peasantry" is totally
vague. Even his grandfather, with whom he lives, is no peasant: As Williams
said of Kettle's analysis of *Tess of the d'Urbervilles*, England has never really
had a peasantry in the past few centuries. Intellectually and culturally,
Mayne is at a voyeuristic distance from his own people. Stephen Smith in *A
Pair of Blue Eyes* feels his distance from his parents more strongly than his
distance from Elfride and her father, though her father will regard his birth-
right as more significant. Ethelberta takes her appropriate place in the ruling
class only in disguise. How could a character of her intelligence and sophistication be a mere servant? In disguise, however, she is, of course, no longer
herself and is thus the victim of a double bind. Cytherea Graye in *Desperate
Remedies* confronts her existence as a figure on the labor market in a newspaper advertisement as "more material" than her real life, and at the height of
her drama recognizes that she is completely alienated from her social image.
Class allots us a place that we can only transgress as we become conscious of
it.

It is clear, however, that if this recognition of the rigors of class division
is radical in Hardy's early fiction, it is certainly not, in any modern or Marxist
sense, socialism. Significantly, in a later reiteration of the "socialist" tendency
of *The Poor Man and the Lady*, Hardy mentions Shaw's use of the disguise
motif from *The Hand of Ethelberta*. Shaw is mentioned several times in the
Life, and at the time Hardy was preparing it Shaw would surely be the most
obvious example of a "socialist" writer. Shaw's social vision was at best radical. The class structure of society is for him a static obstructive milieu, which
is disrupted and transformed by vitality and rationality manifest in a progres-

sive individual. Class is an anachronistic survival. Hardy himself recognizes that this was not a socialist position when he wrote, apparently in 1884: "I am against privilege derived from accident of any kind, and am therefore equally opposed to aristocratic privilege and democratic privilege" (*Life* 204).

Class in the Marxist sense is not a system of social layers; it is the manifestation of a set of relations, specifically relations of production, "relations of effective power over persons and productive forces, not relations of level ownership."[13] Asa Briggs has shown that although this sense of *class* enters the language dramatically in the critical period between the first reform act and the repeal of the corn laws, *class* reverts to something much closer to the eighteenth-century idea of rank at around the time of the second reform bill.[14] This is clearly because arguments in favor of the extension of the franchise wish to widen the legitimation of social groups without altering the actual production relations. It is therefore in the interests of the dominant culture to speak of class as marginal, subject to internal divisions (especially within the laboring class that is divided into labor, aristocracy, and "residuum"), open to individual but not class mobility (the doctrine of self-help). Arnold in *Culture and Anarchy* illustrates the point very well. The classes to Arnold are a given. They do not exist in relation to one another but in parallel, each with a homologous structure. "Culture" is promoted by aliens within those classes who rise above their interests to promote a traditional esprit de corps, the best that is thought and done. Thus class is neither threatened as a mode of social division, nor allowed to be determinant. Its very marginalization ensures its persistence.

Hardy clearly adopts this agenda in these early socially conscious texts. Class is crucially important but as a system of layers. He identifies himself with a radical position simply by recognizing the existence of class (Tories, as Briggs points out, did not like to be reminded of it). But this radicalism goes one stage further than that of more orthodox radicals, for instead of regarding class as a barrier that can be transgressed by individual excellence, vitality, or even culture, Hardy's position is one that makes those qualities redundant. *The Hand of Ethelberta* absolutely confirms this point—only by disguising herself forever will Ethelberta be able to transgress. Even then it is a dangerous procedure. Neigh, for example, sustains his class position only by concealing the source of his wealth, the family knacker's yard.

This observation leads to further discrimination. In *Desperate Remedies, A Pair of Blue Eyes,* and *The Hand of Ethelberta,* the point of transgression and the guarantee of its ultimate failure are a relationship of work. Companion, architect, entertainer—these guarantee the access as by the same token they put the protagonist in the power of those who employ them. This relationship, it is true, is a very marginal feature of the class relations in these texts; but it is not merely a plot device to bring incongruities together, because this functioning is never really transcended. What makes it important, however, is that the most important text of this period, *Far from the Madding Crowd,* precisely does constitute the social relation as a relation of work. Hardy distances this from the actual world of the reader who belongs, presumably, to the madding crowd. But this distancing only clarifies the relationship. Gabriel is thrust into the subordinate position because he is undercapitalized and therefore inadequately insured (see Williams). His dependence on Bathsheba's employment is preluded by the series of disguises he has to adopt to try to acquire a social function, and, of course, he is really in disguise throughout until he resumes his true role as owner of the means of production. Other characters are classified only by the roles they play. Boldwood, for example, is not an aristocrat but only the nearest thing to it by reason of his economic position in the community. Troy ceases to be a sergeant and becomes a gentleman farmer as soon as he has access to the resources of the farm. Class and subordination are in this novel functions of the social relations of production. Society operates through work, and wealth—as Gabriel shows when he reckons wheat as the equivalent of gold after the storm—is expressed in the terms of a developed, wage-based capitalist economy. The reality of class relations is in this novel, heavily disguised as idyll.

The Hand of Ethelberta reverts to contemporary life, and the class system is once more presented as rank. But there are enormous differences from the earlier works. First, as the visit to Neigh's family knacker's yard shows, rank has its actual economic basis. Second, by making herself indispensable to the upper world, Ethelberta turns herself from servant to mistress, which in turn makes her a slave of her own success. The master-servant relationship is, as shown in the parody Manlove practices, a two-way mirror (this is made explicit in *Indiscretion* [32]). More importantly, Ethelberta's manipulative success is challenged by the radical opposition of her stonemason brother, who stands for the class as an active process in opposition to the exploiting class. Gabriel Oak's economic subordination is brought into the urban, contemporary world and calls Ethelberta's mobility a form of treachery. This "comedy in chapters," unlike the Shavian drama it predates, turns into a potential class tragedy: the conflict between collective and personal modes of action that will finally reemerge with *Jude the Obscure*. But this is not merely a matter of representation. There are plenty of representations of this economic relation between classes. Hardy is, I would suggest, almost unique in the midseventies in recognizing this relation to be based only on exploitation. We have only to compare the presentation of class in *Far from the Madding Crowd* and *The Hand of Ethelberta* with Ruskin to see how far out on a limb Hardy is. In *Unto This Last* Ruskin defines wealth as a relationship giving power over others, and he recognizes that this power is the cash nexus that is produced by the division of labor. But in opposition to this view he offers two models of social relationship that are defined by something outside the nexus of cash payment: domestic service and military honor. Hardy seems to satirize this idea explicitly in his novels of the midseventies. Troy's exploitation of the labor relations at Weatherbury shows how effective military ethics are in social life. Ethelbert and Manlove show

how domestic service is totally subordinate to economic need. Not only is the Arnoldian pattern of aliens within a hierarchy questioned by the Ruskinian bid to sustain inequality within a rhetoric of social justice; it is exposed as paternalistic nonsense. But after Sol the stonemason has confronted Ethelberta with her class treachery, where, in the portrayal of social relationships, is Hardy to go?

There is nothing either in Hardy's personal situation or in the general cultural situation in 1876 that would enable him to work out the issues raised in *The Hand of Ethelberta*. The most interesting novels of the same year, Eliot's *Daniel Deronda* and Meredith's *Beauchamp's Career*, show how even within the problematic arena of liberal values there is no visible solution to the political choice between self-fulfillment and self-survival. How much less for the class that has no access to resources except by individual mobility and class betrayal? In Hardy's next novel, *The Return of the Native*, social issues move to the margins. The Heathans are economically very primitive, mixing a marginal market activity based not on production but on collecting, with self-sufficiency, and they thus blend into the landscape, which becomes a generalized objective world for the children of outsiders, widow and retired sea captain, who have no personal economic activity at all. Hardy's concerns are, of course, equally abstracted from the actual historical conditions, resembling the confrontation of the romantic subject with no intractable and impersonal real of "Nature" that we find in Ruskin, Peter, and above all Arnold. The "mind" is modern; the universe it confronts is supposedly "timeless." I have argued elsewhere that Hardy does not merely repeat this modern predicament but represents and goes beyond it, showing subject and object locked in paralytic opposition, but transcended by a necessity that is served neither by romantic rebellion nor by adaptation (which denies inner needs) and that is not available to consciousness separated from action.[15] This opposition is residually manifest in the landscape, which turns out to be not "nature" but, as Eagleton showed, nature as a language,[16] a text on which language is inscribed, its own morphology made up not of a dominant syntax but of many obscure dialectic operations. Opposition of this sort is dramatically evident in the mother's crossing (transgression) of the heath, by which action she confronts the objective world as not merely inscrutable but motiveless, and not therefore supplanting the need to act by wise passiveness.

I think Hardy in this phase is taking upon himself the predicament of what Gramsci would call that of the traditional intellectual with respect to the major discourses within which he can define his being, and shows him confronting an intellectual impasse that cannot be brooked except by transgression of the logical trajectory he confronts. Thus the astronomer of *Two on a Tower* is appropriately awed by the immensity of the universe, but viewing the southern skies, unmapped by his predecessors, he is disgusted by its meaninglessness. He retreats to the alternative discourse of romantic love (the subject as opposed to the object), only to find this no longer available either, to find instead a role as parent, protecting human life in all its insignificance, relating to it by a phrase that in itself is weak and probably borrowed from positivism, but central to Hardy's later develoment: "loving kindness."

The next phase of Hardy's novel writing—which begins late in 1884 as he starts to write *The Mayor of Casterbridge*, ends with the publication of *Tess of the d'Urbervilles*, and results in three novels as accomplished and powerful as the novels of 1876–1884 are confused and even contrived— coincides with the first phase of the socialist revival in England, when for the first time the influence of Marx was an important factor. In 1884 the Democratic Federation became the Social Democratic Federation, and although it was tiny and schismatic, it made a disproportionate impact on the public through the unemployed demonstrations in Trafalgar Square in 1886 and 1887. In 1888 Annie Besant, who was certainly not a Marxist but who was already sufficiently a heroine of revolutionary sexual politics through her divorce and her espousal of birth control, organized the successful strike of Bryant and May match girls. In 1889, the Dock Strike was the first major victory of unskilled organized labour.

Hardy records none of these events explicitly. But we should take note of a number of circumstances. First, even as Hardy left behind the class question in his early novels, his notebooks show him taking an interest in positivism, which prior to the emergence of Marxism was certainly the strongest intellectual system proposing social progress. The English positivists, as Royden Harrison has shown, befriended Marx and were in the seventies an important influence on radical politics.[17] Hardy's personal contact with Edward Beesley, the most left-wing of the positivists, is evident in 1885, when Beesley wrote to Hardy about his defeat at the Westminster election (though we must not make too much of this; Beesley had less contact with the socialist movement in the 1880s). Hardy would have had plenty of access to socialist theory from 1882 onward. Hyndman's *The Historical Basis of Socialism* leaned heavily on Marx, and Bax and Morris brought out *Socialism: Its Growth and Outcome* in 1884. Journals such as *Justice, Commonweal,* and *Today* rehearsed socialist issues. Hardy's two most distinguished rivals, Gissing and James, both brought out novels explicitly dealing with working-class politics—*Demos* and *The Princess Casamassima*. The note of 1884 without a context in *The Life* that I earlier quoted must surely be a response to this "democratic" upsurge. There are many writers to whom Hardy would have been sympathetic who were interested in the movement—Hardy himself mentioned the Belgian socialist, Laveleye. Carpenter, Symonds, Havelock Ellis, Shaw himself—all these writers recognized that the future of their enlightened ideology was bound up with the emancipation of the working class.

Most important, however, is the recruitment of William Morris in 1883 to the revolutionary socialist movement. Morris had been the leading member of the campaign against church restoration to which Hardy was so opposed. He was the heir of Ruskinian aesthetics and, as Hardy had done in *Far from the Madding Crowd*, he secularized Ruskin. Morris attracted great publicity to the socialist movement by getting arrested in 1887. Throughout the 1880s he lectured tirelessly, and produced two socialist stories, *The Pilgrims of Hope* and *A Dream of John Ball*, and many essays expounding socialism, some of which were collected in *Signs of Change* (1888). No writer could ignore the fact that this dreamy Pre-Raphaelite and guardian of traditional craft values was appearing vociferously and articulately on the barricades.

There is a second striking point about the revival of socialism in the 1880s: how bound up it becomes with feminism. Annie Besant is the obvious example, but Olive Schreiner and Margaret Harkness were both friends of Eleanor Marx, whose lecture on "Shelley's Socialism" in 1888 was as much concerned with Shelley's revolutionary sexual politics as with his democratic ideas. It is, of course, not possible to define how much Hardy would have been aware of any of this activity. I am trying only to define what might have been available; it helps to illuminate some of the features of the fiction Hardy wrote in this period. What is crucial is that class politics and sexual politics are part of the same ferment.

Both *The Mayor of Casterbridge* and *The Woodlanders* are, of course, resolutely distanced from these issues. The first is subjected to a precise displacement in time, and the second explicitly displaced geographically outside the gates of the world. Nevertheless, both have connections with the contemporary slum novels of Gissing, James, Besant, and others, as William Greenslade has shown.[18] Mixen Lane has all the marks of Gissing's Litany Lane (*The Unclassed*), and the woods of Little Hintock are repeatedly compared with slums, which in social discourse of the time are treated as natural deformations. In fact, it is common to make the urban working class, outcast London, darkest London, as displaced and exotic as Hardy's Wessex. One could speculate about the motives for Hardy's displacement, but certainly one of the effects is to shift attention from description to processes—that is, the distance creates a space in which histories take place.

The Mayor of Casterbridge is the story of a man of character, but character is conceived literally as bourgeois man, for what else is the mayor but the leading burgher? Hardy draws on Victorian degeneration myths, the nearest in time being Morris's own *Sigurd the Volsung* (1876), which has great similarities—that is, the original self-made man, whose character is unified by his subjective desire, loses to the adaptive divided man who can keep business and pleasure separate, calculate profit rationally, and deploy others effectively without owning them or taking responsibility for them. Henchard and Farfrae are opposed only within the various parameters of self-help—does one rise by overwhelming the objective world or by understanding it? It depends on the complexity of the objective world. What matters, however, from the viewpoint of this argument is that Henchard is reconstructed by the destructive experience of his evolutionary displacement, not as a new man but as one of a crowd, *les misérables*, and in the process, as Showalter has shown, feminized.[19] It is in the double "negation" of this individuality (and that no man remember me) and his masculinity that Henchard is reborn and that the triumph of Farfrae, Newson, and Elizabeth-Jane is so meaningless. The fall of

Henchard replicates the original fall of Gabriel Oak, but the redemption is not a question of rising again; it is a question of embracing obscurity.

The Woodlanders was written between the end of 1885 and the beginning of 1887. Many of Morris's crucial essays appeared in 1885, including "How We Live and How We Might Live," whose title appears to be echoed in Hardy's second paragraph, and "Useful Work and Useless Toil." Some of the Icelandic allusions in the novel, especially to the theft of Marty's locks by "Loki the Malicious" and the explicit comments about the division of labor in the production of Grace's skirt, which is, of course, what gets caught in the mantrap, seem to make this a novel that calls for comparison with Morris. More important than these local details, The Woodlanders inaugurates a general sense of social oppression, of which Marty's useless and piecework labor through the night is the first dramatic instance and the demolition of Giles's cottage the major narrative instance. This general level, however, is clearly abandoned once the story begins to focus on Grace and Fitzpiers. But this general level precisely brings into play the relationship between the social relationship and the gender relationships in the novel, for the economic oppression that is practiced on Marty and Giles by Melbury and Mrs. Charmond is repeated by the gender oppression practiced on Grace and in a sense Mrs. Charmond, and it is at this level that the tensions set up at the beginning of the novel are able to surface and issue in individual rebellion. Again there is a precise parallel to be drawn with Morris, whose Pilgrims of Hope shows the political energies of the commune demanding new attitudes toward sexual relationships and particularly toward monogamy. Divorce, which becomes the central issue of Hardy's novel, is a very central component of the Socialist League's manifesto issued in 1885 (Morris was a founding member of the Socialist League). The sexual politics of The Woodlanders have to be placed in a general world of alienation—all the characters are abstracted from their own lives because the circumstances of their lives are unresponsive to their desires. Hardy's pessimism in this novel, the sense of unfulfilled intention, is a utopian pessimism, deriving from a sense of what things might be. When Grace and Giles think that divorce laws will enable them to possess one another, they are like children in being taken in by lawyer Beaucock's claim that there is no longer one law for the rich and one for the poor. Sherman is right to see The Woodlanders as the novel in which the pessimism closely reflects the class struggles of the time. There is no reason, however, that we should not see it as strategic and conscious. The focus on Grace is a focus on the weakest link in the chain of bourgeois domination.

My intention here is not to provide an analysis of The Woodlanders but only to indicate how close Hardy has come to the same preoccupations as those of Morris, and hence how, indirectly, Marxism has become relevant to his project. Tess of the d'Urbervilles, I think, moves even closer. Its structure is actually best defined in terms of the Marxist model of the base and superstructure. That model is a means of describing the complex relations between the actual means of production (which are the material basis of a society) and the political and cultural structures that are raised on that basis. Of course, these structures do not simply reflect the base, and Marxists who (like Caudwell) tend to see every cultural manifestation as a metaphor for, let us say, capitalism tend to use it reductively. But if we recognize that the base itself is complex—composed not merely of technological resources but also of the social relations by which those resources are put to work—we shall also recognize that the superstructure must act on the base, that there must be levels of discourse more or less reflective of the base, and that the superstructure has its own history and rhythm, lagging behind in some respects, moving forward in others. Were this not so, the history of humanity would be a continuous marking of time.

I have argued in my detailed analysis of *Tess of the d'Urbervilles* that there are three related levels of discourse. There is first of all a complex and contradictory discourse about Nature, and human nature. The overall pattern of the novel denies that Nature has a holy plan. Tess is like a fly upon a billiard table. Her very excellence as a natural phenomenon, her sexual attractiveness, is her downfall. On the other hand, there is a strong sense in the novel—echoing Havelock Ellis and, among others, Morris—that Tess's downfall is only the product of a repressive attitude toward natural sexuality. Both of these approaches are "true"—that is, they are ways of describing reality—but they are dependent on positions of power within that "reality." When Angel feels the ache of modernism, he is merely thinking about the universe: When Tess says we are on a blighted planet, she is thinking about her drunken father and her numerous brothers and sisters. When Alec and Angel give way to desire, it is to destroy another being. When Tess and the other dairymaids run across the fields, it is to express their own generous vitality. The two sources of power in the novel are gender and class. Tess is finally made into a woman by violation and into a field woman by economic oppression. It is the interaction of modernism, sexual equality, and the demand for economic freedom that constitutes the "justice" that is deferred to the President of the Immortals and withheld from the pure woman hanged for being herself. Hardy sent a copy of the first edition of *Tess of the d'Urbervilles* to William Morris. It is a strange act—he did not know Morris personally and Morris almost certainly would not have appreciated the book. But the act tells us something about the project of the novel, as well as something more about the relationship not so much between Hardy and Marxism as between Marxism (in England) and Hardy.

I think it can be argued that if *Tess of the d'Urbervilles* permits and demands a Marxist reading, the texts that follow are much more problematic. *Jude the Obscure* is a novel about working-class experience as a subjective, isolated, and isolating ordeal. The whole point for both Jude and Sue is that there is no cultural home for them, no articulated class experience except that of the class from which they are by their economic position excluded. Accordingly, I do not regard it as any less radical a novel than *Tess of the d'Urbervilles,* but I think we fail to understand how deep it goes unless we acknowledge that it is a novel written by and about someone to whom Marxist answers are not available. I do not think it is difficult to see why Hardy's distance from a socialist analysis grew after 1891. Socialism itself in Britain was undergoing rapid transformation in the early 1890s after the successful resolution of the Dock Strike, the formation of the Independent Labour Party, and the marginalization of Morris himself. Hardy is no possibilist, and possibilism began to dominate the socialist agenda in these years. The radical "revolutionary" position was occupied by issues of gender and aesthetics. The response to *Tess of the d'Urbervilles* was to the idea of the heroine's purity rather than to her economic degradation. It is important to recall that while there was strong hostility to the novel, there was also very strong support for it, even to the extent of Grant Allen dedicating his "hill top novel," *The Woman Who Did,* to the author of *Tess.* Maverick and individualist as Hardy seems to be on the surface, he belongs to a social group as much as anyone does, and the group identified by his work is that of those disaffected intellectuals dominated by what was called the "new spirit." The group of stories written by Hardy in 1891—which make up most of *Life's Little Ironies,* "The Son's Veto" for example, or "For Conscience Sake"— represents class as an agent of sexual respectability and repression. "The Fiddler of the Reels," the great story of 1893, combines a recognition of feminine sexuality (as subversive) with an emphasis on the liberating effect of music. Its ruralist guise does not cloak its affinity with George Egerton. "On the Western Circuit" ironically privileges the erotic as text.

But above all, the novel that intervenes between *Tess of the d'Urbervilles* and *Jude the Obscure* inaugurates a new dimension in Hardy's work. The two versions of *The Well-Beloved*—the serial published in *Illustrated London News* in 1892 and the book published after *Jude the Obscure* in 1897—tell us a great deal about the politics of Hardy's writing. Hillis Miller discusses the two versions with his usual perceptiveness, but by implying that we should read the two versions together, he effectively depoliticizes the texts. In fact, he explicitly compares the novel to Fowles's ideologically pluralist *The French Lieutenant's Woman.*[20] But Hardy gives us two texts, not one text with two endings. The second text is intended to replace the first. That kind of replacement indicates a transition.

The serial version was, according to Miller, written as "something light" to replace the offensive *Tess* for the Tillotson firm. It is, of course, more outrageous than anything in the earlier novel, legitimating as it does an eroticism unrelated to affection or moral stability. At a deeper level, as Swann has suggested, it calls into question empiricist notions of identity, not only by implying that the object of Pierston's love can reappear in different women, but also by having interchangeable names, premarital sex as a custom, and generally a sexual politics that shows "morality" to be relative and historically variable (the lesson Angel Clare learns in Brazil). The serial version stresses Hardy's social message by having Pierston marry Marcia and

Avice III. It also adds a long prehistory of well-beloveds through the letters
he destroys before the story begins. This throws the focus onto the oppression of women. Marcia recognizes that "she was her husband's property, like
one of his statues that he could not sell" (209); Pierston's development, which
emerges dramatically after his marriage to Avice III, is primarily one of his
recognition of the "barbarism" of the age in which marriage laws make it
wrong to commit a simple "act of charity" by letting her go. The story in this
version clearly foreshadows the relationship of Sue and Phillotson. Indeed, it
makes more explicit the wrongness of the husband's imposing his subjective
sexuality on the woman.

Two points emerge from this look at the serial. First, it is clear that the
gender issue, particularly marriage, is the focus Hardy moves toward after
Tess of the d'Urbervilles, because it is there that he has had most response.
Class is very important in *Jude the Obscure*, but it is more inexorable than
sexual politics. Sue and Jude are released from their marital bondage, but
only into deeper economic oppression. There is a Marxist reading of *Jude the
Obscure*, but unlike the reading of *Tess of the d'Urbervilles*, it is not a
reading that fully accounts for the structure. No reading would. *Jude the
Obscure* poses its questions at a level of insolubility that demands not a
Marxist reading but (in my view) a Marxist answer. It is the lack of this
answer that enables Hardy to write as he does. The nearest text available
that proposes answers in Marxist terms, and a novel highly relevant to
Hardy's text, is Morris's *News from Nowhere*. But that too is a text that raises
more questions than answers. There are no easy answers. It is perhaps
significant that Morris, too, ends his literary career in the nineties with
stories about sexuality.

The second point is that when Hardy comes to revise *The Well-Beloved*,
much of this instant social concern goes. The later text is much more the
subjectivist and relativist inquiry Proust was to admire. It is much closer to
the poetry. Hardy's poetry remains, of course, a vigorous challenge to the
dominant lyric tradition that it deploys, making rhythm manifest as meter,
metaphor as simile, "perception" as optics. *The Well-Beloved* in its final
version still outrages the conventions of identity, love, and even time and
place on which much nineteenth-century fiction is based. But it no longer
does so in such an explicit, socially oriented way. To put it another way, while
the first version is positively addressing a debate and an audience, the second, like the poetry, exists within a marked, marginal silence. We lose Hardy
the hilltop novelist, the spokesman of an enlightened avant-garde, and gain
the subversive sage (of course, a subversive sage is still a very paradoxical
and disturbing persona).

The "social" as an explicit area of concern, though it reappears in more
of the poetry than is sometimes acknowledged, is largely allotted to the epic-
drama. *The Dynasts* is a text that none of the critiques I have referred to
really deals with, although it is Hardy's most explicit and sustained intervention in the public domain, and it is one that preoccupies him throughout his

career. The total structure places Hardy very far from any Marxist analysis in the first sense that I have been pursuing. This is not so much because he refuses any notion of historical causality other than the voiceless and mindless will, but rather because there is in *The Dynasts* a radical disjunction between signifier and signified so great as to call in question the function of the signifying process itself. The history the text displays has immense detail and accuracy—if we did not have those daunting photographs of Hardy's Napoleonic library, we would still have an overwhelming sense of how much research is put into it. But it has no before and after. Nothing is changed by the Napoleonic wars; Europe is no different because of them. Neither are the wars really produced. The reader does not need to be aware, for example, that Napoleon is the product of a revolution, rather than just an upstart demagogue. Moreover, this history does not even exist as a moral milieu. It is not very rewarding to try to make discriminations between characters. Some are obviously fatuous (mainly the hereditary monarchs), some are efficient, some have a residual, marginal, private emotional life—but as none of these characters are really able to make choices, none of them are available for praise or blame. History is reduced to spectacle.

John Wain's perceptive comparison of the text to cinema in one sense confirms this view.[21] Not only does the language embody a vivid illusion, but it is an illusion safely on the screen. I think, though, that this idea precisely gives us a purchase on the text. Hardy, as we know, has not been miraculously prophetic by employing a cinematic technique. He would have seen dioramas and phantasmogorias, and some of the illustrations that he had known as a child have this same vivid illusory effect. Spectacle of this sort, however, like the *intention* of some Hollywood movies, is aimed at excluding the spectator from the illusion by awe. *The Dynasts*, I would argue, is a text much less about the Napoleonic wars than about their history. This point is confirmed for me by the overworld, which so far from being a superior consciousness is an excluded consciousness. The Spirits of the Pities, and the Spirits Ironic and Sinister in particular, are responses and postures of the intelligentsia doomed to understand and see but unable to alter in any way what has happened. History, for Hardy, is a text to be read, but not a text that can be altered. In this way, I think *The Dynasts* inscribes the history of the nineteenth-century intellectual. Poets are not, precisely and tragically, the unacknowledged legislators of the world. *The Dynasts* is the morning after *Prometheus Unbound*'s night before.

Critics of Hardy's drama make very little of its title, and yet *dynast* is a rare and strange word. The OED has few references for it; in fact, only one—Muhaffy's *Social Life in Greece* (which Hardy knew)—uses the word in the way Hardy seems to. Milton's "Tenure of Kings" talks of *dynasts* in the context of the *Magnificat;* and it is the Greek text of Mary's praise of God for overthrowing the mighty that Hardy invokes as the only explicit explanation of his title, *at the very end* of the work. *Dynasts* occurs throughout the text in the sense of a social group that has the "making" of history because its desires control the destinies of the lower orders. The high moments of drama are not the political debates, which are wooden and cynical, nor are they the royal passions or military strategems. They are the moments of questioning—deserters, women, ordinary soldiers whose lives are wrecked on behalf of the dynasts. Warfare is "plied by the Managed for the Managers." Managers in the nineteenth century tended to be running workhouses, theaters, or boarding schools. But Hardy is using the term in a very much more modern sense because here it is not the managers who ply, but the managed. Finally, war is the most appalling and unjustifiable division of labor. Milton's text is, of course, antiroyalist. Muhaffy's, too, is also a very political text—not always radical, it is true. But Hardy feels that fiction, particularly Scott's fiction, is necessary because only by departing from the actual history (which is always the history of the rulers) can we enter an unrecorded plea for injustice, and mete out an unreal punishment for it. This is a comment on the repressive silence of the epic. Hardy's text registers the separation of the knowing intellectual from the process that silences the manipulated agents of history.

As noted, this consideration of lexicon is a long way from Marxism in one sense. And it is precisely that absence which *The Dynasts* is about. We have seen Hardy move close to a picture that accords with Marxist perspectives. We also see him move sharply away, into a kind of cosmic wisdom that leaves him in pain and leaves the world he portrays still full of injustice. Marxism was not, in nineteenth-century England, really an available answer. Hardy could not have gone on writing on its basis, because unlike Morris he could not postpone his vision to dream. Hardy is bereft, with a history that is meaningless and a consciousness that is sharp and unresting. What we have to ask is whether Marxism—and if so, in what form—would be an answer to the questions he asks. I believe it is. I will not have proved that point in this essay, but I hope to have shown, at least, that Marxism enables us to go on asking the questions that Hardy poses throughout his life and to which he would not allow answers that were either unrealistic or unjust. He wanted justice *and* realism, and that is a quest we are still embarked upon.

Notes

1. Thomas Hardy, *Jude the Obscure*, ed. Patricia Ingham (Oxford: Oxford University Press, 1985), 356.

2. Thomas Hardy, *The Dynasts*, ed. Harold Orel (London: Macmillan, 1978), 39.

3. Terry Eagleton, *Against the Grain: Essays 1976–1985* (London: Verso, 1986), 40. See also his introduction to *Jude the Obscure* (London: Macmillan, 1974), 9–20; and *Criticism and Ideology* (London: New Left Books, 1976), 94–95, 130–33. Also see nn. 10–15, below.

4. Christopher Caudwell, *Romance and Realism: A Study in Bourgeois Literature*, ed. Samuel Hynes (Princeton: Princeton University Press, 1970), 88–94. This was written, of course, before 1937, but was published too late to have been an influence on most of the other "Marxist" critics I discuss.

5. Raymond Williams, *The English Novel from Dickens to Lawrence* (London: Chatto & Windus, 1970), 95–118. There is a different version in *The Country and the City* (London: Chatto & Windus, 1973), 197–214.

6. C. S. B. Swann, "Hardy's Fiction: 'An Attempt to Give Artistic Form to a True Sequence of Things,' " *Essays in Poetics* 9(1984): 67–101.

7. Arnold Kettle, *An Introduction to the English Novel* (1951; London: Hutchinson, 1961), vol. II, 50–64. See also his "Hardy the Novelist: A Reconsideration" (1966), in *The Nineteenth-Century Novel: Critical Essays and Documents*, ed. Arnold Kettle (London: Heinemann Educational, 1972), 262–73.

8. George W. Sherman, *The Pessimism of Thomas Hardy* (Rutherford, N.J.: Fairleigh Dickinson University Press, 1976).

9. Penny Boumelha, *Thomas Hardy and Women: Sexual Ideology and Narrative Form* (Brighton: Harvester Press, 1982); George Wotton, *Thomas Hardy: Towards a Materialist Criticism* (Dublin: Gill & Macmillan, 1985).

10. Terry Eagleton, *Walter Benjamin: or, Towards a Revolutionary Criticism* (London: Verso, 1981), 129.

11. Florence Emily Hardy, *The Life of Thomas Hardy* (London: Macmillan, 1962), 57–61.

12. Thomas Hardy, *An Indiscretion in the Life of an Heiress*, ed. Terry Coleman (London: Century Publishing, 1985), 49–50. All references are to this edition.

13. G. A. Cohen, *Karl Marx's Theory of History: A Defense*, rev. ed. (Oxford: Oxford University Press, 1979), 83.

14. Asa Briggs, "The Language of 'Class' in Early Nineteenth-Century England," *Essays in Labour History*, eds. Asa Briggs and John Saville (London: Macmillan, 1967), 43–73.

15. John Goode, *Thomas Hardy: The Offensive Truth* (Oxford: Basil Blackwell, 1988).

16. Terry Eagleton, "Nature as Language in Thomas Hardy," *Critical Quarterly* 13(1971): 155–72.

17. Royden Harrison, *Before the Socialists: Studies in Labour and Politics, 1861–1881* (London: Routledge & Kegan Paul, 1965).

18. W. Greenslade, "The Concept of Degeneration, 1880–1910" (Ph.D. diss., University of Warwick, 1982), 111–97.

19. Elaine Showalter, "The Unmanning of the *Mayor of Casterbridge*," *Critical Approaches to the Fiction of Thomas Hardy*, ed. Dale Kramer (London: Macmillan, 1979), 99–115.

20. J. Hillis Miller, introduction to Thomas Hardy, *The Well-Beloved* (London: Macmillan, 1975), 17.

21. John Wain, introduction to Thomas Hardy, *The Dynasts* (London: Macmillan, 1965), ix.

Hardy's Magian Retrospect   Mary Jacobus[*]

For my part, if there is any way of getting a melancholy satisfaction out of life it lies in dying, so to speak, before one is out of the flesh; by which I mean putting on the manners of ghosts, wandering in their haunts, and taking their views of surrounding things. To think of life as passing away is a sadness; to think of it as past is at least tolerable.[1]

*Reprinted by permission of the editors from *Essays in Criticism* 32(1982): 258–79.

Hardy's writing presents one of the most striking instances of literary posthumousness in English literature—a posthumousness as distinct from the furious energies of Yeats's poetic old age as it is from Tennysonian penultimacy. Leaving aside his demise as a Victorian novelist in the 1890s and the belated poetic career embarked on with *Wessex Poems* in 1898, Hardy was himself notably obsessed with the peculiar form of immortality bestowed by living on beyond one's own death. From *Wessex Poems* onwards, every volume ends with a farewell—to youth ("I look into my glass," *Wessex Poems*), to his own ghost ("I have lived with shades," from "Retrospect," *Poems of the Past and the Present*, 1901), to love ("He abjures love," *Times's Laughingstocks*, 1909), to Emma and to the poet himself ("Where the Picnic Was" and "A Poet," respectively the last of the "Poems of 1912–13" and "Miscellaneous Pieces" in *Satires of Circumstance*, 1914). Each of Hardy's farewells remorselessly rehearses an anticipated death: "A few sad vacant hours, / And then, the Curtain." Morbid at worst, bleak at best, imagining one's own death or "dying . . . before one is out of the flesh" may be suspected of holding a melancholy satisfaction beyond the one admitted to by Hardy himself—the satisfaction, perhaps, of compensating for a sense of personal insignificance. " 'He was a man who used to notice such things' " could tell us that Hardy felt unnoticed "already," and not just "Afterwards" (the best-known of his farewells, at the close of *Moments of Vision*, 1917).

These funereal anticipations share a common structure—a self-duplication or doubling that involves an encounter, or, more usually, a dialogue, between Hardy and his ghostly other. Freud reminds us how the double, from being initially an insurance against mortality, becomes a portent of death. Hardy's poetic quest for immortality regularly gives rise to intimations of this kind. In "I have lived with shades," for instance, he looks back at himself from "the To-Be" and fails to recognize the nameless "man / So commonplace" whose "frail speech" and disembodiment are his own: "Into the dim / Dead throngs around / He'll sink. . . ." Later volumes increasingly prefer silence to anonymity—"And my voice ceased talking to me" ("Surview," the final poem of *Late Lyrics and Earlier*, 1922); "Why do I go on doing these things? / Why not cease?" (the last poem in *Human Shows*, 1925); and finally, "He resolves to say no more": "From now alway / Till my last day / What I discern I will not say" (*Winter Words*, 1928). The dialogue of one—"my own voice talking to me"—seems quite accidentally cut short by Hardy's actual death at the age of eighty-seven; for all his scruples about adding to the load of human gloom ("Why load men's minds with more to bear?"), his resolve to say no more would surely, one imagines, have been broken again and again in a final attempt to have the last word before silence and curtain fell for ever.

What seems to be at stake in such farewells is the survival of the poet: that is, his ability to speak from beyond the grave. Hardy's ghostly disappearances are as much a form of self-protection as his silences, rendering him inaccessible instead of insignificant. We literally do not know where to have him. But though he sometimes looks in the mirror and finds nobody there (the Self-Unseeing), his "idiosyncratic mode of regard" is fundamentally self-regarding.[2] The man of "Afterwards" who used to notice such things is a man intent on making us notice his noticings—the unblinking glimpse of a dewfall hawk crossing the shade of night "like an eye-lid's soundless blink"; or the bell whose tolling for the poet's own passing draws together passages as unobtrusive as a hedgehog's across a lawn, or as mysterious as the wheeling of "the full-starred heavens." Here, what is noticed is synonymous with the poet's consciousness. But it would be wrong to suggest that "Afterwards" is really, or even principally, quiet self-advertisement for Hardy's eye for such things half-seen or momentarily glimpsed—that it is, in effect, narcissistic or self-reflecting. Temporal irony and elegy converge, creating a double time-scheme in which elegy belongs to the future ("When the Present has latched its postern behind my tremulous stay"), while noticing drifts towards the past. The eclipse of Hardian conciousness is caught elliptically between tenses (" 'He hears it not now, but *used* to notice such things' "), as if the difference between these unobtrusive passages were that while the hedge-hog keeps on passing, the poet himself has passed on; on the one hand, repetition, and on the other, the past perfect. As writing could be said to be the past tense of noticing, so dying becomes the past tense of passing. The same divided, self-reflexive consciousness afflicts the characters of Hardy's novels, where the cosmic frisson involves walking not simply on one's own grave, but on that of thousands: " 'The best is not to remember that your nature and your past doings have been just like thousands' and thousands', and that your coming life and doings 'll be like thousands' and thousands' " (*Tess of the D'Urbervilles,* ch. xix). So Tess reflects, in a novel originally entitled "Too late, Beloved!" Though Hardy's characters regularly wish them-selves dead, they tend to live on in the ghostly after-life to which Jude consigns himself—a latter-day Job, his voice mingling with other texts from Christminster's past to make him as much belated as ahead of his times. Thus the present for Hardy is never simply time passing, but always a has-been, or a might-have-been: a temporal lack or absence, itself the subject as well as the manner of Hardian elegy.

If the characteristic world of Hardy's fiction, as of his poetry, is not so much the Wessex of the past as the limbo world of "I have lived with shades" (looking before and after), its characteristic mode of irony is temporal. Irony in Hardy's writing becomes less a matter of self-alienation than of time viewed, dizzyingly, from the vantage-point of the future as well as the past. When both time and irony get out of hand, discombobulatingly, even energiz-ingly, they tip over into a special kind of belatedness: that of having seen it all (or having been seen) before. Such seeing swallows up poetic individuality, making a mockery of the quest for literary survival and reducing "afterwards" to the same level as "before"—to "as if it (I) had never been." Hence its desolating implications for the prized individual consciousness of a poem like "Afterwards." Irony works as a defence against the dissolution of individual consciousness by mirroring back the self; though it may involve self-estrangement, or a splitting of self in time, it at least represents a controlled alienation. When irony slips, there occurs a fall into the abyss of non-being ("Into the dim / Dead throngs around /He'll sink . . .") or into the undifferentiated chaos of pre-history—a time-slip, as it were. The slippage of this temporal irony, prompted by the recognition of one's own belatedness (the inability to see oneself as anything but a ghost from the past), characteristically produces in Hardy's writing a peculiar upsurge of imaginative energy in the form of the grotesque—a denial of meaning which, in fragmenting the familiar world of objects and obliterating the present, threatens to undo the integrity of the self.

While ironic doubling provides the consolingly specular mirror of "noticing," or being noticed, the grotesque involves an anarchic overwhelming of the noticer. It signals the moment when irony gives way to incomprehensibility—an unending irony that engulfs the ironist and swamps the seer altogether, leaving him without a stable point of self-reference.[3] Whereas the double at least gives back the self, the proliferating images of the grotesque distort and so deny it, or fracture it into unmanageable plurality. The effect is to defamiliarize that reality by which we know ourselves real, estranging us not only from the world but from ourselves. A comparable moment in Wordsworth's poetry would be the boat-stealing episode in Book I of *The Prelude,* where the "huge Cliff," striding after the boy, displaces his wishful imaginings ("She was an elfin Pinnace . . .") with the primitive shapings of the unconscious; "huge and mighty forms that do not live / Like living men" haunt his dreams and annihilate the familiar forms of Nature ("familiar shapes / Of hourly objects, images of trees, / Of sea or sky," 1805, I. 422–6). In *The Prelude,* Wordsworth immediately goes on to defend himself against such desertion by the object-world, summoning up the reassuring presences which sanctify his poem—"Wisdom and Spirit of the Universe! / Thou Soul that art the Eternity of Thought!"—and insisting on the grandeur, not the littleness, of individual being (". . . until we recognize / A grandeur in the beatings of the heart," 1805, I. 428–9, 440–1). Though in Hardy's writing the experience of personal diminution is itself undiminished (witness the many dwindlings, shrinkings, and disappearances in his poetry), his counterparts to the Spirit of the Universe are the Spirits Sinister and Ironic of *The Dynasts,* another name for the "idiosyncratic mode of regard" by which the incoherence of the universe is anthropomorphized as a universal principle, and subdued to authorial control.

The critical moment in Hardy's writing would therefore come when his irony takes a tumble and the entire novelistic world is put at risk. Just such a moment involving another cliff, the "Cliff without a Name," occurs in his early novel *A Pair of Blue Eyes* (1873). In every sense the most remarkable cliff-hanger of Hardy's career as a serial-writer (it occurs exactly mid-way through the novel and ended the monthly part with a literal "suspense"), the episode also leaves hanging the question of individual survival as it confronts the priggish intellectual, Knight, who has slipped over the lip of a cliff while demonstrating the behaviour of air-currents to the novel's heroine. The lapse allows Hardy to quarry the past like a geologist for the chaos of disintegrated organic forms from which the term "grotesque" is originally derived.[4] Hardy tells us that "It is with cliffs and mountains as with persons; they have what is called a presence"; his heroine (reducing Miltonic sublimity to a feminine shudder) says the death-dealing cliff has "a horrid personality." But Knight is left suspended in "the presence of a personalized loneliness" (ch. xxi). In its "inveterate antagonism . . . to all strugglers for life," the precipice becomes a metaphor for the destructive powers of the imagination, here projected as a landscape hostile to man—not so much impersonal as annihilating to persons: "Grimness was in every feature, and to its very bowels the inimical shape was desolation."

But the most radical assault is on the present: "Not a blade, not an insect, which spoke of the present, was between [Knight] and the past," Hardy tells us. The assault is brought about by accident—"By one of those familiar conjunctions of things wherewith the inanimate world baits the mind of man when he pauses in moments of suspense, opposite Knight's eyes was an embedded fossil. . . ." The literalization here is one of those familiar conjunctions of things and ideas which make Hardy so disconcerting a novelist of contingencies. Suspended in time as well as space, Knight undergoes a free-fall into "the immense lapses of time"—"grand times, but . . . mean times too, and mean were their relics." The embedded trilobite shrinks Knight (man in his noblest form, perhaps?) to the most minimal form of life imaginable, leaving his disembodied consciousness to become the "home," or target, for the novelist's own discomfited imaginings ("There is no place like a cleft landscape for bringing home such imaginings as these"). Hardy's apocalyptic geology disinters not only the strata which record "the immense lapses of time" but the distorted and primaeval forms which threaten to destroy Knight's consciousness, and his own along with it:

> Time closed up like a fan before him. He saw himself at one extremity of the years, face to face with the beginning and all the intermediate centuries simultaneously. Fierce men, clothed in the hides of beasts, and carrying, for defence and attack, huge clubs and pointed spears, rose from the rock, like the phantoms before the doomed Macbeth. They lived in hollows, woods, and mud huts—perhaps in caves in the neighbouring rocks. Behind them stood an earlier band. No man was there. Huge elephantine forms, the mastodon, the hippopotamus, the tapir, antelopes of monstrous size, the megatherium, and the myledon—all, for the moment, in juxtaposition. Futher back, and overlapped by these, were perched huge-billed birds and swinish creatures as large as horses. Still more shadowy were the sinister crocodilian outlines—alligators and other uncouth shapes, culminating in the colossal lizard, the iguanodon. Folded behind were dragon forms and clouds of flying reptiles: still underneath

were fishy beings of lower development; and so on, till the lifetime scenes of the fossil confronting him were a present and modern condition of things. . . . (ch. xxii)

"Was he to die? . . . Was death really stretching out his hand?" The reminder that this is Knight's moment of suspense, not Hardy's, jerks us back from the edge of a different precipice—a vertiginous merging of author and character which threatens to collapse the novelistic illusion into an undifferentiated stream of authorial consciousness. The fossil is dead character, the landscape here no longer literary Wessex but the ancient rock-formations beneath.

In this passage the archaic forms thrown up by Hardy's imagination exceed the bounds of temporal irony (as the force of the passage exceeds its context). Is it an accident that at the point where the novel's "felt life" is most drastically undermined, visible only as a residual relic or fossil, anarchy should enter—along with its partner, simultaneity, closing time up like a fan (or a book) to merge past and present and so controvert the possibility of history altogether? There is now not only no beginning or end, but no significant differentiation between age and age, man and man. "No man was there" unpeoples the novel, leaving a personalized loneliness. Knight's cliff-edge vision is not simply a glimpse into nothingness, but the imagination summoning up the very forms which prophesy its own extinction, as the witches summon up the phantoms of the future before the doomed Macbeth. Such determinism, with its endless backward recession, condemns Knight to non-survival as surely as Macbeth is doomed by his ghostly inheritors. The Cliff without a Name precipitates the temporal vertigo which afflicts consciousness before the death-dealing perspective of time. This is the vision which Hardy attributes not to his own "idiosyncratic mode of regard," but to whatever disowned portion of his imagination turns the past into a monstrous procession of savage beings and extinct creatures. It is not just that the succession of ages, thus unfolded, foretells the death of the individual, or that significant differences are blurred by a chaotic past. Rather, the threat which Hardy confronts is the mind's own effortless spawning of images, the imaginative autonomy which must be buried in the interests of maintaining the realist illusion. Nature sanctifies the powerful image-forming imagination of *The Prelude* by naturalizing it, but in the Wessex Novels landscape provincializes it. Uncovering the draconian forms of primitive imagination, before all forms devolve into the aboriginal, minimally differentiated form of the zoophyte (midway between plant and animal), Hardy throws the organicist order into disarray and momentarily brings to light the imaginatively anarchic basis of his fiction. Though the juxtaposition of Knight and fossil is ironic—accidental, but purposive too—the unfolding of the past which it ushers in establishes a different principle, that of meaningless repetition and purposeless conjunction. Arbitrariness invades the world of the novel, threatening individual consciousness and laying waste the present.

"The yawning blankness / Of the perspective sickens me," writes Hardy elsewhere, of a different absence and another's death (Emma's, in "The Going"). The rift between past and present, like the breach between mind and Nature in *The Prelude*, is the abyss or "yawning blankness" from which an avenging imagination rises up. Where absence makes itself most strongly felt—in loss of familiar objects, in the falling away of the present—or where the writer imagines his own destruction by the very images he invokes, there his imagination seems paradoxically to be most fully in possession. The death of the author, one might say, brings his writing alive, bestowing autonomy, even after-life. One would expect powerful anxieties to attend such self-creating and self-destructive strength, especially in writers ostensibly committed to humanist or Christian affirmation. Musing on the wish for immortality ("The wish, that of the living whole / No life may fail beyond the grave"), Tennyson in an interestingly parallel context ponders the "evil dreams" prompted by the inimical shape of desolation. To the poet of *In Memoriam*, too, the "scarped cliff" has its grim message for individual survival, and by a similar distortion "Man . . . who seemed so fair," "Who rolled the psalm to wintry skies," becomes "No more" than desert dust (the dust of ages); or rather, much worse: "No more? A monster then, a dream, / A discord. Dragons of the prime, / That tare each other in their slime, / Were mellow music matched with him" (st. lvi). The imagining of annihilation here—" 'I care for nothing, all shall go,' " cries Tennyson/Nature—is the annihilation of imagination; the psalm turned to discord, music made monstrous. "Peace," begins the next section. Quieting rough music and banishing his dream, Tennyson (like Wordsworth invoking the Spirit of the Universe) defends against the apocalyptic and destructive qualities of his own buried imagination as, red in tooth and claw, it transforms God into ferocious Nature. The poet who "trusted God was love indeed / And love Creation's final law" turns loveless and lawless himself to become, like Browning's Caliban, the spiteful God of his own uncreation.

As it happens, *A Pair of Blue Eyes* is saturated with quotations from, allusions to, and echoes of Tennyson's poetry, particularly *In Memoriam*.[5] But although the passage would most likely have been in Hardy's mind when he wrote about Knight's ordeal, more is going on in both poem and novel than a mere resurgence of Victorian gloom about evolution and the disappearance of God. In each case, a humane writer is being forced to acknowledge the destructive power of his own imagination, and an aesthete is brought up against the ugliness of his imaginings. Lawlessness and excess ambush the artist's loving control over his work as the ordering and wishfully self-referential aspect of his vision breaks down under the impact of mortality, fragmenting the world into an anti-self called Nature. No longer able to merge with an unbounded and unifying ideal, the aggrandized Romantic self lapses into mid-Victorian gloom and thence into projecting its own avenging rage on the natural world. Instead of endowing Nature with everlasting life, the mind endows it with its own threatened death. In literature, the characteristic form of this failed transcendence and diminished or divided consciousness is the grotesque. Like Tennyson before him, Hardy uses the grotesque to contain the unacceptable facets of his own imagination—reductive, belittling ("He was to be with the small in his death") and, like the Cliff without a Name, possessing a horrid personality; Hardy's humanity and his horridness, after all, are almost equally balanced in plotting the deaths of his characters. But it would be misleading to stress the punitive and self-punishing aspect of the novelist-poet at the expense of the literary tradition activated in his writing. The seepage of draconian slime into Tennysonian ornateness recalls that other master of the grotesque, Browning, who for Bagehot ("Wordsworth, Tennyson, and Browning; or Pure, Ornate, and Grotesque Art in English Poetry," 1864) is the type of the artist dealing "not with what nature is striving to be, but with what by some lapse she has happened to become."

"The most of a realist, and the least of an idealist, of any poet we know," Bagehot's Browning is a poet of disillusion, his art exemplified by "Caliban upon Setebos"—a version, writ large and spiteful, of Tennyson's monstrous dream of discord. Unredeemed man is reduced by "natural" theology to a state of primitive strife with his fellow-creatures in the mud; only "The Quiet" draws the lawless, loveless, and godless universe of the grotesque back towards the realm of irony, hinting at Browning's overarching Christianity. "An exceptional monstrosity of horrid ugliness," huff-puffs Bagehot, "an artist working by incongruity"; "Mr. Browning has undertaken to describe what may be called *mind in difficulties*—mind set to make out the universe under the worst and hardest circumstances."[6] This "mind in difficulties" might be Hardy's own in his most anguished late Victorian mode—or, perhaps, the type of mind listed in Ruskin's *Stones of Venice* account of the grotesque in contrast to "the men who play wisely; who play necessarily; [and] who play inordinately": that is, "those who *play not at all*" (my italics); those, in fact, who display a "diseased and ungoverned imaginativeness" in "the contemplation of great powers in destructive operation, and generally from the perception of the presence of death." Though Hardy can be both wholesomely and rambunctiously playful when he wants, in the context of an early novel like *Under the Greenwood Tree* (1872) or even the doomsday satire of a poem such as "Channel Firing" ("The glebe cow drooled . . . Till God called, 'No . . .' "), his cast of mind has most in common with the kind of grotesque Ruskin labels "terrible." His art, provoked by the mind's confrontation with its own extinction, is equally characterized by its possession of a vision likened (in Ruskin's words again) to a disturbed dream which "comes uncalled, and will not submit itself to the seer."[7] It is in effect such a disturbed dream that baits Knight's mind when the trilobite stares him out of countenance, or that mocks man's vaingloriousness and Pride of Life in "The Convergence of the Twain" with its strange sea-change: "Over the mirrors meant / To glass the opulent / The sea-worm crawls—*grotesque*, slimed, dumb, indifferent" (my italics).

Hardy obviously knew his Ruskin, and the many architectural allusions in his novels give him the chance to show it. In *Far from the Madding Crowd* (1874) the reality that mocks "Troy's Romanticism" (the title of the chapter in which Troy remorsefully plants Fanny Robin's grave with flowers) is conveniently symbolised by a mediaeval gargoyle. "The Gurgoyle: Its Doings" (the following chapter) pours scorn on what Hardy calls "the futility of these Romantic doings" (ch. xlv), just as the gargoyle directs rain water on to Fanny Robin's grave and uproots Troy's newly planted flowers—the doings of the gargoyle acting as a metaphor for those of a punitive author. Having established his Ruskinian credentials ("It has sometimes been argued that there is no truer criterion of the vitality of any given art-period than the power of the master-spirits of that time in grotesque . . ."), Hardy goes on to provide proof of his own art's vitality; the passage presents a standard version of the disorganization of natural forms which in art-historical terms constitutes the essence of grotesque art:

> It was too human to be called like a dragon, too impish to be like a man, too animal to be like a fiend, and not enough like a bird to be called a griffin. This horrible stone entity was fashioned as if covered with a wrinkled hide; it had short, erect ears, eyes starting from their sockets, and its fingers and hands were seizing the corners of its mouth, which they thus seemed to pull open to give free passage to the water it vomited. The lower row of teeth was quite washed away, though the upper still remained. Here and thus, jutting a couple of feet from the wall against which its feet rested as a support, the creature had for four hundred years laughed at the surrounding landscape, voicelessly in dry weather, and in wet with a gurgling and snorting sound. (ch. xlvi)

As with Knight's ordeal on the cliff, the eruption of powerful and anarchic imaginings—the disturbed dream that "will not submit itself to the seer"—is signalled by an excess of monstrous forms. Gurgles and snorts (the oral equivalent of such imagery) emit from an author whose sentiments about graves are elsewhere scandalized by a dog burying a bone instead of a bereaved lover planting rue. ("Ah, are you digging on my grave?" asks the hopeful lady beneath.) Such "satires of circumstance" are a species of vengeance carried out by one part of Hardy's mind on another, or (to use the terms of *The Dynasts*) a confrontation between the Spirit of the Pities and the Spirits Sinister and Ironic.

However, the gargoyle's doings devastate not just a grave, not just buried Hardian sensibility, but Troy's sense of himself: "Almost for the first time in his life Troy as he stood by this dismantled grave, wished himself another man." In a crucial intervention, the authorial voice splits off from the consciousness of his character to ponder his, and our, illusion of being—specifically, of being the hero of the tale:

> It is seldom that a person with much animal spirit does not feel that the fact of his life being his own is the one qualification which singles it out as a

more hopeful life than that of others who may actually resemble him in every particular. . . . Troy had felt, in his transient way, hundreds of times, that he could not envy other people their condition, because the possession of that condition would have necessitated a different personality, when he desired no other than his own. He had not minded the peculiarities of his birth, the vicissitudes of his life, the meteor-like uncertainty of all that related to him, because these appertained to the hero of his story, without whom there would have been no story at all for him. . . . This very morning the illusion completed its disappearance and, as it were, all of a sudden, Troy hated himself. (ch. xlvi)

At the moment when Troy ceases to view himself as singled out, and the man of the present is forced to confront a past that cannot be undone, self-estrangement enters in. The unified consciousness is fragmented as ruthlessly as the gargoyle subverts the organicist order, or mocks the planting of a grave with flowers. By implication, Troy's "story" stops here; no wonder he goes on to discard both clothes and identity—presumed drowned, until he turns up later as a travelling actor in the role of Dick Turpin, the quick-change artist of opportunities he has always in fact been. The moment of self-awareness has fractured his claim to coherence, exposing him (like Hardy's own novels) as only "a series of seemings."[8] The grotesque which in A Pair of Blue Eyes had moved beyond an irony associated with self-alienation seems on the contrary to effect it here. Is this, perhaps, a defensive move on Hardy's part? Hardy's own fiction after all depends on a saving illusion. Troy's disillusion at least allows Hardy to cast out "seemings" with his anti-hero. Reconstituting as well as fragmenting, the gargoyle's doings could be said, paradoxically, to fend off the narrative dissolution which lurks beneath the "organic" surface of Hardy's realism by dissolving the identity of a character instead.

Troy's mephistophelian allure is never quite accounted for, but for Hardy his secret may have lain in his mobility; he is the improviser, gambler, and role-player of picaresque narrative. In this he resembles the type of an artist quite unlike Hardy himself—an artist with no sense of the past and untroubled by incoherence or ironic self-division. It's not surprising that the one novel by Hardy which specifically concerns the artist, The Well-Beloved (1897), should set out to ironize artistic self-division and fixation on the past. An unmistakeably self-mirroring (and to some extent, inevitably self-distorting) work, The Well-Beloved gets sufficiently out of hand—at least in its original version—to qualify as grotesque. Like Mann's Death in Venice (another self-conscious, ironic, and over-schematic account of the artistic temperament), Hardy's portrait of the artist as an old man takes its place alongside his many other fictions of disillusion. A passionate Shelleyan, Hardy, like Browning, saw himself as a failed transcender. This fable of artistic ideals shattered by painful reality is less intellectualized than Mann's Nietzchean depiction of the collapse of Aschenbach's Appollinian aestheticism in the face of Dionysian anarchy and excess, but it is similar in its unmasking of the forces which that art exists to hide: desire and death. Like Mann's hero, Hardy's artist discovers that "Eros is in the word"—that art and eroticism, desire and self-destruction, impel him on his double quest. The stone-sculptor of *The Well-Beloved* is the victim of a compulsion from which he is only delivered by age and the death of the imagination. Pierston is a failed Romantic whose pursuit of the image of the ideal beloved as she flits from form to form, forever eluding his attempts to embody her in that most stony of plastic arts which gives him his name, ends in grotesque tragedy.

Repetition-compulsion (the compulsion to repeat the past by loving the same face incarnated in three generations of women) and art (Pierston's attempts to sculpt the elusive image) converge in Hardy's fable, so that shaping and uncreating are inextricably connected. From the outset, a destructive irony is identified by the novel's Shelleyan epigraph, "One shape of many names"—a reference, presumably, both to the ideal form of the beloved and to "the Spirit of evil" which in *The Revolt of Islam* "reigns o'er a world of woe" (I. xxvii). Though the pursuit inspires his art, Pierston inevitably courts his own death in courting the granddaughter as well as the daughter of his first love, Avice Caro. But the dominant motif in the novel is less the nympholeptic pursuit itself than Pierston's growing self-estrangement— the alienation from an ageing bodily self which mirrors Hardy's own as recorded in a dismal journal-entry of 1892: "I look in the glass. Am conscious of the humiliating sorriness of my earthly tabernacle . . . Why should a man's mind have been thrown into such close, sad, sensational, inexplicable relations with such a precarious object as his own body."[9] In an episode originally published a few weeks later, these inexplicable relations—the theme of Hardy's poem, "I look into my glass"—give rise to a moment of self-confrontation in which Pierston's self-regard, like Hardy's, converts narcissism into the posthumousness which is the special dimension of Hardian irony:

> As he sat thus thinking, and the daylight increased, he discerned, a short distance before him, a movement of something ghostly. His position was facing the window, and he found that by chance the looking-glass had swung itself vertical, so that what he saw was his own shape. The recognition startled him. The person he appeared was too grievously far, chronologically, in advance of the person he felt himself to be. Pierston did not care to regard the figure confronting him so mockingly. . . . But the question of age being pertinent he could not give the spectre up, and ultimately got out of bed under the weird fascination of the reflection. . . . never had he seemed so aged by a score of years as he was represented in the glass in that cold grey morning light. While his soul was what it was, why should he have been encumbered with that withering carcase . . . ?
>
> (Part III, ch. iv)

Instead of pleasurably doubling, the shape that mockingly confronts Pierston undoes the identity of self and image. Its "weird fascination" is that of a spectre, or a portent of death, rather than the ideal love-object or "soul" in whom the artist finds his true likeness (the identification is strengthened elsewhere when Hardy's first thought, which had made the moon an image of the "migratory Well-Beloved," was revised to make Pierston view it as his own "wraith").[10] Hardy afterwards wrote that "There is, of course, underlying the fantasy followed by the visionary artist the truth that all men are pursuing a shadow, the Unattainable"[11]—alerting his readers not simply to the fatality of his fable, but to its self-reflexiveness; "shadow," "shape," "form," and "soul" are the platonic ideals which *The Well-Beloved* pursues implacably to their origin within the artist himself.

But there is in *The Well-Beloved* a distinctively Hardian swerve from Platonic aestheticism to the grotesque—a cynic twist that knits its schematic repetitions into more disturbing meaninglessness. Pierston at his glass is encumbered by the withering carcase of physicality, obsolescence, and death; the novel is not so much an elegy as an outrage, at least as it was originally conceived for serial publication in 1892. In the rewritten ending to the first edition, five years later, Hardy produced a decorous if cynical fable about the artist's *embourgeoisement* and loss of creativity when he resigns himself to reality and humdrum marriage with the woman for whom he had long before jilted the first Avice. The denouement of the serial-version as published in *The Illustrated London News*, though more rough-hewn, had been at once more painful and less self-ironizing; here it had seemed that a vengeful writer was inflicting near-fatal injuries on his artist-surrogate. Pierston, now an old man, leaves the third Avice to her young lover and sets out on a deliberately suicidal voyage, intending literally to drown his sorrows at sea. He regains consciousness after a violent collision with another boat (the reality principle, no doubt) to find himself, not dead, but being nursed by his long-since ex-wife (as she was in the serial version).[12] By now a parodic wreck of her former imperious self, she is an embodiment of Death-in-Life and fitting bride for the relic of an artist: "his wife was—not Avice, but that parchment-covered skull." In the gruesome finale, Pierston first thinks to tear open the wound in his head and "bring eternal night upon this lurid awakening," then bursts into a fit of laughter "so violent as to be in agony" at "a sudden sense of the grotesqueness of things." His last word on his own story has the smack of the gargoyle's derision: " 'it is too, too droll—this ending to my would-be romantic history!' " Like Troy, he not only finds his romantic doings mocked, but experiences his death as the heroic object of his own imaginings. But this time it is Hardy himself, rather than his gargoyle persona, who laughs: the author's own final words and the serial's punch-line were, grotesquely, "Ho-ho-ho."[13]

Elsewhere, the satiric voice is named as that of Despair itself; "Ho-ho!" croaks "the Thing" (Hardy's hopeless other) in "A Meeting with Despair" that takes place in the grotesque landscape of "Childe Roland" ("The black lean land, of featureless contour, / Was like a tract in pain"). That the failure of romantic questers like Pierston tends to lay waste the world around him we have already seen. But while the collapse of the dream by which the artist attempts to guarantee his survival tends also to lay waste the artist himself, it bestows uncanny powers on his art. In the literature of Aestheticism to which *The Well-Beloved* belongs, among many objects the most privileged object of all (as we see in *The Picture of Dorian Gray*) is the image of the artist objectified in his art. It is the failure of objectification—falling back into mere self-revelation—which both destroys the artist and renders his art unstable, giving rise to strange effects. As Dorian's portrait becomes increasingly grotesque once the initial split between artist and object has occurred, so specular relations—however powerfully invested with self-love—prove fantasmatic and disordered, making the world of Hardy's novels not simply self-mirroring (a series of subjective seemings) but darkly distorted. What is involved is not pessimism, or fatalism, but a form of "self-expression" (T. S. Eliot's accusation, levelled at Hardy's insufficient impersonality)[14] in which the compulsion to repeat—at once an erotic attempt to restore a former state and a self-destructive death-wish—can be diagnosed not only in Pierston's sculpture, but in Hardy's writing too. Such repetition is the source of its strange, often disconcerting, but indisputable power.

The same buried patterns at start and end of Hardy's novel-writing career link *A Pair of Blue Eyes* and *The Well-Beloved.* Underlining the elaborate internal parallels in each novel in a famous passage from *La Prisonnière* (*The Female Prisoner*), Proust draws attention to "le parallèlisme entre *La Bien-Aimée* où l'homme aime trois femmes et *Les Yeux bleus* où la femme aime trois hommes" (the parallelism between *The Well-Beloved* where the man loves three women and *A Pair of Blue Eyes* where the woman loves three men). He goes on, using the image of the stone-quarrying island which is the setting of the later novel, to refer to "tous ces romans superposables les uns aux autres, comme les maisons verticalement entassées en hauteur sur le sol pierreux de l'Ile" (all these novels can be superimposed one upon the other, like dwellings vertically stacked up on the stony surface of the Island).[15] The Wessex Edition of the Novels of Thomas Hardy closes up like a fan, leaving the novelist face to face with his beginnings. What is irony within a single novel (the formal mirrorings and inversions of the Hardian plot) becomes repetition when it involves a second, and the result of juxtaposing "tous ces romans superposables" is to turn Hardy's writing into a geological effect of layered texts. The effect is intensified by another and more dizzying form of repetition, crossing the boundaries of life and art: the temporal vertigo, like that of seeing a landscape down the wrong end of a telescope, produced by turning from Hardy's elegies for Emma in the poems of 1912–13 to the scenes of his Cornish courtship in *A Pair of Blue Eyes;* or by finding in *The Well-Beloved* a proleptic account of his later mourning for Emma, once death had made her inaccessible. That Hardy's rewritings are also prewritings, life seeming to imitate art, makes fiction look truer than fact and almost invites us to believe that life (for authors, at any rate) is only writing after all—a perpetual self-invention or self-engendering that alternates with self-destruction; a never-ending ironic process, repetitive rather than temporary.[16] The spiralling imaginings of Hardy's self-consciousness which so often create in his poetic reflections the sense of bodily dwindling or spectrality involve a radical loss, that of the steadying illusion that one's writing has a purchase on reality or that one has oneself a foothold beyond the page. The ability to sustain that loss without losing one's balance altogether may be the essence of the ironist's art; taking a tumble, as Knight does, is to glimpse one's extinction in that of a fossilized zoophyte. But (and this is where his slip becomes heady as well as dizzying) Knight's accident also contains the pay-off for previsioning one's death—the rewards of Hardian posthumousness.

Ultimately, the critical moment in Hardy's writing, that of imagined self-dissolution, permits the threatened or enfeebled consciousness to transfer its own displaced omniscience to the disembodied vision which he calls "magian," rather than surrendering the fantasy altogether. Or, to put it another way, instead of limiting the grotesque and reconstituting it as irony, Hardy is able in his poetry to move beyond it to something nearer the supernatural. In "He resolves to say no more," the final poem of his last volume, Hardy announces: "Let Time roll backward if it will; / (Magians who drive the midnight quill / With brain aglow / Can see it so,) / What I have learnt no man shall know." By implication, he has himself put on the Mage's mantle. The attribution of vast and special powers to the poet is otherwise quite naked. He bears a burden that would cripple others and must be kept from "The blinkered sight of souls in bond" lest it make their lives unendurable—or, like Macbeth's, a weary repetition ("Tomorrow and tomorrow . . ."). Another poem, "The Pedigree," shows "The Mage's mirror" doubling the poet in an infinite regression of diminishing likenesses which obliterates the illusion of unique and unified individual identity with the mockery of its repetitions:

1

I bent in the deep of night
Over a pedigree the chronicler gave
As mine; and as I bent there, half-unrobed,
The uncurtained panes of my window-square let in the watery light
    Of the moon in its old age:
And green-rheumed clouds were hurrying past where mute and cold it globed
    Like a drifting dolphin's eye seen through a lapping wave.

2

    So, scanning my sire-sown tree,
And the hieroglyphs of this spouse tied to that,
With offspring mapped below in lineage,
    Till the tangles troubled me,

The branches seemed to twist into a seared and cynic face
  Which winked and tokened towards the window like a Mage
    Enchanting me to gaze again thereat.

3

    It was a mirror now,
  And in it a long perspective I could trace
Of my begetters, dwindling backward each past each
    All with the kindred look,
  Whose names had since been inked down in their place
    On the recorder's book,   ·
Generation and generation of my mien, and build, and brow.[17]

This is a version of the phantoms that rise before the doomed Macbeth, or
Tess's recognition that her doings are like thousands' and thousands'—the
individual endlessly forestalled by the past ("every heave and coil and move I
made . . . Was in the glass portrayed / As long forestalled"). Unlike Knight's
experience on the cliff, it is not a geological revelation, but it still offers a
pedigree of extinction. All stories became one, as the names "inked down in
their place / On the recorder's book" merge into a family tree that is also a
doomsday book, confronting the poet not only with the repetition of his own
compulsions, but the compulsion of his repetitions—his obedience to an
original "fugleman" or drill-model, "fogged in far antiqueness past surmise
and reason's reach."

    Though the loss of origins might be said to force the writer into regarding
writing as his sole origin, its more radical discomposition lies in making him a
fiction himself instead of the author of fictions: "Said I then sunk in tone, / 'I am
merest mimicker and counterfeit!—/ Though thinking, *I am I, / And what I do
I do myself alone.'* / —The cynic twist of the page thereat unknit / Back to its
normal figure, having wrought its purpose wry. . . ." The cynic twist of the
page—or rather, of the Mage? The "figure" here, at once face and trope, mocks
the written word with its unfolding meaning, its "purport wry." "The Mage's
mirror" becomes a mode of insight, an eye as mute and cold as the moon's or
Hardy's own, whose special power is to undo the present and turn it into
writing. The recognition that "I am *not I*," but controlled by the past—that the
writer is already written, always "Afterwards"—is the temporal irony that
knits a cynic twist into Hardian self-elegy, just as noticing (seeing rather than
seeing into) unknits it again. But along the way, Hardy has granted independent existence to the eye, resourcefully evading the threat to the "I" of his
poem, and making it possible to misread "The Pedigree" as an oblique but
effective defence against extinction. The mere fiction survives, as "eye" if not
"I," leaving an enfeebled authorial persona but a reinforced impersonality. If
the poet himself can't be thought to survive, his poetic vision—sufficiently
detached or alienated from the poet, as moon or Mage—can at least be imagined as doing so. So for all his self-effacements and ghostly aftermaths, a
tenacious confidence underlies Hardy's poetry. His magian retrospect, in

divining the past, annexes to itself the hind-sight that is mourned as unavailable to the poet in the future. It is a vision worth dying for, since it ensures his poetic survival. Or, as Hardy put it himself, with all the confidence of a posthumous imagination, "No man's poetry can be truly judged till its last line is written. What is the last line? The death of the poet. And hence there is this quiet consolation to any writer of verse—that it may be imperishable for all that anybody can tell him to the contrary. . . ."[18]

Notes

1. F. E. Hardy, *The Early Life of Thomas Hardy* (1928), p. 275; an observation recorded in 1888.

2. "Art consists in so depicting the common events of life as to bring out the features which illustrate the author's idiosyncratic mode of regard; making old incidents and things seem as new"; *The Early Life of Thomas Hardy*, p. 294.

3. Cf. Schlegel's essay "On Incomprehensibility," in *Friedrich Schlegel's Lucinde and The Fragments*, trans. Peter Firchow (Minneapolis, 1971).

4. See A. Clayborough, *The Grotesque in English Literature* (Oxford, 1965). The word derives from the fanciful murals with which grottoes were originally decorated.

5. See, for instance, the epigraphs to *A Pair of Blue Eyes*, chs. xx, xxi, xxvi, xxviii; and elsewhere, chs. xi, xxv, xlviii, lxiv, lxv, lxxviii, lxxx.

6. *The Collected Works of Walter Bagehot*, ed. N. St. John-Stevas (13 vols. 1965–), ii. 353, 354, 360.

7. *The Works of Ruskin*, ed. E. T. Cook and A. Wedderburn (39 vols., 1903–12), xi. 152, 166, 162, 178.

8. Preface to *Jude the Obscure* (1895).

9. F. E. Hardy, *The Later Years of Thomas Hardy* (1930), pp. 13–14.

10. The first edition's "wraith" is a revision of the serial reading "sweetheart"; Part III, ch. ii.

11. *The Later Years of Thomas Hardy*, p. 59; a letter originally published in the *Academy*, 3 April 1897.

12. In the earlier version, the plot had turned as much on Pierston's two disastrous marriages—a youthful marriage to the imperious Marcia, and a middle-aged marriage to the third and youngest Avice—as on his pursuit of the thrice-incarnated Well-Beloved.

13. See *Illustrated London News*, 17 December 1892, p. 775.

14. *After Strange Gods: A Primer of Modern Heresy* (New York, 1934), p. 59.

15. *La Prisonnière* (Pléiade ed. Paris, 1923), iii. 377 (translations by Catherine and Dan Majdiak).

16. See Paul de Man's account of the ironic process in "The Rhetoric of Temporality," *Interpretation: Theory and Practice*, ed. Charles Singleton (Baltimore, 1969), pp. 173–209.

17. Cf. Jon Stallworthy's illuminating discussion of Hardy's moon and mirror imagery in "Read by Moonlight," *Essays on the Poetry of Thomas Hardy*, ed. Patricia Clements and Juliet Grindle (London, 1980), 172–88; for Hardy's "ironic and self-effacing" poetic stance, and his relation to the past, see also Samuel Hynes's "The Hardy Tradition on Modern English Poetry," *Sewanee Review*, 88 (1980), 33–51.

18. *The Later Years of Thomas Hardy*, pp. 80–1; a comment of January 1899.

Finding a Scale for the Human:
Plot and Writing in Hardy's Novels   Gillian Beer*

In *The Expression of the Emotions* Darwin describes fear as a primary emotion whose manner of expression has barely changed over millions of years: "We may likewise infer that fear was expressed from an extremely remote period, in almost the same manner as it now is by man; namely, by trembling, the erection of the hair, cold perspiration, pallor, widely opened eyes, the relaxation of most of the muscles, and by the whole body cowering downwards or held motionless."[1] Fear is, in the Victorian anthropological sense, a "survival." Like certain primitive tribes, this primitive emotion survives into the modern world unchanged. Like them, it represents the primal conditions of man and allows us to observe those conditions still at work. Moreover, it occupies the same place in the metaphor of development as do "primitive" peoples: fear is an emotion to be controlled, suppressed, outgrown. Reason is cast as an adult emotion, just as western European man is an "adult" on the scale of development. So, like primitive peoples, fear is to be kept under control. Yet like them, it is still there, not fully left behind, nor entirely dominated. In the arc of development, fear is perceived, disturbingly, as at the base. It retains its insurgent power and is liable—like mutiny—to break out.

The *effort* of empire can be seen in the later-nineteenth-century preoccupation with fear, in a culture which set so much store by courage, or "pluck." It is a preoccupation which then fuels much Edwardian writing, particularly Conrad's works. For example, in *Lord Jim* the atavistic emotion of fear leads Jim to jump overboard, abandoning ship and passengers. His attempt to redeem this failure of nerve takes him at last to the position of wise counsellor of a "primitive" people. In *Heart of Darkness* terror of what will be found at the centre of man's emotions takes the form of a journey into the Amazon jungle and of empire over "primitive" tribes, a journey of self-destruction. In both cases fear of fear is the initiating emotion.

Fear is caused by those who *undergo* fear: servants, animals, women, subject races. Saki in his brief story "Laura" brilliantly condenses the various categories: Laura returns to haunt her friend's husband, as women, otter, and black Nubian servant boy. Children, servants, hunted prey, black races, and women all generate dread here. The fear they feel in the face of the master gives them power to terrify that same master.

In *Daniel Deronda*, George Eliot suggested that "mastering" fear was no answer. It must be entered and used "like a faculty." Hardy wrote in his Journal: "Courage has been idealized: why not fear? which is a higher consciousness and based on a deeper insight."[2] He here inverts the expected

*Reprinted by permission from *Darwin's Plots: Evolutionary Narrative in Darwin, George Eliot, and Nineteenth-Century Fiction* (London, Boston, Melbourne: Routledge & Kegan Paul, 1983).

value placed on fear, while in his attribution of a "deeper insight" he suggests its power in the natural order.

In a journal entry in January 1888 Hardy writes: "Apprehension is a great element in imagination. It is a semi-madness, which sees enemies etc., in inanimate objects." His next entry, a week later, continues: "A 'sensation-novel' is possible in which the sensation is not casualty, but evolution; not physical but psychical . . . whereas in the physical the adventure itself is the subject of interest, the psychical results being passed over as commonplace, in the psychical the casualty or adventure is held to be of no intrinsic interest, but the effect upon the faculties is the important matter to be depicted."[3]

The emphasis here upon the interconnections between "sensation" and "evolution," between apprehension and animism, may lead us a long way into the particular nature of Hardy's creativity. Hardy analysed what he saw as a creative kinship between primitive culture and "highest imaginative genius" in terms of animism. The analysis comes to him with the relish of a fresh notion when Edward Clodd, first president of the British Folklore Society and Darwinist, explained it in terms of cultural development and "survivals":

> December 18. Mr E. Clodd this morning gives an excellently neat answer to my question why the superstitions of a remote Asiatic and a Dorset labourer are the same: "The attitude of man," he says, "at corresponding levels of culture, before like phenomena, is pretty much the same, your Dorset peasants representing the persistence of the barbaric idea which confuses persons and things, and founds wide generalizations on the slenderest analogies." (This "barbaric idea which confuses persons and things" is, by the way, also common to the highest imaginative genius—that of the poet.)[4]

The double sense of apprehension is crucial for Hardy. It includes both the sense of fear and of awakening—and these senses are not opposed or disconnected. Though terror may be an obliterative experience, fear makes keen. It awakens thought and sensation. The self becomes alert, ready, yet passive. And this is very much the situation created in the reader by the contradiction of plot and writing in Hardy's work. We are filled with intolerable apprehensions of what future events may bring, while yet the text in process awakens us to sensation full of perceptual pleasure. It is a state Hardy describes often as part of the experience of his characters. For example, Tess, exhausted, listens to the other women working. She "lay in a state of percipience, without volition, and *the rustle of the straw and the cutting of the ears by the others had the weight of bodily touches*"[5] [my italics]. Touch and hearing lie peculiarly close in his economy of the senses. They are particularly associated with alert passivity.

Hardy acknowledged Darwin always as a major intellectual influence in his work and his way of seeing.[6] Much has been written on the connection and there have been excellent studies of individual novels. In this argument

I want to explore a more general question to do with the relationship of plot and writing. Most commentators have emphasised the point of connection between Hardy and Darwin in terms of pessimism, a sense that the laws of life are themselves flawed. That Hardy did feel this is undeniable. One notices the implicit cultural evolutionism of a passage like this: "The truth seems to be that a long line of disillusive centuries has permanently displaced the Hellenic idea of life, or whatever it may be called. What the Greeks only suspected we know well; what their Aeschylus imagined our nursery children feel. That old-fashioned revelling in the general situation grows less and less possible as we uncover the defects of natural laws, and see the quandary that man is in by their operation" (185).[7]

Aeschylus's imagining has become (by means of evolutionary development) children's feeling. The human quandary is caused by laws themselves defective, and which take no account of us. "A woeful fact—that the human race is too extremely developed for its corporeal conditions, the nerves being evolved to an activity abnormal in such an environment. Even the higher animals are in excess in this respect. It may be questioned if Nature, or what we call Nature, so far back as when she crossed the line from invertebrates to vertebrates, did not exceed her mission. This planet does not supply the materials for happiness to higher existences. Other planets may, though one can hardly see how."[8]

But although he felt the burden of evolution this was by no means all that he felt or all that he makes us feel as a consequence of his familiarity with Darwin's work. Though the individual may be of small consequence in the long sequence of succession and generation, yet Hardy in his emplotment opposes this perception and does so by adopting again the single life span as his scale. Whereas George Eliot's novels, and Dickens's novels, tend to include death, rather than end with death, Hardy's texts pay homage to human scale by ceasing as the hero or heroine dies. The single life span is no longer an absolute but polemical. That is one formal expression of his humanism. It opposes evolutionary meliorism or pessimism by making the single generation carry the freight of signification.

Plot in Hardy is almost always tragic or malign: it involves the overthrow of the individual either by the inevitability of death or by the machinations (or disregard) of "crass casualty." Deterministic systems are placed under great stress: a succession of ghost plots is present. The persistently almost-attained happy alternatives are never quite obliterated by the actual terrible events. The reader is pained by the sense of multiple possibilities, only one of which can occur and be thus verified in time, space, and actuality. The belief in fixed laws is a sustaining element in George Eliot's sense of the moral nature of plot. Fecundity for Zola is life's answer to death. But each of these elements becomes for Hardy part of an ulterior plot, beyond the control of humankind. Near the beginning of *Tess of the D'Urbervilles* Hardy comments sardonically: "Some people would like to know whence the poet whose philosophy is in these days deemed as profound and trustworthy as his song is breezy and pure, gets his authority for speaking of 'Nature's holy plan.' " Darwin had sought to share Wordsworth's testamental language in his image of "Natural Selection," which identified nature with benign planning and makes of natural selection a more correct form than man's merely artificial selection.[9] Hardy reads such plans as plot; plot becomes malign and entrapping, because it is designed without the needs of individual life in mind. Human variety is oppressed by the needs which generate plot. Angel Clare begins to free himself from his class-bound assumptions of working people's uniformity:

> Without any objective change whatever, variety had taken the place of monotonousness. His host and his host's household, his men and his maids, as they became intimately known to Clare, began to differentiate themselves as in a chemical process. The thought of Pascal's was brought home to him: "A mesure qu'on a plus d'esprit, on trouve qu'il y a plus d'hommes originaux. Les gens du commun ne trouvent pas de différence entre les hommes." ("The more intelligence one has, the more one finds how many original people there are. Ordinary people do not discern the difference between persons.") The typical and unvarying Hodge ceased to exist. He had been disintegrated into a number of varied fellow-creatures—beings of many minds, beings infinite in difference.

But even as he becomes aware of fellow creatures "infinite in difference," the action of his sexual presence is producing uniformity, as the dairymaids writhe in the power of their own unasked for sexuality, "an emotion thrust on them by cruel Nature's law."[10]

In reading Hardy's work we often find a triple level of plot generated: the anxiously scheming and predictive plot of the characters' making; the optative plot of the commentary, which often takes the form "Why did nobody" or "had somebody . . . ," and the absolute plot of blind interaction and "Nature's laws." These laws cannot be comprehended within a single order. In Hardy's novels all scales are absolute, but multiple. So he includes many time-scales, from the geological time of Egdon Heath to the world of the ephemerons. The idea that nature is adapted to man is expressive of morbid states of mind in *Tess of the D'Urbervilles* so that "at times her whimsical fancy would intensify natural processes around her until they seemed part of her own story." This way lies the plot of paranoia where exterior, interior, and ulterior fuse so that the question of the source of the plot (in the clinic of the head, in the chaos of the universe) cannot be redeemed.

The emphasis upon systems more extensive than the life span of the individual and little according to his needs is essential to Hardy's insight. Much of the grandeur of his fiction comes from his acceptance of people's independence and self-assertion—doomed and curtailed persistently, but recuperating. But further underlying that emphasis upon the individual is the paradox that even those recuperative energies are there primarily to serve the longer needs of the race and are part of a procreative energy designed to combat extinction, not the death of any individual.

Alongside the emphasis on apprehension and anxiety, on inevitable overthrow long foreseen, persistingly evaded, there is, however, another prevailing sensation in Hardy's work equally strongly related to his understanding of Darwin. It is that of happiness. Alongside the doomed sense of weighted past and incipient conclusion, goes a sense of plenitude, an "appetite for joy." This finds expression—as it must if at all—in the moment-by-moment fullness of the text. In "Song of Myself" Whitman (who is quoted in *Tess*) wrote: "I have heard what the talkers were talking, the talk of the beginning and the end, / But I do not talk of the beginning or the end. / There was never any more inception than there is now, / Nor any more youth and age than there is now, / And will never be any more perfection than there is now, / Nor any more heaven or hell than there is now. / Urge and urge and urge, / Always the procreant urge of the world."

At each moment the world is complete, though urged onwards always by procreation. Whitman's is a powerful alternative to that form of evolutionary thinking which sets the past aspiring to become present, and the present imagining a more satisfying future. Whitman's sense of the world's fullness is yet linked to that "appetite for joy" which Hardy saw as charging life equally with rapture and disaster. Sexual joy is always dangerous, not only because of the possibility of loss, but because it is linked to *generation*, the law which rides like a juggernaut over and through individual identity and individual life spans.

> She clasped his neck, and for the first time Clare learnt what an impassioned woman's kisses were like upon the lips of one whom she loved with all her heart and soul, as Tess loved him. "There—now do you believe?" she asked, flushed, and wiping her eyes.
> "Yes. I never really doubted—never, never!"
> So they drove on through the gloom, forming one bundle inside the sail-cloth, the horse going as he would, and the rain driving against them. She had consented. She might as well have agreed at first. The "appetite for joy" which pervades all creation, that tremendous force which sways humanity to its purpose, as the tide sways the helpless weed, was not to be controlled by vague lucubrations over the social rubric. (*Tess*: 218)

The impassioned moment is seized through touch and temperature, the most intimately present of sense-experience. Then the language turns aside, first into the imagery of the sea and of motion (still perpetuating the bodily experience of the lovers). The sense of power and of helplessness changes into the jarring abstraction of the "vague lucubrations over the social rubric," facetiously orotund. The reader must work for meaning, instead of being immersed in meaning—and the sense and sound alike rebuff readers, and distance lovers.

Hardy comments on another natural drive, separate from that of procreation although often associated with it: "the determination to enjoy": "Thought of the determination to enjoy. We see it in all nature, from the leaf on the tree to the titled lady at the ball. . . . Like pent-up water it will find a chink of possibility somewhere" (August 1888).[11] In "The Dorsetshire Labourer" (1883) he sees the refusal to believe in happiness among "the labouring classes" as a class-bound condescension and satirises such views: "Misery and fever lurk in his cottage, while to paraphrase the words of a recent writer on the labouring classes, in his future there are only the workshop and the grave. He hardly dares to think at all. He has few thoughts of joy, and little hope of rest." In contrast, Hardy asserts, a real observer would discover a diversity of character, life and moods. "He would have learnt that wherever a mode of supporting life is neither noxious nor absolutely inadequate, there springs up happiness, and will spring up happiness, of some sort or other. Indeed, it is among such communities as these that happiness will find her last refuge on earth, since it is among them that a perfect insight into the conditions of existence will be longest postponed."[12] Again, the creative contradiction is set out. "There springs up happiness" as against "the conditions of existence": sensations against laws; writing against narrative. In a comparison of George Eliot and Hardy, one of their earlier critics, Oliver Elton, defined the difference between them thus: "While exhaustively describing life, she is apt to miss the spirit of life itself. Its unashamed passion, its careless gaiety, the intoxication of sunshine—so far as she understands these things, she leaves us with the feeling that she rather distrusts them."[13] Hardy's work, in contrast, is characterised by these qualities. He does not distrust passion, gaiety and sunshine but he records how through event and time they are threatened, thwarted, undermined. And how for each organism, and through writing, they are recuperated.

He describes not only the "fearful joy," the "killing joy" of sexual arousal, but placable, unnoticed happiness, something so "matter of course" that no one comments on it. So only Eustacia sets out to *act* in the Mummers' play; the rest go through the motions in a way that Hardy thoroughly naturalises by means of the metaphor of mushrooms: "The remainder of the play ended: the Saracen's head was cut off, and Saint George stood as victor. Nobody commented, any more than they would have commented on the fact of mushrooms coming in autumn or snowdrops in spring. They took the piece as phlegmatically as did the actors themselves. It was a phase of cheerfulness which was, as a matter of course, to be passed through every Christmas; and there was no more to be said" (*Return*: 157).

Metaphor in the following passage is slight and is used only laterally, comparing one natural form to another ("almost feline" . . . "toads made noises like very young ducks") until the last phrase, "their drone coming and going like the sound of a gong." The propinquity of the human here barely disturbs the animate.

> The month of March arrived, and the heath showed its first faint signs of awakening from winter trance. The awakening was almost feline in its

stealthiness. The pool outside the bank by Eustacia's dwelling, which seemed as dead and desolate as ever to an observer who moved and made noises in his observation, would gradually disclose a state of great animation when silently watched awhile. A timid animal world had come to life for the season. Little tadpoles and efts began to bubble up through the water, and to race along beneath it; toads made noises like very young ducks, and advanced to the margin in twos and threes; overhead, bumble-bees flew hither and thither in the thickening light, their drone coming and going like the sound of a gong. (*Return*: 207)

The same comedy of propinquity and complementarity is present in most of the descriptions which release pleasure, the human presence delicately stopping and completing the whole:

When Elizabeth-Jane opened the hinged casement next morning the mellow air brought in the feel of imminent autumn almost as distinctly as if she had been in the remotest hamlet. Casterbridge was the complement of the rural life around; not its urban opposite. Bees and butterflies in the cornfields at the top of the town, who desired to get to the meads at the bottom, took no circuitous course, but flew straight down High Street without any apparent consciousness that they were traversing strange latitudes. And in autumn airy spheres of thistledown floated into the same street, lodged upon the shop fronts, blew into drains, and innumerable tawny and yellow leaves skimmed along the pavement, and stole through people's doorways into their passages with a hesitating scratch on the floor, like the skirts of timid visitors.[14]

The problem and the poignancy of narrative for Hardy was the gap between sensation and recall: "Today has length, breadth, thickness, colour, smell, voice. As soon as it becomes *yesterday* it is a thin layer among many layers, without substance, colour, or articulate sound" (27 January 1897).[15]

His writing seeks the palpable. It is in the present moment that human knowledge is realised and human happiness is experienced. The present is part of the material order as the past can no longer be. Hardy, in fact, shares that Romantic materialism which we have already dwelt on in Darwin's writing.

Observation is charged with sensory power. In both writers the material world is described simultaneously in terms which may lend themselves to an optimistic or pessimistic interpretation, but which function *as terms* through the pleasures of observation. The rapid changes of scale and distance shift the writing between tabulation, recurrence, the single instance, diversity recorded, the historical sense of physical life experienced again and again.

With respect to plants, it has long been known what enormous ranges many fresh-water and even marsh-species have. . . . I think favourable means of dispersal explain this fact. . . . Wading birds, which frequent the muddy edges of ponds, if suddenly flushed, would be the most likely to have muddy feet. Birds of this order I can show are the greatest wanderers, and are occasionally found on the most remote and barren islands in the open ocean; they would not be likely to alight on the surface of the sea, so that the dirt would not be washed off their feet; when making land, they would be sure to fly to their natural fresh-water haunts. I do not believe that botanists are aware how charged the mud of ponds is with seeds. . . . I took in February three table-spoonfuls of mud from three different points, beneath water, on the edge of a little pond; this mud when dried weighed only 6¾ ounces; I kept it covered up in my study for six months, pulling up and counting each plant as it grew; the plants were of many kinds, and were altogether 537 in number; and yet the viscid mud was all contained in a breakfast cup! Considering these facts, I think it would be an inexplicable circumstance if water-birds did not transport the seeds of fresh-water plants to vast distances, and if consequently the range of these plants was not very great. (376–7)

Darwin's provisional explanation takes the form of description with a strangely imagined participation in the flight of the wading birds with their muddy feet, their sudden flight, their powers of wandering, their avoidance of the sea and seeking for fresh water. Then the perspective changes suddenly from ranging mind's-eye to the experimental observer, with his pleasure in "pulling up and counting each plant as it grew" and the precise largesse of the number 537. Darwin combines the domestic object of the breakfast cup of mud and the free space of the ocean-ranging birds to reach a conclusion cast in negatives which delay—and reinforce—its inevitability.

"Herons and other birds, century after century, have gone on daily devouring fish; they then take flight and go to other waters, or are blown across the sea." Darwin's writing represents the pleasurability of the physical process; it registers the felicity, as well as the difficulty, of life's multiple scales and sensations. His evidence is not experimental solely, but imaginative, relying on a felt and learnt identification with alien forms of life.

His range of reference, his sense of lateral experience, finds a new place for man within the natural order, unnamed among many creatures in "the entangled bank." Yet his writing also amplifies that image by granting to the human observer the power simultaneously to observe and identify with all other forms of life: the kicking ostrich, the worm "crawling through the damp earth," "how much the fruit of the different kinds of gooseberries differ in size, colour, shape, and hairiness," "humble-bees" which alone can reach the nectar of the purple clover.

He is "humbly recording diverse readings" of the phenomena of life, and that, Hardy declares, is the "road to a true philosophy of life." What Hardy wrote in justification of *Poems of the Past and Present* in 1902 has its application also to the textuality of his novels: "Unadjusted impressions have their value, and the road to a true philosophy of life seems to lie in humbly recording diverse readings of its phenomena as they are forced upon us by chance and change."[16] Hardy and Darwin concur in that chance and change are not intermitting conditions in their work. Rather, they are the permanent medium of experience and thus of language. But both of them also insist on repetition as a basic organisation for all experience within the natural order. Heron, ants, plants, exist juxtaposed in the same intensity of physical recall, focused by the strain and the release of fitting them close to the human.

> When the nest is slightly disturbed, the slaves occasionally come out, and like their masters are much agitated and defend the nest: when the nest is much disturbed and the larvae and pupae are exposed, the slaves work energetically with their masters in carrying them away to a place of safety. . . . During the months of June and July, I have watched for many hours several nests in Surrey and Sussex, and never saw a slave either leave or enter a nest. (214–15, Darwin)

> In front of her a colony of ants had established a thoroughfare across the way, where they toiled a never-ending and heavy-laden throng. . . . She remembered that this bustle of ants had been in progress for years at the same spot—doubtless those of the old times were the ancestors of these which walked there now. She leant back to obtain more thorough rest, and the soft eastern portion of the sky was as great a relief to her eyes as the thyme was to her head. While she looked a heron arose on that side of the sky and flew on with his face towards the sun. He had come dripping wet from some pool in the valleys, and as he flew the edges and linings of his wings, his thighs, and his breast were so caught by the bright sunbeams that he appeared as if formed of burnished silver. (296, Hardy)

Hardy's writing is characterised by creative vacillation, by a shiftiness which survives the determinations of plot. Life is devious and resourceful, constantly reassembling about new possibilities which lie just off the path of obliterative energies of event.[17] Happiness and hap form the two poles of his work.

Happpiness here does not share in the powers of narrative. Indeed it is almost always at odds with narrative, because it is at odds with succession. Happiness is, rather, constellatory, "a series of impressions" at most. His sentences cull material from quite diverse worlds, and contradictory discourses, making no attempt to homogenise the varying densities into one stream: "He might have been an Arab, or an automaton; he would have been like a red-sandstone statue but for the motion of his arm with the dice-box" (243). "The sloping pathways by which spectators had ascended to their seats were pathways yet. But the whole was grown over with grass, which now, at the end of summer, was bearded with withered bents that formed waves under the brush of the wind, returning to the attentive ear Aeolian modulations, and detaining for moments the flying globes of thistledown" (*Mayor*: 99). Hardy's associative ear sets "Arab" and "automaton" alongside each other, while the sense of each word demands a completely different contextuality from the reader. Time and dimensions shift. Similarly the dialect word "bents" and its modifier "withered" gather an auditory pattern composed of "w"s, "r"s, and "b"s: "was bearded with withered bents that formed waves under the brush of the wind." Then that pattern peters out and instead we have the classical-scientific discourse of "Aeolian modulations" (with its own strong auditory resolves of "m," "l," and "n" which are carried forward into "moments" . . . "flying globes," "thistledown"). The reconciling pleasures of the ear sustain but do not disguise the semantic leaps.

Hardy like Darwin places himself in his texts as observer, traveller, a conditional presence capable of seeing things from multiple distances and diverse perspectives almost in the same moment.

> A traveller who should walk and observe any of these visitants as Venn observed them now could feel himself to be in direct communication with regions unknown to man. Here in front of him was a wild mallard—just arrived from the home of the north wind. The creature brought within him an amplitude of Northern knowledge. Glacial catastrophes, snow-storm episodes, glittering auroral effects, Polaris in the zenith, Franklin underfoot,— the category of his commonplaces was wonderful. But the bird, like many other philosophers, seemed as he looked at the reddleman to think that a present moment of comfortable reality was worth a decade of memories. (*Return*: 109)

The eye of the writing moves far and near, not so much dwelling in multiple minds, as in George Eliot, as creating a shifting space and changing scales. Ear and touch become identified.

> Throughout the blowing of these plaintive November winds that note bore a great resemblance to the ruins of human song which remain to the throat of fourscore and ten. It was a worn whisper, dry and papery, and it brushed so distinctly across the ear that, by the accustomed, the material minutiae in which it originated could be realized as by touch. It was the united products of infinitesimal vegetable causes, and these were neither stems, leaves, fruit, blades, prickles, lichen, nor moss.
>
> They were the mummied heath-bells of the past summer, originally tender and purple, now washed colourless by Michaelmas rains, and dried to dead skins by October suns. So low was an individual sound from these that a combination of hundreds only just emerged from silence, and the myriads of the whole declivity reached the woman's ear but as a shrivelled and intermittent recitative. Yet scarcely a single accent among the many afloat to-night could haven such power to impress a listener with thoughts of its origin. One inwardly saw the infinity of those combined multitudes; and perceived that each of the tiny trumpets was seized on, entered, scoured and emerged from by the wind as thoroughly as if it were as vast as a crater. (*Return*: 78)

This vacillation of memory and material, near and far, of tactile and abstract makes for a kind of liberty for the reader, even though an unstable liberty. It is something to set against the dogged interpenetration of event by which his plots overdetermine outcome. We always sustain until the last moment a passionate sense of possible happiness: he sustains hope by different levels of plot, liberty by multiple perspectives. And the drive of his plots is so crushing precisely because of the full sense of *life* elated in us by the range of sense perceptions which throng his writing. The intricate affinity of touch and sound keeps the reader alert and close. Looking back on a novel by Hardy many readers are afflicted and aghast. But he is also one of the most popular and widely read of writers: we enter his works not only to be chagrined and thwarted, but also sustained by the moment-by-moment plenitude of experiences offered us. Traumatised by conclusion, the reader in retrospect almost forgets the bounty of text. Forgetting and having are both crucial in Hardy.

Derrida's contraries of play and history are helpful here. The text in process is at present occurring and need not have reference to the absent origin. It permits a sense of free play for the reader. But the mega-plot may also be borne in micro-form within a single sentence, so that we have in much of Hardy's writing *both* the "broken immediateness" (l'immediatété rompue) which Derrida associates with Rousseau, *and* what he casts as Nietzschean: "the joyous affirmation of the free play of the world."[18]

Two elements of Darwin's theory had a peculiarly personal significance in Hardy's writing—and they were elements which pointed in differing directions, forming a contradiction where Hardy could work. The first element was Darwin's insistence on "normative felicity": despite the suffering in the natural world, survival depended on a deep association of life and pleasurability.

Darwin's other emphasis was upon imperfect adaptation.[19] Although the individual organism is guided by pleasurability and "well being," the process of development by means of accumulated variations has not assured complete congruity between need and adaptation.

Maladaptation, "the FAILURE OF THINGS to be what they are meant to be," obsesses Hardy.[20] In the light of this emphasis his apparently lack-lustre praise of Tess as "an almost standard woman" can be properly read as superlative, a part of that argument about the significance of individual and species which preoccupied Darwin too. But the "almost" is also important—its force is insensitive rather than demurring. "New Year's thought. A perception of the FAILURE OF THINGS to be what they are meant to be, lends them, in place of the intended interest, a new and greater interest of an unintended kind."[21]

The urgency of intended happiness, intended perfection, pervades Hardy's text, but its poignancy derives from the failures of perfection, the unfulfilled, the skewed, and disturbed. That is what allows the reader to recognise and yearn for the shadow plots of achievement and joy which can never fully manifest themselves. The shifts between the perfect and the blighted, between the benign and the grotesque, are mediated through anthropomorphic imagery, which shifts the boundaries between people and objects, "representing the persistence of the barbaric idea which confuses persons and things." Carpenter had suggested that evolutionary theory disturbed all such demarcations, showing the vacillations between mollusc and man and the continuance of common forms still capable of change. Darwin expressed deep emotional and intellectual problems through the struggle to control anthropomorphism in "the face of nature." Visage and surface, "physiognomy," elide the distinctions between man and the natural world. "It was at present a place perfectly accordant with man's nature—neither ghastly, hateful, nor ugly: neither commonplace, unmeaning, nor tame; but, like man, slighted and enduring; and withal singularly colossal and mysterious in its swarthy monotony. As with some persons who have long lived apart, solitude seemed to look out of its countenance. It had a lonely face, suggesting tragical possibilities" (*Return*: 35).[22]

Instead of man disjunct from all other aspects of the material order, or at the pinnacle of hierarchy, he must now find a place in a world of "horizontality," as it comes home to Clym in *The Return of the Native.* "It gave him a sense of bare equality with, and no superiority to, a single living thing under the sun."

So the problem of finding a scale for the human becomes a besetting preoccupation of Hardy's work, a scale that will neither be unrealistically grandiose, nor debilitatingly reductive, which will accept evanescence and the autonomy of systems not serving the human, but which will still call upon Darwin's oft-repeated assertion: "the relation of organism to organism is the most important of all relations" (e.g., 14:449). Darwin offers no privileged place to the human, but by appropriating older myth-metaphors such as the tree of life, he might seem to restore a continuity or wholeness to the human. In *The Woodlanders* Hardy re-uses the image of the tree, first in the abbreviated anthropological/psychological riposte of the old man whose life is literally dependent on the tree which has grown alongside his life's span; then through the entire imagery of work which places the human at the service of the natural world, and most strikingly in passages such as this, in which the human is seen as part of (not fully in control of) natural process. The human body is everywhere suggested in the description, the perfect exists alongside the warped and stunted; sound and touch are scarcely separable:

> They went noiselessly over mats of starry moss, rustled through interspersed tracts of leaves, skirted trunks with spreading roots whose mossed rinds made them like hands wearing green gloves; elbowed old elms and ashes with great forks, in which stood pools of water that overflowed on rainy days and ran down their stems in green cascades. On older trees still than these huge lobes of fungi grew like lungs. Here, as everywhere, the Unfulfilled Intention, which makes life what it is, was as obvious as it could be among the depraved crowds of a city slum. The leaf was deformed, the curve was crippled, the taper was interrupted; the lichen ate the vigour of the stalk, and the ivy strangled to death the promising sapling. (82)[23]

Variation is here perceived not as creative divergence, but as marred and interrupted form. The *Unfulfilled* Intention, the "struggle for life" is evident and botched: as he writes in a later scene, the trees are "close together, wrestling for existence, their branches disfigured with wounds resulting from their mutual rubbing and blows." He calls directly here on Darwin's extended description of the "great tree": "At each period of growth all the growing twigs have tried to branch out on all sides, and to overtop and kill the surrounding twigs and branches, in the same manner as species and groups of species have tried to overmaster other species in the great battle for life" (171). Similarly, his description of "Dead boughs scattered about like ichthyosauri in a museum" condenses the time scale in Darwin's similar description: "From the first growth of the tree, many a limb and branch has decayed and dropped off; and these lost branches of various sizes may represent those whole orders, families, and genera which have now no living representatives, and which are known to us only from having been found in a fossil state" (172).

But the intervention of the human form disturbs in Hardy's writing the assurance of Darwin's tree. The woodland is simultaneously a scene of decay, deformation, new growth and "starry moss." Hardy is acutely alert to diverse time-scales, and to the extent to which the oblivious interaction of these differing scales make up the mesh of event and experience: "a few short months ago . . . down to so recent a time that flowers then folded were hardly faded yet." In his journal in December 1865 he notes: "To insects the twelvemonth has been an epoch, to leaves a life, to tweeting birds a generation, to man a year" (157). And in *Tess* that observation has become both more reductive and more voluptuous. Time-jars are the norm.

> In the ill-judged execution of the well-judged plan of things the call seldom produces the comer, the man to love rarely coincides with the hour for loving. Nature does not often say "See!" to her poor creature at a time when seeing can lead to happy doing; or reply "Here!" to a body's cry of "Where?" till the hide-and-seek has become an irksome, outworn game. We may wonder whether at the acme and summit of the human progress these anachronisms will be connected by a finer intuition, a closer interaction of the social machinery than that which now jolts us round and along; but such completeness is not to be prophesied, or even conceived as possible. (67)

Exuberant life is diminished within the scale of the writing which surveys it. The most fortunate creatures are those who dwell entirely within a single time-scale: for human beings empathy with such life can be only momentary. Our habitual experience is of multiple time which brings with it the incommensurate: Mrs Yeobright, on her journey across the heath to renew contact with Clym and Eustacia, sits down beside a pond:

> Occasionally she came to a spot where independent worlds of ephemerons were passing their time in mad carousal, some in the air, some on the hot ground and vegetation, some in the tepid and stringy water of a nearly dried pool. All of the shallower ponds had decreased to a vaporous mud amid which the maggoty shapes of innumerable obscure creatures could be indistinctly seen, heaving and wallowing with enjoyment. Being a woman not disinclined to philosophize she sometimes sat down under her umbrella to rest and to watch their happiness, for a certain hopefulness as to the result of her visit gave ease to her mind. (285)

The "ephemerons" live a life of ecstatic enjoyment; the term "ephemeron" names their time-span as brief and yet the effect of the description is of ceaseless activity, unstoppable delight. By naming them "ephemerons" Hardy calls into play those alternative time-scales which the human must always inhabit—and within our reading here diverse time-codes are at jar. Mrs Yeobright is recovering hope, but the reader (with the foreknowledge of the book's title *The Closed Door*) previsions a time beyond the end of her walk, and that not hopefully. *Human* anxiety and envy are encoded in the half-repudiation of the creatures' enjoyment: "the maggoty shapes of innumerable obscure creatures could be indistinctly seen, heaving and wallowing with enjoyment."

The two major emotional and creative problems with evolutionary theory forced on Hardy were to find a scale for the human, and a place for the human within the natural order. Like Darwin, an ambiguous anthropomorphism pervades his writing—an anthropomorphism which paradoxically denies human centrality and gives the human a fugitive and secondary role in his system of reference but not in his system of values.

Egdon is fitted to survive because it is not exceptionally steep or flat, and not subject to man's husbandry. The "finger-touches" it has felt are "of the last geological change." "Those surfaces were neither so steep as to be destructible by weather, nor so flat as to be the victims of floods and deposits. With the exception of an aged highway, and a still more aged barrow presently to be referred to—themselves almost crystallized to natural products by long continuance—even the trifling irregularities were not caused by pickaxe, plough, or spade, but remained as the very finger-touches of the last geological change" (*Return*: 36).

Hardy's reading and his observation alike made him hyper-conscious of multiple scale, multiple time, and of the unique problem consciousness created in persuading the human to attempt to live in all of them. "At night, when human discords and harmonies are hushed, in a general sense, for the greater part of twelve hours, there is nothing to moderate the blow with which the infinitely great, the stellar universe, strikes down upon the infinitely little, the mind of the beholder; and this was the case now" (*Two on a Tower*: 83).[24] The human body is implicit in these descriptions of magnitudes; it comes to the surface of language to reach out, or be struck: "even the trifling irregularities were not caused by pickaxe, plough, or spade, but remained as the very finger-touches of the last geological change. . . . At night . . . there is nothing to moderate the blow with which the infinitely great, the stellar universe, strikes down upon the infinitely little, the mind of the beholder."

What to Darwin was in the main wonderful—the sense of history prolonged beyond consciousness, of modes of existence independent of our observation—to Hardy was more often a source of oppression and disruption. He dwelt most happily within bounds, but his writing all has to do with the crossing of bounds—of time, of space, of relationships too. We see the paradox intensely marked in the biographical fact that he disliked to be touched, while his writing is permeated with experiences of touch, texture and temperature. His hyper-sensitivity to tactual experience is related to the problem of finding a scale for response and experience.

In Hardy's early novel, *A Pair of Blue Eyes*, a scene occurs which is often referred to in discussions of his relation to evolutionary ideas and specifically to Lyell's discussions of geological time; Knight finds himself clinging to a cliff face, about to fall; opposite Knight's eyes was an imbedded fossil, standing forth in low relief from the rock. It was a creature with eyes:

> The eyes, dead and turned to stone, were even now regarding him. It was one of the early crustaceans called Trilobites. Separated by millions of years in their lives, Knight and this underling seemed to have met in their place of death. It was the single instance within reach of his vision of anything that had ever been alive and had had a body to save, as he himself had now.
>
> The creature represented but a low type of animal existence, for never in their vernal years had the plains indicated by those numberless slaty layers been traversed by an intelligence worthy of the name. Zoo-phytes, mollusca, shell-fish, were the highest development of those ancient dates. The immense lapses of time each formation represented had known nothing of the dignity of man. They were grand times, but they were mean times too, and mean were their relics. He was to be with the small in his death.[25]

Man here still feels himself at the summit of creation—the *incongruity* of companionship with minute fossil life thwarts him. Yet kinship is acknowledged, the creature had "been alive and had had a body to save, as he himself had now."

Lyell's tone of melancholy puzzlement over the machine of the universe becomes militant in Hardy:

> Why the working of this same machinery should be attended with so much evil, is a mystery far beyond the reach of our philosophy, and must probably remain so until we are permitted to investigate, not our planet alone and its inhabitants, but other parts of the moral and material universe with which they may be connected. Could our survey embrace other worlds, and the events, not of a few centuries only, but of periods as indefinite as those with which geology renders us familiar, some apparent contradictions might be reconciled, and some difficulties would doubtless be cleared up. But even then, as our capacities are finite, while the scheme of the universe may be infinite, both in time and space, it is presumptuous to suppose that all sources of doubt and perplexity would ever be removed. (*Principles of Geology*, vol. ii, ch. xxix, p. 144 (10th edition))

The absolute gap between our finite capacities and the infinite time and space of the universe burdens Hardy's texts with a sense of malfunction and apprehension. There is a collapse of congruity between the human and the objects of human knowledge and human emotion. In such a situation finding a place and scale for the human becomes a matter not of the appropriation of space, the colonising of experience, but rather of identification, a willingness to be permeated, to be "transmissive." Passivity is naturalised at the level of description as well as of character.

In *The Return of the Native* the topic of the book is the near impossibility of return. In an evolutionary order it is not possible to choose to return to an earlier state. "In Clym Yeobright's face could be dimly seen the typical countenance of the future" (185). Clym "the native" comes back to Egdon, wanting to become again an "inhabitant" but wanting also to educate and develop the other inhabitants. Thereby he becomes an invader—an alien force which disrupts and changes. He wishes to "revert . . . to ancestral forms" (*The Origin of Species*: 77) but "by the experiment itself the conditions of life are changed." His determination to remain in Egdon rather than to move on disrupts his relations to his mother and to Eustacia Vye. At the centre of the book's record, though, is the description of Clym, half-blind, working as a furze-cutter on the heath. In this passage a momentary completeness is achieved.

> His daily life was of a curious microscopic sort, his whole world being limited to a circuit of a few feet from his person. His familiars were creeping and winged things, and they seemed to enroll him in their band. Bees hummed around his ears with an intimate air, and tugged at the heath and furze-flowers at his side in such numbers as to weigh them down to the sod. The strange amber-coloured butterflies which Egdon produced, and which were never seen elsewhere, quivered in the breath of his lips, alighted upon his bowed back, and sported with the glittering point of his hook as he flourished it up and down. Tribes of emerald-green grasshoppers leaped over his feet, falling awkwardly on their backs, heads, or hips, like unskillful acrobats, as chance might rule; or engaged themselves in noisy flirtations under the fern-fronds with silent ones of homely hue. Huge flies, ignorant of larders and wire-netting, and quite in a savage state, buzzed about him without knowing that he was a man. In and out of the fern-dells snakes glided in their most brilliant blue and yellow guise, it being the season immediately following the shedding of their old skins, when their colours are brightest. Litters of young rabbits came out from their forms to sun themselves upon hillocks, the hot beams blazing through the delicate tissue of each thin-fleshed ear, and firing it to a blood-red transparency in which the veins could be seen. None of them feared him. (262)

Everything is particular; the pleasures of touch are augmented by our pleasures of sight, which he lacks. The persistent anthropomorphism calls attention to the human and comically, throw-away, dislimns human boundaries; "unskilled acrobats," "silent ones of homely hue," "flies, ignorant of larders and wire netting." Man is here familiarised with other creatures; the weight of the bees who "tugged at the heath and furze-flowers" is enlarged as under a microscope to equality with the human inhabitant. Bodily temperature is again the medium of pleasure and of experience, and is felt as much *by means of* the young rabbits who "sun themselves upon hillocks, the hot beams blazing through the delicate tissue of each thin-fleshed ear" as through Clym's presence. The "entangled" or "tangled bank" which in Darwin's text is peopled by plants, birds, insects, and worms, here has room also for man, not set apart from other kinds. "None of them feared him."

All the separate time- and space-scales for a short while are in harmony. Because Clym's world is "limited to a circuit of a few feet from his person" and because of the "monotony of his occupation," he is not distinguished from the rest of the natural order. His coat is now like that of Egdon Heath itself as it was described in the first chapter: "Civilization was its enemy; and ever since the beginning of vegetation its soil had worn the same antique brown dress, the natural and invariable garment of the particular formation." The topographical "features" and "surface" of the introductory description are here present as human face, but a face almost indistinguishable from the heath ("the minor features of the heath . . . the white surface of the road" are here countered by "a brown spot in the midst of an expanse of olive-green gorse"). The fullness and the quirkiness of this central description are both equally unforgettable. The reader is offered plenitude, but a plenitude which cannot rest easy with itself for long.

The "return of the native" can be achieved only within the smallest extent of time and space. The rest of the book shows Clymn obliged to re-emerge from the pleasures of "forced limitation."

In *Tess* there occurs a somewhat similar moment of completeness which openly washes away all "distinction between the near and the far" and in which "Tess was conscious of neither time nor space." Here Hardy brings out the animistic sense that all life is equally alert and equally passive. The atmosphere is so *"transmissive"* "that inanimate objects seemed endowed with two or three senses, if not five." "An auditor felt close to everything within the horizon." In this soundless landscape Tess moves, hearing only the sound of Angel's strings and drawn towards them:

> It was a typical summer evening in June, the atmosphere being in such delicate equilibrium and so transmissive that inanimate objects seemed endowed with two or three senses, if not five. There was no distinction between the near and the far, and an auditor felt close to everything within the horizon. The soundlessness impressed her as a positive entity rather than as the mere negation of noise. It was broken by the strumming of strings. . . . The outskirt of the garden in which Tess found herself had been left uncultivated for years, and was now damp and rank with juicy grass which sent up mists of pollen at a touch; and with tall blooming weeds emitting offensive smells—weeds whose red and yellow and purple hues formed a polychrome as dazzling as that of cultivated flowers. She went stealthily as a cat through this profusion of growth, gathering cuckoo-spittle on her skirts, cracking snails that were underfoot, staining her hands with thistle-milk and slug-slime, and rubbing off upon her naked arms sticky blights which, though snow-white on the apple-tree trunks,

made madder stains on her skin; thus she drew quite near to Clare, still unobserved of him. (150)

Viscous substances, rank smells, slime and stickiness: the unweeded garden is a "profusion of growth" but it is described in language which registers disturbance and repugnance—a disturbance and repugnance which yet yield to voluptuous acceptance. Tess registers but does not describe. She is immersed in this sticky life-and-death, yet not in alienated consciousness of it. The language of description is interposed, but "transmissive." Here hyperfecundity, the activity of growth, permeates language, even transgresses language. Resistance to such fullness is felt in the writing, but also calm.

Life in Hardy never falters, but the individuals who live it barely survive the books' length.

In his last two novels, *Tess* and *Jude,* generative plot threatens and squanders individuality. Tess is a late representative of a "great family." Darwin's "great family" of all life is narrowed again to that of privilege. Angel thinks "The historic interest of her family—that masterful line of d'Urbervilles—whom he had despised as a spent force, touched his sentiments now" (364). But she is also, through her mother and as vitally, a representative of that fecundity which has allowed those outside the parkland to endure, while the "great family" withers away. Hardy was fascinated by theories of descent—he read Weismann on heredity, just as earlier he had read *The Origin* and *The Descent.*[26] Angel Clare imagines himself as the "new" man and is unable to understand that Tess is a possible form for the "new" woman—both survivor and intelligent forerunner. In that sense Tess dies, wasted. But the book (which is imbued with Max Müller's solar mythology and with sun worship) properly gives us back the scale of Tess's life. It is for this reason—that writing still predominates over plot—that we feel Tess's story as less bleak than that of Jude and Sue.

Tess is jubilant as well as terrible. Jude and Sue on the other hand see themselves as precursors, and can achieve their full value only *as* precursors of a "new" order. The death of their children (murdered by little Father Time in a late-Malthusian tragedy, "Done because we are too menny") leaves Jude and Sue as aberrant, without succession, and therefore "monstrous" in the sense that they can carry no cultural or physical mutations into the future and must live out their lives merely at odds with the present.

In the late works plot dominates "apprehension." The Romantic materialism which Hardy shared with Darwin threatens to wither in the face of the urgency of succession. Society has set too much store by ideas of succession, heredity and progress. Renewal, and the lateral range of sensation, are endangered by the insistence on development.

Already in a journal entry in 1876 Hardy had registered something closer to a hardening than a merging: "If it be possible to compress into a sentence all that a man learns between 20 and 40, it is that all things merge in one another—good into evil, generosity into justice, religion into politics, the year into the ages, the world into the universe. With this in view the evolution of species seems but a minute and obvious process in the same movement."[27] To Darwin, the plot that his own writing proposed seemed (or needed to seem) benign. Hardy perceived the malign tautology latent in it: the "struggle for life," or, even more, "the survival of the fittest," pre-emptively extolled the conquerors. Those who survived were justified. But he shared with Darwin that delight in material life in its widest diversity, the passion for particularity, and for individuality and plenitude which is the counter-element in Darwin's narrative and theory. Hardy set out the contra-diction. Like Darwin, he feels the problem of anthropomorphism in describ-ing a natural order not centred on man, but although he often registers grotesque interruption through allusions to the human body, yet his writing conjures the intimacy of the senses by means of which we apprehend the material world.

Plot—that combination of the inexorable and the gratuitous—in *Jude* annuls writing. But in all other of Hardy's works there is, as in Darwin, a strongly surviving belief in the "recuperative powers" which pervade both language and the physical world.

Notes

1. Charles Darwin, *Expression of the Emotions in Man and Animals*, preface by Konrad Lorenz (Chicago and London, 1965):360–1.

2. Florence Emily Hardy, *The Early Life of Thomas Hardy 1840–1891* (London, 1928): 253. Hereafter *Early Life*.

3. *Early Life*: 268.

4. *Early Life*: 301–2.

5. Thomas Hardy, *Tess of the D'Urbervilles: A Pure Woman Faithfully Presented*, ed. P. N. Furbank (London, 1975): 316. All page references are to this edition.

6. At the end of his life Hardy listed thinkers important to him as "Darwin, Huxley, Spencer, Comte, Hume, Mill," cited Carl J. Weber, *Hardy of Wessex: His Life and Literary Career* (New York, 1965): 246–7. In the *Early Life* he claimed to have been "among the earliest acclaimers of *The Origin of Species*": 198. See Peter Morton, *"Tess of the D'Urbervilles*: A Neo-Darwinian Reading," *Southern Review*, 7 (1974): 38–50; Roger Robinson, "Hardy and Darwin" in *Thomas Hardy: The Writer and His Background* (New York, 1980): 128–50; Elliot B. Gose, "Psychic Evolution: Darwinism and Initiation in *Tess*," *Nineteenth Century Fiction*, 18 (1963): 261–72; Perry Meisel, *Thomas Hardy: The Return of the Repressed* (New Haven and London, 1972); Bruce Johnson, " 'The Perfection of Species' and Hardy's *Tess*," in *Nature and the Victorian Imagination*, ed. G. B. Tennyson and U. C. Knoepflmacher (Berkeley, 1978): 259–77. Meisel and Johnson are particularly impressive in their grasp of the implications of Darwin's thought for Hardy.

7. *The Return of the Native*, ed. Derwent May (London, 1975). All page references are to this edition.

8. *Early Life*: 285–6.

9. For discussion of Darwin's debt to Wordsworth see Edward Manier, *The Young Darwin and His Cultural Circle* (Dordrecht, 1978): 89–96; Marilyn Gaull, "From Wordsworth to Dar-win," *The Wordsworth Circle*, 10 (1979): 33–48.

10. *Tess*, ed. cit: 146, 174.

11. *Early Life*: 279.

12. "The Dorsetshire Labourer," *Longman's Magazine* (1883).

13. Cited in Gordon S. Haight, *A Century of George Eliot Criticism* (London, 1966): 192.

14. *The Mayor of Casterbridge*, ed. I. Gregor (London, 1976).

15. Florence Hardy, *The Later Years of Thomas Hardy* (London, 1930).

16. H. Orel, ed., *Thomas Hardy's Personal Writings* (London, 1967): 39.

17. John Bayley, *An Essay on Hardy* (Cambridge, 1978), discusses the unaccording, oblivious quality of Hardy's writing.

18. Jacques Derrida, "Structure, Sign, and Play in the Discourse of the Human Sciences," *The Structuralist Controversy: The Languages of Criticism and the Sciences of Man*, ed. Richard Macksey and Eugenio Donato (Baltimore and London, 1970):264.

L'immédiateté rompue est donc la face triste, négative, nostalgique, coupable, rousseauiste, de la pensée du jeu dont l'affirmation nietzschéene, l'affirmation joyeuse du jeu du monde et de l'innocence du devenir, l'affirmation d'un monde de signes sans faute, sans vérité, sans origine, offert à une interprétation active, serait l'autre face.

(Broken immediateness is thus the sad, *negative*, nostalgic, guilty, Rousseauist facet of the thinking of freeplay of which the Nietzschean *affirmation*—the joyous affirmation of the freeplay of the world and without truth, without origin, offered to an active interpretation—would be the other side.) [The translation is from Macksey and Donato's text.]

19. "Natural selection will not produce absolute perfection." Darwin cites the bee's sting, which causes its death.

20. *Early Life*: 163. (1 January 1879).

21. R. H. Hutton, writing in 1854, shows how the problem of "essence" in taxonomy had already entered literary language: "Just as science finds the type of a class of flowers which actual nature seldom or never does more than *approach*, so that in a certain sense science knows what the flower *ought* to be, while nature never quite produces it." He then discusses Shakespeare's Cleopatra as an example. *Prospective Review*, 10 (1854): 476.

22. See the discussion above: 112–115. [Ed. note: Beer's reference is to an earlier section of her book.]

23. *The Woodlanders*, introd. David Lodge (London, 1975): 82.

24. *Two on a Tower*, introd. F. B. Pinion (London, 1976): 83.

25. *A Pair of Blue Eyes*, ed. Ronald Blythe (London, 1976): 222.

26. August Weismann, *Studies in the Theory of Descent* (London, 1882). Hardy said that he read him in 1890 "having finished adapting *Tess of the d'Urbervilles* for the serial issue." *Early Life*: 301.

27. *Early Life*: 146–7.

Passion in Context   Barbara Hardy*

Hardy's lyrics show his restraint in emotional representation. His eloquence is muted, pure, stark, and intense, startling us by quiet means, letting feeling well up in the spaces between utterances, or resound after

*Reprinted by permission from Barbara Hardy, *Forms of Feeling in Victorian Fiction* (London: Peter Owen, 1985).

silence. In "Overlooking the River Stour," he spends almost the whole poem on brilliantly incised visual images—swallows, moorhens, kingcups—of a world of non-human nature outside his window. Then he shocks us by uttering a feeling for what was not seen, or regarded, inside the room, revealing regret and remorse, while refusing to relate. The reticence of "the more" is strong and delicate: "And never I turned my head, alack, / While these things met my gaze / Through the pane's drop-drenched glaze, / To see the more behind my back. . . . / O never I turned, but let, alack, / These less things hold my gaze!"

In a similarly reserved poem, "After a Romantic Day," Hardy once more lets feeling's pressure stir through ellipsis, curtness, understatement, and implication:

> The railway bore him through
> An Earthen cutting out from a city:
>   There was no scope for view,
> Though the frail light shed by a slim young moon
>   Fell like a friendly tune.
>   Fell like a liquid ditty,
> And the blank lack of any charm
>   Of landscape did no harm.
> The bald steep cutting, rigid, rough,
>   And moon-lit, was enough
> For poetry of place: its weathered face
> Formed a convenient sheet whereon
> The visions of his mind were drawn.

Here he is able not only to represent feeling, but also, within the purity of lyric, to meditate on that feeling, to show and to marvel at a fullness of feeling which needs no objective correlatives, in life or art, though that blank and bald cutting acts as a functional negation of the objective correlative. Hardy's caressing touch passes over those untold visions of his mind, the experience reverberating for the man who has just passed through it, and into whose silence it enters, creatively. Emotion fills the imagination, to the brim. What rings for him, without symbol or name, speaks silently to us. Hardy's lyric poetry, like all great lyric poetry, depends on a refusal to give, in complete or elaborate form, characters and histories. It respects the intimacy and mystery of what John Stuart Mill called the "deeper and more secret workings of human emotion."

In the novels the conditions are different. The means are narrative and dramatic. Lyricism is present in the service of narrative and dramatic forms, dwelling intensely on emotional experiences which are fully placed in character, history, and environment. T. S. Eliot, who discussed Hardy's art (in *After Strange Gods*) entirely in terms of its emotional expression, found it lacking in affective differentiation, accusing Hardy of being concerned not with minds but with passions, and of handling them as states of "emotional paroxysm" in which, Eliot proposes, human beings are all alike. Hardy is a novelist of violent feeling; in his Preface to the first edition of *Jude the Obscure,* his most tragic, dogmatic, and illustrative novel, he speaks of showing "the strongest passion known to humanity," and of telling "without a mincing of words, of a deadly war waged between flesh and spirit." The epigraph to Part First, "At Marygreen," is a quotation from Esdras about men running "out of their wits" for women, but the implied violence and extremity do not prepare us for the analytic nature of the novel. Its characters are represented through the continuity, variety and rhythm of their emotional lives. Those lives move in and out of crisis with a full sense, on the part of their author, of the individual creature and the external conditions. Like George Eliot, Hardy disagrees with Novalis in order to emphasize a belief that tragedy is created from within and from without. Jude is frustrated by birth and class but also by the motions of his sexual appetites. It is important to see that Hardy does not mark him out as singular in sexual vitality but as a common and natural example, not differentiated by a special flaw. What is special is his intelligence and personality, not his desires. Like *Jane Eyre* and *Villette,* the novel offers its version of the conflict and communion of reason with passion. Hardy finds powerful images for Jude's passionate pull away from the rational course, from self-improvement, from study, from the world of his candle's light on the book:

> It had been no vestal who chose *that* missile for opening her attack on him. He saw this with his intellectual eye, just for a short fleeting while, as by the light of a falling lamp one might momentarily see an inscription on a wall before being enshrouded in darkness. And then this passing discriminative power was withdrawn, and Jude was lost to all conditions of things in the advent of a fresh and wild pleasure. . . . (Part 1, Chapter 6)
>
> In short, as if materially, a compelling arm of extraordinary muscular power seized hold of him—something which had nothing in common with the spirits and influence that had moved him hitherto. This seemed to care little for his reason and his will, nothing for his so-called elevated intentions, and moved him along, as a violent schoolmaster a schoolboy he has seized by the collar, in a direction which tended towards the embrace of a woman for whom he had no respect, and whose life had nothing in common with his own except locality. (Part 1, Chapter 7)

The analysis is conducted by narrator and character. The character is allowed to understand the conditions of his passion, while the narrator remarks the irrelevance of insight. This is not a conflict between mind and appetite, though the divided self is shown in that image of brief illumination, "the light of a falling lamp." Sexual desire is shown through a refusal to personify rather than through personification, signified in a passive voice, "this passing discriminative power was withdrawn." The images which follow are partial personifications, organs and not wholes, held at arm's length by a scrupulous assertion of comparison, "In short, as if materially." The personified power seems the more active for being peculiarly specialized, nothing but arm, convincingly called "compelling" and "extraordinary." When one image is changed for another, there is the bizarre juxtaposition of the isolated arm and the "violent schoolmaster," and the schoolmaster simile then interacts grotesquely with the literal, unfigurative acts and characters, "in a direction which tended towards the embrace of a woman for whom he had no respect." This rhetoric has a particular reference: the images of the schoolmaster and the inscription on the wall derive from Jude's love of learning, while their implications of force make plain the natural power he is up against. When Hardy presents emotional crisis it is not, like Charlotte Brontë and George Eliot, to emphasize moral debate and division, but in order to show the overwhelming power of passion, even when working in and on high intelligence. Charlotte Brontë's Reason would be irrelevant here, not because Hardy is showing a weak man, but because he is showing an overwhelming force. Within the fully delineated social circumstance, the force defeats Jude's passionate aspirations. But Eliot is wrong: passion is placed and differentiated by character.

Hardy does not write allegories of passion in which the forces are evenly matched, and tends to avoid decisive crises of passion. He shows few moments of high affective drama, where a moment's decision can influence the whole life. Far from showing character in states of emotional paroxysm, he prefers to show the combination and accretion of many impassioned occasions. Where the crisis of passion occurs, it is often offstage, narrated rather than dramatized in present-tense intensity. Sometimes the expected passion is displaced, as in *Tess of the d'Urbervilles*. The celebrated seduction is neither shown nor related, and the murder of Alex D'Urberville is narrated indirectly and curiously, first through the bloodspot on the ceiling, then in Tess's singular confession. The expected passions are guilt, fear, or remorse, but what Angel (and the reader) hear is innocent and expectant love:

> I have done it—I don't know how. . . . Still, I owed it to you, and to myself, Angel. I feared long ago, when I struck him on the mouth with my glove, that I might do it some day for the trap he set me in my simple youth, and his wrong to you through me. He has come between us and ruined us, and now he can never do it any more. I never loved him at all, Angel, as I loved you. . . . only, Angel, will you forgive me my sin against you, now that I have killed him? I thought as I ran along that you would be sure to forgive me now I have done that. It came to me as a shining thing that I should get you back that way. (Chapter 57)

Angel interprets this simplicity and candour as delirium, comes to judge it as sanity. She asks forgiveness, not for murder, but for unchastity. Hardy brilliantly endows her with perverse feelings whose perversity is comprehensible. The naive words and form of the narration are both pure and grotesque. Angel first thinks she is speaking metaphorically, then that she is exaggerating: "By degrees he was inclined to believe that she had faintly attempted, at least, what she said she had done; and his horror at her impulse was mixed with amazement at the strength of her affection for himself, and at the strangeness of its quality" (Ibid). The "phase" in which this chapter appears is ironically called "Fulfilment." Tess's insistence on the fulfilment of love overrides our expectations of a fulfilment of revenge or justice. Angel's feelings perfectly match hers, at last: like her he is confused, excited and unable to reason. Her assurance puts refusal out of the question: love utters an imperative. Her language infects his: the free indirect style which registers his response takes on her matter-of-factness and simplicity: "It was very terrible if true; if a temporary hallucination, sad. But, anyhow, here was this deserted wife of his, this passionately-fond woman, clinging to him without a suspicion that he would be anything to her but a protector. He saw that for him to be otherwise was not, in her mind, within the region of the possible. Tenderness was dominant in Clare at last" (Ibid).

The penultimate chapter of the novel, the last in which Tess appears, continues this guilt-free imperative and unjudging response. The simple assumptions of love, on which Tess had once acted and expected Angel to act, overcome reason and morality. The passionate faith first assumes and then creates a responsive tenderness. The novel has shown feelings and relationships conditioned and constricted by social laws, and now insulates feelings from convention for a brief space. The completeness of the tacit asking and giving makes any suggestion of sexuality irrelevant; this is one of those rare occasions in fiction when the lover's closeness may or may not be sexual. What is stressed is the unconditional, the relaxed freedom of an enclosed but private time and place, out of time and place: "I am not going to think outside of now. Why should we! Who knows what to-morrow has in store?" (Chapter 58). Her command of the present almost casts a charm over time, "But it apparently had no sorrow." There follows a passage of time-lapse which is tenderly appropriate to this time-haunted novel, for these time-haunted lovers:

> They were indisposed to stir abroad, and the day passed, and the night following, and the next and next; till, almost without their being aware, five days had slipped by in absolute seclusion, not a sight or sound of a human being disturbing their peacefulness, such as it was. The changes of the weather were their only events, the birds of the New Forest their only company. By tacit consent they hardly once spoke of any incident of the past subsequent to their wedding-day. The gloomy intervening time seemed to sink into chaos, over which the present and prior times closed as if it never had been. Whenever he suggested that they should leave their shelter, and go forwards towards Southampton or London, she showed a strange unwillingness to move.
>
> "Why should we put an end to all that's sweet and lovely!" she deprecated. "What must come will come." And, looking through the shutter-chink: "All is trouble outside there; inside here content."
>
> He peeped out also. It was quite true; within was affection, union, error forgiven: outside was the inexorable. (Ibid.)

There is a double current of feeling, as the reader's expectation and tension move across the enclosure and stasis of the characters. The naive style is used in Tess's mild and surprised observation of her past gentleness, "Yet formerly I could never bear to hurt a fly." It is used also in the lovers' literal-minded acceptance of "content" within and "trouble" outside, as she looks through the shutters and he then peeps out to see and accept what her simple vision sees, "It was quite true." The naively registered emotional state can be seen as that of abnormal shock, for both, but it is also structural, presented as a form of the defiant, rational, and tranquil rejection of social circumstance which the novel has been pleading for since Tess's seasonal recuperation. Hardy presents a two-faced situation. It is disturbed and abnormal, if we judge by the conventional standards the novel has been subverting, but understandable and admirable, if we can imagine the severance of the individual from the larger world. Hardy is no fantasist, and sets a limit to this episode of rational madness. The feelings of loving union and harmony are rendered mildly, in an understatement entirely fitted to the narrative rhythm, establishing a lull before the expected storm. It is right that the suspension of law and convention should be initiated by Tess, who has always been capable of pure, unconventional feeling, not only in her recuperation, but in her later empirical expectations of Angel's love and sympathy. The replacement of guilt by love is in keeping with her rejections of history, both naive and intelligent. She refused Angel's characteristically improving offer of history lessons on the grounds that all she will learn is her descent from a line of identical victims, "there is set down in some old book somebody just like me" (Chapter 19), and her fear of tomorrows "all in a line, the first of them the biggest and clearest, the others getting smaller . . . very fierce and cruel" (Ibid.) is equally eloquent of her sense of what is threatening to the individual in the inescapable environment. Angel diagnoses her sense of historical melancholy as the "ache of modernism," ironically placed, in a character with a fine sense of instinctive and untutored feelings, able, like Angel's music, to "drive such fancies away": it is these natural feelings which help her, the pure, or natural woman, to revive and rally, to defeat or resist the larger environment, in brief but significant episodes. In this final episode of love and death, Hardy assimilates the individual drama through cadences of expectation, tension, fulfilment, and shock, to his larger structure of natural motion, change, loss, and renewal. This is the cyclical form with which he rejects George Eliot's ethical relish at the determination of deeds. Hardy shows that the deeds of Tess and Angel have determined events, but he knows, and also shows, and makes them come to know, that deeds don't necessarily determine emotions. Here, where there might be guilt and horror, there is love.

Tess is simple but ruminative. At the beginning of the novel, when she compares earth to a blighted fruit, she reflects on experience, and at the end she reflects both on the relaxation and the tension, the freedom and the limits, of love's five days of borrowed time and space. Angel's loving becomes purified, in Hardy's sense of the word. It is eased and simplified as he gives not only what she asks but more, what she asked on their marriage: "I do love you, Tess—oh, I do—it is all come back!" The future is held at bay, and there is a return, an undoing of the past. They feel nothing "subsequent to their wedding-day." Angel's earlier sophistry about loving someone who wasn't there is finally revised and dismissed. Tess's outside was her inside too, a natural integrity. Their discovery of each other, and Angel's self-discovery, are not projected in any imaginable social paradigm, but in this repose and interval between the discovery of murder, "Drip, drip, drip," and the final arrest, both inexorable social acts of cause and effect. Tess is allowed a final rebellious questioning, this time not of society but of Heaven which turns out to be emptier than earth, "I wanted so much to see you again. . . . What—not even you and I, Angel who love each other so well?" The following image of the landscape's massive refusal to answer is sensuously and symbolically exact: "the whole enormous landscape bore that impress of reserve, taciturnity, and hesitation which is usual just before day." The humanizing of nature is gently done, in a transference of feeling which just stops short of personification. Nature seems sympathetic, but like humanity, cannot console. Hardy sets the individual feelings, as Lawrence saw, against the natural landscape, and he shows the frail connection between the human and the non-human phenomenal world. His assertion of the connection and the separation, at this point of crisis and conclusion, defines the loneliness of the human pair, as the environment closes around them after an interval which lets them love.

What Hardy does is not at all what Eliot accuses him of doing. Far from showing paroxysms of passion in which character and circumstance are undifferentiated, he takes imaginative pains to place the episodes of passion in the total structure of the work. Tess and Angel not only feel characteristically, but their acts of feeling are in accordance with the novel's argument and story, with everything that has gone before. Angel's early love for Tess, which he comes to discard as an ignorant love for her shell, is justified as the right reading of integrity, the perfect response to the natural, pure, and whole person. Tess's dreamlike appreciation of the honeymoon interlude is entirely in keeping with her closeness to nature and to her awareness of social constriction. Hardy's methods of dramatizing intense feeling lucidly insists on such continuities.

It is also true that he links the crisis of feeling with a world beyond the work of art. He is not only interested in individualizing feeling, and placing it in the sequence of narration, but he is also constantly aware of the relation of individual feeling to larger traditions and rituals. The force of the episode in Bramhurst Court comes not only from the pressure of all that precedes it in the novel, but from the immediate pressure of a sense of ritual. The coming-together in the empty house is the honeymoon the lovers have been denied, perversely placed after a killing not a wedding. This is clear from the explicit revision of the past, the bed, the return to past feeling, the housekeeper's view of "A genteel elopement" and the lovers' refusal to think of anything "subsequent to their wedding-day." The re-enactment also recalls the previous crossing of ritual, when the wedding-night was marked by Angel's somnambulist laying of Tess in the tomb. Hardy enlarges and solemnizes the individual occasion by relating it to social tradition, but always shows the individual variation. In *Tess,* the ritual enlargements come closer to perversion, for worse and for better, than to renewal. There is a simpler process of ritual enactment when Tess and Angel discover Stonehenge, and she is arrested as she wakes from a sleep on the sacrificial slab. She has been right about history, her nature and her doings "have been just like thousands' and thousands'." Hardy links the moment of passion to the book's past and the historical past beyond the book. The passions are individualized, sometimes through astonishing displacements, but they are related to those ceremonies and rituals through which the individual can express and order feeling. The novelist renews the ritual, as he intensifies and reveals the nature of such feeling and such ceremony.

In *The Mayor of Casterbridge* Hardy's combination of ritual and particularity irradiates the commonplace and domestic scene, but also domesticates and realizes solemnity and melancholy. Like Dickens, Hardy uses comedy to release and to ground pathos, as in the rendering of Susan Henchard's death. Elegy and eulogy are spoken by the Mistress Quickly-like Mrs Cuxsom in a garrulous, circumstantial, solemn, and delicate narration:

> Mrs Cuxsom, who had been standing there for an indefinite time with her pitcher, was describing the incidents of Mrs Henchard's death, as she had learnt them from the nurse.
>
> "And she was as white as marble-stone," said Mrs Cuxsom. "And likewise such a thoughtful woman, too—ah, poor soul—that a' minded every little thing that wanted tending. 'Yes,' says she, 'when I'm gone, and my last breath's blowed, look in the top drawer o' the chest in the back room by the window, and you'll find all my coffin clothes; a piece of flannel—that's to put under me, and the little piece is to put under my head; and my new stockings for my feet—they are folded alongside, and all my other things. And there's four ounce pennies, the heaviest I could find, a-tied up in bits of linen, for weights—two for my right eye and two for my left,' she said. 'And when you've used 'em, and my eyes don't open no more, bury the pennies, good souls, and don't ye go spending 'em, for I shouldn't like it. And open the windows as soon as I am carried out, and make it as cheerful as you can for Elizabeth-Jane.' "
>
> "Ah, poor heart!"
>
> "Well, and Martha did it, and buried the ounce pennies in the garden. But if ye'll believe words, that man, Christopher Coney, went and dug 'em up, and spent 'em at the Three Mariners. 'Faith,' he said, 'why should death rob life o' fourpence? Death's not of such good report that we should respect 'en to that extent,' says he."
>
> "'Twas a cannibal deed!" deprecated her listeners.

"Gad, then, I won't quite ha'e it," said Solomon Longways. "I say it today, and 'tis a Sunday morning, and I wouldn't speak wrongfully for a zilver zixpence at such a time. I don't see noo harm in it. To respect the dead is sound doxology; and I wouldn't sell skellintons—leastwise respectable skellintons—to be varnished for 'natomies, except I were out o' work. But money is scarce, and throats get dry. Why *should* death rob life o' fourpence? I say there was no treason in it."

"Well, poor soul; she's helpless to hinder that or anything now," answered Mother Cuxsom. "And all her shining keys will be took from her, and her cupboards opened; and little things a' didn't wish seen, anybody will see; and her wishes and ways will all be as nothing!" (Chapter 18)

The Shakespearian echoes are clear, "as white as marble-stone" recalling Falstaff's death-bed, in the vivid and thematic narrative detail, and the blend of humour and sadness fully drawn from the chief narrator and the chorus. We are moved out of sorrow into robust humour, and back again to pathos in the final invocation of the stubbornly surviving and mercilessly exposed household gods. This intense and balanced invocation of literature and custom is only the poetic conclusion to a long scene, where Hardy contrives to give us the unexpected rather than the predictable and universal. As Mrs Henchard lies dying she is watched by Elizabeth-Jane, her daughter, and the vigil is a fine instance of Hardy's restraint:

To learn to take the universe seriously there is no quicker way than to watch—to be a "waker," as the country-people call it. Between the hours at which the last toss-pot went by and the first sparrow shook himself, the silence in Casterbridge—barring the rare sound of the watchman—was broken in Elizabeth's ear only by the time-piece in the bedroom ticking frantically against the clock on the stairs; ticking harder and harder till it seemed to clang like a gong; and all this while the subtle-souled girl asking herself why she was born, why sitting in a room, and blinking at a candle; why things around her had taken the shape they wore in preference to every other possible shape. Why they stared at her so helplessly, as if waiting for the touch of some wand that should release them from terrestrial constraint; what that chaos called consciousness, which spun in her at this moment like a top, tended to, and began in. Her eyes fell together; she was awake, yet she was alseep. (Chapter 18)

Hardy neatly displaces the girl's sense of bewilderment and doubt, slightly but sufficiently particularizing the "things around her" to make them stare at her "helplessly" as he moves her from metaphysical confusion to sleep. Her mother speaks "without preface, and as the continuation of a scene already progressing in her mind" as she talks about her wish for Elizabeth-Jane's marriage, and the succeeding dialogue is unmarked by unusual feeling, snatched out of ordinariness and made strange by the circumstances:

"You remember the note sent to you and Mr Farfrae—asking you to meet some one in Durnover Barton—and that you thought it was a trick to make fools of you?"

"Yes."

"It was not to make fools of you—it was done to bring you together. 'Twas I did it."

"Why?" said Elizabeth, with a start.

"I—wanted you to marry Mr Farfrae."

"Oh mother!" Elizabeth-Jane bent down her head so much that she looked quite into her own lap. But as her mother did not go on, she said, "What reason?"

"Well, I had a reason, 'Twill out one day, I wish it could have been in my time! But there—nothing is as you wish it! Henchard hates him."

"Perhaps they'll be friends again," murmured the girl.

"I don't know—I don't know." After this her mother was silent, and dozed; and she spoke on the subject no more.

Some little time later on Farfrae was passing Henchard's house on a Sunday morning, when he observed that the blinds were all down. (Ibid.)

It is strikingly different from the death-scenes in Dickens where every detail is magnified, and extraordinary. Hardy's taste is for a mingling of the ordinary with the extraordinary, sometimes to transform object into symbol, but sometimes in order to register the proximity of low and high feeling. This is to combine expectation with surprise.

Understatement makes its bid for pathos, as in Henchard's will. His death is briefly narrated by Abel Whittle, "he couldn't eat—no, no appetite at all—and he got weaker; and to-day he died. One of the neighbours have gone to get a man to measure him," to which Farfrae says, "Dear me—is that so!" and Elizabeth says nothing. Like Susan Henchard's death, this is an off-stage event, Hardy frequently avoiding the actual dying. After this laconic report there follows the reading of the will:

"MICHAEL HENCHARD'S WILL

"That Elizabeth-Jane Farfrae be not told of my death, or made to grieve on account of me.
    "& that I be not bury'd in consecrated ground.
    "& that no sexton be asked to toll the bell.
    "& that nobody is wished to see my dead body.
    "& that no murners walk behind me at my funeral.
    "& that no flours be planted on my grave.
    "& that no man remember me.
"To this I put my name.
        "MICHAEL HENCHARD." (Chapter 45)

Once more particularity refreshes ritual in the pathetic spelling-mistakes and the reversal of customary last wishes for ceremony and memorial. Elizabeth reads the "bitterness" and responds first with remorse, then acceptance, "there's no altering—so it must be." The solemn formalizing of bitterness, self-pity, and pride is characteristic of the man who sold his wife by auction and brought the wedding present of the caged bird. The act of control is both dignified and indulgent, like all Hardy's acts. But pathos is dismissed, as the narrator changes her word "bitterness" to the compassionate word, "anguish." Elizabeth's response to this request is itself in character:

> She knew the directions to be a piece of the same stuff that his whole life was made of, and hence were not to be tampered with to give herself a mournful pleasure, or her husband credit for large-heartedness.
>
> All was over at last, even her regrets for having misunderstood him on his last visit, for not having searched him out sooner, though these were deep and sharp for a good while. From this time forward Elizabeth-Jane found herself in a latitude of calm weather, kindly and grateful in itself, and doubly so after the Capharnaum in which some of her preceding years had been spent. As the lively and sparkling emotions of her early married life cohered into an equable serenity, the finer movements of her nature found scope in discovering to the narrow-lived ones around her the secret (as she had once learnt it) of making limited opportunities endurable; which she deemed to consist in the cunning enlargement, by a species of microscopic treatment, of those minute forms of satisfaction that offer themselves to everybody not in positive pain; which, thus handled, have much of the same inspiring effect upon life as wider interests cursorily embraced. (Chapter 45)

We moved from lyricism to narration, and from the isolation and anguish to the tranquil passions of Elizabeth, one of Hardy's conspicuous survivors. The narrative on the last page expands the novel more extensively than the hand-in-hand departure of Angel and Liza-Lu in *Tess*, or the grim arrangements of Arabella at the end of *Jude*. The conclusion to *The Mayor of Casterbridge* wrings out of the narrator the marvellously reluctant admission, "minute forms of satisfaction that offer themselves to everybody not in positive pain." The introduction of Elizabeth-Jane's moderate happiness joins but does not diminish the sense of tragedy. It endorses anguish by reluctance and qualification, and also by the insistence that Elizabeth-Jane is aware of the exceptional ease of her case and so refuses to be "demonstratively thankful."

One of Hardy's finest uses of ritual comes at the end of *The Woodlanders*, where Marty South visits the grave of Giles Winterbourne. It is a subtly constructed conclusion, rising out of a lower-key passage which creates a strong contrast and a smooth transition. *The Woodlanders* and *The Trumpet-Major* are the only Hardy novels to end on a tragic tone. They have a divided plot, and do not concentrate on a central tragic destiny like that of the last novels, which need, like Shakespearian tragedies, to follow intense anguish with recovery or reordering. A farewell to comedy in a choric discussion of women's wiles, and the climates of courtship, acts as a bridge passage to Marty's elegy. As Upjohn and the other rustics talk, they see "a motionless figure standing by the gate," recognize her, comment, "'a was always a lonely maid" and go "homeward," to think "of the matter no more." The novel ends with Marty's last speech. It is all ritual, and all character:

As this solitary and silent girl stood there in the moonlight, a straight slim figure, clothed in a plaitless gown, the contours of womanhood so undeveloped as to be scarcely perceptible in her, the marks of poverty and toil effaced by the misty hour, she touched sublimity at points, and looked almost like a being who had rejected with indifference the attribute of sex for the loftier quality of abstract humanism. She stooped down and cleared away the withered flowers that Grace and herself had laid there the previous week, and put her fresh ones in their place.

"Now, my own, own love," she whispered, "you are mine, and only mine; for she has forgot 'ee at last, although for her you died! But I— whenever I get up I'll think of 'ee, and whenever I lie down I'll think of 'ee again. Whenever I plant the young larches I'll think that none can plant as you planted; and whenever I split a gad, and whenever I turn the cider wring, I'll say none could do it like you. If ever I forget your name let me forget home and heaven! . . . But no, no, my love, I never can forget'ee; for you was a good man, and did good things!" (Chapter 48)

The traditional flowers of elegy, funeral and vegetation rite are the trees of the local woods, the timber Giles and Marty planted and worked with. The feeling of love and praise is joined to the passion of jealous and triumphant possessiveness. The familiar promise to remember is uttered as a claim to be faithful, and not to forget, as Grace has forgotten. The customary praise of funeral oration and epitaph is individual and justified in the case of this good man. What Marty does is common, as she visits the grave and puts her fresh flowers on it, but it is particular, as she clears away the withered flowers she and Grace had put there together. Its appeal is enlarged and solemnized, but it is wholly individual, remembering the pattern, process, and passions of this novel. It is interesting to see that Hardy's narrator doesn't entirely match the impression of the dramatic speech, as if commentary were outrun by embodiment, the tale wiser than the artist. She had not rejected sex for abstract humanism.

In these instances of passionate drama, comedy co-operates with pathos and tragic awe but is kept distinct from it. In *Under the Greenwood Tree*, Hardy blends the comic and the serious in one medium. He uses exaggeration and irony to poke gentle fun at Dick Dewy's romantic loving, but not destructively. His passionate absorption is amusedly and tolerantly related by a voice speaking from weathered experience like that of the tranter or the shoemaker, who has passed through the first climates of courtship but are never cynical or cruel enough to solve Dick's puzzle about his elders' unromantic attitudes to love. The medium is a steady and consistent one, sustained throughout the short novel, to report and register a range of comic and serious feelings. . . .

Hardy's realization of the life before and after the paroxysm, his sense of the preparations and aftermath of passion, shows itself sometimes in comic language. Timothy Fairway in *The Return of the Native*, for instance, speaks with a joviality tempered by lyricism, about the passing of desire:

"Ah, Humph, well I can mind when I was married how I zid thy father's mark staring me in the face as I went to put down my name. He and your mother were the couple married just before we were, and there stood thy father's cross with arms stretched out like a great banging scarecrow. What a terrible black cross that was—thy father's very likeness in en! To save my soul I couldn't help laughing when I zid en, though all the time I was as hot as dog-days, what with the marrying, and what with the woman a-hanging to me. . . ." (Book 1, Chapter 3)

As in *Under the Greenwood Tree*, the contrast and pattern is in essence that of some of the painter Munch's most terrible contrasts between age, middle age, and youth, but shown in Hardy with comic impartiality, wryness, and that light but controlled touch which he shares with Timothy Fairway, Gabriel Oak, and some of his other characters.

Although Hardy can speak and show the clarity and force of passion, he can also relax intensity to show the emotional life between crises, thus shaping the full curve of feeling. He shows the pathways to passion. He shows the interaction of two (and more) people's passionate lives. Sue and Jude are responsive to each other's feelings, and Sue is especially vulnerable, and especially dangerous, through her nervous, doubtful, uneasy susceptibilities, sexually fearful, capricious, vain, affectionate, tender. Hardy, like Lawrence, shows the passions we name with dangerous confidence, and the states of feeling too mixed or complex to be tamed by names. (It is ironic that Lawrence, who so attacked our simplification and classification of feeling, should have so simplified Hardy, but of course it is easier to urge our own complexities of passion than to understand other people's.) Philotson, Sue's husband, explains to his friend that he cannot say what Sue feels for Jude, "A curious tender solicitude seemingly." And he knows that she can perhaps not find a word for it herself, "though her exact feeling for him is a riddle to me—and to him to, I think—possibly to herself" (Part 4, Chapter 4).

Sue's incapacity for sexual relationships[1] collaborates fatally with her courageous social subversions, and clashes fatally with Jude's needs for a physical and intellectual elective affinity. In some ways they feel together, as in mortification. In some ways they are strikingly different, and Hardy contrasts Jude's emotional solidity and simplicity with Sue's emotional epicureanism:

> They strolled undemonstratively up the nave towards the altar railing, which they stood against in silence, turning then and walking down the nave again, her hand still on his arm, precisely like a couple just married. The too suggestive incident, entirely of her own making, nearly broke down Jude.
> "I like to do things like this," she said in the delicate voice of an epicure in emotions, which left no doubt that she spoke the truth.
> "I know you do!" said Jude. (Part 3, Chapter 7)

Such epicureanism plays its subtle part in that other novel of strong passion and violent upheaval, where man and nature luridly light each other:

The Return of the Native. We think of the grand passions of Eustacia Vye, but the only feeling she is really clear about is that of restless longing and discontent, and her tragedy, to some extent like Jude's and Sue's, rests on a lack of grand and ruling passion. These are modern children, self-conscious, analytic, divided, looking over the verge of passion almost before they experience passion, wanting to feel, and over-rehearsing feeling. Hardy, like Forster, knows that human beings are often wrecked and bewildered by feeling that they ought to feel more, or feel differently, from how they actually feel. Like Stendhal's Julien Sorel, Eustacia tries on the fit of different feelings. The rehearsal sometimes moves into genuine action, sometimes not:

> She was at the modulating point between indifference and love, at the stage called "having a fancy for." It occurs once in the history of the most gigantic passions, and it is a period when they are in the hands of the weakest will.
>
> The perfervid woman was by this time half in love with a vision. The fantastic nature of her passion, which lowered her as an intellect, raised her as a soul. If she had had a little more self-control she would have attenuated the emotion to nothing by sheer reasoning, and so have killed it off. If she had had a little less pride she might have gone and circumnambulated the Yeobright's premises at Blooms-End at any maidenly sacrifice until she had seen him. But Eustacia did neither of these things. She acted as the most exemplary might have acted, being so influenced; she took an airing twice or thrice a day upon the Egdon hills, and kept her eyes employed. (Book 2, Chapter 3)

This interest in emotional uncertainty reaches its comic, not always controlled form, in that strange novel, *The Well-Beloved,* where Hardy's sense of the fitfulness, arbitrariness, and discontinuity of feeling is shown in the wry instance of a middle-aged man, who—unlike others, observes the novelist's gentle irony—has not sailed past the passions into calm seas.

Notes

1. The best discussion of Sue Bridehead is John Goode's "Sue Bridehead and the New Woman," in *Women Writing and Writing about Women,* M. Jacobus (ed.) (London, 1979).

The Rhetoric of Silence in Hardy's Fiction
Wayne C. Anderson*

Hardy's notebooks are terse and spare, composed for the most part of matter-of-fact observations on business and the daily routine.[1] Of the few

*Reprinted from *Studies in the Novel* 17(Spring 1985):53–68. © 1985 by North Texas State University. Reprinted by permission.

passages recording specific scenes or moments, the most significant have to do with silence. "Lonely places in the country each have their own peculiar silences," Hardy notes in an early memoranda book, and some years later he remarks, "I sometimes look upon all things in nature as pensive mutes."[2] Human silences compel him as well. "Write a list of things," he reminds himself in 1885, "which everybody thinks and nobody says." In another notebook he quotes from the maxims of the Spanish Jesuit Balthasar Gracium, "Keep always something behind in store.—Even in one's knowledge there should be force in reserve" and "Reticence is the seal of capacity."[3] Such admonishments take on greater interest in light of Hardy's reticence as a person. The editors of the notebooks and letters agree that he was a man of "profound reserve," "furtive," "elusive," "invariably oblique," "reticent." Millgate describes Hardy's boyhood habit of "sitting by, silent and unnoticed, while his parents and their relatives and friends sang, played, joked, and talked together," a habit that in Millgate's view eventually results in the "attitude of uninvolved spectatorship" characteristic of his narrative voice.[4]

I want to argue that silence is also a major preoccupation in Hardy's novels, and moreover, that the rhetoric of Hardy's fiction is fundamentally a rhetoric of silence. My discussion has two parts. In the first I try to show the depth and complexity of the silences in Hardy's major fiction by focusing in detail on a representative scene from *The Return of the Native*. Before going on to consider the larger issues, I want to establish that silences do exist in Hardy's language and that they are an integral part of characterization, plot development, and point of view. In the second section I turn to the rhetorical consequences of these silences, particularly in *The Return of the Native*, *The Mayor of Casterbridge*, and *Tess of the d'Urbervilles*. Here I want to suggest that the rhetoric of silence in Hardy's fiction is a strategy for eliciting our own acts of interpretation as readers. The various and subtle silences of Hardy's language are important because they demand reading, because they force us in the act of reading to experience what Hardy regards as our basic human responsibility for discovering truth.

1

The long opening scene of *The Return of the Native* illustrates the importance of silence at every level of Hardy's fiction. The setting is the "untameable," "unenclosed" landscape of Egdon heath, an "unmoved" and "inert" wasteland resisting roads and plows and any human inscription. Egdon is a place of "incredible slowness," of "understatement and reserve," of silence. It is true that the heath has its own "linguistic peculiarity"—the eerie whisper of wind blowing through the "mummified heath bells"—but this "wild rhetoric of night" only accentuates the absence of speech. It is alien, nonverbal, a reiteration of mere physical presences. And it originates from the silence of nature: "So low was an individual sound from these [heath bells] that a combination of hundreds only just emerged from silence" (pp. 33–36, 78).[5]

Hardy's prolonged description of the heath in this opening chapter is itself a kind of silence. As Genette says of similar moments in Flaubert, when the narrator dwells on the particulars of setting "the narrative seems to fall silent and become frozen under what Sartre was to call 'the great petrifying gaze of things.' " In focusing on externalities at the expense of explicit narrative commentary, Hardy, like Flaubert, sends discourse "back to its silent underside."[6]

Against this backdrop two travelers encounter one another, the reddleman walking beside his spring van, and an old man walking home across the heath, a "decaying officer" who we later learn is Captain Vye, Eustacia's grandfather. After exchanging greetings the two continue together in silence. The reddleman "showed no inclination to continue in talk," and their combined presence is momentarily absorbed into the silent landscape: "There were no sounds but that of the booming wind upon the stretch of tawny herbage around them, the crackling wheels, the tread of the men, and the footsteps of the two shaggy ponies which drew the van." At first this silence is companionable, Hardy says. It does not convey "any sense of awkwardness," since chance companions frequently "plod on for miles without speech" in the loneliness of the country. Here "contiguity amounts to a tacit conversation." But the silence of contiguity is immediately displaced by the reddleman's frequent trips to the back of his van, a nonverbal gesture which incites the old man's curiosity:

> when [the reddleman] returned from his fifth time of looking in the old man said, "You have something inside there besides your load?"
> "Yes."
> "Somebody who wants looking after?"
> "Yes."

Both men are slow to speech, and when they do talk their language is clipped and spare. The captain is curious. But despite his obvious interest the reddleman refuses to relay any information about his passenger other than the simple fact that he has given her a ride from Anglebury:

> "I know the town well [the captain replies]. What was she doing there?"
> "Oh, not much—to gossip about."

After a few more questions, the reddleman puts an end to the brief conversation: "Tis no matter. . . . Now, sir, I am sorry to say that we shall soon have to part company" (pp. 37–40).

The silence here is a silence of secrecy, a withholding of information and interpretation. At the same time we can gather that it is a silence of intense feeling. The ellipsis records what we later learn are Diggory's complex and passionate feelings about Thomasin. Later, too, we learn that Diggory's silence about Thomasin's misfortune and about his own desires is a sign of his integrity, his honest devotion and selflessness. Here there are few words. Blank space begins opening up in the text, sentences breaking down from block paragraphs to indented dialogue, dialogue in which each response is barely a sentence or a word. Gaps begin opening up within sentences, dashes and ellipsis violating the syntax. Hardy is sensitive to the nuances of conversation, which depend as much on silence as on speech—the silence of the listener, the silence of hesitations and gaps, of the necessary "switch-pauses" that allow one speaker to stop talking and another to begin, only here accentuated and intensified, made to represent the strain of undisclosed knowledge, the pressure of curiosity.[7]

More than that, Hardy himself is silent. We know that he is an omniscient narrator. "On the evening under consideration it would have been noticed that . . ." he says, signalling that the story has already taken place and that as narrator he is in possession of all the facts (p. 36). But he withholds information and interpretation throughout this long scene—it extends over the first six chapters of the novel—and remains silent about important details, avoiding explicit interpretation and commentary. His "authorial silence" is that of an outside observer forced to make inferences and read meanings on the basis of external data.[8] "The great thinker," Hardy quotes in a notebook from Frederick the Great, "is distinguished from other men by his superior power of building an hypothesis. He co-ordinates the facts better."[9] By adopting the stance of authorial silence, Hardy puts himself in the position of building hypotheses and coordinating facts.

Silence deepens in the rest of the scene. Our first glimpse of Eustacia is of a mysterious form rising above the distant outline of the barrow. She is unnamed. Hardy merely observes her silent presence from a distance, objectively describing her movements: "The figure perceptibly gave up its fixity, shifted a step or two, and turned around. As if alarmed, it descended on the right side of the barrow, with the glide of a water-drop from a bud, and then vanished. The movement had been sufficient to show more clearly the characteristics of the figure, and that it was a woman's" (p. 41). The silence of the figure and Hardy's own chosen silence about her identity force him into the "as if" constructions, as well as into conditional and hypothetical phrasing— "to see it move would have impressed . . ." "had a looker on been. . . ." The silences are even more marked when we finally see Eustacia in full. She has waited near her signal fire "dead-still," in "extraordinary fixity." Hardy notes that throughout the night she has "indulged" in only three utterances, and these are fragmentary: a sigh, a laugh, and the single word, "Yes." Observing only what can be seen at the moment, restricting himself to empirically grounded conjectures ("proved," "as if"), Hardy withdraws in this protracted description to an oddly detached point of view (pp. 77–80). Miller has used the metaphor of distance to describe this stance—Lodge has compared it to the perspectives of film-making—but it seems to me that silence is a more provocative term.[10] It suggests the mood and tone of the prose, its reticence and carefulness about disclosure, and in this way links Hardy's narrative stance to the relationship of characters and the quality of landscape within the narrative.

When the characters do speak to each other in this opening scene, their conversation is governed by pauses, hesitations, refusals to speak, and nonverbal gestures. When Mrs. Yeobright confronts her niece about the aborted wedding and the return in disgrace, their conversation is riddled with gaps. "I am—not married," Thomasin replies, "faintly." "Excuse me—for humiliating you, aunt, by this mishap." When questioned further she repeatedly cries, "I cannot explain," silent tears conveying the depth of her feeling (pp. 66–67). Her subsequent conversation with Wildeve is marked by "murmurs," "faint" replies, and "short" rejoinders. Wildeve's taciturnity is a sign of his sullenness and glibness, Thomasin's of her anxiety and shame. The full range of feelings in this situation is communicated only by what nonverbal communication scholars have labelled "affect displays," emotion registered in bodily expression[11]—Thomasin's "large eyes" flying from Mrs. Yeobright's to Wildeve's face, Wildeve's "brief, tell-tale look" toward Eustacia's signal fire (pp. 68–75). Eustacia and Wildeve's eventual meeting is the culmination of this rhetoric. Their signals are the nonverbal gestures of the fire and of a stone thrown in the adjacent pond. In her coquettishness Eustacia subsequently "cries under her breath," "murmurs," stalls, pauses to tease and sulk. Her rhetoric of evasiveness and withholding—indicated by ellipsis and dashes—"silences" Wildeve, who looks at her "quietly" and answers in monosyllables (pp. 84–88). To borrow again from Genette's reading of Flaubert, these moments of pause and omissions are "doubly silent," first "because the characters have stopped talking in order to listen to the world and to their dreams," second "because this interruption of dialogue and action suspends the very speech of the novel and absorbs it, for a time, in a sort of unspoken interrogation."[12]

Only the minor characters in *The Return of the Native* are in any way noisy or talkative. After leaving us with the enigmatic exchange between the reddleman and the captain, Hardy turns to a description of the singing, dancing, and frolicking of the furze-cutters around their Guy Fawkes fire. The long stretch of narration and brief conversation is suddenly broken up by an extended dialogue among the characters, and in dense Dorset dialect. The furze-cutters spend the evening telling stories, a fact that Hardy repeatedly emphasizes, calling our attention to the "speaker," the "narrator," the "audience" for the stories—to the fact of language being spoken (pp. 48–49). The furze-cutters do the work of narration that Hardy to this point refuses to do, gradually conveying the facts of plot and scene—Thomasin and Wildeve's relationship, Clym's pending return, and so on.

It is not insignificant that when Mrs. Yeobright intrudes upon the furze-cutter's bonfire she immediately silences the gathering. "I'm sorry to stop the talk," she says, and her replies to questions are "quiet." Hers is the silence of a superior toward inferiors, betokening "a certain unconcern at their presence," thus "indirectly implying that in some respect or other they were not up to her level" (pp. 58–60).[13] More importantly, the contrast between the loudness of the furze-cutters and the dignified silence of Mrs. Yeobright suggests how carefully Hardy orchestrates silence and speech, silence and sound, throughout this long and important scene. The scene has a musical structure, the narrative rising and falling in pitch and volume, bursts of noise punctuating significant silences. It is a *tour de force* of silence, a blending together of silences on every level—silences of characters, silences between characters, silences before, after, and within speech, authorial silence—silences betokening embarrassment, courtship, guilt, shame, honesty, passion, devotion, and always, in the background, the brute and indifferent presence of the heath.

But while the silences of the first few chapters of *The Return of the Native* are particularly intense and sustained, silence is by no means unusual in Hardy. The opening scene on the heath is only a more extended example of the way silence functions throughout *The Return of the Native, The Mayor of Casterbridge,* and *Tess of the d'Urbervilles.* All of Hardy's major landscapes are silent—the streets of Casterbridge are "curiously silent" (p. 205); the absolute "soundlessness" of the dairy impresses Tess "as a positive entity rather than as the mere negation of noise" (p. 150). All of Hardy's main characters are typified by silence—Henchard's "taciturnity" is "unbroken," "marked" (p. 37); Tess is "soft and silent," characterized by "mute obedience," "dumb and vacant fidelity" (pp. 176, 215, 257). Silence is the key to the relationships among the characters at every point in the major novels, governing the way they communicate with each other. There is the silence of embarrassment and awkwardness, the silence of anger and estrangement, the silence of mutual understanding and intuitive compatibility, the silence of ineffable feeling, the silence of violent action, the silence of nonverbal gesture—silences of many shades and resonances.[14] Silence permeates the novels. It is for precisely this reason that so many of the major scenes in Hardy's fiction are virtual pantomimes, tableaux, or what Irving Howe calls "dumb shows."[15] When Lucetta, Elizabeth-Jane, Henchard, and Farfrae inadvertently find themselves sharing tea, Hardy notes that there were "long spaces of taciturnity" between their scattered bits of conversation when even the "click of a heel on the pavement" outside the window was audible (pp. 196–97). Hardy observes of Jude and Sue in *Jude the Obscure* that "there was ever a silent conversation passing between their emotions, so perfect was the reciprocity between them" (p. 2211). Clym and Eustacia's love transcends expression: they "remained long without a single utterance for no language could reach the level of their condition" (p. 21). Arabella hits Jude with a pig's pizzle to attract his attention (pp. 61–62); Wildeve uses a moth to extinguish Eustacia's candle flame and thus signal his presence outside (p. 278). As Hardy says of the townspeople of Casterbridge, his characters "[speak] in other ways than by articulation." For them, "space, the arms, the hat, the stick, the body throughout [speak] equally with the tongue" (p. 89).

And informing these silences at important points in all the major novels is the authorial silence Hardy demonstrates in the opening of *The Return of the Native*. In the beginning of *The Mayor of Casterbridge* Hardy again introduces his characters with silent detachment, withholding omniscience and limiting himself to inferences based on the observation of externals. As we shall see, though he engages in much omniscient commentary about Tess, he employs authorial silence at several key moments. In *Jude the Obscure* Hardy seems to employ authorial silence whenever he comes to describe Sue's behavior; he rarely allows us to glimpse what is taking place *in* her mind. Here, as with the other dimensions of silence, the opening of *The Return of the Native* is the prototype of a narrative strategy that in subsequent novels may become less forced or strained but is always a fundamental element of pacing and plot development. Here and on every level the introductory chapters on the heath are representative of the silences that dominate Hardy's fiction.

2

What makes these silences significant is their rhetorical impact on us as readers. A rhetoric of silence conditions our response to character, landscape, and plot development in Hardy's fiction, eliciting—demanding—our participation in the act of narrative. Virginia Woolf has observed that with Hardy's characters "we do not remember how they have lived" or "how they have talked and changed and got to know each other, finely, gradually, from step to step and from stage to stage."[16] I think this is true, in part, because Hardy's characterizations depend on silence. He does not present his characters in the conventional way of the novel—through self-revelation, dialogue. As readers we need to be alert to the subtleties of the nonverbal in Hardy's prose, subtleties made still easier to overlook or undervalue by Hardy's own silences, his own decision not to disclose meaning directly. Hardy's novels have been attacked because they are too carefully staged, each scene and movement too mechanically, too carefully worked out. Perhaps this quality of the prose is ultimately a product of silence. Hardy's authorial silences and the silences of his characters require a focus on external gesture and formal movement, as well as meticulous attention to the inferences justified by detail.

What the rhetoric of silence requires is an attentiveness from us as readers. A silence does not readily disclose its meaning. It exists by definition in the absence of speech, in the absence, therefore, of explicit explanation. It requires interpretation, an act of reading.

Captain Vye discerns "a moving spot" down the road which he assumes is a vehicle of some sort, then, as it draws closer, perceives to be a spring van. The driver walking beside it is clothed in red, a silent fact that the Captain immediately interprets: "The old man knew the meaning of this. The traveller with the cart was a reddleman." Diggory's subsequent silences about his passenger force more difficult acts of reading. "You have a child there, my man?" "A young woman?" "Your wife?" Because Diggory refuses to divulge any substantial information, the captain is forced to construct his own hypothesis. Silence necessitates reading: "Who is she? One of the neighbourhood?" "A nice-looking girl, no doubt?" (pp. 39–40).

The heath-folk gather around the Guy Fawkes bonfire and look across the way at another fire, oddly brilliant even after the others have died: "This quiet eye had attracted attention from time to time; and when their own fire had become sunken and dim it attracted more." Grandfer, Fairway, and the others proceed to speculate about the nature of the fire, its approximate distance, its fuel, how much longer it will burn, whose fire it is, what it means. Simply by reading the light of this "quiet eye" they are able to conclude that Eustacia is responsible for the blaze and that she has used a large quantity of her grandfather's "cleftwood," although the reason for this waste of fuel is unclear (pp. 55–56). Like all the heath-folk, the furze-cutters are necessarily expert at interpreting the data of the heath, drawing conclusions from minute detail when ready explanations are not available.[17]

Given the silences they must constantly confront, all of Hardy's major characters are required to be readers. Elizabeth-Jane finds herself in the awkward position of observing the silent and elliptical courtship of Lucetta and Farfrae: Lucetta's embarrassed pauses and blushes when she meets Farfrae on the street; her odd evasiveness whenever he is mentioned; her obvious gestures of rejection toward Henchard—all silences, all nonverbal clues. Eventually she is about to interpret these silences, even though Lucetta has told her nothing of her true feelings: "A seer's spirit took possession of Elizabeth, impelling her to sit down by the fire and divine events so surely from data already her own that they could be held as witnessed." Suddenly she knows that Lucetta is in love with Farfrae: "The fact was printed large all over Lucetta's cheeks and eyes to any one who could *read* her as Elizabeth-Jane was beginning to do" (p. 187, italics mine). Tess's silent refusals to discuss marriage, her silent, repressed uneasiness after accepting, force Angel into readings: he regards her attentively, "conn[ing] the characters of her face as if they had been hieroglyphics," studying her expressions like "one deciding on the true construction of a difficult passage" (pp. 203, 245).

The idea of reading is just as important and pervasive in Hardy's fiction as the idea of silence. His characters are continually engaged in acts of reading, from the reading of books and letters to the reading of people and situations. Moreover, silence and reading are almost always aligned in Hardy. Silence creates texts, and texts, after all, are silent. "Writing has this strange quality," Socrates explains to Phaedrus, a quality it shares with painting. If one asks the creatures in a painting any question, "they preserve a solemn silence." If one questions written words in the hope of better understanding their meaning, "they always say only one and the same thing."[18] So, too, with the silent texts in Hardy. They simply reiterate themselves rather than refining, extending, explicating their mysteries.

From this perspective silence can have dark thematic implications. Sometimes Hardy seems to be suggesting that there is no meaning behind the silent texts of experience, or that correct reading of these texts is impossible. Betrayed or trapped by words, Hardy's characters become isolated in their own subjectivity. They cannot say what they mean, what they feel, lapsing into silences that lead to further alienation and loss. Silence can also suggest the absolute neutrality of nature in human affairs. The heath "thrills silently in the sun" as Mrs. Yeobright turns from the closed door of her son's house, indifferent to her suffering, indifferent to her impending death (p. 93). Nature is "ruled" by silence when Alec seduces Tess, merely reiterating itself, unconcerned with Tess's catastrophe: "All material objects around announced their irresponsibility with terrible iteration," Hardy says, after Angel rejects Tess on their wedding night (p. 254). Silence shows the ratio of landscape to character; the silences of individuals are absorbed into the greater silence of brute matter.

The larger and more disturbing silence in this respect is the silence of God. "Where was the providence of her simple faith," Hardy asks during Tess's seduction: "Perhaps, like that other god of whom the ironical Tishbite spoke, he was talking, or he was pursuing, or he was in a journey, or he was sleeping and not to be awakened" (p. 101)—i.e., he does not answer her; to her cries he is silent. "Do you think we shall meet again after we are dead?" Tess asks Angel as they wait at Stonehenge:

> He kissed her to avoid a reply at such a time.
> "O Angel—I fear that means no!" said she, with a suppressed sob. "And I so wanted to see you again—so much, so much! What—not even you and I, Angel, who love each other so well?"
> Like a greater than himself, to the critical question at the critical time, he did not answer; and they were again silent. (p. 417)

The reference here is to one of the great and troubling silences of the New Testament, Christ's silence to the charges of the high priest before the Crucifixion; the earlier reference is to one of the many instances of God's silence in the Old Testament.[19] Both suggest Hardy's rejection of the Judeo-Christian tradition, his inability to make the leap of faith which transcends God's apparent absence.[20] The "Immanent Will" that governs Hardy's universe is "a consciousness infinitely far off, at the other end of the chain of phenomena, always striving to express itself, and always baffled and blundering."[21] It cannot answer the critical question at the critical time.

But it is precisely because of these larger silences that Hardy's characters are called to act. Silence leads to freedom and responsibility. Neher observes that "the word binds and obligates; it defines the infinite. Only silence leaves being and nothingness their limitless potential."[22] Hardy puts if this way. Given that there is no external authority establishing the validity of our actions, given that there is no a priori set of values, each person must "make a philosophy for himself out of his own experience."[23] The emphasis in

Hardy's fiction is not on passivity or resignation but on the active interpretation and shaping of the silent texts of our experience. Elizabeth-Jane, as Millgate notes, is representative of the "distinctively Hardyean voice and point of view."[24] She recognizes that the world's silences call for quietude in us. Experience has taught her that "the doubtful honour of a brief transit through a sorry world hardly called for effusiveness." But at the same time she has come to see that in the absence of external authority we have the responsibility of making these "limited opportunities" "endurable." By "a species of microscopic treatment," a strategy of "cunning enlargement," we can discover in the "minute forms of satisfaction" available in our everyday life an "inspiriting power" sufficient to make meaning (p. 332). Hardy's suggestion is that in a world of silences we are called to read. In a world where God is silent, we must build hypotheses by which to live; in a world where nature is silent, we must create our own order and meaning; in a world where the people around us are silent, we must struggle to establish love and relationship.

More importantly for our purposes, the cunning enlargement of particulars is also involved in Hardy's authorial silence. In effect Hardy puts himself in the position of reading the silences of character and landscape. "That she was tall and straight in build, that she was ladylike in her movements, was all that could be learnt of her just now," "a few additional moments proved," "[i]t might reasonably have been supposed that"—in his description of Eustacia, Hardy restricts himself to reading what he can from her silent figure as she waits on the barrow for Wildeve (p. 77). Eustacia does not reveal herself, does not speak for herself, and Hardy will not speak for her. Her silence forces him into the inferences and "as if" conjectures I noted earlier. Like the furze-cutters admiring Eustacia's fire, he is the outside observer trying to comprehend something beyond his immediate understanding. Hardy even becomes involved in interpreting the composition and significance of the fire: "One reason for the permanence of the blaze was now manifest," he observes when he can seize on the necessary facts, "the fuel consisted of hard pieces of wood, cleft and sawn" (p. 81).

All this has an impact on us as readers. Because the characters have not divulged any information, because Hardy has not given us the full context, we, too, have to work to understand the meaning of events. We are like Captain Vye, straining to understand who is in Diggory's van. We are like the heath-folk conjecturing about Eustacia's fire. We, too, have to infer meaning from scattered minutiae, and only after carefully assembling the detail do we finally understand that the blaze is a signal fire to Wildeve and thus symbolic of all the central events in the novel. With Hardy we must read the silent figure of Eustacia, gradually gaining a sense of the whole from a collection of particulars. In the darkness of the night on the heath, we must struggle to see; everything is in shadow, a correlate of silence, a concealing.[25]

Hardy soon moves into omniscience after concluding these introductory chapters, descending into Eustacia's mind and telling us in great detail what he knows about her motives and impulses. *The Mayor of Casterbridge, Tess of the d'Urbervilles,* and *Jude the Obscure* depend on the careful psychological discriminations that Hardy makes as omniscient narrator. The silences we have seen are brief moments in what are otherwise extended omniscient narratives. In an important letter Hardy separates himself from the objective experimentation of James and argues that a novelist is obligated to shape and interpret his material by directly intervening in the narrative rather than letting events simply take place before the reader's eyes without any indication of their significance.[26] Indeed, the silences of his characters, their long and solitary work in the fields, their wordless brooding and suffering, force him into omniscient commentary. It would be tedious to spend the bulk of the narration inferring inner qualities from superficial detail. The demands of pacing exposition require him to employ omniscience and tell us what Tess or Henchard are thinking beneath their silent exteriors. If anything, Hardy's fiction suffers from excessive commentary. We know too well what Hardy thinks, what Hardy wants us to feel.

But in the midst of such pervasive commentary and shaping, the presence of periodic silences is all the more significant. Over the course of the novels silences signal crucial meanings, prepare and educate us for what Hardy will eventually explain in full. Hardy indulges in much omniscient commentary throughout the beginning of *Tess of the d'Urbervilles,* but he shifts point of view after Tess's seduction. Here he describes Tess walking home after her experience with Alec, then stops, pauses, and begins Chapter 14 with a long look at the villagers harvesting the wheat, gradually moving from a panoramic description of the landscape to a description of the workers to a description of one particular worker. "The eye returns involuntarily to the girl in the pink cotton jacket," he says, "she being the most flexuous and finely-drawn figure of them all." He goes on to describe the exact position of her bonnet and the color of her complexion (which "may be guessed from a stray twine or two of dark brown hair"), drawing conclusions only where he can fix on a specific external detail. The woman is silent in her work, the others are silent about her, and he must hypothesize: "Perhaps one reason why she seduces casual attention is that she never courts it." Hardy is silent here on a fundamental level. He does not tell us that this is Tess, or what has happened to her since her return, or what is taking place in her thoughts. It is not just that Hardy is trying to create suspense; as readers we immediately know the identity of this striking figure. Instead, Hardy wants us to join him in studying the evidences of Tess's character, to experience for ourselves her strength and beauty, her unusual charisma. He wants us to draw our own conclusions and thus substantiate in advance what he will later assert about Tess's personality and actions. Moreover, Hardy is silent about the crucial fact of Tess's baby. We must surmise from her blushing, her anxious looks, her apparent anticipation that the children approaching the field are bringing Tess's baby for nursing (pp. 115–18). Certainly Hardy resorts to silence at this juncture in part for the purposes of propriety—all the references to

Tess's baby were omitted in the serial version of the novel—just as he passes over other sexual details in silence, politely fading out, as it were, at the crucial point in Tess's seduction. But even in the revised text he prefers to let us come to the knowledge of the child ourselves and in the process come to the knowledge of Tess's dignity and self-possession. Hardy does not want us to anticipate any particular bit of information. Rather he wants us to engage in the act of anticipating, of reading, of interpreting.

Long stretches of omniscient narration take up the center of *Tess of the d'Urbervilles*. Hardy clearly identifies with Tess, cares about her intricate motives, and he follows all the twists and turns of her thinking. But near the end of the story authorial silence again becomes significant. Tess is silent when Alec offers to lodge her destitute family, breathing more quickly but saying nothing (p. 378). There is then a significant gap, a literal blank space on the page, between phase six and phase seven of the novel in which Hardy shifts from the scene at the d'Urberville tomb to Clare's return from Brazil without telling us what has happened in the intervening weeks or months (p. 389). Instead we must accompany Angel as he begins inquiring after Tess, all the time puzzling over her odd silences at the tomb, her ambivalent silences in response to Alec's new advances. We, too, must interpret Joan d'Urberville's reluctance at the threshold of her new house, her withholding of information; we, too, must search through the streets of Sandbourne, wondering what choices Tess has made. "Where could Tess possibly be," Angel asks himself, "a cottage girl, his young wife, amidst all this wealth and fashion?" In the absence of exact knowledge, we must "ponder," "conjecture"—read (pp. 396–99). Of course, at this point we know more than Angel; we have already guessed that Tess has joined Alec. But Hardy continues to unfold the scene detail by detail, surface by surface, even at the end when Tess appears in a cashmere dressing gown at the top of the stairs. It is appropriate that Angel's reading of this silent sign issues into speechlessness. "Speech was as inexpressive as silence," Hardy says, although, ironically, the very breakdown of language is an index to the intensity and pathos of Angel's feeling (pp. 400–01). The key is Hardy's refusal to fill in the gaps left by Angel's speechlessness. As readers we must fill in the gaps—the gaps draw us into the narrative.

As Wolfgang Iser puts it, "the unwritten aspects of apparently trivial scenes and the unspoken dialogue within the twists and turns not only draw the reader into the action but also lead him to shade in the many outlines suggested by a given situation, so that they take on a reality of their own."[27] Iser is referring here to the "gaps" or "blanks" that exist in any work of fiction, gaps that in Hardy are magnified and extended. As Hardy himself puts it in the preface to *The Dynasts*, the reader must become a "performer," a "utility-man of the gaps," supplying particular details whenever the poem is necessarily sketchy and general.[28] In the face of the silences in Hardy's fiction, we must also become "utility-men of the gaps," "performers" in the narration. Indeed, the gaps or silences in the opening of *The Return of the Native* not only require such participation, they encourage it. "The imagina-

tion of the observer," Hardy says of Eustacia's distant form, "clung by preference to that vanished, solitary figure, as to something more interesting,
more important, more likely to have a history worth knowing" than characters more visible in the scene (p. 42). Silence stimulates our curiosity, entices
our interest.

Hardy later tells us the meaning of each of these silences. We are never
on our own for very long in Hardy's fiction. Like Thackeray in Iser's analysis,
Hardy is a figure at the "half-way point" in the development of the novel from
Fielding to Joyce, neither fully omniscient nor entirely detached.[29] My argument is that Hardy intervenes with commentary only after a moment of
silence, of what both Iser and Ingarden would call "indeterminancy," in
which we must discover or anticipate the meaning ourselves.[30] He tells us
meaning only after we have experienced it, made it. In this way Hardy's
silences and the silences of his characters converge, our interpretations as
readers paralleling and confirming the interpretations required of every character. Even as Clym or Elizabeth-Jane or Tess struggle to read the silent texts
of their own experience, we must cunningly enlarge the particulars of
Hardy's silences to create satisfactory readings of our own.

Notes

1. I would like to thank the Vice Chancellor for Academic Affairs and the Excellence
Foundation at the University of North Carolina at Greensboro for giving me a summer research
grant in 1983 to research and write this article.

2. *The Personal Notebooks of Thomas Hardy*, ed. Richard H. Taylor (New York: Columbia
Univ. Press, 1979), p. 9; Florence Emily Hardy, *The Life of Thomas Hardy* (New York: Macmillan, 1928), I, 150. There are many similar passages. See *Life*, I, 123, 216, 267; II, 13.

3. *Life*, I, 211; *The Literary Notes of Thomas Hardy*, ed. Lennart A. Björk (Göteborg,
Sweden: ACTA Universitatis Gothoburgensis, 1974), I, 52.

4. *Personal Notebooks*, p. xi; *The Collected Letters of Thomas Hardy*, ed. Richard Little
Purdy and Michael Millgate (Oxford: Clarendon, 1978), I, vii; Michael Millgate, *Thomas Hardy:
A Biography* (New York: Random House, 1982), p. 42. Hardy describes himself in this way: "A
shrewd man who knew me at this time (aet. 26) said, Here is a man who, when he is silent will
never begin to speak; and when he once begins to speak, will never stop" (*Literary Notes*, I, 4).

5. My primary texts are from *The New Wessex Edition* of Hardy's novels, ed. F. N.
Furbank (London: Macmillan, 1975). Subsequent references appear in the text.

6. Gerard Genette, *Figures of Literary Discourse*, trans. Alan Sheridan (New York: Columbia Univ. Press, 1982), p. 194.

7. See Judee K. Burgoon and Thomas Saine, *The Unspoken Dialogue: An Introduction to
Nonverbal Communication* (New York: Houghton Mifflin, 1978), p. 231.

8. Wayne Booth defines authorial silence as "the manner in which [the author] leaves his
characters to work out their own destinies or tell their own stories" (*The Rhetoric of Fiction*;
[Chicago: Univ. of Chicago Press, 1961], p. 273). Silence is opposed to "commenting" throughout *The Rhetoric of Fiction*; it is the central metaphor for the "effacement" of the author (p. 50).
Interestingly, Booth returns to the notion of authorial silence in the postscript to the recent
second edition of *The Rhetoric of Fiction* (Chicago: Univ. of Chicago Press, 1983), expanding the
term to encompass a broader range of effects: "When we think about the 'uses of silence' . . . we

should thus think not only of the silences employed in modern works that give the illusion of the author's disappearance. What is left unsaid is as revealing in Homer or Fielding [and, I would add, in Hardy] as in Samuel Beckett" (p. 423). I am very much indebted to Booth's notion of authorial silence, and his notion of rhetoric, throughout my discussion.

9. *Literary Notes,* I, 52.

10. In his description of Hardy's detached and distant point of view, Miller refers to the narrator "quietly watching on the sidelines" (J. Hillis Miller, *Thomas Hardy: Distance and Desire* [Cambridge, Mass.: Harvard Univ. Press, 1970], p. 6). Lodge notes how the "cinematic novelist" "deliberately renounces some of the freedom of representation and report afforded by the verbal medium" (David Lodge, "Thomas Hardy as Cinematic Novelist," in *Thomas Hardy After Fifty Years,* ed. Lance St. John Butler [Totowa, N.J.: Rowan and Littlefield, 1977], p. 80). Notice how silence is implicit in both these formulations.

11. Burgoon and Saine, p. 58.

12. Genette, p. 194.

13. See T. J. Bruneau, "Communicative Silences: Forms and Functions," *Journal of Communication,* 23 (1973), 32, 39.

14. See Barbara Hardy, *Tellers and Listeners: The Narrative Imagination* (London: Athlone Press, 1975), p. 175: Hardy's "crises and climaxes turn on confidence, confession, warning, encouragement, revelation, history, and on reticence, lies, secrets, and silences. What is told, and what is withheld make up the tragic or comic pattern of his people." This is an important point, but Hardy does not go on to develop it.

15. Irving Howe, *Thomas Hardy* (New York: MacMillan, 1967), p. 31. Like many critics Cecil notes that Hardy's "creative impulse seems to have instinctively expressed itself in picture," but he goes on to note that the silence that necessarily accompanies these picture: "the dramatic moment expresses itself in action rather than words" (Lord David Cecil, *Hardy the Novelist,* in the Norton Critical Edition of *The Return of the Native,* ed. James Gindin [New York: Norton, 1969], pp. 457–58). Beach observes that as in a movie, Hardy tells his story "with the least possible help from the printed legend." "The action is not a matter of dialogue and debate; it is a simple affair of physical action" (Joseph Warren Beach, *The Technique of Thomas Hardy,* in the Norton Critical Edition of *Mayor,* ed. James K. Robinson [1977], p. 311). But while silence is occasionaly noticed in passing in Hardy criticism, no one has explored its importance in full.

16. Virginia Woolf, *The Common Reader,* in *Hardy: The Tragic Novels,* ed. R. P. Draper (New York: MacMillan, 1975), p. 74.

17. Norman Page approaches the same idea from the standpoint of Hardy's "pictorial art," though not in as much detail (Norman Page, *Thomas Hardy* [Boston: Routledge and Kegan Paul, 1977]). One of Hardy's favorite devices, Page notes, is to " 'show' the reader an object and to leave him to draw his own conclusions from it. . . . The ideal reader is expected to share this skill with some of his characters—the countryman's ability to observe the world around him and interpret visual evidence that might be overlooked by a less attentive viewer" (p. 73). The reader is thus "prompted by a visual sign to construct the 'story' or situation represented by the picture" (p. 74).

18. Plato, *Phaedrus,* trans. H. N. Fowler, in Thomas W. Benson and Michael H. Prosser, eds., *Reading in Classical Rhetoric* (Bloomington: Indiana Univ. Press, 1969), p. 38.

19. Matthew XXVI: 62–63: "And the high priest arose, and said unto him, Answerest thou nothing? What is it which these witness against thee? But Jesus held his peace"; I Kings XVIII: 27: "Elijah mocked them, and said, Cry aloud: for he is a god; either he is talking, or he is pursuing, or he is in a journey, or preadventure he sleepeth, and must be awaked."

20. See André Neher, *The Exile of the Word: From the Silence of the Bible to the Silence of Auschwitz,* trans. David Maisel (Philadelphia: The Jewish Publication Society of America, 1981), for an interesting meditation on God's silences in the Jewish tradition. In Neher's view God's silences are ultimately a form of revelation in themselves, the *via negativa* of faith.

21. From an interview, quoted in Millgate, p. 410.

22. Neher, p. 50.

23. *Life*, II, 91.

24. Millgate, p. 253.

25. James Kincaid argues that as readers our response to Hardy depends "on what is not explicitly there, on crucial absences, often emphasized as absences" (James R. Kincaid, "Hardy's Absences," in *Critical Approaches to the Fiction of Thomas Hardy*, ed. Dale Kramer [New York: Barnes & Noble], 1979, p. 202). But as his argument proceeds it becomes clear that absence for Kincaid equals "incoherence" rather than gaps or silences in the conventional sense. His notion is that Hardy deliberately offers a number of possible readings of any given event without defining which is valid. He "plays with the very authenticity of the text, asking whether this text or any text can be truly read"; his characters are "surrogates for the reader's similarly hubristic quest for discovering coherent meaning" (pp. 209–10). While I share Kincaid's interest in the notion of "reading" and of "texts," my concern is not with whether or not Hardy offers us a definitive interpretation of events or thinks that such an interpretation is possible. My argument is that the rhetoric of silence encourages us to see the importance of the act of reading in and of itself.

26. *Letters*, III, 183. Hardy's reference is to the "slice-of-life" school of fiction writing.

27. Wolfgang Iser, *The Implied Reader* (Baltimore: Johns Hopkins Univ. Press, 1974), p. 276.

28. Quoted in Millgate, p. 430.

29. See Iser, pp. 102–03.

30. See Iser, *The Act of Reading* (Baltimore: Johns Hopkins Univ. Press, 1978), pp. 170 ff. and Roman Ingarden, *The Literary Work of Art* (Evanston: Northwestern Univ. Press, 1973), pp. 246 ff. This is not to suggest that Iser and Ingarden agree on the function of indeterminacy. Iser objects that Ingarden gives too much priority to the text as a fixed determiner of meaning— to the notion that the unity of a text is brought about by "acts of concretization" which the text itself dictates—and not enough to the reader who constructs the text. Iser's point is that readers can construct texts in many and varied ways.

Emma Hardy's Helping Hand   Alan Manford*

It has long been known that the holograph manuscripts of several of Thomas Hardy's novels contain not only his own handwriting but also that of his first wife, Emma. This fact and certain comments attributed to Emma Hardy have led to speculation about her role in the writing of Hardy's novels.[1] Speculation may be a fascinating literary game, but ultimately we must rely upon harder evidence, and in this case the most important evidence is what is actually in the manuscripts.

Several excellent studies have focused upon the manuscripts, but the question of Emma's role has often been of little or no importance to these studies, which have also tended to concentrate on one particular novel in isolation from the others. R. L. Purdy comes the nearest to giving a full

*This essay was written specifically for this volume and is published here for the first time by permission of the author.

picture of the amount of Emma's handwriting in the manuscripts. Unfortunately, Purdy's figures err on the cautious side; he does not specify on which leaves he has identified Emma's hand, and he does not stipulate the criteria he uses to distinguish the two hands.[2]

It is thus my intention in the first part of this essay not only to raise several issues concerning this subject, but as far as possible to clear away some of the misinformation and misunderstanding that surround it. I aim to do this primarily by providing a more reliable basis upon which to assign the hands to the two writers.

Why do we need to identify Emma Hardy's hand in Thomas Hardy's manuscripts? The answer may seem self-evident, but it is worth stating nevertheless. There are in fact several reasons that it is important to distinguish the two hands (all of which offer scope for further research once Emma's hand has been identified).

First, it is important to be sure what in the manuscripts is in Emma's hand so that her role in the writing of the novels can be properly determined. Was she merely an amanuensis, or did she make unsolicited alterations to Hardy's words? If the latter, what is the nature of such alterations?

Second, it is important for the textual editor (who deals with the minutiae of the texts) to know which parts are in Emma's hand so that he or she can identify, analyze, and take into account Emma's spelling, hyphenation, and punctuation practices.

Third, it is important for the scholar to be able to judge whether the appearance of Emma's hand in the manuscript coincides with and thus identifies passages with which Hardy was having particular difficulty. Indeed, what light in general might a study of Emma's role shed on Thomas Hardy's working habits?

Finally, a biographer of Hardy, or indeed any student of the couple's relationship, might like to know that we can positively identify Emma's hand on the verso of a leaf in the extant manuscript of *Jude the Obscure* (which did not serve as printer's copy). Is it ominous that this is all that appears of Emma's hand in this particular manuscript, in view of the deep rift the novel is said to have caused between the couple? Or is it surprising to find that Emma may actually have been involved with this novel even on such a small scale (and, who knows, she may even have helped with a manuscript for printer's copy, which is not extant)?[3] The biographer might also be interested in the possibility that the addition "I see now how this inequality may be made a trouble to us" in the manuscript of *A Pair of Blue Eyes* (f. 110) may be in Emma's hand; and to know that the addition in *Two on a Tower* (f. 338) "what woman has a right to blight a coming life to preserve her personal soul?" *is* in Emma's hand.[4]

A second question is, Why is it necessary at this time satisfactorily to distinguish the two hands? The answer is contained in the discrepancies and disagreements that exist between the published attempts to differentiate between the two hands. Not only are there disagreements about the actual words reckoned to be in Emma Hardy's hand and discrepancies concerning the number of manuscript leaves attributed to her, but analyses of the two hands have been contradictory and generally unsatisfactory in that they have tended toward being subjective and imprecise. They have been based on insufficient observation and an inadequate understanding of the nature of handwriting, and they refer too loosely or only partially to the evidence of the manuscripts themselves. A more systematic approach is called for.

Most studies either have selected certain letterforms that are claimed to be typical of one hand or the other or have resorted to vague generalizations about the appearance of the hands; others have combined these two approaches. The weakness of the first approach is that the supposedly distinguishing letterforms have not been chosen on any objective, scientific basis and can thus be very unreliable evidence. The weakness of the second approach is that descriptions of the two hands would need to be extremely precise in order to enable someone else to confirm one's observations of the differences. Moreover, much of the more problematic material appears in the manuscripts as interlined additions, which might be written with a different pen and for which the reduced writing space would have a cramping effect, possibly altering the appearance of a script. Efforts to distinguish the hands need to take this feature into account. It is worthwhile to review briefly a few instances of the shortcoming of the haphazard methods and criteria that have been used to differentiate the two hands.

One of the first scholars to deal with the problem of identifying the hands was Carl J. Weber. He maintained that "the author and his wife wrote in styles of penmanship sufficiently alike not to attract the immediate notice of a careless reader, but a deliberate examination of their differing ways of shaping 'd,' 'r,' and 's' will soon enable the reader to separate the writing of the author from that of his wife."[5] Not only does Weber here fail to specify which forms of these particular letters he associates with which writer, but I would question whether these three letters are in any case sufficient or even the most useful choices as distinguishers. My own analysis confirms that the first two are relevant, but it is difficult to understand why Weber should mention *s*, in that even in the leaves of the *Two on a Tower* manuscript reproduced with his article it does not appear a very meaningful distinction.

R. L. Purdy gives figures for the extent of Emma's hand in each of the manuscripts, but does not give any explanation of how he distinguishes the two hands. In a letter to me he has remarked that he found Emma's ampersands and final *y*'s very characteristic. Whether these were inadequate criteria or whether his study of this aspect of the manuscripts was necessarily cursory (in view of the immense ground he had to cover when preparing the bibliography), the fact is that several of his figures are inaccurate.[6]

In 1962 C. J. P. Beatty and Robert Gittings corresponded through the pages of *TLS* concerning the latter's edition of Emma Hardy's *Some Recollections*. Beatty, as well as picking up a few slight misreadings, challenges

Gittings (and his coeditor, Evelyn Hardy) not only over editorial policy but about whether certain readings are in Hardy's or Emma's hand.[7] Beatty does not, however, attempt to justify on what grounds he distinguishes the two hands.

Nonetheless, in defending his judgment in assigning certain words and phrases to the hand of either Emma or Thomas Hardy, Gittings makes several points about Hardy's handwriting:

> The tail of the "y" in "very" turns up. In Hardy's hand the final "y" always has a straight tail, as it has *in his own signature*. Moreover, the ampersand sign "&" is not in his decorative and highly characteristic style, as it appears elsewhere in the manuscript. . . . The words "their nature" in square brackets are not certainly in Hardy's hand. The turned-up final "y" in "poetry" indicates this. Compare also the "p" which differs from those in Hardy's pencilled note.[8]

These remarks are particularly interesting in that they are primarily concerned with interlinear additions. Let us examine each of Gittings's criteria. First, the statement that "in Hardy's hand the final *y* always has a straight tail, as it has *in his own signature*," is demonstrably untrue, as an examination of Hardy's signatures on his letters to Macmillan (now in the British Library), for example, would show. Although in this particular case Gittings is correct to assign this emendation to Emma, in fact the probability of Hardy using a straight-tail *y* is only marginally greater than that of Emma doing so. The ampersand is extremely useful in distinguishing the two hands, but Gittings is missing the important difference between the forms most commonly used by Hardy and Emma (as shown in my own analysis later in this essay). The decorative ampersand sometimes used by Hardy in interlineations is not a reliable distinguisher, because Emma also uses it.[9] Similarly, there is no certainty that because one *p* differs from another in Hardy's hand it is therefore not by Hardy: Although *p* can be a useful distinguisher, there is often a great similarity between the *p*'s of Hardy and Emma. The judgment that "the calligraphy is far more spreading" than usual to be Hardy's is an example of vague generalization about the appearance of the writing: How much writing "spreads" might depend greatly on how much space it has, and, unless we are being precise over measurements, it is a very relative quality. Moreover, I agree with Beatty that this particular reading is in Hardy's hand.

Dale Kramer first pointed out that "further research with other manuscripts is needed" to determine Emma Hardy's role in her husband's literary affairs.[10] He also states that the "research should not be done entirely by the literary scholar" and to illustrate his point discusses the shortcomings of the criteria used by Weber and Gittings. He suggests that the individual manuscripts "seem to have their own criteria for distinguishing the handwritings," which is a theory worth serious consideration, in that hands possibly change with time and with the state of mind and health of the writers. For the manuscript of *The Woodlanders* Kramer claims that the most useful criterion is the *th* combination (in which Hardy seldom crosses the *t*, while Emma invariably does). These remarks are essentially true, but based on observation and random comparisons rather than on systematic analysis.

In 1973 Christine Winfield, in an article about the manuscript of *The Mayor of Casterbridge,* quite rightly says: "One other preliminary factor to be considered in any textual study of Hardy's work is the similarity between Hardy's handwriting and that of his first wife Emma"; she adds that "the extent of Emma's contribution at least deserves consideration."[11] She also makes the relevant point that "the script of the interlinear elements of the text is slightly more difficult to identify, since Hardy's style of writing in this area tends to differ somewhat from his usual hand." It is regrettable that despite remarking that "the differences between the two scripts are small enough almost to escape notice on a cursory reading" (and, one might therefore assume, would require precise means to distinguish them), and despite her identification of leaves of the extant manuscript that contain Emma's hand corresponding almost exactly to my own (so it would be interesting to know what means Winfield used to identify them), she passes over the problem of distinguishing the two hands by referring in a footnote to the fact that Weber mentions the problem "with use of inadequate criteria" and Kramer "much more satisfactorily." Moreover, she dismisses the entire issue: "Assuming however that Emma was simply transcribing and not creating revisions, the identification of the handwriting is not of great importance." That Winfield is probably, although not absolutely certainly, correct and that the scope of her study is far wider than merely a consideration of the two hands in the manuscript excuse her, but it is a pity she is not forthcoming about how she distinguishes between them.

Lennart A. Björk, editor of Hardy's literary notes, offers some comments that have a general usefulness in this context:

> Emma Hardy's hand is regularly sloped to the right; her husband's gives a slightly more irregular impression, heightened by the fact that in his hand the arch of *h* and the minims of *m, n,* and *u* are often splayed. Individual letters are otherwise not unequivocally safe criteria. Normally, however, the following traits are recognizable: his *d* is more often than not round-backed, hers straight-backed; his *t*, when crossed at all, usually has a stroke at the head of the stem, hers is crossed below the head.[12]

Björk is sensibly cautious about applying individual letters as "unequivocally safe criteria." One can also see what he means about the regular slope of Emma Hardy's hand and the more irregular impression given by Thomas's. Impressions can be elusive, however, and it would certainly be true to say that much of Thomas's hand also slopes distinctly to the right. Although the general impression of regularity of slope may be useful when one is faced with a few lines of text, it would be difficult to argue that it should carry much weight when one is dealing with individual words.

Patricia Ingham is correct in her identification of Emma's hand in a deleted line on the verso of a leaf in the manuscript of *Jude the Obscure*. Her only comment on how this identification was made is the following: "This is my own opinion. I am grateful to R. E. Alton . . . who kindly compared the two hands and expressed the view 'it could be E. L. H. It has much of the sharpness of her hand and the slope.' "[13] R. E. Alton's judgment (as represented here) seems not only tentative, as is understandable in the circumstances, but also somewhat vague. What exactly anyone else is to make of "the sharpness of her hand and the slope" is very much open to question.

In an article with which I would otherwise not disagree, Suleiman M. Ahmad states:

> It is not necessary to be a handwriting expert to distinguish Hardy's hand from Emma's. Their scripts show similarities but are not identical. Generally speaking, Emma's is more angular and deliberate. Seldom therefore do we find words joined together in her script, nor do we find many t's left uncrossed. Hardy's script, on the other hand, is more fluent: more often than not he joins "of" and "to" to the following word, and his "t" in the combination "th" is very rarely crossed. The distinctive feature, however, should be sought in the way Emma shapes certain letters. Her initial small "h" and "b" as well as her "r" are almost consistently different from Hardy's. "It is quite impossible to describe adequately the formation of a written letter," says McKerrow; but by careful observation the Hardy student can acquire the "feel" of the scripts in question and assign each to the writer without much difficulty.[14]

Although several of Ahmad's observations here are sound, I am uncertain exactly what he intends by "more angular and deliberate," while my own studies would not confirm the usefulness of the initial *h* or *b*. Just how optimistic his last comment is should be apparent from what I have already said—if it were possible to "assign each to the writer without much difficulty," why has there been so much disagreement in the relatively few studies already published? The quotation from McKerrow is apt and lies at the root of the inadequacy of attempts to analyze the difference between the hands of Hardy and Emma. If describing the formation of written letters proves impossible, however, it is quite possible to illustrate the different letterforms to which one is referring.[15] Moreover, the spurning of systematic study in favor of a reliance on "feel" is far from satisfactory and did not prevent Ahmad from overlooking that the versos of sheets 105 and 106a of the manuscript he was studying (*A Pair of Blue Eyes*) contain words in Emma's hand.

If the criteria and methods hitherto used to distinguish between the hands of Thomas and Emma Hardy are unsatisfactory, how *are* the hands to be distinguished? If we discount these what might be called "rule-of-thumb" methods of identifying the hands, what do we use instead?

I contend that the weakness of the use of idiosyncratic letterforms for the purpose lies not in any inherent inadmissibility of the method. It is, rather, that in order to apply such a method one must first of all identify the most relevant distinguishing criteria by means of a logical, statistically accurate procedure, and then apply those criteria cautiously and systematically. In 1976 I attempted to do both these things with respect to the writing in the manuscript of *The Woodlanders*.[16] After further consideration, I would make certain modifications to what I proposed then, and now suggest the following as at least a possible way forward.

As I have argued above, the various criteria offered by literary scholars as a means of distinguishing the two hands have many shortcomings. Apart from the criteria not being arrived at in a statistically satisfactory way, the main shortcoming is that no writer will invariably form any given letter in one particular way, and forms claimed to be distinctive of either Hardy's or Emma's hand undoubtedly do occur in the other's handwriting. It is thus a matter of establishing the probability of a particular form belonging to one hand, rather than categorizing forms as being exclusively either Hardy's or his wife's.

It is also important to establish this probability for as large a number of significant characters as possible, for the simple reason that the more characters one can distinguish, the more chance there is of significant characters occurring in any particular sample of writing. By *significant* in this context I mean letters (or letter-combinations, or other forms such as the ampersand) that prove the most useful in distinguishing the two hands; this is a relative quality, in that our purpose is one of comparing two particular hands rather than offering a definitive description of one hand. Thus, if we take certainty to be 1.00, a character for which the probability is 0.99 of the one writer using a certain form and 0.95 of the other writer using the same form would *not* be significant, because it would not offer a reliable distinction, the two writers using the same form with relatively the same frequency. However, a character for which the probability is only 0.55 of the one writer using a certain form might be useful in distinguishing the hands if the probability were only 0.14 of the other writer using the same form.

To establish a set of criteria for distinguishing the two hands in the manuscript of *The Woodlanders*, I carried out a statistical analysis of each hand, based on two samples of five leaves that in each case are undisputably wholly in the hand of the same writer (discounting any interlineations).[17] The chosen leaves are spaced throughout the manuscript, and a leaf in one hand has a counterpart in the other that is a near neighbor.

To give figures that might be applied more generally to all Hardy manuscripts, I have repeated this procedure, taking a similar sample from the manuscript of *The Return of the Native*.[18] Only a few manuscripts still contain a sufficiently large sample of Emma's writing to enable this procedure to be carried out with statistical validity. Choosing *The Return of the Native* has the advantage in that it is one manuscript upon which there seems to be agreement about the number of leaves in Emma's hand, and it is also nicely distant from *The Woodlanders* in time of composition.

The accompanying table shows my findings. How these are calculated is perhaps best demonstrated by an example. In the sample of Emma's hand from *The Return of the Native* and *The Woodlanders,* the total number of *th* combinations was 338, and the number of times the uncrossed version occurred was 66; the probability of Emma writing an uncrossed *th* is therefore 66/338, or 0.20. The total number of *th* combinations in the sample of Thomas Hardy's hand was 345, and the number of the uncrossed version was 337; the probability of Hardy writing an uncrossed *th* is therefore 337/345, or 0.98. From these figures it can be said that for an uncrossed *th* appearing in these manuscripts, if Hardy had written it then the probability that he would have used this form is 0.98, while if Emma had written it then the probability that she would have used this form is only 0.20. We can therefore say that the particular character is more likely to have been written by Hardy, although it could be by his wife.

There is generally a reasonable degree of consistency between the figures for *The Woodlanders* and those for *The Return of the Native.* There are, however, some discrepancies that confirm Dale Kramer's remark that the individual manuscripts "seem to have their own criteria for distinguishing the handwritings." Thus, for example, Emma's hand in *The Return of the Native* contains a higher proportion of curved-back *d*'s and a lower proportion of straight-backed *d*'s than in *The Woodlanders;* Thomas Hardy's preference for one form of *f* is far less marked in *The Return of the Native* than in *The Woodlanders;* and the figures for final *g* and final *y* (not given here) are so inconsistent between the two manuscripts as to be, on this evidence, unreliable distinguishers (other than within individual manuscripts).

How can such figures be put to practical use in distinguishing the two hands? The relative probability of the word or words being in the hand of each writer could no doubt be calculated by multiplying together the probability figures (as given in the table) for each occurrence of significant characters in the word or words, and thus arriving at a mathematical probability. This, however, may be carrying statistical zeal too far, and it is perhaps sufficient to apply the knowledge of the relative probabilities of as many as possible of the significant characters. To illustrate, the interlineation above line 4 of f.314 of *Two on a Tower* runs: "*the* names & memories *of their* owners" (my italics).[19] An examination of all the significant characters here (that is, those in italics) and a careful weighing of their relative probabilities would demonstrate that these words are almost certainly in Emma's hand.

If this is a satisfactory means of distinguishing the two hands, what implications are there (other than purely bibliographical)? In what ways can a knowledge of who wrote what in the manuscripts contribute toward our understanding and appreciation of Thomas Hardy's novels? What might we learn about such matters as Hardy's working methods and Emma's role in

Statistical Analysis of Handwriting Samples from *The Woodlanders* and *The Return of the Native*

Character	Form	Probability Thomas Hardy	Probability Emma Hardy
&		0.98	0.01
		0.02	0.99
k		0.76	0.01
		0.22	0.00
		0.02	0.28
		0.00	0.70
th		0.00	0.78
		0.98	0.20
		0.02	0.02
r		0.53	0.07
		0.33	0.00
		0.10	0.93
		0.03	0.00
f		0.41	0.05
		0.15	0.92
		0.23	0.00
		0.21	0.01
d		0.62	0.40
		0.24	0.00
		0.13	0.03
		0.01	0.57
p		0.88	0.10
		0.12	0.90
T		0.91	0.10
		0.06	0.60
		0.06	0.05
		0.00	0.25

The probability figure is given to the second decimal place and is arrived at by dividing the number of occurrences of a particular character form by the total occurrences of the character in all its forms.

relation to those methods? What light might be shed on such aspects as development of plot and characterization? To suggest answers to some of these questions, I shall focus upon the manuscript of *The Woodlanders*.[20]

Dale Kramer (in "Revisions and Vision") has already carried out a thorough examination of the revision within this manuscript.[21] What follows here should be seen as a supplement to that study rather than a correction of it. Kramer's main aim was to explore Hardy's craftsmanship as evident in the manuscript; mine is to highlight the part played by Emma Hardy.

The manuscript of *The Woodlanders* is perhaps the obvious choice for such a study, in that it contains the largest number of leaves in Emma's hand extant in any of Hardy's novels, and as such possibly offers the best evidence of how the couple may have worked together. The manuscript, which served as printer's copy for the novel's serialization in *Macmillan's Magazine* from May 1886 to April 1887, consists of 498 sheets numbered consecutively from 1 to 491 (with 7 supplementary sheets). Purdy identifies 106 of these sheets as wholly or partly in Emma's hand. Kramer claimed to be able to distinguish only 65 (although he would now, I am sure, recognize that there are many more).[22] My own reckoning of the leaves wholly or partly in Emma's hand is 128 (plus one verso and false starts on the versos of 3 others). To say the least, this is a considerable amount (more than a quarter of the manuscript), and there are many implications, ranging from what exactly her role was and how she carried it out, to what effect she might have had on the meaning and the styling of the text.[23]

What, then, can an accurate knowledge of the handwriting in the manuscript of *The Woodlanders* tell us? One general point to be made is that although the presence of Emma's hand might indicate places in the manuscript where Hardy was having difficulty, to assert that this is usually the case is a dangerous generalization, in that the logical conclusion is that he was having problems in all installments except that for October. It would be more accurate to say that Emma was helping as a copyist most of the time Hardy was working on his final draft and was saving him some of the drudgery of writing out. That some of her contributions occur at points where he may have been experiencing difficulty is thus to an extent coincidental in the case of this manuscript.[24] It is, however, true that Emma's writing sometimes presents material of a later date than the surrounding leaves. An example is f.121 (which, unlike those before and after, bears an unaltered foliation): This leaf concerns the rustic chorus of Tangs senior and Creedle discussing the imminent death of South and the implications that this event has for Giles Winterborne. Whether this scene marks a completely different way of introducing this particular strand of Giles's ill fortune is impossible to know for sure, but it would seem that the original sheet was at least so heavily revised as to need recopying.

One other instance is worth noting. Chapter 44 begins on the bottom of f.437 (which is a composite leaf, the top in Hardy's hand, the bottom in Emma's) and continues on f.438 and onto the additional leaf f.438a—both in Emma's hand. That this material is a later addition is further borne out by the fact that the foliation of ff.439–45 (that is, the rest of the chapter) originally ran as ff.438–42. This later material deals with Grace sickening, taking the phial of medicine left by Fitzpiers, recovering, visiting Marty, and going with Marty to Giles's grave. Whether this material represents additional ideas or merely an extension of what was in the earlier draft is difficult to say. The business of the phial had already been prepared for on f.429 (unless that is a later reworking), and the mourning of Grace and Marty continues from f.439 onward. It seems probable that the extra material comes out of an attempt to emphasize the irony surrounding Fitzpiers's saving of Grace's life and to smooth the way for their eventual reconciliation.

As far as the Hardys' actual working methods are concerned, it is evident that Emma helped throughout the writing of the manuscript's final draft. Her contribution is spread throughout, but not evenly. The portion sent to the printer for October contains no leaves in her hand; the July and August portions contain only 7 between them; yet the other portions (with one exception) contain from 9 to 16 (disregarding leaves with her writing on their verso). The outstanding exception is the penultimate installment, that for March: Of the 38 leaves, 26 contain Emma's hand. Only 10 of the 128 leaves are isolated: The leaves with her writing tend to be grouped, most frequently in threes or fours, and there are two runs of 8 leaves (both in the March portion).

It is further evident that the Hardys often worked on the copying simultaneously and even interchanged copying of the same leaf. Approximately half the leaves containing Emma's hand are entirely in her hand (apart from later revisions), but others show Hardy and Emma taking up the writing of leaves begun by the other, and even on occasion resuming and re-resuming after the other (for example, on f.360 Emma writes lines 2–13 and 17–22; on f.443 she writes lines 1–4 and 6–7). Most leaves in Emma's hand show that they were copied by her from Hardy's foul papers: They are neat and have many instances of what appear to be simple copying errors. The leaves also bear witness to the fact that Emma usually copied carefully and with critical judgment.

There are a few exceptions to her general care. For example, some leaves that Emma had to copy contained the form "Winnifred," and she was probably entrusted to transcribe it as "Grace" on her own judgment. On one occasion she forgot to do so, despite having already made the change in two other instances on the same leaf (f.72). The appearance of the form "Winnifred" here has a threefold significance: It reveals a name used in an earlier draft; it shows that Emma was probably copying closely what was in front of her; and it shows that she did not always apply full critical intelligence to the task. On another occasion she remembered while in the act of writing and managed only to put "Win" before correcting herself (f.60).

Many of Emma's errors are minor spelling slips (which she often corrects herself), but there is one instance of an error that probably caused Hardy to remold a sentence in order to make sense. It comes near the end of Chapter 34, when Fitzpiers has unwittingly taken Melbury's horse instead of the one he is accustomed to, and has been thrown near a chestnut tree. Melbury has followed him. At this point Emma wrote: "When he reached the chestnut he saw Fitzpiers dismounted, thinking something was wrong & <in[*or* on]> after feeling about for a minute or two discovered Fitzpiers lying on the ground" (f.340).[25] Whether the main flaw here is that something (such as "was missing") has been omitted after the first "Fitzpiers" or that the poor punctuation makes the meaning unclear, Hardy nevertheless found it necessary within the manuscript to revise the sentence to the following: "Thinking something was wrong the timber-merchant dismounted as soon as he reached the chestnut, & after feeling about for a minute or two discovered Fitzpiers lying on the ground."

There is also, I believe, evidence that at least some of the leaves may have been written from dictation. Apart from the number of alterations made by Emma as she copied, this "evidence" is in the form of errors that may have occurred *because of their sound.* The spelling "Bocock" (ff.385 and 386: for "Beaucock") could be the result of Emma's writing down the sound without seeing the word. Both instances of this misspelling occur in passages later deleted by Hardy. The example of f.385 is in a passage that contains two alterations in Emma's hand: "<It had> Its tenour was very different from Winterborne's by the same post. It had been written <th[e]> late on the evening before Bocock's." This might be further evidence that at this point Hardy was dictating (and making changes as he proceeded). On f.394 Emma writes the correct form, "Beaucock," which may indicate that this leaf was copied, not dictated.

Emma's writing what she heard rather than saw might also be the cause of another misspelled name, "Winterbourne" (f.121—thrice—and f.205), and a number of other slips that could have been made for the same reason. There is one such slip on f.303: "one of the business men in the neighbourhood." Hardy altered this in the manuscript to "busiest." F.33 has the following: "before them; <H>hence the <tails>, tales, chronicles." The first alteration may be the result of Hardy's changing a period to a semicolon while dictating. The word *tails* may have been written down because it came at the end of a dictated phrase, but Emma did not realize that its homophone was intended until the next phrase was given. The form "Burgesse's" (f.361: corrected by Hardy to "burgesses' ") might also have originated because Emma was using her ears rather than her eyes. The correction "barbar<ic>ous' (f.80) might be another example of a change made during dictation.

Such examples (some of which might be mere copying errors) do not necessarily constitute proof that any of the manuscript of *The Woodlanders* was dictated, but they do indicate the possibility. Likewise, the occurrence of the form "Mrs. Cs estate" (f.303), with "Charmond's" interlined above, might also indicate dictation: That is, the shorthand form was used for speed, to be filled out at later leisure.

The final two main points that can be confirmed by accurate knowledge of the handwriting both involve revision in the manuscript. First, Hardy usually revised most of Emma's fair copies, and second, there is evidence of Emma's making changes. The first point is an affirmation of one of Hardy's main characteristics as a writer (that is, his seemingly irrepressible urge to tinker with a text at any opportunity). In view of what I am about to say, it is also perhaps reassuring.

Apart from the effect that so much writing in Emma's hand might have on what we can call the novel's surface aspects (spelling, punctuation, hyphenation, italicization), everyone concerned with an appreciation of Hardy's art will want to know whether there is any evidence that Emma may have exercised an influence on the development or expression of the novel's meaning—that is, upon the words. As the answer to this is that there is such evidence, the student of Hardy will therefore no doubt further wonder about its nature and extent, and particularly whether it has any discernible influence on such matters as characterization, plot, and style.

There are no easy or unequivocal answers to this last question, mainly because even though we can positively identify Emma's hand making revisions, we do not know ultimately whether they were made under Hardy's instruction, written or oral, or on Emma's own initiative. Nevertheless, if we may set aside this uncertainty and assume for the moment that the changes to the text made in Emma's hand were carried out upon her own initiative and not at Hardy's bidding, what picture do we obtain of the overall effect her interventions had upon the text?

All the changes made in Emma's hand are minor and consist of a single word or short phrase; most can best be classed as stylistic. Some, however, bear upon characterization, and others, if not exactly concerned with plot, at least constitute comment on the action or affect the order in which the tale is told.

A simple example of a single-word revision that bears upon characterization is on f.23, where Emma interlines the word *afterwards:* "he was <then> /afterwards/ very miserable at what he had done." This passage refers to Melbury's feeling at having stolen the sweetheart of Giles Winterborne's father; the revision ties in with Melbury's way of acting impulsively and considering the consequences "afterwards." Whatever his later remorse, however, his dominating motive is usually self-interest. There are more significant revisions concerning the characters of Grace, Giles, Fitzpiers, and Mrs. Charmond, and their various relationships.

On f.80 Grace and Mrs. Charmond are talking about mantraps. Mrs. Charmond makes a remark full of innuendo about their "ominous significance where a person of our sex lives," and Emma writes: "Grace was bound to smile; but that side of womanliness was one which <sh> her inexperience had no great zest in contemplating." The change from the probable "she" to "her inexperience" is made in the act of writing and serves to widen the gulf in worldliness between the two women. Further down the same leaf another revision applies the epithet "almond" to Mrs. Charmond's eyes (Emma wrote: "her <ey> almond eyes"). Most of the other details about Mrs. Charmond in this paragraph are in Hardy's hand and are written later. The word *almond* is consistent with the idea of "long eyes so common to the angelic legions of early Italian art" and may also be intended to convey the bittersweet uncertainty of the almond's fruit. Two other changes in Emma's hand concern Mrs. Charmond's appearance and the art with which she adds to nature. On f.314

Emma writes: "the touches of powder on her <face> handsome face for the first time showed themselves as an extrinsic film." The addition of the word *handsome* either has ironical undertones or suggests that beneath all the powder there really is a handsome woman. On f.360 Emma writes: "Felice Charmond was a practical hand at make-ups, as well she might be, & she had so skillfully padded & painted Fitzpiers /with the old materials of her trade/ in the recesses of the lumber-room." The insertion "with the old materials of her trade" seems to be in Emma's hand, although there are later revisions to this passage by Hardy: The words refer to Mrs. Charmond's former profession as an actress and serve to emphasize how involvement with that profession is fundamental to Mrs. Charmond's character.

Another change concerns Mrs. Charmond's relationship with Grace. When Melbury goes to Mrs. Charmond to persuade her not to take Grace's husband, he argues that there had once been a bond of affection between the two women until "you dropped her /without a reason,/ & it hurt her warm heart more than I can tell you" (f.315). This is all in Emma's hand, including the interlineation: There was a reason (that Mrs. Charmond feared Grace's proximity would cause her own attractiveness to appear the less), but neither Grace nor Melbury would be aware of it (and indeed at the time Melbury had attributed Mrs. Charmond's coldness to Grace's association with Giles). For Melbury to use the phrase *without a reason* in his tête-à-tête with Mrs. Charmond seems quite natural, however, and the memory of the true reason would be an added barb causing this allusion "to touch her more than all Melbury's other arguments."

Two examples of an epithet being added or suppressed provide a contrast in the way that the reader's sympathies can be gently influenced. On f.336, when Fitzpiers has gone to comfort Mrs. Charmond instead of showing solicitude for his wife, Melbury considers that Fitzpiers should have stayed home or ridden to meet "his <wife> ailing wife." Emma added the epithet as she was writing, and its effect is to heighten how uncaring Fitzpiers is being toward Grace. In comparison, the reader's sympathy for Mrs. Charmond's death is reduced by the change "Discussion of <poor Felice> the almost contemporaneous death of Mrs. Charmond" (f.444). Pity for her is lessened by the distancing effect of substituting the more formal "Mrs. Charmond" for "Felice," by the deletion of the sympathy-evoking "poor," and by the less immediate phrase "the almost contemporaneous death of" (it is thus not Mrs. Charmond that is being discussed, but the impersonal idea of her death).

There are a number of changes concerning the relationship between Giles and Grace. When Giles is finding that he cannot bring himself to tell Grace that they will not be able to marry, he offers "her his arm with the most <formal> /reserved/ air" (f.393): "formal" would tell us about Giles's manner, but "reserved" tells us more about the inner thoughts that lie behind his demeanor. Their relationship when Grace stays in Giles's hut is carefully handled. Thus decorum is preserved by Giles preparing everything necessary for breakfast from "about the <premises> precincts" (f.408); and by his insistence that he should not see her—"<I will come again in the evening> /Put my breakfast on the bench/" (f.408). When Grace discovers the pitiful condition to which Giles has been reduced because of her, the extremity of his state and its inherent danger are emphasized by the inter-lined addition "Both his clothes & the straw were saturated with rain" (f.418); and in the resulting surge of emotion she is allowed to address him "O my Giles" after "Giles" was deleted, replaced by "friend," and then reinstated (f. 418). After Giles's death, Grace "had tried to persuade herself that he might have died of his illness even if she had not <gone to him> /taken possession of his house/" (f.438a); this revision diminishes the sense of Grace's wanton abandonment and emphasizes that in effect she ousted Giles from his house, which consequently increases her guilt over contributing to his death.

There are likewise revisions that have a bearing upon the character of Fitzpiers and his relationship with Grace. In the passage in which Fitzpiers is watching the different methods employed by people opening the gate outside his window, several changes are made within two lines: "<& rep> who passed & repassed <by that> along that route. <He pe> Being of a philosophical stamp he perceived that" (f.152). The first two are trivial (one probably a copying error, the other a minor verbal alteration), but the third adds an important comment on Fitzpiers's character. There is a distinct element of the Peeping Tom here, and the description of Fitzpiers as "being of a philosophical stamp" might seem to offer some justification for what he is doing. It is significantly not justified as scientific interest, however, and many of Fitzpiers's actions spring from motives that are less laudable and more impractical than purely scientific.

The difference between how we are meant to view the relationships of Giles with Grace and of Fitzpiers with Mrs. Charmond is carefully adjusted by the insertion of the value-laden word *spiritual:* "it was yet infinite <in> / in spiritual/ difference" (f.420). A change further down the same leaf serves to depersonalize the relationship between Grace and her husband (at the point when Giles is near death): Fitzpiers is described as "a man who, if it were possible to save Winterborne's life, <was the> had the brain most likely to do it." The change from a probable structure of "was the man to do it" to "had the brain . . ." subtly places the relationship between Grace and Fitzpiers on a more professional footing here: The emphasis is on Fitzpiers's skill as a doctor, not his qualities as a human being. Conversely, an insertion later in the manuscript personalizes an abstract statement, but again serves to count against Fitzpiers: "the man whom /Grace's/ fidelity could not keep faithful was stung into a passionate frame of mind concerning <Grace> her by her avowal of the contrary" (f.441). This passage is later revised by Hardy, but these two early changes were made by Emma as she wrote (inserting "Grace's" led to the deletion of "Grace," which was done immediately after she had written the word). It is no longer the intangible quality of fidelity, but specifically "Grace's," and it is therefore more reprehensible that

Fitzpiers should not have responded in a morally correct way, rather than being perversely more aroused by her avowed lack of fidelity.

A little further on in the story, when Grace is being brought round to the idea of reaccepting Fitzpiers, one added detail demonstrates how this acceptance is seeping into her mind. She receives a letter from him, the perusal of which "had a certain novelty for her.<but the chief &> She thought that, upon the whole, he wrote love-letters very well. But the chief" (f.446). The inserted sentence shows that she is finding something to admire him for, and, as it happens to be love letters, that he has already established a way back to her heart.

It would perhaps be astounding if the manuscript contained evidence to suggest that Emma had a major, direct influence on the novel's plot. There is no such dramatic evidence; however, there are minor points. The time element, for example, is affected in one small instance. Grammer Oliver informs the ailing Grace that the phial originally left by Fitzpiers for Giles had been left at the house by Marty "when she came <yester> this morning" (f.437). The change makes no fundamental difference to the plot; but it seems more likely that, in view of Grace's grave condition, the medicine would have been brought to her on the same day that it had been delivered to the house, rather than on the following day.

Another change (unless merely the correction of a copying error) occurs when Fitzpiers has gone off on the mare Darling, ostensibly to visit a patient. Emma wrote: "He had not reached home at bedtime, but there was nothing singular in this, though she was not aware that he had any patient more than five or six miles distant in that direction. <He did> The clock had struck two" (f.274). It is impossible now to know what sentence was to be introduced by "He did," but it is evident that a change of mind occurred, whether substantial or merely concerned with expression.

There are other similarly enigmatic false starts. Thus, when Giles and Melbury are about to drink some cider together while Melbury bares his soul, Emma wrote: "<Gra> He drew out the cider mug" (f.306). If this was not a mistake, what was the original intention? Had Melbury been on the point of bringing Grace into the conversation before they began drinking? In the section containing the interview between Melbury and Mrs. Charmond, Emma wrote: "<So h> 'Yes, what is it' " (f.312). Was Mrs. Charmond originally to have said something different? Was Melbury to have done or said something at this point? Further on in the interview (when Mrs. Charmond is denying knowledge of any gossip) is this false start: "<What> Tell me of it" (f.314). Is this a change of expression? Was Mrs. Charmond to ask, "What gossip?"

If it is difficult to know why these changes were made, the effect of most of the stylistic changes in Emma's hand is clearer. There are up to eighty of these changes. Although a few are interlineations, most were made by Emma as she copied out the text. Many involve the substitution of words with different shades of meaning: for example,

<fetched> called for (f.42); <So> Accordingly (f.52); <said> enquired (f.58); <look at> /regard/ (f.72); <old things> /memories/ (f.72); <grassy> /green/ (f.152); <Ah> "Ha-ha-ha," (f.153); <without> having no (f.181); <unconscious> automatic (f.281); <suspected> /wondered if/ (f.281); <shed> shelter (f.306); her <mind> wish (f.416); <terrible> /dreadful/ (f.417); <think> look upon her (f.419); <woo> [start of "woods"] copses (f.434); <suffered> /endured/ (f.469).

Other stylistic revisions spring from slight changes of emphasis that involve a revised construction or the addition of words: for example,

<rendering it> rendering that labour (f.42); looked <into> quietly into (f.78); The <girl> next was a girl (f.153); something <quite> which had little connection (f.185); what he thought <visible> he saw written (f.186); <he came> /he had come/ (f.187); <a specially> a comfortable place (f.187); <He soon per> The shape resolved itself into (f.189); The <weather was> /morning had been/ windy (f.266–67); hitched Darling to <one of the low> a bough hanging a little below the browsing line (f.335); The /Hintock/ woods (f.401); <a> /an ordinary/ (f.409); <climbing> /trying/ to climb it (f.416A); worthy <of the> to possess the (f.427); the /true/ conditions (f.441); to <enter> adopt this mode of entry (f.457).

I list so many examples to bring home the possible extent of Emma's influence. The occasional alteration does not matter that much, perhaps, but we are faced here with an accumulation of changes in a hand that is not the author's own. Even to dismiss most of these alterations as "stylistic" is hardly satisfactory, in that we cannot divorce style and meaning. There are several rays of hope for those who like matters to be straightforward and would rather not entertain the thought that a manuscript may contain nonauthorial words. First, several of the alterations I mention are on leaves that may well have been dictated by Hardy (and the correction is thus a change of mind while dictating). Second, some of the alterations seemingly by Emma could result from her accidentally beginning to copy passages already—but perhaps lightly—deleted by Thomas, or passages where the way Thomas had made the revision rendered his intention not obvious at first glance. Third, as I have already emphasized, whatever is in the manuscript underwent many subsequent rounds of authorial scrutiny as the text passed from edition to edition. Moreover, the corrections in Emma's hand seem in general to accord well with the meaning and mood of the manuscript.

Before leaving the subject, however, I would like to refer to a piece of discarded writing in the manuscript that (unless one is absolutely convinced of the "dictation theory") is less easy to dismiss. This particular piece of discarded writing contains what appears to be drafting by Emma. All of f.275 is in her hand. She originally continued onto f.276, but wrote only two lines with revisions before the sheet was abandoned (the verso was later used for f.282). The revisions on this former f.276 are also in Emma's hand. She first wrote: "Fitzpiers wished her good-bye with affection even tenderness &

then passed through the gate & ambled down the steep bridle-track to the valley." She then deleted "wished her good-bye" and interlined above it "bade her adieu," which sounds less coldly formal than "wished her good-bye," although there may be an ironic undercurrent that it is "adieu" and not "au revoir." The words "& mounted" were inserted after "affection," but a change places them after "tenderness"; Emma had in fact moved this from f.275, where she wrote "watched <him mount> the mare brought round." All the added words on the discarded f.276 are undoubtedly in Emma's hand, and they are retained in Hardy's final draft in his own hand on f.276: "Fitzpiers bade her adieu with affection, even with tenderness, mounted his horse, passed through the gate, which Grace held open for him, and ambled down the steep bridle-track to the valley." Into this passage Hardy inserted some three and a half lines written on f.275 verso, and later made one or two further changes in the printed texts. It should, however, be noted that the exact phrase of Emma's first addition is retained throughout, as is the idea of Fitzpiers mounting his horse.

It cannot be proved whether any of the changes in the manuscript were made by Emma of her own accord. There are clearly in the manuscript of *The Woodlanders* many instances of revisions in her hand that are difficult to explain away, and it is certainly possible that she may have made a number of minor changes. Whether the presence of words and phrases possibly coined by Emma rather than by Hardy himself constitutes coauthorship or corruption of Hardy's artistic and aesthetic integrity is a philosophical question that I do not propose to grapple with here. My own feeling is that, even if Emma were responsible for all the changes I have attributed to her hand, they are by no means so extensive as to justify the term *collaboration:* Hardy was indisputably in charge of the manuscript text of *The Woodlanders*.

Nevertheless, even if Emma Hardy merely acted as a scribe, the fact that she, rather than Hardy, wrote a fifth of the printer's copy must have had a direct influence on the novel's transmission (particularly on its styling). It is for this, more than any other, reason that it is important to establish as accurately as possible which parts of the manuscript are in Emma's hand.[26]

I offer the preceding comments based upon what might be called an interim or provisional method of distinguishing the two hands; but although I hope to have shown that the statistical method outlined above is more satisfactory than a more general classifying of characteristics as belonging to one hand or the other, I am conscious that refinements could be made. To go further with my method may, however, be unnecessary. We are now moving into an age that seeks ever-greater precision, and, to achieve it, is prepared to harness the powers of modern technology. The use of computers is already well established in bibliography and textual editing, and it seems only a matter of time before technology is applied to the problem of distinguishing the hands of Thomas and Emma Hardy. Indeed, precedents already exist.

Colette Sirat argues that traditional paleography is inadequate in describing writing, in that it relies on the use of terms that are literary and vague.[27] Although she is not concerned specifically with nineteenth-century English script, her point is amply borne out by the review I have made above of attempts to describe the hands of Hardy and Emma. Sirat further argues that it is necessary to define, circumscribe, and measure certain of the factors of writing, which can be done accurately only with the aid of the techniques used by the most exact sciences (such as optics). She describes several of these techniques, two of which are particularly worth our serious consideration here.

The first technique involves the projection of the manuscript onto a TV screen that is linked to an electronic brain. An example of the application of this method to distinguish hands is the work of B. Arazi.[28] Arazi took specimens of the handwriting of thirteen different persons; these texts were scanned horizontally and vertically and digitized, using the values zero and one for the background and written line, respectively. From the scannings he drew histograms of the run-lengths of the zero values. States the abstract of Arazi's article: "It is shown that the similarity between the histograms of two samples of the same person's handwriting is greater than that between the histograms of samples of two different persons' handwriting. It is also shown how some characteristics of a handwriting can be measured quantitatively."[29]

This sounds very promising, in that if such a process could provide us with a clear distinction between the hands of Thomas and Emma Hardy, there should be no arguing with science. But apart from the cost of the equipment involved, and the knowledge and expertise needed to produce meaningful results (to say nothing of the difficulties that literary folk might encounter trying to make sense of scientific terminology), there is one particular problem peculiar to our purposes that might prove difficult for this method. I refer to the presence of interlinear insertions in the Hardy manuscripts. Arazi scans scripts "written with the same spacing between lines."[30] Not only would the interlineations interfere with the scanning of the script written on the lines, but it might be invalid to scan the interlineations themselves, in that they were not written in spaces that might be comparable. Arazi's method as it stands would thus seem to be helpful for identifying hands in manuscript passages of fair copy, but would not be of help in deciding about the more problematic interlineations.

The second method of analyzing scripts "scientifically" comes out of the work of the Laboratoire de Physique Generale et d'Optique (*Laboratory of general physics and optics*) of the Université de Besançon, where a group of researchers under the direction of J. C. Vienot studied the writing of Heine and his secretaries. Many of the published findings are written by J. Duvernoy. One of the basic techniques was to analyze the deviance of a letter from a "model" of that letter (the model being, as I understand it, the ideal form originally learned by the writer). It is claimed that this method, which uses a highly mathematical process, allows not only separation of different hands but also (because a writer's hand diverges further from the model with time) the dating of texts.[31] This method sounds marvelous. Unfortunately, however, the same problems arise as those mentioned with regard to Arazi's methods. And there are further problems for the English-speaking literary scholar, because the literature outlining and explaining these techniques is either written in very technical French or translated into even more impenetrable English, accompanied by mathematical diagrams, formulas, and graphs. Moreover, from the literature itself one gains the impression that the techniques need refining and must be carefully applied to avoid error; for example, in one article Duvernoy discusses the possibility of errors if the theoretical model is applied "beyond its own limitations."[32]

It would nevertheless seem that these technological processes, once sufficiently refined, might offer (at the risk of being termed sledgehammers to crack a tiny nut) something approaching a firm response to literary questions involving handwriting—if not to the question of authority, at least to that of whose hand has written what.

Notes

1. See, for example, Frank A. Hedgcock, "Reminiscences of Thomas Hardy," *National and English Review* 137(1951): 222.

2. Richard Little Purdy, *Thomas Hardy: A Bibliographical Study* (Oxford: Clarendon Press, 1954; rev. 1968).

3. Purdy (88) suggests that printer's copy for the serialization of *Jude the Obscure* was a typescript, although Hardy talks of "restoring the MS. of *Jude the Obscure* to its original state" for the first edition (Florence Emily Hardy, *The Life of Thomas Hardy: 1840–1928* [London: Macmillan, 1928], 268).

4. The manuscript of *A Pair of Blue Eyes* is in the Berg Collection (New York Public Library); quotations from this manuscript are with the permission of the curator of the Henry W. and Albert A. Berg Collection, the New York Public Library, the Astor Lenox and Tilden foundations, and the trustees of the Hardy estate. The manuscript of *Two on a Tower* is in the Houghton Library, Harvard University; quotations are by permission of the Houghton Library.

5. Carl J. Weber, "The Manuscript of Hardy's *Two on a Tower*," *Papers of the Bibliographical Society of America* 40(1946): 5.

6. For example, Purdy identifies 1 leaf with Emma's writing in *The Trumpet-Major* (there are 2 leaves); 28 leaves in *Two on a Tower* (there are 40 leaves, as well as others with interlineations in her hand); and 106 in *The Woodlanders* (see later in this essay).

7. *Times Literary Supplement*, 1 June 1962, 420.

8. *Times Literary Supplement*, 8 June 1963, 429.

9. See, for example, the manuscript of *The Woodlanders*, f.23, line 22.

10. Dale Kramer, "A Query concerning the Handwriting in Hardy's Manuscripts," *PBSA* 57(1963): 357–60.

11. Christine Winfield, "The Manuscript of Hardy's *Mayor of Casterbridge*," *PBSA* 67(1973): 35. The other quotations in this paragraph are also from p. 35.

12. *The Literary Notes of Thomas Hardy*, vol. 1, ed. Lennart A. Björk, I (Göteborg, Sweden: Acta Universitatis Gothoburgensis, 1974), xxxii.

13. Patricia Ingham, "The Evolution of *Jude the Obscure*," *Papers of the Bibliographical Society of America* 70(1976): 35 n.

14. Suleiman M. Ahmad, "Emma Hardy and the MS. of *A Pair of Blue Eyes*," *Notes and Queries*, n.s. 26 (1979): 320–21.

15. Indeed, McKerrow does just this: Ronald B. McKerrow, *An Introduction to Bibliography for Literary Students* (Oxford: Oxford University Press, 1927), 343, 349. Anyone wishing to see extended samples of the hands of Thomas and Emma Hardy can find them in *The Return of the Native: A Facsimile of the Manuscript with Related Materials*, ed. Simon Gatrell (New York and London: Garland, 1986).

16. Alan Manford, "Materials for an Edition of Thomas Hardy's *The Woodlanders*" (M.A. thesis, University of Birmingham, 1976), 73–79.

17. The leaves in Hardy's hand were ff.7, 156, 276, 342, and 387; and in Emma's hand, ff.8, 154, 275, 340, and 386. In all cases interlinear writing was discounted, as it is always possible that such writing could be in a different hand or have different letterforms because of the reduced space for writing.

18. The leaves in Hardy's hand were ff.7, 53, 57, 134, and 195; and in Emma's, ff.6, 54, 59, 135, and 194. The manuscript is in the library of the University College, Dublin.

19. Reproduced in Weber, 4.

20. The manuscript of *The Woodlanders* is in the Dorset County Museum; quotations are with the kind permission of the trustees of the Thomas Hardy estate and the trustees of the Thomas Hardy Memorial Collection. My thanks also to Mr. R. N. R. Peers for his helpfulness when I have consulted materials in the museum.

21. Dale Kramer, "Revisions and Vision: Thomas Hardy's *The Woodlanders*," *Bulletin of the New York Public Library* 75(1971): 196–230, 248–82.

22. Purdy, 56. Dale Kramer, "A Query Concerning the Handwriting in Hardy's Manuscripts."

23. These are the folios with Emma Hardy's hand: 8, 23–24, 31–32, 32 verso, 33, 35, 42–43, 45–46, 50, 52–54, 58, 60–61, 72–75, 78–80, 91, 99, 121, 152–55, 181–83, 185–87, 189–91, 194, 204–7, 266–68, 271–75, 281–83, 303–6, 310–16, 335–37, 339–41, 345, 360–61, 382–83, 385–86, 393–95, 398–401, 404, 407–9, 415–16, 416A, 416B, 417–20, 426–29, 434–38, 438A, 440–47, 455–58, 469–71, 476–78. There is deleted material in her hand on the versos of 54, 282, and 388.

24. For example, of the eight leaves inserted immediately before f.85, Emma is responsible for only two and a half—a not-excessive amount, in view of the proportion of her hand in the entire manuscript.

25. When transcribing manuscript material I place deleted matter within angled brackets and interlineations between strokes.

26. For a practical editorial viewpoint, see Thomas Hardy, *The Woodlanders*, ed. Dale Kramer (Oxford: Clarendon Press, 1981), 59–61. Among other points (including ones concerning similarities in the two writers' treatment of punctuation and spelling), Kramer emphasizes that "the decisive point regarding the significance of Emma's assistance is that Hardy did not send to the printers unexamined copy of hers," and that "the most persuasive reason not to reject the manuscript as copy-text because Emma helped prepare it is that those pages and parts of pages written by her are closer to the original source—Hardy's own draft—than is any printed version" (*61*).

27. Colette Sirat, *L'Examen des écritures: l'oeil et la machine (The examination of writings: the eye and the machine)* (Paris: Centre National de La Recherche Scientifique, 1981).

28. B. Arazi, "Handwriting Identification by Means of Run-Length Measurements," *IEEE Transactions on Systems, Man, and Cybernetics*, vol. SMC-7, no. 12 (1977): 878–81.

29. Ibid., 878.

30. Ibid., 878.

31. J. Duvernoy, "Optical Pattern Recognition and Clustering: Karhunen-Loève Analysis," *Applied Optics* 15(1976): 1584–90.

32. J. Duvernoy, "Erreurs liées à la détermination des facteurs de forme en traitement optique de l'information" ("Errors tied to the determination of factors of form in the optical treatment of information"), *Optics Communications* 16(1976): 350–55.

Individual Novels

Far from the Madding Crowd as an Introduction to Hardy's Novels

Roy Morrell*

This novel is more typical of Hardy than a casual reading and a simplifying memory might indicate. The end, for example, is emphatically not a romantic happy-ever-after affair. We need not take Joseph Poorgrass's final "it might have been worse" at quite its long-face value; and we can see the title of the final chapter ("A Foggy Night and Morning") as perhaps Hardy's way of touching wood: there is, indeed, a suppressed and sober, but none the less noticeable, elation about the tone of the end; but the fact remains that Gabriel is no Prince Charming for a girl of three- or four-and-twenty. Ahead of Gabriel and Bathsheba is no romance, but a reality that Hardy represents as more valuable, a reality of hard and good work on the two farms:

> He accompanied her up the hill, explaining to her the details of his forthcoming tenure of the other farm. They spoke very little of their mutual feelings; pretty phrases and warm expressions being probably unnecessary between such tried friends. Theirs was that substantial affection which arises (if any arises at all) when the two who are thrown together begin first by knowing the rougher sides of each other's character, and not the best till further on, the romance growing up in the interstices of a mass of hard prosaic reality . . . (LVI).

The trend of thought should by this time be familiar enough; but the passage also illustrates Hardy's "hard prosaic"—sometimes awkward—way of thinking and writing, born of a conviction that the truth must be told, even if it cannot always be told attractively.

The distinction Hardy draws between romance and reality does not appear only at the end of the book; it is worked into the scheme of the whole. In contrast to Gabriel Oak, the two other main male characters, Troy and Boldwood, one actively and the other passively, represent aspects of romantic unreality. Boldwood is the dreamer himself, and the unreality is in the way he approaches Bathsheba, seeing in her not a woman of flesh and blood,

*Reprinted by permission from *Thomas Hardy: The Will and the Way* (Kuala Lumpur: Oxford University Press, 1965).

but a romantic dream. Troy, on the other hand, approaches Bathsheba realistically enough; but he is approached romantically *by her*: he seems to her a romantic figure, and initially, an escape from a dilemma into which the circumstances of her real everyday life have thrown her. Boldwood, for Bathsheba, has represented a certain social goal: propriety and respectability. For a short time, while he seems inaccessible, these things seem attractive to her; and it is these values that he tries to insist upon: the formal rightness of her keeping her "promise," her duty to reciprocate the love she has aroused in him. There is cruelty in Boldwood's romanticism, in the way he insists that she shall adhere to his idea of her (as there is cruelty in Angel's romanticism, and Knight's and Clym's); but Boldwood suffers more than he makes Bathsheba suffer, and the wildness and unhappiness of his love is conditioned by his dream and his distance from reality: "The great aids to idealization in love were present here: occasional observation of her from a distance, and the absence of social intercourse with her . . . the pettinesses that enter so largely into all earthy living and doing were disguised by the accident of lover and loved-one not being on visiting terms; and there was hardly awakened a thought in Boldwood that sorry household realities appertained to her . . ." (XIX). But Boldwood remains just as blind to realities when he gets to know her. After the disappearance of Troy, he again nourishes his love, but "almost shunned the contemplation of it in earnest, lest facts should reveal the wildness of the dream" (XLIX). It is a "fond madness": and the anticlimax is the discovery (while Boldwood is in prison, awaiting trial) of all the jewellery and clothing labelled "Bathsheba Boldwood," bought for a woman who had never promised to marry him (LV).

Hardy is disparaging romance, the dream and the dreamer. He is suggesting, instead, that one should live—not in accordance with nature—but in accordance with reality. And this point is made clearly by the three choices open to Bathsheba: Oak, Boldwood, and Troy. Boldwood, of course, ceases to attract her as soon as he forces his attentions on her: and there is a gentle irony in the fact that she sees in Troy, who has taken her away from Boldwood, something of what Boldwood has seen in her: a figure of romance, someone from another world. But it is not only Troy's glamour; it is also that "arch-dissembler"[1] Nature that prompts Bathsheba to love Troy. She goes to meet him, hesitates, and then surrenders her heart, in the chapter called "The Hollow amid the Ferns." The scene is one of great natural beauty, of lush growth:

> . . . tall thickets of brake fern, plump and diaphanous from recent rapid growth, and radiant in hues of clear and untainted green.
>
> At eight o'clock this midsummer evening, whilst the bristling ball of gold in the west still swept the tips of the ferns with its long, luxuriant rays, a soft brushing-by of garments might have been heard among them, and Bathsheba appeared in their midst, their soft, feathery arms caressing her up to her shoulders. She paused, turned, went back . . . (XXVIII).

But again she changes her mind, and goes on to the meeting place, a hollow where the fern "grew nearly to the bottom of the slope and then abruptly ceased. The middle within the belt of verdure was floored with a thick flossy carpet of moss and grass intermingled, so yielding that the foot was half-buried within it." Nature is softly inviting and reassuring her. She surrenders to Nature as much as to her lover,—to her own natural womanliness which, Hardy tells us, she normally had too much sense to be quite governed by (XXIX). The treatment of this theme is more subtle, perhaps, and certainly more extended, in *Tess;* but it is effective in *Far from the Madding Crowd,* all the same.

Bathsheba's third possibility is Oak; whose name at least cannot be made to suggest *compliance* with nature, but rather sturdy resistance, hard use and endurance. The distinction Hardy draws at the beginning of the novel (II) between the intermingling sounds of one vast integrated body of Nature over Norcombe Hill, and the "clearness" and "sequence" of the "notes of Farmer Oak's flute,"[2] runs right through the book. Gabriel Oak is not a part of Nature. He may be a countryman, but he is always a human being, fully conscious of his human responsibility, always ready to modify, to deflect, to improve, Nature's workings; always, that is, after his first setback. A "natural" sequence of events destroys his sheep; but he does not see himself as a victim of fate—as Troy would have done, or Henchard ("I am to suffer, I perceive"). He realizes he is ruined, and that, not having insured his sheep, he himself is to blame. And his second thought is that things would be even worse if Bathsheba had married him: "Thank God I am not married: what would she have done in the poverty now coming upon me?" Thereafter he intervenes in the natural sequence of events in as timely a fashion as he can. He prevents the fire from spreading to the ricks and buildings of Bathsheba's farm (VI); he cures the poisoned sheep (XXI); he saves Bathsheba's harvest from the storm (XXXVI, XXXVII); and he tries to intervene, but unsuccessfully, before Boldwood's optimistic dreams lead to disaster (LII, iii and vi), and before Bathsheba gives way to her infatuation for Troy: ". . . But since we don't exactly know what he is, why not behave as if he *might* be bad, simply for your own safety? Don't trust him, mistress . . ." (XXIX)— Gabriel's version of Hardy's own advice to take "a full look at the Worst." But Oak's attitude towards Nature is best seen in the account of the storm, because here Nature appears in her two aspects: creator and destroyer. She is prepared, but for Gabriel, to destroy the harvest she has bounteously created; and it is Gabriel's appreciation of the bounty, his sense of its meaning in terms of human life and sustenance, that makes him put forth all this strength to save the bounty from the destruction and to pit himself against the whole scheme of things, the whole trend of circumstance at that time. He fights not only against elemental nature, but against "nature's" hold on the humanity around him: Troy's insidiously easy-going ways (" 'Mr Troy says it will not rain, and he cannot stop to talk to you about such fidgets' "), the only too natural sleepiness and inertia of the drunken workfolk in the barn, and his own natural fears when the threat of the lightning becomes too great. The critics who suppose that Hardy shared and advocated the philosophic resignation of some of his rustics should read again the thirty-sixth and thirty-seventh chapters of *Far from the Madding Crowd*: if ever a man had the excuse of surrendering, of saying "It was to be," Oak has the excuse on the night of the storm. Instead, he fights.

Yet throughout his fight, there remains a sense in which Nature's opposition is "neutral"; nothing is purposely aimed against Oak. The changes mount against him; but they are still chances. And he seeks to keep ahead of them; he gets a lightning conductor improvised. Had there been any malicious purpose, an earlier flash of lightning would have struck him down. It is a fight between a man intelligently directing his efforts and "senseless circumstance." Oak persists; and he wins. He is not quite alone; in the latter part of the night he is helped by Bathsheba. The scene is one of many in the novels that vividly suggest the need of the human pair for each other, the individual's comparative—sometimes complete—helplessness alone.

There is another side to Gabriel's feeling for Nature: he fights her successfully because he understands and can sympathetically interpret the doings not only of his sheep, but also of Nature's smaller creatures—slug, spiders, and toad (XXXVI). He seeks to learn from Nature; for instance, from the sprig of ivy that has grown across the door of the church tower, proving that Troy has *not* been in the habit of entering here modestly and unobserved (as Bathsheba too readily believes), and that Troy is, therefore, a liar (XXIX). Nature is one of Gabriel's resources; but he is never controlled by her, nor, in any Wordsworthian sense, does he ever trust her. The essential thing about Gabriel is not that he is in contact with Nature, but that he is in contact with reality. He neither evades it nor resigns himself to it; he makes something out of it.

This point is effectively made by a metaphor embodied in an incident early in the book, just at the turning point of Oak's fortunes, when he has proved he can survive even the worst that life has to offer and when his luck (if such a word can be used) is at last on the mend. He is drinking cider in the Malthouse, and has just endeared himself to the Weatherbury folk by refusing the luxury of a clean cup:

> "And here's a mouthful of bread and bacon that mis'ess have sent, shepherd. The cider will go down better with a bit of victuals. Don't ye chaw quite close, shepherd, for I let the bacon fall in the road outside as I was bringing it along, and may be 'tis rather gritty. There, 'tis clane dirt; and we all know what that is, as you say, and you bain't a particular man we see, shepherd."
>
> "True, true—not at all," said the friendly Oak.
>
> "Don't let your teeth quite meet, and you won't feel the sandiness at all. Ah! 'tis wonderful what can be done by contrivance!"
>
> "My own mind exactly, neighbour." (VIII)

The incident is a precise metaphor of what Oak has been doing in the wider sphere of his life: he has had his share of "unpalatable reality," but by contrivance he has managed to find life's grittiness not so "unpalatable" after all.

Hardy's attitudes and themes in this novel are, indeed, typical; what is not typical is the method: he is presenting his main theme—the value of pessimism as a practical policy (". . . You cannot lose at it, you may gain . . .") through a pessimist, a central character who is successful. He is presenting it, that is, positively, instead of through the failure of a hero who is too optimistic or unrealistic. The total pattern, however, is not so different: there are unrealistic people (as we have seen) who are foils to Oak, just as in the other novels there are realists, like Farfrae, who are foils to the unsuccessful heroes. An advantage of *Far from the Madding Crowd* as an introduction to Hardy's novels is just that it *is* positive, and provides a basis for understanding the irony of most of the others.

Despite Meredith's advice that he should avoid the direct and positive method, Hardy has given us, in Gabriel Oak, as positive a model—after one or two initial overconfident slips—as Egbert Mayne. I see this as not without significance: Hardy wished, without doubt, to clarify the values for his readers. The fire in *Desperate Remedies*[3] that seems to proceed haltingly, and to wait every now and then—but quite in vain—for some intelligent intervention, becomes the fire Oak sees at Weatherbury (VI): it has already reached the stage of accelerated climax; but, even so, a man like Oak who can act promptly and courageously, is able to intervene, and to organize the firefighting, and he is just in time to prevent the spread of the flames to the farm buildings and to other ricks.

But the Weatherbury fire can serve as an illustration of Hardy's development in a more important respect. The point of the incident is not only to show how the courage and intelligence of a superior man can help the ordinary community when by itself that community is helpless; but also to show how that man gets a job. Oak has failed to get work at the hiring fair, and he is in desperate straits; but through the fire, and his ability to swallow his pride even when he discovers that the owner of the farm is Bathsheba, the woman who once rejected him, he gets the employment he needs. Hardy here embodies in action and incident what in *Desperate Remedies* had to be expressed in an explicit statement. What Edward Springrove reminds Cytherea, ". . . that the fame of Sir Christopher Wren himself depended upon the accident of a fire in Pudding Lane,"[4] is transposed from the key of the young architect to that of the countryman, and presented not in words, but in action. And there are other examples. We have already remarked that Hardy's note about the "figure" that "stands in our van with arm uplifted, to knock us back from any pleasant prospect we indulge in as probable" is paraphrased in *Desperate Remedies*, Hardy explaining that "a position which it was impossible to reach by any direct attempt was come to by a seeker's swerving from the path." Less than four years later, this does not have to be phrased at all. It becomes the sequence of events at the beginning of *Far from the Madding Crowd*: Gabriel, indulging in the "pleasant prospect" of success as a sheep-farmer, and even at one point accepting as "probable" his marriage with Bathsheba, is "knocked back." He is ruined. At Casterbridge hiring fair, subsequently, he fails to get a job as bailiff or even as shepherd. But then, "swerving from his path," he gradually contrives to reach all his original objectives, one by one: he becomes a shepherd, a bailiff, the owner of Boldwood's farm, and eventually Bathsheba's husband.

Let us now consider such of Hardy's favourite narrative devices as may be illustrated from *Far from the Madding Crowd*, beginning with two of the most important: the highly-charged expressionistic incidents that have been called "grotesques," and his contrasts. These ironical contrasts may be partly accounted for by Hardy's modest wish—expressed indeed at this very period of his life—to be considered a good hand at a serial."[5] But this is certainly not the whole truth. Hardy's belief in the eternal possibility of change was something fundamental; and some of the contrasts he suggests are far more elaborate than anything required by the suspenses and sequels of a magazine serial story. In *Far from the Madding Crowd* it happens that one of the most extraordinary of Hardy's "grotesques" has an important place in one of his series of ironical contrasts; we shall therefore be able to discuss them together. But first a word about the "grotesques," since they have proved to be critical stumbling blocks: Hardy risked the sleepwalking scene in *Tess*, and the trilobite and cliff rescue in *A Pair of Blue Eyes*, and other such scenes, because he saw their function as transcending their awkwardness and lack of realism. And they may fulfil their function not despite their awkwardness, but because of it. Read in their full contexts, they set chords vibrating through the whole novel. The sleepwalking scene, with its central incident of Angel carrying Tess precariously along the plank above the flooded waters of the Froom, reminds us of Tess's complete helplessness in Angel's care; and of Tess's responsibility too, since a false move on her part will be fatal; above all, the precariousness is a reminder that the happiness of both is in the balance; Angel's placing of Tess in the coffin powerfully suggests that he is killing his love for her; and, behind the mere fact of the sleepwalking, is the hint that Angel does not know where he is going. It is Tess, indeed, who finally takes control, leading Angel back to safety; this is an indication that the salvation may be in Tess's own hands. Through the very incident—if she tells Angel about it—she may help him to clarify his feelings. The cliff scene in *A Pair of Blue Eyes* is less complex; but this too might be taken primarily as an indication of the deep need of Elfride and Knight for each other, while subsidiary details suggest the completeness with which Elfride has renounced all thought of marrying Stephen. These are but suggestions; with the most interesting expressionistic scene in *Far from the Madding Crowd* I will try to give the implications a little more fully: it is the scene where the grotesque gurgoyle spouts water over Fanny's grave and undoes all that Troy's remorseful labour has accomplished.

The first irony is Troy's astonishment. He feels he has turned over a new leaf and made a virtuous show of remorse; but finds that " . . . Providence, far from helping him into a new course, or showing any wish that he might adopt one, actually jeered his first trembling and critical attempt in that kind . . ." (XLVI). But Hardy, in the preceding chapter, "Troy's Romanticism," had shown Troy's activities in a different light. After a long and tiring day, in which he had walked to Casterbridge and back, arranged for a headstone to be inscribed and dispatched, and finally toiled at the grave late into the night, planting flowers by the light of a lantern, Troy had taken shelter in the church porch, and fallen asleep. "Troy," Hardy remarks, "had no perception that in the futility of these romantic doings, dictated by remorseful reaction from previous indifference, there was any element of absurdity." Here, then, is another and a greater irony: in the contrast between the immense trouble that Troy takes, to prove his love for Fanny now she is dead, and his neglect of her during her lifetime. Seen in this light, the gurgoyle's mockery is but a picturesque projection, an image, of Hardy's own feelings about Troy. But even if we share Troy's view[6] that Fate cruelly prevents him from adequately displaying his remorse, we certainly cannot suppose it was Fate that had stopped him from marrying Fanny: it was injured pride. And is not this the explanation of his present defeat? His pride is hurt; the approving pat on the back that he expects from Providence has not come. If he had been thinking, not of the hurt to himself, but simply of what could be done to repair the damage, he could have done it; and with a quarter of the effort he had spent toiling by lantern-light the night before. Hardy pushes this point home, as there is no need to remind the reader, by showing Bathsheba doing simply and easily what Troy thinks it is useless to attempt: gathering up the flowers and replanting them, cleaning up the headstone, and arranging for the pipe in the gurgoyle's mouth to be deflected. For Troy such actions are impossible: "He slowly withdrew from the grave. He did not attempt to fill up the hole, replace the flowers, or do anything at all. He simply threw up his cards, and foreswore his game for that time and always. . . . Shortly afterwards he had gone from the village." He has no intention of returning to Bathsheba's farm; and surely the greatest irony of all is that in his remorse for the past, he is neglecting the present. He regrets having neglected Fanny when she was alive; but, repeating the same pattern, he is neglecting the woman—in every way Fanny's superior—whom he has actually married.

Indeed, as one contemplates the situation, the ironies seem to multiply. There is the fact that Troy, of all people, should not be surprised at what the rain can do: only a few weeks before, the storm he confidently predicted would not happen, did happen, and would have ruined him and Bathsheba but for Oak's courage. Then he had blamed the rain for all the money he had lost at the Budmouth races. And this reminds us that the money he spent on Fanny's grave, like that he lost on the horses, was not even his own; it was Bathsheba's. And again the realization is forced upon us that from the rain and the gurgoyle Troy had suffered no tangible harm; his ego was hurt, his gesture spoilt: nothing else. But the world of *Far from the Madding Crowd* is, after all, one where more is at stake, sometimes, than the success of a gesture; and beyond the ironies of what Troy had left undone, and still leaves undone, there is the further ironic contrast between the way Troy is immediately and utterly defeated by the mere *appearance* of disaster and difficulty, and the way Oak has fought against what might have been a real disaster and at the real risk of his life. Many facets of Troy's character are recalled as we ponder over the incident; and in particular his weakness for display: a small point is the splendid impossibility of the lie about his modestly entering the church in such a way as to avoid being seen, and the blindness of Bathsheba in believing him.[7]

The occasional importance of images in Hardy's narrative method is not likely to be overlooked. Discussion of these has proved easy, and sometimes uninformative. When Bathsheba first meets Troy, the gimp on her dress is caught in one of his spurs, and as Troy seeks to disentangle it, the lantern throws their shadows against the trees of the fir plantation so that "each dusky shape" becomes "distorted and mangled till it wasted to nothing" (XXIV). It is easy to see this as a "proleptic image," a hint of the trouble in store for them when their lives become entangled. But why "when"? Why not "*if* their lives become entangled"? Why should Bathsheba ignore a danger that almost everyone else in Weatherbury sees clearly? There is no need to repeat what I have already stressed:[8] that far more striking images—such as those which predict death and disaster for Gabriel before the storm—indicate not a determined future, but undetermined possible dangers that can be averted.

But there is one image in *Far from the Madding Crowd* on which it is necessary to comment, since it has escaped the notice of other critics. Gabriel is investigating an unfamiliar light (II), and finds that it comes from a shed set into the hillside. He peers through a hole in the roof, and finds himself looking down upon a young woman whom he at first does not recognize, seeing her "in a bird's eye view, *as Milton's Satan first saw Paradise.*" There are ways of dealing with things as awkward as this: some critics may say that Hardy does not know what he is doing; that he is writing here without inner conviction; others may ridicule Hardy's attempt to display his book knowledge. But there is only one way of reading this in good faith: to assume that Hardy meant what he said. And Hardy is not parading his own book knowledge: *Paradise Lost* was one of Gabriel Oak's books, we discover later (VIII); and we are following *Gabriel's* eyes, *his* impressions, *his* slight feeling of guilt, as he peers into the hut. There is nothing satanic about Gabriel; and indeed there is something very unsatanic about his name; all the same, he would like to intrude, and does in fact later intrude, upon this girl's life. The function of the image is, indeed, clear: it strikingly raises the question whether the intruder is always evil, or whether he can be—as Gabriel turns out to be, by and large—a good angel.

It is through this image, in fact, that we approach the social theme of the book—in so far as it has one: the strengthening of a rather backward, pleasant, easy-going rural community by two newcomers, two intruders. The Weatherbury folk are too close to nature; ignorant, lazy, rather irresponsible, and superstitious: it is significant that when Bathsheba, against her better judgement and under Liddy's persuasion, consults the "Sortes Sanctorum," a rusty patch on the page indicates how often the Bible has been used before for this purpose. In all kinds of small ways the country people show that they are not adapting themselves for survival under new conditions of life, and weaknesses are creeping in. They need someone like Bathsheba, an unconventional woman, whose parents were townsfolk, to come and take a personal interest in the farm, to sack the dishonest bailiff, and take full responsibility herself. The workfolk are capable enough, but they are useless in an emergency: they get flustered or they are tipsy; and they have none of the new skills and scientific knowledge that enable Gabriel Oak to operate upon the sheep that have poisoned themselves in the young clover. But more than this, they need Oak's new conscientiousness, his firmness, his readiness, his refusal to let personal griefs affect his actions (he is contrasted strikingly in this respect with Boldwood, whose preoccupation with grief—as we learn when Gabriel meets him the morning after the storm—has caused him to neglect his harvest). Neither Oak's new skills nor the qualities of his character were learnt from the Weatherbury community; he brings them—as Bathsheba brings her vitality and unconventionality—from outside. They are strangers in a sense that even Troy is not; Troy slips only too readily into the easy-going country morality. Gabriel and Bathsheba have all the strength of newcomers, outsiders, who revitalize the old stock.

I have mentioned the fact that Bathsheba allows herself to be influenced by the irresponsible and romantic Liddy in the Sortes Sanctorum scene and the sending of the valentine. This does not contradict my argument: it is a lapse on Bathsheba's part, and she pays dearly for it. And every detail of the episode is interesting as revealing that Bathsheba is all the time aware of the more sensible course; for instance she reverses the conditions of the toss because she thinks the book is more likely to fall open: ". . . Open Boldwood—shut, Teddy. No; it's more likely to fall open: Open, Teddy—shut, Boldwood" (XIII). It falls shut. And Bathsheba, who knows perfectly well what she wants to do, and what she ought to do, acts instead as she is directed by chance. It is an interesting illustration of the fact that human beings who are capable enough of acting independently of chance, and more intelligently, sometimes choose to put themselves in chance's hands. The relevance of this point to incidents in the other novels (for instance, Elfride's decision that her horse shall choose her direction for her) needs no emphasis; nor need we stress the irony with which Hardy links Bathsheba's foolish and, indeed, disastrous action with the Sortes Sanctorum and tossing of a hymn book, and so, by ironic implication, with the workings of Providence.

So often is Hardy's attitude to change misunderstood, that it is perhaps worth adding that chances, in his books, are not always disastrous ones; and there is an instance in *Far from the Madding Crowd* of a singularly fortunate chance: Bathsheba happens to pass near Gabriel's hut and to notice that both ventilators are closed. Her chance discovery saves Gabriel's life.

> "How did you find me?"
> "I heard your dog howling and scratching at the door of the hut when I came to the milking (it was so lucky, Daisy's milking is almost over for the season, and I shall not come here after this week or the next). The dog saw me, and jumped over to me, and laid hold of my skirt. I came across and looked round the hut the very first thing to see if the slides were closed. My uncle has a hut like this one, and I have heard him tell his shepherd not to go to sleep without leaving a slide open . . ." (III).

But there is more to it than the lucky chance of Daisy's milking not being quite over: the event is nearly a disaster; and the disaster is prevented only because the person happening to come by was—by Wessex standards—remarkably responsible, and intelligently alert to the worst contingencies.

A final point: Hardy was much interested in what one may call the psychology of the "object": the distress and sudden weakness felt by someone—often a woman—when she discovers she is being talked about, and has thus become an object in the eyes of others. Tess's "feminine loss of courage" at Emminster is caused by overhearing Angel's brothers talking about her;[9] Sue cannot ignore the gossip she overhears about herself and Jude;[10] Elfride is horrified to find that Knight is writing an article about her;[11] even Ethelberta is disconcerted at overhearing some gossip about her own future;[12] and, as we might expect, Hardy explicitly theorizes about this human weakness in *Desperate Remedies*.[13] Bathsheba is vexed that Gabriel has seen her unconventional behaviour on horseback; and she is indignant at his tactlessness in letting her know. None the less, the fact that she knows he has seen her, and is critical of her conduct, makes her a little dependent on him; she finds herself sounding him as to what others are saying about her, and seeking Gabriel's good opinion. Her self-justifications and confidences are not just a narrative device: Hardy is doing more than conveying to us a few facts we should otherwise not know—Bathsheba's doings in Bath, for instance—he is showing her becoming more and more dependent upon Gabriel and Gabriel's approval. At the same time Gabriel himself is becoming more and more the controlling centre of all the activity on the two farms; and from looking *to* him, Bathsheba gradually finds herself looking *up* to him.

Romantic Westerners are sometimes a bit surprised that Bathsheba marries Oak; but between the man we meet in the opening pages, pleasant and unassuming but tactless and just a shade too confident, and the Gabriel Oak of the last chapters, there are many subtle differences; and perhaps her choice is not so surprising. In the East, feelings are reversed: surprise is sometimes felt that *he* could have brought himself to marry *her*. She had slighted him, as Japanese and Chinese readers point out, and she was not an easily controllable woman. Not many English people react in this way because, I suppose, we share Gabriel's liking for a woman who is exceptional. And also, surely, because we have learnt to understand his great merits; first, he leaves pride and pique to fools like Troy, and second, we feel he can cope even with Bathsheba: there has been nothing so far that he has failed to cope with. We have learnt to accept, as one of the greatest of qualities, Oak's adaptability; and, at the end of the book, we take Hardy's point that it is a special sort of goodness to arrange to go to California, if that seems best, and then to be able, equally easily, to cancel such plans when, at the last moment, the factors in the situation change, and he can marry Bathsheba after all.

Notes

1. *Early Life*, p. 231; *Life*, p. 176.

2. See p. 16 above. [Ed. note: Morrell's reference is to the first chapter of his book.]

3. See above, pp. 53 ff. [Ed. note: Morrell's reference is to his preceding chapter.]

4. *Desperate Remedies*, II, 2.

5. *Early Life*, p. 131; *Life*, p. 100.

6. Shaw once complained that his critics always agreed with his sentimental heroines; one might say with equal truth that Hardy's critics always agree with his fatalists. It is odd that Troy gets little sympathy from the critics, *except at this point*—where he gets no sympathy from Hardy.

7. It is possible that Hardy got the hint for Troy's lie from an inscription in Puddletown ("Weatherbury") Church which reads: "*Huc ades non videri sed audire et precari.*"

8. See pages 12–13 and 19 above. [Ed. note: Morrell's reference is to the first chapter of his book.]

9. *Tess*, XLIV.

10. *Jude*, V.vi.

11. *A Pair of Blue Eyes*, XVIII.

12. *The Hand of Ethelberta*, XXV.

13. " . . . We do not much mind what men think of us . . . provided that each thinks and acts thereupon in isolation. It is the exchange of ideas about us that we dread . . ." (*Desperate Remedies*, I.5).

The "Poetics" of *The Return of the Native*

John Paterson*

If *The Return of the Native* suggests the most formal and even the most literary of Hardy's experiments in prose fiction, it is perhaps because his imagination was dominated at this juncture, as it had not been before and as

*Reprinted from *Modern Fiction Studies* 6(1960): 214–22. © 1960 by Purdue Research Foundation, West Lafayette, Indiana 47907. Reprinted with permission.

it would not be again, by the legend and literature of Greece and Rome. This influence is first of all apparent in the dubious doctrine the novel was evidently designed to dramatize: "The truth seems to be that a long line of disillusive centuries has permanently displaced the Hellenic idea of life. . . . What the Greeks only suspected we know well; what their Aeschylus imagined our nursery children feel."[1] But it is also apparent in the frequency of the novel's references to Homer, Virgil, Aeschylus, and Sophocles as well as to more modern practitioners of epic and tragic form: e.g., Dante, Shakespeare, Milton, and (through Handel) Racine.[2]

That this influence entered the novel more especially as a dramatic influence Hardy was himself to acknowledge later. There is a virtue, he wrote of his late play, *The Famous Tragedy of the Queen of Cornwall*, in preserving the unities: "the only other case I remember attempting it in was *The Return of the Native*."[3] Hence the limitation of the action to the narrow space of Egdon Heath and of the time to a year and a day. Beyond this, Hardy employed, in Eustacia's moments of crisis, the convention of the set speech; dissociated the community of humble peasants from the gentility of the heath to create a rough equivalent of the Greek chorus; and, though compelled against his better judgment to add a sixth book,[4] originally conceived the novel in terms of five books in imitation, evidently, of the five acts identified with classical tragedy.

If a direct formal and structural correspondence was intended, however, it must in the process of composition have lapsed or become diffused. The claims of the main characters to aristocratic standing are, in the first place, seldom convincing: they qualify at best as a species of stuffy provincial gentility. The stress of the novel falls, in the second place, not on one major figure but on several, the image of Eustacia Vye dominating, if at all, only after a debilitating struggle with the competing images of Thomasin, Clym, and Mrs. Yeobright. Its center of gravity is in fact so unstable that its intensity as tragedy is ultimately dispersed, the complication of its plot suggesting more the loosely-fashioned pastoral romance of *Far from the Madding Crowd* and *The Woodlanders* than the rigorously-structured drama of Sophocles and Aeschylus. The novel displays, finally, infiltrations of romantic sympathy altogether foreign to the tragic vision of things. Unpersuaded of the existence of a just cosmic order, it fails to command, in the presence of human defeat, the detachment and equanimity of the classical imagination.[5] As features of form and structure, then, the preservation of the unities and the five-"act" division appear either as arbitrary or as ornamental.

In the end, however, the structure of the novel, its principle of organization, is less architectural than poetic or musical. For if Hardy failed to produce a formal and structural parallel with Greek tragedy, he managed to achieve, consciously or unconsciously, a reasonable artistic equivalent. By the sheer and almost systematic accumulation of allusions to the geography and history, the legend and literature, of classical antiquity, he evoked the large and heroic "world" out of which Greek tragedy came and, by so doing, fixed the otherwise purely local action of the novel within a frame of reference that gave it dignity and meaning.[6] Thus the domestic landscape of Wessex is everywhere transfigured by the heroic landscape, real and imaginary, of an older and grander civilization. Egdon Heath recommends itself to the diminished modern consciousness as "the new Vale of Tempe" (p. 5); the little hills on its lower levels look from Rainbarrow on a misty morning "like an archipelago in a fog-formed Aegean" (p. 100); and Budmouth combines, in the unsophisticated imagination of the heath-folk, "a Carthaginian bustle of building with Tarentine luxuriousness and Baian health and beauty" (p. 108). An ordinary chimney fire becomes, in the perspective of this novel, "an Etna of peat" (p. 160).

More significantly, Egdon Heath itself is altogether transfigured in being juxtaposed with the grisly underworld of the ancients and, though less frequently, with its Christian equivalent. This identification is established immediately in the first chapter where, described as a "Titanic form" ("Every night its Titanic form seemed to await something" [p.4]), the heath suggests Tartarus, the gloomy foster-home of rebel-gods. Soon afterward, Egdon is called upon to evoke the Limbo of Dante's (and Virgil's) imagination: "The whole black phenomenon beneath represented Limbo as viewed from the brink by the sublime Florentine in his vision, and the muttered articulations of the wind in the hollows were as complaints and petitions from the 'souls of mighty worth' suspended therein" (p. 17). This image is elaborated in the setting of the novel's third chapter, where the fires that flare in the darkness suggest the inflammable landscape of the Christian Hell. Later still, the heath provokes a reference to "Homer's Cimmerian land" (p. 60), the dark region at the outer rim of the world and the traditional location of the entrance to Hades.

If Egdon Heath suggests the grim underworld of the Greek and Christian imaginations, the main characters of the novel naturally suggest its ghostly and tormented inhabitants. Egdon is explicitly identified as Eustacia's "Hades" (p. 77). The dignity that sits upon her brow is defined as "Tartarean" (p. 77) and her removal from Budmouth to Edgon, like that of the Titans to Tartarus, as a banishment (p. 78). When Mrs. Yeobright and Olly Dowden go down from Rainbarrow into the darker regions below, the vocabulary and imagery overwhelmingly suggest a descent into the underworld of the dead: "Down, downward they went, and yet further down—their descent at each step seeming to outmeasure their advance. Their skirts were scratched noisily by the furze, their shoulders brushed by the ferns, which, though dead and dry, stood erect as when alive." The situation of the two women at this point is designated, in fact, a "Tartarean situation" (p. 38). Even the phlegmatic and apparently imperturbable Diggory Venn is seen in the same hyperbolic terms: as one who has suffered the pangs of unrequited love, he is said to have "stood in the shoes of Tantalus" (p. 94).

Moreover, throughout the novel character and scene and incident are constantly evaluated, or more accurately, transvaluated, according to a scale provided by classical history and literature. Johnny Nunsuch's suspension between the vague menace of the reddleman and the certain wrath of Eustacia Vye is defined as "a Scyllaeo-Charybdean position" (p. 84). His dying mother in his arms, Clym proceeds "like Aeneas with his father" (p. 348) and, having learned the import of her last words, endures the anguish of Oedipus: "his mouth had passed into the phase more or less imaginatively rendered in studies of Oedipus" (p. 384). Indeed, as the symbol of the diminished consciousness of modern times, Clym's is explicitly contrasted with the heroic consciousness of Hardy's prelapsarian Greeks: "Should there be a classic period to art hereafter, its Pheidias may produce such faces" (p. 197).

While Clym suggests the deterioration of "the Hellenic idea of life," Eustacia suggests its anachronistic and hence foredoomed revival. When she is not being victimized by the gods and goddesses, she is visualized as one of them herself, her approximation to divinity providing the dominant note of the "Queen of Night" chapter. "Eustacia Vye was," the chapter begins, "the raw material of a divinity. On Olympus she would have done well with a little preparation" (p. 75). "The new moon behind her head," the chapter records elsewhere, "an old helmet upon it, a diadem of accidental dewdrops round her brow, would have been adjuncts sufficient to strike the note of Artemis, Athena, or Hera respectively." (p. 77). Eustacia occasionally recalls the statuary of ancient Greece with its imagery of god-like heroes and heroic gods. "One had fancied," Hardy remarks, "that such lip-curves were mostly lurking underground in the South as fragments of forgotten marbles" (p. 76). And the wound which she sustains at the hands of Susan Nunsuch is later said to look "like a ruby on Parian marble" (p. 219). Elsewhere, informed that her association with Wildeve is likely to damage her character, Eustacia is "as unconcerned at that contingency as a goddess at a lack of linen" (p. 109).

Also, throughout the novel the image of Eustacia Vye inevitably inspires allusions to the history and legend and literature of an exotic antiquity. Her profile justifies comparison with that of Sappho (p. 62); in moments of calm, she suggests the Sphinx (p. 75); she is said to have "pagan eyes, full of nocturnal mysteries" and moods that recall the lotus-eaters (p. 76). When she does not choose to be direct, she can "utter oracles of Delphian ambiguity" (p. 82); and her dream is described as having "as many ramifications as the Cretan labyrinth" (p. 138). On the occasion of the Christmas party she plays the Venus to Clym's Aeneas: "When the disguised Queen of Love appeared before Aeneas a preternatural perfume accompanied her presence and betrayed her quality" (p. 167). And prevented by her disguise from exercising her charms on Clym, she has "a sense of the doom of Echo" (p. 169). In by far the most dazzling of her classical associations, Eustacia is established, in virtually explicit terms, as a lineal descendant of Homeric kings: "Where did her dignity come from? By a latent vein from Alcinous' line, her father hailing from Phaeacia's isle?" (p. 78). Identified by Mrs.

Yeobright as a bandmaster from the island of Corfu (p. 239)—Phaeacia's isle—Eustacia's father will be described more spectacularly by Thomasin as "a romantic wanderer—a sort of Greek Ulysses" (p. 251).

Nothing contributes more, however, to the transfiguration of the novel's essentially domestic action than the Promethean theme and image. At the very least, the legend of the fallen god more narrowly delimits the field of the novel, exerts a stricter control over its form and meaning, than the rather widespread context provided by the system of classical allusions. It creates, indeed, a frame of reference that operates within, and cooperates with, the larger classical frame of reference.

The Promethean theme and metaphor are already active, if only indirectly, in the Tartarean analogy alluded to earlier. For the image of a "Titanic form" that "seemed to await something" suggests nothing so much as the figure of Prometheus awaiting the promised liberation from the torments of his imprisonment. Furthermore, the bonfires that have been lit ostensibly in observance of Guy Fawkes day are charged with a specifically Promethean significance: "To light a fire is the instinctive and resistant act of man when, at the winter ingress, the curfew is sounded throughout Nature. It indicates a spontaneous, Promethean rebelliousness against the fiat that this recurrent season shall bring foul times, cold darkness, misery and death. Black chaos comes, and the fettered gods of the earth say, Let there be light" (pp. 17–18). Elsewhere Clym Yeobright himself is created in the image of the fallen god: "As is usual with bright natures, the deity that lies ignominiously chained within an ephemeral human carcass shone out of him like a ray" (p. 162). In his role of the reformed Promethean, he is later called upon to sound that note only too baldly: "Now, don't you suppose, my inexperienced girl," he tells that unregenerate fire-worshipper, his wife, "that I cannot rebel, in high Promethean fashion, against the gods and fate as well as you" (p. 302).

As this reference may have indicated, however, the Promethean passion of the novel particularly concentrates itself in the image of Eustacia Vye. Her dialogue and, in general, the terms of her thinking and feeling have a rhetorical quality that unmistakably suggests the generic heroine of Greek tragedy, if not Prometheus himself. Thus she can confess to "an agonizing pity for myself that I ever was born" (p. 232) and aspire "to look with indifference upon the cruel satires that Fate loves to indulge in" (p. 243). Death seems to her the only relief "if the satire of Heaven should go much further" (p. 305); and she is said to have good grounds for asking "the Supreme Power by what right a being of such exquisite finish had been placed in circumstances calculated to make of her charms a curse rather than a blessing" (p. 305). "How I have tried and tried to be a splendid woman," she cries finally in her denunciation of the gods, "and how destiny has been against me! . . . I was capable of much; but I have been injured and blighted and crushed by things beyond my control! O, how hard it is of Heaven to devise such tortures for me, who have done no harm to Heaven at all!" (p. 422).

The Promethean motif affects the substance of the novel in an even more subtle and indirect way. In the fire-imagery, by inference Promethean, with which the text is virtually saturated, it becomes chemically active at the vital center of the novel. This is already apparent in the major imagery of scene and incident. The darkness of the heath is shattered in the third chapter by the grotesque bonfires that mark the anniversary of the Gunpowder Plot. In the almost parabolic episode of Chapter IV, Book Fourth, Wildeve makes his presence known to Eustacia by releasing at her window a moth that perishes in the flames of her candle. On the day of Mrs. Yeobright's death, the universe of Egdon Heath is visualized as almost literally on fire: "The sun had branded the whole heath with his mark, even the purple heath-flowers having put on a brownness under the dry blazes of the few preceding days. Every valley was filled with air like that of a kiln, and the clean quartz sand of the winter water-courses, which formed summer paths, had undergone a species of incineration since the drought had set in" (pp. 326–7). And Mrs. Yeobright subsequently dies what amounts to a symbolic death-by-fire: "The sun . . . stood directly in her face, like some merciless incendiary, brand in hand, waiting to consume her" (p. 342). Finally and most conclusively, Eustacia Vye herself perishes in the same fatal flames: she is burned in effigy by Susan Nunsuch (pp. 424–5), and acting out the parable of the moth-signal and making Susan's prophetic magic good, she hurls herself into what is called, inevitably, "the boiling *caldron*" of the weir (p. 441).

The Promethean theme is expressed and supported not alone by the major imagery of action and setting, but also by the minor imagery, the local fire-imagery, with which the language of the novel is from beginning to end surcharged. Egdon's "crimson heather" is "*fired*" to scarlet by the July sun (p. 283). In the presence of Eustacia Vye, "*the revived embers* of an old passion *glowed* clearly in Wildeve" (p. 73) who sees himself as having upon him "the curse of *inflammability*" (p. 71). And from the ravine which is the site of Diggory's encampment, Eustacia sees "a sinister redness arising . . . dull and lurid like *a flame in sunlight*" (p. 174). "Why," Mrs. Yeobright cries, disappointed in her hopes for her son, "should I go on *scalding* my face like this?" (p. 256). After her death Clym's eyes will be "lit by a hot light, *as if the fire in their pupils were burning up their substance*" (p. 366).

The fire-imagery is never more emergent than when Eustacia Vye commands the attention of the novel. Thus the colour of her soul is fancied as "*flame-like*" (p. 76). "A *blaze* of love, and extinction" she prefers characteristically, to "a lantern glimmer of the same" (p. 79). Antagonized by Wildeve's cool manner, indignation spreads through her "like subterranean *heat*" (p. 72) and elsewhere angered by the reddleman, she lets him see "*how a slow fire could blaze on occasion*" (p. 107). She resembles the tiger-beetle "which, when observed in dull situations, seems to be of the quietest neutral colour, but under a full illumination *blazes* with dazzling splendour" (p. 104). And when she laughs and opens her lips, the effect is at once more and less than human: "the sun shone into her mouth as into a tulip, and *lent it a similar scarlet fire*" (p. 104).

After her first meeting with Clym, she is *"warmed with an inner fire,"* but is later alarmed at the thought of a rival like Thomasin "living day after day in *inflammable* proximity to him" (p. 171). After their first kiss, Clym fears his mother will ask, "What red spot is that *glowing* upon your mouth so vividly?" (p. 225). In her quarrel with Mrs. Yeobright, Eustacia speaks out "with *a smothered fire* of feeling" and "*scalding* tears" trickle from her eyes (pp. 288–9), events justifying Clym's allusion to their "*inflammable* natures" (pp. 293–4). In the period after Mrs. Yeobright's death, Eustacia will be "*seared* inwardly" by the secret she dares not tell (p. 367).

The fire-imagery joins, then, with the specific allusions to, and evocations of, the Prometheus story to frame and transvaluate the otherwise purely domestic action of the novel. In their association with fire, Clym, Mrs. Yeobright, Wildeve and, above all, Eustacia are identified as Promethean figures. Consumed in the flames of their own passion and in effect defeated by their own aggressive humanity, they stand in opposition to Thomasin, Diggory, and the modest members of the peasant community who are more reluctant to play with fire and to invite the retribution of jealous gods.[7]

The Promethean and classical analogy is not of course sustained throughout. The inspiration of the serial novelist is intermittent, tends to flag and falter.[8] Hardy sometimes shifts his focus from the classical to the Elizabethan: at the scene of Mrs. Yeobright's death, for example, Egdon Heath suddenly suggests the landscape of *King Lear;* and when the indignant husband melodramatically confronts the erring wife, the scene suggests a domestic nineteenth-century notion of Jacobean grand drama. Even more crucially, the characters and incidents and scenes are not always equal to their heroic analogues; and when this is the case, the classical frame of reference merely serves to expose their insufficiency. The analogy with Oedipus, for example, far from celebrating the image of Clym Yeobright, merely indicates how appallingly far short of the tragic king he really falls.

For the most part, however, the major imagery of the novel is equal to its formidable frame of reference. Egdon Heath eventually connotes much more than the provincial landscape it denotes: it is a stage grand enough to bear the weight of gods and heroes; more specifically, it is Tartarus, the ancient underworld of the fallen Titans; and more specifically still, it is the prison-house of Prometheus, the fire-bearing benefactor of mankind. Similarly, Eustacia Vye is more than just another of Hardy's foreign and slightly spoiled aristocratic girls impatient of their dreary confinement in the provinces: she is the reincarnation not, perhaps, of any specific heroine of classical tragedy but, certainly, of the "idea" of such a heroine; and her kinship is, in this sense, more with Clytemnestra and Antigone than with Felice Charmond and Lucetta La Sueur. Moreover, the action of *The Return of the Native,* which is perhaps intrinsically less an action of antique nobility and grandeur than a domestic action peculiar to ballad and pastoral romance, is placed in a medium of analogy, a frame of reference, that creates an illusion of antique nobility and grandeur. Whereas the larger classical frame of reference creates an heroic context in which the local elements of the narrative achieve by analogy a measure of status and dignity, the Promethean frame of reference defines in more specific terms the evaluating of transvaluating context.

In the last analysis, then, the artistic unity and coherence of the novel do not depend on those purely external features of form and structure represented by the preservation of the unities and the organization in five "acts." They depend, rather, on the application of a significant frame of reference and on the activity of a meaningful pattern of images. In this sense the novel obeys not so much the architectural concept of form favored by the Greek dramatists as the musical or poetic—i.e., less clearly rational—concept of form favored by modern experimenters in prose fiction. Consciously or unconsciously, Hardy contrived in *The Return of the Native* that technique of spatialization which has been described as the twentieth century's particular contribution to the form of the novel.[9]

Notes

1. Thomas Hardy, *The Return of the Native*, Harper's Modern Classics (New York, 1922), p. 197. All page references, henceforward to be incorporated in the text, will be to this volume. The italics in the passages dealing with Hardy's fire imagery are, of course, mine.

2. Eustacia's moods are said to recall "the march in 'Athalie' " (p. 76).

3. Florence Hardy, *The Later Years of Thomas Hardy* (New York, 1930), p. 235.

4. See Hardy's footnote (p. 473) disclaiming responsibility for the sixth book.

5. Hardy managed only once, perhaps, and that was in the making of *The Mayor of Casterbridge*, to approximate the conditions of traditional tragedy. See John Paterson, "*The Mayor of Casterbridge* as Tragedy," *Victorian Studies*, III (December 1959), 151–172.

6. In establishing his heroic context, Hardy evoked the antiquity of the Celts and Hebrews as well as that of the Greeks. The classical allusions, however, far outnumber the Celtic and Hebraic.

7. Hardy tended up to a certain point to see all men as Promethean martyrs. Certainly, Diggory's red color would suggest that only the middleclass apotheosis enforced by the extraneous Book Sixth kept him out of the company of the defeated romantics: Clym, Eustacia, Wildeve and Mrs. Yeobright. And our first glimpse of the country-folk is of an almost demoniacal crew dancing about an impious bonfire. In the end, however, they are, like Thomasin, fully adjusted to the limitations of the human condition and hence untouched by the ecstasies and frustrations of the Promethean passion.

8. A study of the manuscript and variant editions does indicate, however, that Hardy was not wholly unaware of this sensitive inner movement of the novel. See John Paterson, *The Making of* The Return of the Native, University of California Publications, English Studies, No. 19 (Berkeley, 1960), Ch. V.

9. Joseph Frank, "Spatial Form in Modern Literature," in *Critiques and Essays in Criticism*, ed. Robert Wooster Stallman (New York, 1949), pp. 315–328.

The Buried Giant of Egdon Heath

Avrom Fleishman*

> I tell of Giants from times forgotten,
> Those who fed me in former days. . . .
>
> —Völuspa Saga

> Agog and magog and the round of them agrog. To the continuation of
> that celebration until Hanandhunigan's extermination!
>
> —Finnegans Wake

One would search long for a commentator on *The Return of the Native* who has failed to locate the story of Clym Yeobright and Eustacia Vye in the elaborated space of its landscape. Still it may be said that Egdon Heath has not been recognized as a figure in its own right—in both narrative senses of "figure," as person and as trope. One of the closest observers of the novel, John Paterson, has listed some of the heath's associations: ". . . it is a stage grand enough to bear the weight of gods and heroes; more specifically, still, it is the prison-house of Prometheus, the fire-bearing benefactor of mankind."[1] Paterson and others have supported such identifications by quoting the novel's repeated attribution of Promethean characteristics to the major characters. Hardy is never one to make his classical allusions evasively; the demonic rebelliousness of Eustacia and the bonded martyrdom of Clym are steadily projected upon the heath in the mode of scenic amplification. Yet the felt connection between the human actors and their inanimate setting exceeds the scope of metonymic associations like the scene-act ratio of Kenneth Burke. The ruling passions of the protagonists in *The Return* and the awesome powers of the heath need to be treated as forces of a like nature— the heath manifesting the same impulses as do the fictional characters.

To return to the setting of Hardy's first major novel is to seize his imagination at an originative position, where his sense of the past and his complex feelings about modern life intersected at a place with which he identified himself. Throughout his career, Hardy was inclined to express his strong response to the history-laden landscape of his shire in images of a special kind—special, that is, when compared with those of other Victorian novelists but commonplace in the tradition of local observers with a bent for narrative explanation. He was born, it will be recalled, in a cottage on the edge of the fourteen miles or so of high ground that has come to be identified with Egdon Heath, and he built his home, Max Gate, near its southwest flank five years after writing *The Return*.[2] In 1878, the year the novel was published, the Folk-Lore Society was founded in London, and at about this date Hardy joined the Dorset Natural History and Antiquarian Field Club. To the latter he also delivered a paper on "Some Romano-British Relics Found at Max Gate, Dorchester"[3]—found, that is, during the digging of

*Reprinted from *Fiction and the Ways of Knowing: Essays on British Novels*. © 1978 by the University of Texas Press. By permission of the author and the publisher.

foundations for his house. These delvings in the earth encouraged Hardy in a long series of reflections on the presence underfoot of a many-layered past: beginning as early as the passage in *The Return* on Clym's attendance at the opening of a barrow (book III, chapter iii); continuing with the account of unearthed Roman skeletons in *The Mayor of Casterbridge* (chapter xi); and developing a fine blend of fascination and detachment in poems like "The Roman Gravemounds" and "The Clasped Skeletons."

The sense of the past, it has been abundantly demonstrated, touches Hardy's work at innumerable points, but one may by isolated for the present discussion: his adumbration of an animate (or once-animate) being dormant in the earth, whether in the form of a buried skeleton incarnating the ghosts of the past, or of a quasi-human figure underlying or constituting certain topographical features (usually hills), or of a *genius loci* residing not in an aerial or other evanescent medium but in the soil of the place itself. It will be seen that some such preternatural beliefs are at work amid the rationalist skepticism which Hardy tried to maintain and that, while his own beliefs are not to be equated with those of the peasants in his tales, his absorption in them resembles the intellectual sympathy which modern anthropologists and folklorists have been recommending.

The prime instances of buried figures in the Hardy country are, quite naturally, those associated with a number of massive formations which surpass anything comparable in the southwest—the region of England perhaps most densely populated by ancient remains. Foremost is Maiden Castle, a Celtic hillfort a few miles south of Dorchester, which Hardy described as "an enormous many-limbed organism of an antediluvian time . . . lying lifeless, and covered with a thin green cloth, which hides its substance, while revealing its contour."[4] Comparable in fame and grandeur is the Cerne Abbas giant, with his club and explicit phallus, on a hill seven miles north of Dorchester in a region Hardy favored for his rambles; it is mentioned in *Tess of the d'Urbervilles* and other writings, most saliently when described by the local peasantry in *The Dynasts* as a malevolent ogre, comparable to Napoleon.[5]

Besides those and other gigantic erections in the vicinity, like Stonehenge, additional outcroppings of the land contour Hardy's writings. In a poem titled "The Moth-Signal," specifically set on Egdon Heath and reminiscent of an incident in *The Return*, the waywardness of modern domestic life is seen from the perspective of a dweller in the earth: "Then grinned the Ancient Briton / From the tumulus treed with pine: / 'So, hearts are thwartly smitten / In these days as in mine!' "[6] Hardy takes up the point of view of an inhabitant of the heath in a more personal way in another poem, "A Meeting with Despair" (noted in the manuscript as set on Egdon Heath):

> As evening shaped I found me on a moor
>   Sight shunned to entertain:
> The black lean land, of featureless contour,
>   Was like a tract in pain.

"This scene, like my own life," I said, "is one
    Where many glooms abide;
Toned by its fortune to a deadly dun—
    Lightless on every side."

.   .   .   .

Against the horizon's dim-discernèd wheel
    A form rose, strange of mould;
That he was hideous, hopeless, I could feel
    Rather than could behold.

Although Hardy metaphorically identifies the pattern and tone of his life with the heath's, he resists the insinuations of the apparition—named "Despair" in the title but referred to only as "the Thing" in the poem itself—so as to argue that the glowing sunset portends better prospects for the future. In a voice we recognize as that of the stupid giant of fairy tales, his interlocutor replies, "Yea—but await awhile! . . . Ho-ho!—/ Now look aloft and see!" More striking, perhaps, than either the poem's finale (with the loss of light and portent of defeat) or the similarities between its treatment of Egdon Heath and the novel's is the encounter with an abiding presence there—the black lean land, featureless, in pain, from which a hideous, hopeless form arises.

These poems call to mind others in which one of the most familiar features of Hardy's style, personification, is employed in its mode of gigantism. The best-known instance of this trope is found in "The Darkling Thrush": "The land's sharp features seemed to be / The Century's corpse outleant. . . ." In the periodical publication of the poem, its original title emphasized this figure rather than the thrush: "By the Century's Death-bed" enforces the idea not simply of a localized spirit but of the entire earth as a body suffering a secular decline. A more sharply focused version of this image occurs in the poem "By the Earth's Corpse" (from the same volume as "The Darkling Thrush"), in which Time and "the Lord" conduct a dialogue on the themes of guilt and repetition, while placed like mourners near "this globe, now cold / As lunar land and sea," at some future time "when flesh / And herb but fossils be, / And, all extinct, their piteous dust / Revolves obliviously. . . ."

The most highly developed vision of the earth as an organic, vaguely human being is, however, that of *The Dynasts*. A stage direction of the "Fore Scene" is justly famous for its panoramic sweep, anticipating (but still surpassing) the movement of the camera eye in epically scaled movies: "The nether sky opens, and Europe is disclosed as a prone and emaciated figure, the Alps shaping like a backbone, and the branching mountain-chains like ribs, the peninsular plateau of Spain forming a head. . . . The point of view then sinks downwards through space, and draws near to the surface of the perturbed countries, where the peoples, distressed by events which they did not cause, are seen writhing, crawling, heaving, and vibrating in their various cities and nationalities." With the return to this vision in the "After Scene," Europe is "beheld again as a prone and emaciated figure. . . . The lowlands look like a grey-green garment half-thrown off, and the sea around like a disturbed bed on which the figure lies." In this instance, human forms in the mass join with geographical features to create the image of a total organism: the earth itself (or its European portion) as a giant, going through the stages of awakening, struggle, and exhaustion—a composite being living out the disturbances and sufferings of humankind.

Is it this (or a related) giant who confronts the reader from the title of the opening chapter of *The Return*: "A Face on which Time makes but Little Impression"? The rhetoric of the so-called pathetic fallacy suggests that it is a creature on the scale of the earth: it "wore the appearance of an instalment of night" and, reciprocally, "the face of the heath by its mere complexion added half an hour to evening."[7] Not only are vital reflexes, human apparel, and personal physiognomy suggested, but the sustained comparison of Egdon Heath and mankind is raised from mere analogy to essential identity: "It was at present a place perfectly accordant with man's nature—neither ghastly, hateful, nor ugly: neither commonplace, unmeaning, nor tame; but, like man, slighted and enduring; and withal singularly colossal and mysterious in its swarthy monotony. As with some persons who have long lived apart, solitude seemed to look out of its countenance. It had a lonely face, suggesting tragical possibilities" (I, i, 35). It is on the basis of this profound identity that the epithets used for the heath come to resonate like personal designations: "Haggard Egdon," "the untameable, Ishmaelitish thing that Egdon now was," "the people changed, yet Egdon remained." In the most pathetic of these characterizations, the place is defined in relation to other natural forces in a style usually reserved for romantic fiction: "Then Egdon was aroused to reciprocity; for the storm was its lover, and the wind its friend." But the role hardly suits a figure that has emerged as not merely humanized but on a larger-than-individual scale: "singularly colossal and mysterious in its swarthy monotony." Such a colossus can be a hero only of a special sort.

In inventing the name itself, Hardy seems to have had in mind not a place-name but a personal one. Its closest analogue is a forename: *Egbert*, from Old English *ecg* ("sword") and *bryght* ("bright")—the latter term also appearing in the chief surname used in the novel. *Egdon* would be its derivable opposite: the second syllable is equivalent to *dun*, the word used since Anglo-Saxon times to describe the natural shades of landscape, animals, and atmosphere in a dull, brown grey range. (But compare the Celtic name of Maiden Castle: *mai dun* ["strong hill"].) Etymology resolves nothing, but this name goes beyond the expansive suggestiveness of well-wrought place-names in fiction, encouraging instead the identification of a personal presence by a favored technique of characterization.

If these two processes are indeed comparable—if a somewhat amorphous terrain is presented here in the manner in which fictional characters are conventionally introduced—we shall have to revise our expectations of the role of landscape in this novel more radically than we may be prepared to do. Landscape is not satisfied to act in *The Return of the Native* as a background, with human subjects in the foreground (although some positioning of people against a background of natural elements is at work, e.g., in the chapter entitled "The Figure against the Sky"). Instead, Egdon Heath becomes one of the principal agents of the action, a protagonist in the classical sense of the dramatic actor, and probably the most memorable figure to emerge from the events. The title of the novel has been given some new turns in recent criticism, so as to widen its reference beyond the donnée of Clym's return to Wessex.[8] If its individual implications are taken seriously, the title refers somewhat sardonically to Clym's return to the native state in the course of the action; it also suggests more broadly the heath's renewed prominence in the life of the characters and of the modern age generally. "The Return of the Native" would name, then, a story about Egdon Heath.

The operation of these narrative traits makes the term "personification" no longer adequate to describe the process by which Egdon Heath is generated by the text. When natural categories are fixed, one may speak about the ascription of human characteristics to inanimate beings or about the representation of an abstract or other impersonal entity in human terms. But Egdon is not so clear-cut: it is never given as entirely on one side of the animate/inanimate polarity before being assimilated to the other. Even in the opening chapter, the metaphoric expressions by which it is rendered human are immediately posited as literal (or as leading to literal statements about the heath's role in human psychology): "Then [in storms, etc.] it became the home of strange phantoms; and it was found to be the hitherto unrecognized original of those wild regions of obscurity which are vaguely felt to be compassing us about in midnight dreams of flight and disaster, and are never thought of after the dream till revived by scenes like this" (I, i, 35). Without drawing conclusions about Hardy's version of the unconscious, we find his prose moving from the metaphoric level (movement of storms ‖ movement of phantoms), to statements that posit the heath as the original model of dream landscapes, to a final suggestion of its function as a permanent index of the unconscious "regions" of the mind itself. So steadily cumulative is this assimilation of the heath to the animate level that toward the close of the novel, as intensity of style mounts in tempo with intensity of action, we are prepared to take in stride such passages as this: "Skirting the pool [Eustacia] followed the path towards Rainbarrow, occasionally stumbling over twisted furze-roots, tufts of rushes, or oozing lumps of fleshy fungi, which at this season lay scattered about the heath like the rotten liver and lungs of some colossal animal" (V, vii, 370). While it is Eustacia who is stumbling toward her death, it is the heath that is seen here as a dismembered giant—neither clearly human nor, as Lawrence thought, merely bestial but a "colossal animal" who is martyred and distributed in a spectacular way.

While the interconnections of the animate and the inanimate must be deduced from the rhetorical modes of the opening chapter, later passages state their inherent identity in the heath with some urgency. The chief of these occurs in the first description of Eustacia Vye:

> There the form stood, motionless as the hill beneath. Above the plain rose the hill, above the hill rose the barrow, and above the barrow rose the figure. Above the figure was nothing that could be mapped elsewhere than on a celestial globe.
>
> Such a perfect, delicate, and necessary finish did the figure give to the dark pile of hills that it seemed to be the only obvious justification of their outline. Without it, there was the dome without the lantern; with it the architectural demands of the mass were satisfied. The scene was strangely homogeneous, in that the vale, the upland, the barrow, and the figure above it amounted only to unity. Looking at this or that member of the group was not observing a complete thing, but a fraction of a thing. (I, ii, 41)

Hardy employs the term "organic" in the next sentence to describe the internal relations of the "entire motionless structure"; we may apply it equally to the tenor of his thinking in this passage. Although the human figure is to be regarded esthetically as a "necessary finish" and a satisfaction of an "architectural" demand, it is more fundamentally a "fraction" of a larger "unity." Nor is the heath complete without the person: it needs it as its "obvious justification," to become a "homogeneous" being in its own right. The text speaks of this organic unity of the human and the nonhuman "members" of Egdon Heath as "a thing" and elsewhere adds, "a thing majestic without severity, impressive without showiness, emphatic in its admonitions, grand in its simplicity"(I, i, 34).

Although Eustacia is most striking in her unwilling assimilation into Egdon Heath, other characters exhibit a spectrum of possible relations to it, ranging from identification to detachment. Although the gigantic "thing" takes in both human beings and the heath, there are a number of possible modes of integration, which various characters explore. The peasants live in wary observance of the land and its seasons, but their limited mentalities are none too gently satirized in Hardy's folkish chapters. The reddleman, Diggory Venn, shows himself adroit not only in the world of commercial and (eventually) erotic competition but is especially competent among the highways and byways of the heath. (It is noteworthy that he gets no particular credit for this intimacy with the heath, as measured by the conventions of heroic stature; given Hardy's view of him as an "isolated and weird character"—in the "Author's Note" of 1912—he is scarcely ennobled by his numerous displays of omnicompetence.) It is Clym who displays the most complex relation to the heath, being the one who exercises a series of considered choices in the matter. In his first characterization, his constitution or generation by the place is stressed: "If any one knew the heath well it was Clym. He was permeated with its scenes, with its substance, and with its odours. He might be said to be its product" (III, ii, 197). At the end of his series of ideological shifts and personal misfortunes, he stands before the heath in an alien position, as of one face impervious to another: ". . . there was only the imperturbable countenance of the heath, which, having defied the cataclysmal onsets of centuries, reduced to insignificance by its seamed and antique features the wildest turmoil of a single man" (V, ii, 342). But the most extreme separation from the heath—indistinguishable from a kind of rationalistic stupidity—is represented by the pragmatic objectivity of Thomasin Yeobright: ". . . Egdon in the mass was no monster whatever, but impersonal open ground. Her fears of the place were rational, her dislikes of its worst moods reasonable" (V, viii, 380).

Despite their differences, the characters have a common connection with the heath, a unity of fate that is consistently figured in allusions to Prometheus: "Every night [the heath's] Titanic form seemed to await something; but it had waited thus, unmoved, during so many centuries, through the crises of so many things, that it could only be imagined to await one last crisis—the final overthrow" (I, i, 34). The iconography of Prometheus chained to a mountain in the Caucasus is strikingly transmuted in this and similar passages: the *scene* of suffering becomes the sufferer (Egdon is not Caucasian but Titanic), while at least part of the demigod's character is ascribed to the land itself in its "unmoved" martyrdom. Yet the myth's primary orientation toward apocalypse (the final overthrow of Zeus) is, as we shall see, fully employed in *The Return*.

The heath's Promethean, long-suffering form of resistance is picked up in the characterization of the human actors but is resourcefully applied as a differentiating factor. The peasants' lighting of fires to celebrate Guy Fawkes Day, although localized as a modern British survival of the ritual death and rebirth of the year, is seen as the expression of a universal need: "Moreover to light a fire is the instinctive and resistant act of man when, at the winter ingress, the curfew is sounded throughout Nature. It indicates a spontaneous, Promethean rebelliousness against the fiat that this recurrent season shall bring foul times, cold darkness, misery and death. Black chaos comes, and the fettered gods of the earth say, Let there be light" (I, iii, 45). Here humans, heath, and Titans are seen on the same side, resisting—or at least protesting—an imposition from without, the fiat of a being or realm representing black chaos, winter, and death. Humanity joins with the land itself in "Promethean rebelliousness," and it is with one voice that they register their counterfiat; theirs is the voice of the "fettered gods" or Titans, which proclaims light—a biblical equivalent for the Promethean fire that is the subject of this passage.

The chief characters are, however, subtly distinguished in their articulations of this rebellion and thus in their associations with the band of "fettered gods." Eustacia is described from the first in terms derived from the preceding passage: "Egdon was her Hades, and since coming there she had imbibed much of what was dark in its tone, though inwardly and eternally unreconciled thereto. Her appearance accorded well with this smouldering rebelliousness. . . . A true Tartarean dignity sat upon her brow . . ." (I, vii, 94).

The term found in both passages, "rebelliousness," is linked to its consequences of banishment or living burial, whether of humans in Hades or of
Titans in Tartarus (the variability of mythological traditions is exploited here
to make these roughly equivalent terms for confinement in the earth). It is
notable that this passage begins by emphasizing Eustacia's unwilling bondage in Egdon, the setting of her unsatisfactory station in life, but it gradually
identifies her with the heath insofar as the latter, too, is unreconciled to its
bound condition under the fiat of the ruling gods.[9]

Precisely the opposite shift occurs in the course of Clym's characterization: beginning as one fully at home on the heath—"its product"—he becomes so thoroughly acclimated in his return to the soil that he renounces
rebelliousness: "Now, don't you suppose, my inexperienced girl, that I cannot rebel, in high Promethean fashion, against the gods and fate as well as
you. I have felt more steam and smoke of that sort than you have ever heard
of. But the more I see of life the more do I perceive that there is nothing
particularly great in its greatest walks, and therefore nothing particularly
small in mine of furze-cutting" (IV, ii, 276–277). Clym's liberal renunciation
of the Promethean stance is part of an explicit cultural theme in the novel,
concerned with the vulnerability of the modern mind by virtue of its skeptical intelligence, its loss of traditional, organizing mythologies (a loss and a
vulnerability in which Hardy felt himself implicated). But Clym's career also
involves a break with the creaturely tendency to rebellion against earthbound suffering, a separation from the Titanic "fettered gods" with whom
Eustacia, involuntarily, associates herself. And it is this loss of Promethean
vision that is his true undoing, for he sees "nothing particularly great in
[life's] greatest walks" or, by the same token, in the heath's.

Having detected the signs of a giant figure buried in the verbal integu-
ment of *The Return*, noted its provenance in Hardy's imaginings of his native
place, and considered its shadowy relations with the characters of the drama,
what can we say of the wider significance of this massive presence? The
range of relevant contexts extends to the margins of the human imagination,
for giants have populated not only folk and fairy tales, cosmogonies and
epics, but also topographical prominences the world over. It is evident that
Hardy would have known the Greek versions of this mythology, as well as its
variants among the English Romantic poets; it is perhaps less known that he
was attentive to local legends accounting for curious outcroppings by tales of
giants buried or sleeping in the land. Hardy recorded one such topographical
fable in his notebook: "The Legend of the Cerne Giant. He threatened to
descend upon Cerne and to ravish all the young maidens on a particular
night and to kill the young men next day. Goaded to desperate courage they
waylaid and killed him, afterwards cutting his effigy on the hill. He lived
somewhere up in the hills, was waited on by wild animals and used to steal
the farmers' sheep, eating one a day. The *Giant's Head Inn* nearby evidently
related to the tradition."[10] This explanatory tale registers what may be called

the subdued-ogre variant of topographical gigantism but, as this is only one in a range of possibilities, a brief review of the alternatives will suggest a need for closer inspection if we are to single out the special face of Egdon Heath.

In contrast to the subdued ogre, the Titan lore with which Egdon Heath is associated stands in a tradition of proto- or prohuman giants reaching back to classical myth and descending to Hardy by way of Aeschylus and Shelley. Unlike the dead and buried giant whose form is left in the shape of hills or in markings upon them, the bound and tortured colossus of the Promethean strain is often placed within caves or in the rock face—the better to express his continued protests in the form of rumblings, quakes, and other seismic phenomena. While the subdued ogre testifies to past victories by humanity, or at least by the local inhabitants, the bound Titan testifies to the present dominance of inimical powers and encourages continued but passive resistance to them. Hardy stands with his poetic master Shelley in removing the Titanic will from Aeschylus' mythic drama—making outspoken resistance like Eustacia's futile while establishing Egdon Heath as a figure of patient though brooding endurance.

A further extension of this long-suffering martyr to earthbound existence lies in a train of apocalyptic heroes of folk tales and legendary history around the earth. This figure is known to the Aarne-Thompson motif index under the rubrics "Culture hero still lives," "Culture hero asleep in mountain," and "Culture hero's expected return."[11] Examples may be drawn from history (Charlemagne asleep within the Unterberg), religion (Balder and a host of other deities), or a mixture of history and myth (Arthur being the foremost example, one who is at home in the west of England). Neither dead and buried nor bound and rumbling, the culture hero looks to the promised future, and his legends partake of a popular apocalyptic impulse independent of religious eschatology. Common to these figures is their human scale; although invested with supernatural graces, they avoid the grotesquerie of gigantic expansion. Yet they are akin to the buried giants in their generalized potentiality: it is man himself who lies sleeping but latently liberated in these tales. Moreover, in some of his most spectacular variants, this sleeping savior is localized not merely under a hill or at a place but within an entire landscape: as Blake's Albion is the incarnation not merely of a national leader but of the land itself and the race's destiny.

Beyond Hardy's interest in topographical legends and primordial rituals, he was inevitably exposed to giant figures in the course of his lifelong absorption in the Romantic poets. It is well known that he considered Shelley "our most marvellous lyrist"[12] and quoted or alluded to his work perhaps more often than to any other, barring the Bible and Shakespeare. Although he devoted lavish encomiums to several favorite lyrics, Hardy clearly found *Prometheus Unbound* more to his fictional purpose. While it is relatively unrewarding to retrace the specific transactions with that epic-drama in *The Return*'s Promethean imagery, there are important elements of Shelley's poetic mythology in Hardy's world view. Most striking in the action of both poem and novel is the appearance of the earth itself as a force in human destiny: for Shelley, this force is associated with the mysterious role of the earth-dwelling giant, Demogorgon, while for Hardy it is localized in Egdon Heath. The two are not the same, nor do they entail fully commensurate ideas of fate or necessity, but they are individualized figures of natural power abiding in the earth, with enormous regenerative potential. Indeed, the ambivalent reactions of awe and fascination generated by Demogorgon's gross majesty are akin to those inspired by Egdon's characterization.

Even more may be suggested, if without perfect assurance: the prescientific geological theories which have been shown to be at work behind Shelley's phrase "the breathing earth,"[13] as well as other references to animate underground expressions of the human condition, may have a place in the substructure of Hardy's setting. Earl Wasserman's studies of the poem's complex imagery of volcanism, earthquakes, and other geological processes reveal an ambiguity in Shelley's use of the figure which is matched in Hardy: ". . . the single dominant image of the breathing earth symbolizes such opposite values as the volcanic disordering of the earth by Prometheus' curse and enchainment and also the revolutionary eruption that removes Jupiter. . . . Volcanoes are catastrophic, but they also can stir the lethargic earth to action and to new forms." This mixture of rocklike, impervious, but restive power, subdued to long endurance yet rancorous in its arrested potentiality—along with quirky manifestations of smoldering hostility and a threat of direr disturbances—makes up the heroic stature of Shelley's earth demon and Hardy's heath. In both writers, the pathetic and the promising elements of the human condition are attached to the figures of giants; for Shelley, Prometheus and Demogorgon convey humanity's spiritual bondage and potential liberation; for Hardy, Egdon Heath combines the exhalations of age-old suffering and the expectancy of long-looked-for awakening: "The sombre stretch of rounds and hollows seemed to rise and meet the evening gloom in pure sympathy, the heath exhaling darkness as rapidly as the heavens precipitated it. . . . The place became full of a watchful intentness now; for when other things sank brooding to sleep the heath appeared slowly to awake and listen" (I, i, 33–34).

The common fund of traditional lore for both conceptions lies in the classical mythology and localized legends of the Titans. Whether associated with Prometheus or Demogorgon,[14] whether connected with volcanoes and earthquakes or the formation of islands and mountain ranges, the Titans play a vigorous role both in Romantic poetry and in Hardy's latter-day version of its themes. The long theomachy of the Olympians and the Titans is a malleable political paradigm and has been adapted to national interests far beyond its Greek source; most germane for English myth makers is the exiling of the defeated deities not to subterranean Tartarus but to an Atlantic island. The inevitable association of one of their number, Atlas, not only with the lost island of Atlantis but also with the British Isles[15] provides abundant opportunities for the poets to connect the origins of Britain with a primal act of cultural rebellion, an exiled condition, and a foretold apocalypse.

Blake was well informed of such imaginative possibilities and, while Hardy's involvement with Blake has yet to be adequately assessed, it is clear that his sense of Titanic powers at work and at rest beneath the soil of England is matched only by Blake's among the English poets. While Hardy carefully selects the Titanic features of his landscape—seeing, e.g., Rainbarrow as a "wart on an Atlantean brow" (I, ii, 41)—Blake works out the features of his Albion in spectacular detail:

> London is between his knees, its basements fourfold;
> His right foot stretches to the sea on Dover cliffs, his heel
> On Canterbury's ruins; his right hand covers lofty Wales,
> His left Scotland; . . .
>
> .   .   .   .
>
> He views Jerusalem & Babylon, his tears flow down,
> He mov'd his right foot to Cornwall, his left to the Rocks of Bognor.
> He strove to rise to walk into the Deep, but strength failing
> Forbad, & down with dreadful groans he sunk upon his Couch
> In moony Beulah. . . .[16]

Lest there be any doubt about Blake's identification of Albion with a Titanic source, he makes this point explicit in the "Descriptive Catalogue" to his paintings, with regard to the lost "Ancient Britons": "The giant Albion, was Patriarch of the Atlantic; he is the Atlas of the Greeks, one of those the Greeks called Titans." And again in "A Vision of the Last Judgment": "He is Albion, our Ancestor, patriarch of the Atlantic Continent, whose History Preceded that of the Hebrews & in whose Sleep, or Chaos, Creation began. . . ." The generation of Blake's ideas from among the syncretic mythographers and their complex developments in the fabric of his poetry are matters to be followed up in other commentaries.[17] But we can see in his poetic mythology and Hardy's a common concern to identify the sources not only of the present nation but of the land itself with a Titanic giant whose traces still lie open to inspection in the formations of the soil of England.

What emerges from these poetic and fictional versions of Britain's antediluvian history is a pattern of original settlement by gigantic creatures, following defeat and exile; their withdrawal, whether from renewed defeat or other calamity, into the earth (a significant variation on most myths of chthonic ancestors, who emerge *from* the native soil); and their dormant persistence under the feet of the present inhabitants, while awaiting a threatened cataclysm and possible restoration. Although human fate is inextricably bound up with the primal structures of the land and its speculative inhabitants, their restoration has no simple issue; the rising of the sleeping giants by no means guarantees a permanent liberation from their common oppression—and may portend the opposite. Thus Blake names one of the sons of Albion as Hylé (Greek for primal matter) and identifies him with Gog, taken in the biblical sense of the baser form of man.[18] Though *Jerusalem*'s climactic awakening of the sleeping giant, Albion, redeems all his sons in a general easement, the term Gog is again used to suggest that the terrible aspect of humanity's gigantism can never finally be put down. As Frye explains, "if behind the Bible there is the memory of an age of murderous ogres who perished in a stench of burning flesh, then in front of it there is an apprehension of a returning power of gigantic self-destruction. The former survives in the Bible as the Covering Cherub; the latter is portrayed as the giants Gog and Magog who return with the full power of darkness after the millennium."[19]

Sifting through his web of folklore—both popular and poetic, markedly British and within Hardy's favorite range of reading—which of the strains of gigantism can be found uppermost in *The Return*? It is clear that the first type, the subdued ogre, is furthest from prominence, although Egdon has its baleful features; Hardy is least interested in celebrating humanity's past triumphs over chthonic powers in nature, for his view of both emphasizes their unity. The bound Titan, on the other hand, is the figure most obvious in the language of the text, and it seems evident that Hardy establishes in the Titanic heath the burden of a mankind forced to submit to an order of things that can only be explained (if it can be explained at all) as deriving from an arbitrary, if not a malevolent, authority. Yet space should be made for the third type of giant, not so much rebellious as long-suffering, dormant but expectant, who is implicated in the common fate of man and nature yet looks forward to an ultimate liberation.

In transforming *The Return* from the "ballad and pastoral romance" elements of its "Ur-novel,"[20] Hardy was applying to a more profound level of folklore, where reside the popular imaginings of origin, authority, and apocalypse which are given scope in giant lore. And, in effecting a "classical transvaluation" into the tragic mode, Hardy was drawing on a potentiality in Aeschylus which inspired Shelley, perhaps too avidly, in his *Prometheus*: the opening to the future which inspires hope. Egdon Heath carries, among its many resonances of power and endurance, a vibration not so much stoical as regenerative and creative—whatever the failures of its denizens to make much of their connections with it. This potentiality need not be—indeed resists being—specifically tied to historical events, either past revolutions or future ones.[21] In underscoring the action of *The Return* with traces of apocalyptic promise, Hardy adds to a long tradition of English poetic figures—from Blake's, to Yeats' Rocky Face and Thomas' White Giant,[22] who mark the intimations of aeonian change in the contours of the land.[23]

Notes

1. "The 'Poetics' of *The Return of the Native*," *Modern Fiction Studies* VI (1960): 214; Paterson has also published a monograph on the composition of the novel: *The Making of The Return of the Native*, University of California English Studies, no. 19 (Berkeley and Los An-

geles, 1960). The folkloric aspects of the novel have been recognized at least since Ruth A. Firor's *Folkways in Thomas Hardy* (Philadelphia and London, 1931), esp. pp. 265–268.

2. For a map that shows these positions clearly, see F. E. Halliday, *Thomas Hardy: His Life and Work* (New York, 1972), facing the acknowledgments page. More detailed maps of the region are to be found in F. B. Pinion, *A Hardy Companion: A Guide to the Works of Thomas Hardy and Their Background* (London, New York, etc., 1968), pp. 313, 411 ff. Hardy's own sketch map of the fictional heath is reprinted in many editions.

3. The paper is reprinted in *Thomas Hardy's Personal Writings: Prefaces, Literary Opinions, Reminiscences*, ed. Harold Orel (Lawrence, Kan., London, etc., 1966), pp. 191–195; in this volume, see also "Shall Stonehenge Go?" "Maumbury Ring," and other pieces on Dorsetshire antiquities. Also see Richard M. Dorson, *The British Folklorists: A History* (Chicago and London, 1968), pp. 202 ff., for the vigorous activity in folklore and mythological studies during the period of Hardy's creation of a virtual county history in his fiction.

4. "A Tryst at an Ancient Earthwork," in *A Changed Man and Other Tales* (Wessex edition [London, 1912 ff.], vol. XVIII, p. 174). For a succinct description of Maiden Castle, see *Atlas of Ancient Archeology*, ed. Jacquetta Hawkes (London, New York, etc., 1974), p. 34.

5. The story is told in part I, act II, scene v, in a setting specified as "Rainbarrows' Beacon, Egdon Heath."

6. *Collected Poems of Thomas Hardy* (New York, 1964), p. 370; other quotations of the poetry are from this edition.

7. I quote the New Wessex edition (London, 1974) as most generally available (although not a definitive text), by book, chapter, and page numbers, parenthetically. The present quotation is from bk. I, chap. i, p. 33.

8. Perry Meisel's *Thomas Hardy: The Return of the Repressed: A Study of the Major Fiction* (New York and London, 1972) makes its Freudian point by its very title; also, for references to the Promethean theme, see p. 78.

9. Cf. J. Hillis Miller, *Thomas Hardy: Distance and Desire* (Cambridge, Mass., 1970), p. 91: "The heath is neither a character in itself nor merely a dark background against which the action takes place. The heath is rather the embodiment of certain ways in which human beings may exist. Diggory Venn and Eustacia Vye rise out of the heath as versions of two of these ways, Diggory the detached waiting and watching expressed by the heath, Eustacia the tragical possibilities of violence and infinite longing the heath contains."

10. *Thomas Hardy's Notebooks* . . ., ed. Evelyn Hardy (New York, 1955), pp. 65–66; entry dated 12 September 1888. To this variant, compare the version recorded by the folklorist Gomme, reprinted in *A Dictionary of British Folk-tales in the English Language*, ed. Katherine M. Briggs (Bloomington, Ind., 1971), pt. B, vol. I, p. 611. Also see Robert Hunt's *Popular Romances of the West of England* . . . (London, 1865), an attractively presented collection of legends that Hardy may well have known, for it is close to his topographical interests. Its first section is "The Giants" and includes the story of Corineus and Gogmagog (to be discussed below), as well as tales of giant passions highly accordant with his fictional themes.

11. Stith Thompson, *Motif-Index of Folk Literature* . . . (Bloomington, Ind., 1955), vol. I, nos. A570, A580. For other instances directly related to Hardy's interests, see E. W. Baughman, *Type and Motif-Index of the Folktales of England and North America*, Indiana University Folklore Series, no. 20 (The Hague, 1966), under the same index numbers.

12. *The Life of Thomas Hardy: 1840—1928*, by Florence E. Hardy [*sic*] (London, etc., 1965 [1928; 1930]), p. 17. For other references to and quotations from Shelley in Hardy's works, see Pinion, pp. 213–214.

13. *Prometheus Unbound*, II, ii, 52. For a discussion of the geological and meteorological phenomena, see Earl R. Wasserman, *Shelley's Prometheus Unbound: A Critical Reading* (Baltimore, 1965), pp. 147 ff.; the subsequent quotation is from p. 163 (also included in his later *Shelley: A Critical Reading*).

14. Wasserman finds Demogorgon cast in the role of "Typhon and the other volcanic giants or Titans who, like Prometheus, rebelled against Jove" (*Shelley's* Prometheus Unbound, p. 159), but this by no means precludes his conventional identification with philosophical necessity or, as M. H. Abrams would claim, with "process."

15. Robert Graves, *The Greek Myths* (Harmondsworth, Eng., 1962 [1955]), I, 40 and 145–147.

16. *Milton*, bk. II, pl. 39; *Complete Writings of William Blake*, ed. Geoffrey Keynes (London, New York, and Toronto, 1966 [1957]), p. 531. The subsequent quotations are from pp. 578 and 609 of this edition.

17. See Edward B. Hungerford, *Shores of Darkness* (Cleveland and New York, 1963 [1941]), pp. 46 ff.; also Harold Bloom, *Blake's Apocalypse: A Study in Poetic Argument* (Garden City, N.Y., 1965 [1963]), p. 108.

18. *Jerusalem*, chap. iii, pl. 74, p. 715 (in the Keynes edition); cf. the penultimate plate of poem, where the "Triple Headed Gog-Magog Giant / of Albion" is again recalled, in the midst of a redemptive apocalypse.

19. *Fearful Symmetry: A Study of William Blake* (Boston, 1962 [1947]), p. 399. Gog and Magog, who combine elements of the legendary giant of hills and heaths, the dead and buried but ultimately to return hero, and the original British race—the earthborn and earthbound dwellers in the land—are known in English popular culture, though perhaps better in their London than their West Country representations. The first is a ubiquitous figure of the Western imagination, in time, place and cultural level—from the book of Genesis to Andrew Sinclair's recent novel, *Gog*. In ancient legends of Alexander the Great, Gog and Magog are his enemies and, once conquered, are sealed behind a wall in the Caucasus; indeed, Robert Graves has suggested by analogy the equation of Gog with Prometheus (*The White Goddess: A Historical Grammar of Poetic Myth* [London, 1962 (1948)], p. 237). But Gog's British fortunes seem more closely linked with his bad reputation in both the Old and New Testaments (Ezek. 38–39, Rev. 20), which colors his role in Cornish legend with connotations of the forces of Satan. When Spenser and Milton retell Geoffrey of Monmouth's story of Gog's and the other resident giants' defeat by the Trojan conquerors of England, the legend certifies the cultural triumph of a higher race over the autochthonous one (*The Faerie Queene*, II, x, 6–11; III, ix, 49–50; *The History of Britain . . .*, bk. I). Yet this morality has not prevented the giant statues of Gog and Magog in the Guildhall of London from being carried in procession on the Lord Mayor's Day (usually November 9, close on the Guy Fawkes' dying-and-reviving-year festivals enacted in *The Return*)—when they are not so much exhibits of conquered savages as impressive old friends. The most recent effort to recover Gog's English traces, T. C. Lethbridge's *Gogmagog: The Buried Gods* (London, 1957, pp. 10 ff., as this does not appear to be a scientifically verifiable investigation, it should be treated as suggestive, not decisive), describes his pattern found in the Gogmagog Hills of Cambridgeshire. In an expanded scene around the Cerne Abbas giant, Lethbridge detects a sacred combat for possession and renewal of the earth. In this conjectural interpretation, the male figure is both Gog and the Sun, the female is Magog and Epona (the ancient British horse goddess), and the other male participant is the demon of darkness, winter, and death—the archetypal antagonist of Frazerian fame.

20. Terms used in Paterson, *The Making of* The Return, esp. p. 167; for the next quoted phrase, see p. 164.

21. As in Derwent May's introduction to the New Wessex edition of the novel (pp. 14–15): "Egdon's 'Titanic' form, as Hardy more than once calls it, suggests first of all the brute, mindless strength of the earth-giants; but he does not leave the suggestion there. At times, he says, the heath, like the fallen Titans, seems to be waiting for what he ambiguously calls 'the final overthrow.' Revolution, in short, is in the air. We quickly associate the idea with much that the countrymen artlessly say [about the Napoleonic Wars]. . . . Even in the lost villages of Wessex, that unprecedented event in modern history, the French Revolution, has left its faint trace."

22. The latest entries in this line are Jeremy Hooker's volume of poems on the Cerne Abbas figure, *Soliloquies of a Chalk Giant* (London, 1974), and George Barker's "Dialogues of Gog and Magog," in *Dialogues, etc.* (London, 1976).

23. Although it has yet to be demonstrated that Hardy included Vico in his studies of history and mythology, he could have found in *The New Science* an imaginative interpretation of the giant figure much in accord with his own habits of thought. For Vico, the underlying principle in Promethean and other myths of chained or buried giants is connected with the origins of authority: "Authority was at first divine; the authority by which divinity appropriated to itself the few giants . . . by properly casting them into the depths and recesses of the caves under the mountains" (*The New Science*, trans. T. G. Bergin and M. H. Fisch [Ithaca, N.Y., 1948; Italian: 1725–1730], ¶ 369 f.). One may follow out in *The New Science* the process by which the giants came to check their bestial habits, learned to bury their dead in the mountains—where "enormous skulls and bones have been found and are still found"—and developed the "heroic education" and "poetic morals" which are Vico's terms for civilization. How Joyce took possession of this giant lore is well known; given his interests in repressive authority and latent liberation, Hardy might well have done so, too.

Middling Hardy Simon Gatrell*

Since the publication in 1912 of Hardy's *General Preface to the Novels and Poems*, which appeared in the first volume of the Wessex Edition, the history of the study of his novels has been (by and large) one of the acceptance of Hardy's own distinction between seven novels of character and environment which constitute the centre of his achievement, and seven other novels which are peripheral, experimental, trivial, or just downright bad. Richard Taylor, in his recent book *The Neglected Hardy*, has in some measure fixed this distinction, writing as he does of Hardy's "lesser novels"; it is a division that I find unjustifiable. If such a league-table approach to Hardy is inescapable—and it does have the novelist's sanction—then there must be a fresh valuation which recognizes that there is a middle category of Hardy novels, one that includes *Under the Greenwood Tree* as well as *The Trumpet-Major, Far from the Madding Crowd* as well as *Two on a Tower:* a group of novels in which Hardy is not aiming for the intensity and heroism of *Tess of the D'Urbervilles* or *The Mayor of Casterbridge*, but has different and equally valuable goals which are also more or less satisfactorily achieved.

Such a revaluation is properly the subject of a book rather than an essay, and here my aim is exploratory. The passage I wish to explore is that stretch of six rather lost years in Hardy's creative life from 1879 to 1884, which saw the publication of *The Trumpet Major, A Laodicean* and *Two on a Tower*, as well as one or two of Hardy's better short stories, including "Fellow-Townsmen" and "The Distracted Preacher"—a period which falls into the

*Reprinted from *Thomas Hardy Annual No. 4*, ed. Norman Page (London: Macmillan, 1986). Reprinted with permission by Macmillan, London and Basingstoke, and by Humanities Press, International, Inc., Atlantic Highlands, N.J.

middle of Hardy's fictional career, but in which he wrote none of the novels he later characterized as being "of character and environment." Yet there is at least one structural way in which these middle novels can be seen as part of the pattern that begins with *Under the Greenwood Tree* and ends with *Jude the Obscure*. It will not be controversial to propose that in *Under the Greenwood Tree* of 1872, *Far from the Madding Crowd* of 1874, and *The Return of the Native* of 1878, Hardy can be seen, amongst other things, working gradually towards the complete integration of the natural environment with the image and thematic structures of the novel, reaching a kind of climax of intensity in Egdon Heath and its dwellers. I would contend that in 1878 Hardy felt that he could go no further along that line, and sought about for another non-human medium that could function symbolically and as an organizational principle for plot and character. I would then go on to suggest that a similar pattern of experiment leading to achievement can be found in the three middle Hardy novels that are my present subject, in which Hardy attempts to discover to what extent *buildings* can embody the essentials of his human story in the way that the Heath does in *The Return of the Native*.

Of course this is not to say that buildings were not sometimes important elements in the earlier novels; and indeed if one considers, say, the narratorial debate about the value of medieval barn, church and castle in *Far from the Madding Crowd,* it can be seen that they have already carried *thematic* significance. It is also true that other critics before now (the latest being Peter Casagrande) have seen an architectural element in the middle Hardy novels; but I think none has seen it in quite this way, or as having the importance that I do.

It would be as eccentric to suggest that an exploration of the role that buildings might play in his fiction was the primary impulse behind *The Trumpet-Major*, as to suggest that Hardy was conscious in *Under the Greenwood Tree* of the role that the natural environment might undertake; he was interested, rather, in writing a historical novel, a novel of the period of the Napoleonic wars; and, rather more surprisingly, he wanted to write a comedy. It is, however, possible to show that the historical and comic action of *The Trumpet-Major* is contained, and to an extent embodied, by the significant dwelling-places in the novel—Overcombe Mill, Oxwell Hall, the buildings of Budmouth, and the military camp on the down. These structures, permanent or temporary, are at least half-integrated into the historical theme of the book. The nearest that Hardy comes to a statement of an idea of history is when, in chapter 13, Anne Garland is in Budmouth and sees the King on the Esplanade. The narrator observes of her that she "felt herself close to and looking into the stream of recorded history, within whose banks the littlest things are great, and outside which she and the general bulk of the human race were content to live on as an unreckoned, unheeded superfluity." From time to time through the novel the reader is also an observer on the banks of this stream, visiting Captain Hardy, watching the *Victory*, even seeing Anne dip a toe into it as she speaks with the King. But the moving-water metaphor finds an expression also in Hardy's summary of *un*recorded history at the end of chapter 3: "Thus they crossed the threshold of the mill-house and up the passage, the paving of which was worn into a gutter by the ebb and flow of feet that had been going on there ever since Tudor times." The mill-house, like the family of the miller, is for Hardy a representative part of the unhistory of the country, what we now know as local history, and which many consider to be the only sure basis of any historical knowledge; in this, as in other things, Hardy was ahead of his time. The solid virtues of miller and mill are early established, and never lost sight of; their long-established foundations, their usefulness, their value to the community. We might to advantage compare both family and building with the Poysers and their farm in George Eliot's *Adam Bede*.

If this distinction between recorded and unrecorded history underlies the action, then the mill-house and its garden and river may also be seen to embody part of the action itself. It is described thus in chapter 2:

> Overcombe Mill presented at one end of the appearance of a hard-worked house slipping into the river, and at the other of an idle genteel place, half-cloaked with creepers at this time of the year, and having no visible connexion with flour. . . .
>
> In the court in front were two worn-out millstones, made useful again by being let in level with the ground. Here people stood to smoke and consider things in muddy weather; and cats slept on the clean surfaces when it was hot. In the large stubbard-tree at the corner of the garden was erected a pole of larch-fir, which the miller had bought with others at a sale of small timber in Damer's Wood one Christmas week. It rose from the upper boughs of the tree to about the height of a fisherman's mast, and on top was a vane in the form of a sailor with his arm stretched out. When the sun shone upon the figure it could be seen that the greater part of his countenance was gone, and paint washed from his body so far as to reveal that he had been a soldier in red before he became a sailor in blue. The image had, in fact, been John, one of our coming characters, and was then turned into Robert, another of them. This revolving piece of statuary could not, however, be relied on as a vane, owing to the neighbouring hill, which formed varying currents in the wind.

The double nature of the building in this description is appropriate to the inhabitants of its partitioned state at the beginning of the novel, the idle Garlands and the busy Lovedays. As the two families grow closer and become united by marriage, so the external and internal dividing lines of the house become blurred and broken down. Discarded fragments of the mill machinery are found further useful functions to serve; and the weathervane, with its interchangeable figure that alters direction when the wind blows, anticipates accurately in its complication the relationship between Anne Garland and Miller Loveday's two sons. Even the final detail of its unreliability as a vane finds an echo by the end of the novel, in Hardy's demonstration that Anne's choice between the two sons is not made under the influence of any recognizable rational or moral breeze, but rather by the unaccountable breath of her own instinct, which proceeds from heaven knows where.

Both the mill and Oxwell Hall, the second important dwelling in the novel, were originally manor-houses, and both have undergone a social decline; but whereas the mill has turned from pleasure to fruitful industry, the Hall has become a farm through neglect rather than design, and its function as byre, yard and farmhouse is presented in terms of decay, at odds with the original grandeur. There has been no loving care, no conscious transformation; in short, no money has been spent on the building and no attention paid to its structure. It is as if old Derriman, whose home it is, camps rather than lives there; and both man and house are crippled with miserliness.

If Derriman's occupation of Oxwell Hall seems impermanent, almost as if he were squatting, the third structure in which I am interested is impermanence itself—not a building at all, but the tented camp of the soldiers on the down above Overcombe. The camp is the connection between the stream of history that runs through Budmouth for the span of the King's presence and the permanent unhistorical unmetaphorical streams that run past the mill and the Hall; it is on the fringes of both, it has a foot in either world, entertained by one, serving the other; temporary, movable, evanescent, the conductor through which Anne and others reach in to recorded history. It is the temporary home of Anne's temporary lover, whose temporary stay on the earth ends upon an indefinite but historical bloody battlefield in Spain. The transient nature of his canvas dwelling balances the mercurial flighty nature of Bob Loveday, helping us to accept Hardy's choice for Anne.

It must be accepted that Hardy has not fully integrated into the texture of *The Trumpet-Major* his perception of the historical opposition between the two erstwhile manor-houses on the one hand and King George's Budmouth on the other, or of that between the mill and the Hall; much in the novel remains episodic. But it seems right to see the novel as in part the beginning of a search for correspondence between theme and character and building.

Indeed it may be that Hardy only discovered how fruitful such a structural pattern might be in the course of writing *The Trumpet-Major*; it cannot be coincidental that George Somerset, the hero of his next novel, *A Laodicean,* is an architect. Unfortunately if it *was* Hardy's intention to explore further the role that buildings might play in his fiction, the serious illness he contracted while writing the novel undermined his purpose. It is only in the first two parts of the novel and at the very end that we can see how the approach might have developed.

When, in the novel's second chapter, Somerset traces a telegraph wire through an arrow-slit in the wall of a feudal castle, the action becomes an occasion for reflection on the contrasts between new and old, between Victorianism and medievalism, couched at times in paraphrase of Matthew Arnold:

There was a certain unexpectedness in the fact that the hoary memorial of a stolid antagonism to the interchange of ideas, the monument of hard distinctions in blood and race, of deadly mistrust of one's neighbour in spite of the Church's teaching, and of a sublime unconsciousness of any other force than a brute one, should be the goal of a machine which beyond everything may be said to symbolize cosmopolitan views and the intellectual and moral kinship of all mankind. In that light the little buzzing wire had a far finer significance to the student Somerset than the vast walls that neighboured it. But the modern fever and fret which consumes people before they can grow old was also signified by the wire; and this aspect of today did not contrast well with the fairer side of feudalism—leisure, lighthearted generosity, intense friendships, hawks, hounds, revels, healthy complexions, freedom from care, and such a living power in architectural art as the world may never again see.

This contrast between new and old is taken up and reflected in other ways: the medieval castle belongs to Paula Power, the daughter of a successful entrepreneur; she lives only in a fragment of the structure, and Somerset, in exploring Stancy Castle, comes across her modernized rooms; the narrator reflects that "These things, ensconced amid so much of the old and hoary, were as if a stray hour from the nineteenth century had wandered like a butterfly into the thirteenth, and lost itself there." She lives in the castle with the daughter of the last de Stancy to own his feudal inheritance, and just as the structure contains new and old, so Paula and Charlotte de Stancy represent new and old. Charlotte inherits the de Stancy face, and its feudal attitudes; but her father is very different, having accepted his social decline, and being insistent above all upon frugality. The house in which he now lives reflects this, and embodies the oppositions voiced in the first paragraph quoted earlier. Initially the suburban villa is described in the language of an estate-agent's dream, in which the irony is unmistakable: "Genuine roadside respectability sat smiling on every brick of the eligible dwelling" (p. 47). But in the following paragraph the tone changes dramatically: Somerset notices "a canary singing a welcome from a cage in the shadow of the window, the voices of crowing cocks coming over the chimneys from somewhere behind, and the sun and air riddling the house everywhere." And this alternation of irony and appreciation continues throughout the description, so that in these first chapters of the novel we have modern pettiness and modern brilliance set against medieval splendour and medieval darkness and decay; and this theme operates through both characters and buildings, only to get lost in the search for incident to fill out episodes which became all that Hardy could cope with in his illness. But at the end of the novel it resurfaces in the destruction by fire of Stancy Castle, and the proposal of Somerset, now married to Paula Power, to design a new house, eclectic in style, to stand beside the ruins of the old. And though they have made this commitment to the new eclectic, the last words of the daughter of the quintessentially

Victorian success, the railway entrepreneur, are: "I wish my castle wasn't burnt; and I wish you were a de Stancy."

In *A Laodicean* we can see what Hardy might have done; in *Two on a Tower* the symbolic substructure of the novel, based on buildings, is as successful and multifaceted as that based on Egdon Heath in *The Return of the Native*. The novel begins rather deceptively: "On an early winter afternoon, clear but not cold, when the vegetable world was a weird multitude of skeletons through whose ribs the sun shone freely, a gleaming landau came to a pause on the crest of a hill in Wessex." The detail from the vegetable world and the mention of Wessex seem to suggest that this might be the first sentence of a novel like *The Woodlanders*; but the presence of a gleaming landau represents the true note of the novel more accurately: even though Mrs. Charmond might have possessed such a carriage, one cannot imagine Hardy beginning *The Woodlanders* with a reference to it. The reference to Wessex is especially misleading, for *Two on a Tower* shares none of that community of spirit, place and culture. This novel could have been located anywhere, and the precise topography of its action in relation to any map of Wessex remains undiscoverable, being both vague and inconsistent (as Frank Pinion points out in his "Glossary of Place Names" appended to his New Wessex edition of the novel). What is important, however, is the relative location of the buildings that are significant. The salient features are two groupings: the tower on Rings Hill, the temporary hut at its foot and the farmhouse in Welland Bottom, which lie to the north of the turnpike road; and Welland House and Church to the south. It will be seen, then, that the crest of the road on which the heroine of the novel causes her landau to be halted divides her great House from the column in which the following paragraphs show her to be interested; and this physical division is echoed in the structure of the novel.

The tower is a very ancient and a very potent symbol; critics who have said anything about *Two on a Tower* have had their say on its significance; and I shall prove no exception. There is at the outset a relationship between Viviette Constantine's husbandless state and the phallic shape of the tower; though the conscious reason for her interest in it is the broad view obtainable from its summit, yet it seems probable that the subconscious motive is sexual in origin. And when she has been jolted across the arable land in her carriage, has climbed the hill, and reaches the foot of the column, Hardy provides a description which seems to me to possess an erotic charge of some strength:

> The gloom and solitude which prevailed around the base were remarkable. The sob of the environing trees was here expressly manifest . . . some boughs and twigs rubbed the pillar's sides. . . . Below the level of their summits the masonry was lichen-stained and mildewed, for the sun never pierced that moaning cloud of blue-black vegetation. Pads of moss grew in the joints of the stonework, and here and there shade-loving insects had engraved on the mortar patterns of no human style or meaning; but curious

and suggestive. Above the trees the case was different: the pillar rose into
the sky a bright and cheerful thing, unimpeded, clean and flushed with
sunlight. (ch. 1)

And it is indeed true that she finds sexual satisfaction as a result of entering
the tower; but Hardy's symbolic design is subtle and complex, and before
that occurs we are invited to read the passage I have just quoted in a slightly
different light, and the tower sheds its sexual role, as will be seen later. In
the meantime it is worth examining the other external symbolic burdens that
the tower carries in these introductory chapters.

In describing its situation the key words that Hardy uses are "isolated"
and "insulated"; in modern usage we would, I think, consider these two words
related, but distinct in meaning, but in 1800 this was certainly not the case,
and it is not clear how close they had become by 1882. Both words are
relatively recent additions to English. "Insulate," a characteristic Renaissance
formation from the Latin *insula* or *insulatus,* meant originally "to make into an
island by surrounding with water." The first figurative uses of the past partici-
ple are recorded early in the eighteenth century, with the meaning "standing
apart" or "solitary"; it is more difficult to know when its present primary sense
(deriving particularly from use in connection with electricity) of "prevention
from escape by a surrounding medium" became current figuratively.

"Isolate" is a still more recent acquisition; the verb is in fact a back-
formation from "isolated." This entered the language through the use in the
later eighteenth century of the French *isolé* to represent the figurative use of
"insulated" which was growing at the same time. By 1800 *The British Critic*
could write "The affected, frenchified and unnecessary word *isolated* is not
English, and we trust never will be."

It seems clear from Hardy's use that he did consider them distinct, and I
believe that this distinction is important for him. The tower, we are told in
the first page, stands upon a circular isolated hill, amidst an extensive arable
field, with no track, let alone a road, approaching it. It appears, as Norman
Page has pointed out, like an enchanted castle whose access is surrounded by
tests of the seeker's endurance.[1] It is one of the thematic ironies of this novel
that the conventional pattern of sexual relationships is reversed, and it is so
in this aspect as elsewhere. The traditional fairy-tale arrangement is inverted, and it is the princess who is in quest of adventure, perhaps erotic
adventure, and who stumbles on a beautiful youth in a tower—Swithin St
Cleeve, guardian of the key to the column, and passionate astronomer, who
has set up his telescope on the summit. That the tower is isolated by the field
allows them to keep their meetings there secret; that it is insulated by the
field preserves the charge of emotional and spiritual love that is generated
within it. These qualities of isolation and insulatedness remain in force in
some measure to the end of the novel.

As well as a phallic image and an enchanted dwelling, the column also
looks from a distance like a telescope; it is built in the plain unfluted Tuscan

Doric order of architecture to make the resemblance stronger, and it is itself a hollow tube pointed at the stars, and the fittest place for Swithin's observatory. For John Bayley in his fine essay in the first volume of *The Thomas Hardy Annual* (1982) "It is the tower that is in the imaginative foreground, and the tower is only incidentally an observatory. In one aspect it is a strange man-made object in its natural setting: in another, a symbol of marriage itself. Or at least of a love-relation involving marriage." It seems to me, though, that love and looking at the stars are fused in the symbol of the tower rather than separated.

Once we gain the interior of the tower, and once we see the relationship between astronomer and lady grow, the pure exteriority of the symbol fades and in its place comes what Yeats (with his genius for symbol) represented by tower and winding stair, the union of masculine and feminine, direction and indirection, aspiration and emotion, body, perhaps, and soul—as Bayley says, a symbol of marriage itself. Hardy refers often enough to the spiral staircase to make this apparently anachronistic connection with Yeats not merely an intellectual exercise. And as we see the growth of love within the tower, Hardy disentangles the physical element of the relationship between Swithin and Viviette from the emotional and spiritual, and locates it at the foot of the tower, in the darkness of the plantation. It is at the foot of the tower that Swithin is enlightened by the gossip of the workfolk, but it is outside the tower, in the hut that Viviette has paid for, that the physical expression of their relationship is centered. And that opening description takes on a different aspect in the light of this development, contrasting as it does the brightness and clarity of the tower's summit with the suggestive darkness of its base.

The hut is built near the foot of the tower so that Swithin can have somewhere to sleep after late nights at work at the top and avoid disturbing his grandmother in the farmhouse at Welland Bottom. At the same time as he recognises his love for Viviette, he (as far as the novel is concerned) abandons the farmhouse; and the only shelter for his body that we are told about until Viviette sends him away from her is this cabin. It is thus directly connected with their relationship; it is, as Swithin says, the "palace" to which he brings Viviette back from their wedding at Bath (with its proleptical ironic reference to Viviette's subsequent marriage to Bishop Helmsdale), it is their bridal chamber, and later it is where their son is conceived. Its relation to the tower is indicated again on the morning after the lovers' first night together: they sit outside eating breakfast while "at their elbow rose the lank column into an upper realm of sunlight which only reached the cabin in fitful darts and flashes through the trees" (ch. 20)—a passage consciously echoing the first description of the tower, and directing the reader to the separation that has taken place of the physical and the spiritual aspects of love. They never make love on the tower, and when, in a 1912 revision, Viviette makes time to visit Swithin after their marriage and the resumption to outward appearances of their separate lives, it is in the hut, not the tower, that they meet.

For a while the tower and the hut are bound together in the gloomy and passionate darkness that surrounds them, and, though hidden, the lovers' relationship is whole. But eventually circumstances combine to drive Viviette to sacrifice her happiness to Swithin's future, one might almost say to his ambition, and to send him abroad to study the strange stars of another hemisphere. The idea, the spirit of their love survives, as the tower survives, but the physical reality of their relationship is broken, as the hut is dismantled on Swithin's departure. And more, as it is dismantled, Viviette has the timbers numbered so that it can be re-erected in exactly the same form as before, when Swithin returns, just as she hopes that when he comes back he will help to reconstruct their relationship on the same terms as before. The cynical speech of the workman who takes down the cabin relates to both the hut and what it symbolizes: "the young man would as soon think of buying a halter for himself as come back and spy at the moon from Rings-Hill Speer, after seeing the glories of other nations and the gold and jewels that were found there . . ." (ch. 37).

For Swithin, the tower has always been an observatory, and only passingly the vessel of his emotional awakening; from time to time Hardy has shown us Swithin in the character of the scientist with no horizons beyond those he scans; even in love he has none of the emotional surcharge that fires Viviette—he remains practical and as nearly detached as his eager love permits. They only marry so that his work may continue without interruption from the frustrations of unsatisfied love. The tower, as I have said, looks like a telescope, and in its role as aspirational structure it is the fit home for intellectual activity—this has been recognized from Milton's philosopher in *Il Penseroso* to Shelley's Prince Athanase. Yet Hardy is ambivalent both about science and the scientific temperament as it is embodied in Swithin. In one sense it is admirable, expressing Man's great desire to expand his knowledge beyond its perceived bounds, and to increase thereby his stature. But at the same time it can be arid and inhuman when measured by other criteria, and Swithin is saved from this aridity by Viviette, saved from excluding from his life human relationships, and love as the intensest of those relationships, in order to stretch human knowledge. Thus, as I have said, the symbol of the hollow tower twined by its winding stair. And when Swithin abandons Viviette to take up his legacy and sails for South Africa, he leaves that saving grace behind.

The tone of the narrative towards his astronomical work at Cape Town has altered quite substantially from the eager interest that both narrator and Viviette show towards his activities on the tower's top. This is made clear both discursively and through image and symbol. As he receives Viviette's letter explaining her marriage to the Bishop, his response is "as one who suddenly finds the world a stranger place than he thought; but is excluded by age, temperament and situation from being much more than an astonished spectator of its strangeness" (ch. 40). At the end of three years' work in Cape Town, Swithin has achieved much; but the narrator chooses to commence the description of his achievement thus: "His memoranda of observations had accumulated to a wheelbarrow load . . ." (ch. 41). And at the end of a passage about the nature of his work there is this: "In these experiments with tubes and glasses, important as they were to human intellect, there was little food for the sympathetic instincts which create the changes in a life. . . . Swithin's doings and discoveries . . . were, no doubt, incidents of the highest importance to him; and yet from an intersocial point of view they served but the humble purpose of killing time, while other doings, more nearly allied to his heart than to his understanding, developed themselves at home" (ch. 41). That the attitude to the scientific work is dismissive seems evident, more vividly so in the image of the wheelbarrow than the succeeding generalization perhaps. Still more interesting in this context is a slightly earlier passage that describes the setting up of Swithin's telescope at the Cape: "Unable to get a room convenient for a private observatory he resolved at last to fix the instrument on a solid pillar in the garden; and several days were spent in accommodating it to its new position." And in case the reader should miss the point, the next sentence makes a reference which must cause him to pause and consider: "In this latitude there was no necessity for economising clear nights as he had been obliged to do on the old tower at Welland" (ch. 40). We see here how in abandoning Viviette, putting his astronomy before his human relationship, he has caused the tower to harden and diminish, becoming "a solid pillar," excluding the possibility of "intersocial activity," remaining aridly functional.

When he does return to Welland it is only because he has finished his work, not because Viviette is again a widow, or because she has also returned. There is no hut for him, and he comes back to the farmhouse in the Bottom, where amongst others he meets Tabitha Lark, of whom more anon. Intending, the day after his return, to visit Viviette at the great House, his attention is attracted to the tower by a transitory effect of light, which shows a figure at its summit. He changes direction towards it, "for the spot seemed again like his own."

When Swithin re-enters the tower he finds Viviette and their son at the top. As the narrator points out, "The Swithin who had returned was not quite the Swithin who had gone away," and he is shocked by her faded aspect into silence, which she interprets accurately and tells him to leave her:

"Swithin, you don't love me," she said simply. And it is true. But what Swithin has to offer her is marriage, not in the same spirit of passionate love symbolized by the combination of tower and cabin, but in the spirit of loving-kindness, of which the narrator says that it is a sentiment perhaps in the long run more to be prized than lover's love. Swithin turns on the stair, reascends, and embraces and kisses Viviette, but she cannot survive the intensity of her passionate renewal of joy and dies in his arms.

It then becomes a question of whether the novel is in part at least not another of Hardy's essays on the destructiveness of lover's love and the value of loving-kindness; of whether in this context the tower is not also in opposition to the cabin, the light to the darkness. As I said earlier, the complexity of Hardy's symbolism in this novel is greater than one might imagine.

And even this is not the last word from the tower: in an addition to the past paragraph of the novel made in the first edition, Swithin looks up for assistance with the insensible Viviette and sees "Tabitha Lark, who was skirting the field with a bounding tread—the single bright spot of colour and animation within the wide horizon." She is "skirting the field," she has nothing to do with the tower, and yet it has been made sufficiently clear to us, even without this final hint, that Tabitha is a much more appropriate mate for Swithin. We may, though, imagine that he will never experience with her the union of passion and spirit that the tower and cabin have symbolized; nor will he experience the destructiveness that the union can bring.

Michael Millgate has pointed out that there are three groupings of buildings, the Bottom, Welland Village and Welland House and Church, and relates them to social groupings in the novel; he feels also that there is something too contrived, artificial, unengaged about the patterning—as if Hardy were rather mechanically performing an exercise in novel-construction.[2] I have tried to suggest that Hardy goes rather further and deeper than this in his use of buildings, and I want now to take up one of Millgate's groupings, Welland House and Church, and consider how it relates to the Rings-Hill Speer and its cabin, and how House and Church relate to each other.

The first description we have of the church is at the beginning of chapter 11: "The heavy, many-chevroned church, now subdued by violet shadow except where its upper courses caught the western stroke of flame-colour, stood close to her grounds . . ." and a paragraph later, as Viviette enters the church: "The semi-norman arches with their multitudinous notchings were still visible by the light from the tower window, but the lower portion of the building was in obscurity. . . ." The most striking feature of these passages is the deliberate way in which they echo the first description of the tower, with its contrast between the darkness of the lower part shaded by trees and the brightness of the upper, flushed in sunlight. When revising the manuscript Hardy was perhaps worried that this parallel might escape his readers, and so in the second passage he altered "visible by the light from the west window" (the original reading) to "visible by the light from the tower window." This church is Viviette's spiritual, aspirational home, as Ring's-Hill Speer is Swithin's, its tower standing up to Heaven as the column stands up to the heavens, its roots in the Christian burial ground which joins it to Welland House, as Speer and cabin are rooted in the prehistoric pagan burial ground on which they are built.

This parallelism is best shown within the two characters by comparing the sense of absence from himself that Swithin experiences when examining and pondering the stars with this description of Viviette's experience in church: "She knelt till she seemed scarcely to belong to the time she lived in, which lost the magnitude that the nearness of perspective lent it on ordinary occasions, and took its actual rank in the long line of centuries. Having once got out of herself, seen herself from afar off, she was calmer. . . ." It is further evidence of the conscious intention within this passage that "seen herself from afar off," the core of the connection with Swithin's seeing himself in relation to the far-off galaxies, was only added in the first edition.

The parallel is inescapable; but once it has been established, Hardy is mainly concerned to show the basic contrast between the two—even in its darkness the tower has life and energy associated with it, whereas the church is associated with oppression and death.

In the description I have already quoted, there were other revisions in the manuscript: the opening words "The heavy, many-chevroned church, now subdued by violet shadow," with their emphasis on *heavy* and *subdued*, originally read "The quaint and handsome church, now bathed in violet shadows," with a quite different effect. The church is also described at the time of the confirmation service; the girls in their white dresses "lighted up the dark pews and grey stonework to an unwonted warmth and life. On the south side were the young men and boys, heavy, angular and massive, as indeed was rather necessary, considering what they would have to bear at the hands of wind and weather before they returned to that mouldy nave for the last time" (ch. 24). And again the emphasis is on heaviness and death, an emphasis which here too has been reinforced through an alteration to the manuscript: the "warmth and life" that the girls bring to the dark pews, with its implication that without them it is cold and dead, was originally merely "gaiety." It is in this place that we see Viviette praying for strength to give up Swithin and, when she has married him, attempted to confirm him in the Christian faith; in view of the way that the building has been described, we should not be surprised to discover that it lays a dead hand upon her love.

When Viviette goes into the church in Chapter 11, intending to resign Swithin to "some maiden fit and likely to make [him] happy," she is saved from her sacrifice and her sin in one stroke by the news that she is a widow; but it is no coincidence that playing the organ, as Viviette sits beneath the tables of the law, is Tabitha Lark, who is indeed a "maiden fit." And at the confirmation service, Viviette's visible triumph over Swithin's instinctive scientific paganism, the narrator insistently makes the same point: "Handsomest woman in the church [Viviette] decidedly was; and yet a disinterested spectator who had known all the circumstances would probably have felt that, the future considered, Swithin's more natural mate would have been one of the muslin-clad maidens who were to be presented to the Bishop with him today." And though Tabitha is not being "presented," but is again playing the organ, Swithin has more direct and intimate contact with her than with his wife.

These two passages might be held coincidental—after all an organist is likely to be found in the church—were it not that in the first the organist was originally the schoolteacher, and only in a revision Miss Lark, and in the second the incident in which Swithin and she converse was heavily revised to augment the solicitude with which he attends to her distress, and were it not also that there is a third scene in the church in which Hardy is drawing still more deeply upon the parallel symbolism I have noted. While Swithin is waiting for an appointment with the Bishop in the graveyard, he enters the church and ascends the tower in order to see what is going on in the adjoining garden of Welland House. As he observes Viviette together with her brother and the Bishop, and is in the dumb-show of receiving blown kisses from her, Tabitha Lark suddenly appears at his side of the tower. Swithin is surprised, and with some reason; though she says she has come to play the organ, her motive in ascending the tower can hardly be the simple curiosity to know what he was looking at that she suggests. This is underlined by their conversation, which takes a turn equally surprising to Swithin and the reader:

> "The Bishop is a striking man, is he not?"
> "Yes, rather," said Swithin.
> "I think he is much devoted to Lady Constantine, and I am glad of it. Aren't you?"
> "Oh yes—very," said Swithin, wondering if Tabitha had seen the tender little salutes between Lady Constantine and himself.
> "I don't think she cares much for him," added Tabitha judicially. "Or even if she does, she could be got away from him in no time by a younger man."
> "Pooh, that's nothing," said Swithin impatiently. (ch. 27)

And with this rather inadequate remark the dialogue terminates. The tone and intention here are hard to assess. It almost seems that Tabitha is teasing Swithin, and Swithin perhaps suspects it; but either way it suggests a greater intimacy between the two, particularly on Tabitha's part, than we might otherwise have suspected—and again the evidence for this connection is provided in the church (and here in the tower of the church) which is Viviette's spiritual resort, and which thus may be seen to betray her. That, as far as the reader is concerned, the relationship between Swithin and Tabitha is seen until the end of the novel entirely within the context of the church may be held to indicate strongly that their future is to be joined there in matrimony; and the last pages of the novel can only reinforce this impression.

"Lady Constantine was," the narrator explains, "necessarily either love or *dévote*"; but we might consider that for most of the novel she is both. And there is a third strand to her temperament: the woman of convention who is responsive to the codes of society in general and her own class in particular. It is this motive in her that insists upon keeping the marriage with Swithin secret, and it is this side of her character that is embodied in her House, her retreat, almost empty, dark, secure. There is a revision in the manuscript near the beginning of chapter 38 which illustrates Hardy's awareness of the potential of this connection between Viviette's commitment to society and great houses. She is sitting in a train taking her to Southampton, where Swithin is, as she thinks, on board a ship about to leave harbour; in the first manuscript version the narrator indicates her anxiety by commenting that "The lovely scenes through which she was dragged had no points of interest for her now." But in reconsidering the passage Hardy realised that he could express the same anxiety in a way that also directed the reader's attention to her major underlying preoccupation; and it becomes "The changeful procession of country seats past which she was dragged, the names and memories of their owners, had no points of interest for her now" (ch. 38). Welland House, then, symbolizes Viviette's sense of her position in the county, about which she is extremely sensitive; and it represents a refuge to which she can retire if she wishes, when her strength outside is insufficient to resist the forces attempting to break down her allegiance to the county code.

The central action of the second half of the novel is Viviette's decision to postpone her remarriage to Swithin for five years so that he can enjoy the fruits of her legacy and advance his position in astronomy. The narrator sees this as heroic self-sacrifice, almost martyrdom; and stresses the way in which the essentially Christian virtue of altruism and self-sacrifice conquers both her desire for Swithin and her desire for social conformity: "Thus she laboured, with a generosity more worthy even than its object, to sink her love for her own decorum in devotion to the world in general, and to Swithin in particular" (ch. 35). The human greatness of this act is beyond doubt, but its relation to the building symbolism already established and to subsequent events undermines the premises upon which it was built.

Her renunciation might be seen as wrapped around with betrayal; it is in the cabin which has been their bridal chamber that Viviette comes upon the document which leads to their separation; it is in the Great House, which represents in such tangible form her commitment to the values of her society, that she decides to set aside those values; we have already seen how the church, whose moral teaching she is following here with such pain to herself, is offering Tabitha Lark as her replacement. Hardy admires her action, recognizes the love that inspires it, but believes that it is fundamentally misguided.

It is not chance that leads Viviette and Swithin to make love in the cabin on the night that they part for good, nor is it accident that Viviette becomes pregnant; it is the expression of their need for each other beyond considerations of wealth or ambition, and as such must have a powerful effect upon their lives; it is, one might say, the cabin's amends for its previous betrayal. As soon as she realizes she is pregnant, her need for marriage, for social conformity, increases beyond the power of her altruism to inhibit it, and she frantically tries to reach him before he leaves—but in vain. At approximately the same time the Bishop of Melchester renews his offer of marriage to her (urged by Viviette's brother), and she accepts him. Her need to conform to social convention might be seen as the revenge of the House over the morality of the church.

In all this the tower has remained inviolate; the observatory has been removed, but the walls and the winding stair within do not change; it is still the seat of that love which goes beyond the physical, and which Hardy believes to be the most important element in human life. He has examined scientific aspiration, social codes, religious morality, and found them all insufficient without that union of two people in loving-kindness that is symbolized by the tower. Viviette has shown her greatness of spirit throughout the novel, but Hardy has shown that it is based on wrong assumptions. By herself she is not strong enough to move beyond the conventions which she acknowledges, and Swithin is too weak to help her. He accepts her decision that they should part partly through ambition, partly because he has no will to oppose to hers to the end. Thus it is right that they should meet for the last time on the tower, and it is beyond doubt that she should die from joy—it is the most generous ending that Hardy could conceive. Swithin is simply not great enough for her.

I began this discussion by pointing out the isolation of the tower, and one might say that isolation is pervasive: we are confronted with human isolation in face of the stars; Viviette is isolated in her House from all that she is accustomed to; indeed Welland itself is isolated. In face of all this isolation Hardy proposes that it is only the human loving relationship that keeps this isolation at bay; and without that, science, society and church are sterile, even deadly.

We are not used to thinking of comedy, of lightness of touch, as virtues inhabiting Hardy's greatness; we are not used to thinking that his significant purposes might be achieved by other means than through the interrelationship of man and his natural environment in a tragic mode; yet that we should do will only increase our estimation of Hardy as a writer. And so it can be claimed that *Two on a Tower* and *The Trumpet-Major* are middling Hardy novels, not to be neglected and discarded but to be examined for their evidence that Hardy could achieve fine work beyond the bounds of Wessex tragedy.

Notes

1. Norman Page, *Thomas Hardy* (1977) p. 111.
2. Michael Millgate, *Thomas Hardy: His Career as a Novelist* (1971) p. 190.

Thomas Hardy's *The Mayor of Casterbridge:* Reversing the Real   George Levine*

> I like a story with a bad moral. My sonnies, all true stories have a coarseness or a bad moral, depend upon't. If the story tellers could have got decency and good morals from true stories, who'd ha' troubled to invent parables?
>
> —Reuben Dewey, in *Under the Greenwood Tree*

*Reprinted from *The Realistic Imagination: English Fiction from Frankenstein to Lady Chatterley* (Chicago and London: University of Chicago Press, 1981). © 1981 by the University of Chicago.

1

Reuben Dewy seems a comic apologist for the later Hardy, in whose novels we find stunning reversals of the emphases and assumptions that guided realists through the first half of the nineteenth century. For Hardy, whose reserved hostility to the arbitrariness and cruelty of most social conventions is well known, the fullest truth inheres not in the moral ideals of modern civilization but in the essential passions and energies of human nature. These may be detected most convincingly in the unself-conscious traditions of societies, close, in their rhythms and morals, to the processes of nature, in which sporadic violence is a norm, and only barely touched by the movements of history. Or, more interestingly, the energies are most vividly present in those characters who have, for whatever reason, been touched into at least a primitive consciousness of the constrictions imposed by tradition, by social expectations, by moral ideals. The emphasis in Hardy shifts, not so much from the "ordinary," as from the realist's conception of ordinariness. His protagonists, from Dick Dewy to Michael Henchard, are all, in some respects, quite ordinary; yet they increasingly become focuses of tragic intensity. Their desires are not the romantic dreams to be mocked and minimized by wise or ironic narrators, but the stuff of nature and of tragedy.

In Hardy's fiction the realist's acceptance of compromise becomes itself a social convention, or an ideal either deadening when it is pursued without consciousness of the pain of experience, or almost unattainable but by hard discipline. The disenchanted acceptance of the ordinary and decent in the sharp sunlight that banishes the fantasies of romance; the recognition of the needs of others and of the limitations of the self; the revelation like Gwendolen Harleth's, that "her horizon was but a dipping onward of an existence with which her own was revolving";[1] the discovery of one's own mixed nature, of the flaws in one's lover, of the insuperable pressures of society—all of these normal consequences of the realities of Victorian fiction become in Hardy not less inevitable, but less a means to moral growth, and less adequate as a summary of reality. They become, rather, almost unendurable occasions for the tragic. Hardy's fiction gives the impression that, although the narrator does what he can to minimize them, the stakes have been raised, not only far beyond the Trollopian norm, but to the level of the absolute. There are, to be sure, characters in his novels who make the compromise, but the focus is on a prior reality. Hardy's protagonists seem to echo the experience of Victor Frankenstein, whose history is a sequence of waverings between an absolute ideal and a domestic compromise. One feels, retrospectively, a Hardyesque quality to Frankenstein's last uncompromising recovery of his dream amid the vision of failures and compromises: "Yet another may succeed."

Indeed, in Hardy, the compromise with the dream of large romantic aspiration has itself something of the quality of romantic dream about it. That is, such compromise is intrinsically unavailable to the instinctively aspiring protagonists who, like Frankenstein, are impelled not by any moral consideration it may at any moment rationally offer, but by a longing for the absolute and for the pure power of the self triumphant. If *Under the Greenwwod Tree* ends with one of those ironically imagined compromises, as a comedy, it nevertheless has within it the elements that will later make for tragedy. And it points forward, beyond its own pages, with a pleasant and satisfying humor that belies the seriousness of the possibilities: " 'O, 'tis the nightingale,' murmured she, and thought of a secret she should never tell" (ch. 5, p. 237).

In later work, the attempt to limit aspiration is clearly a dream. When, in *The Woodlanders,* Dr. Edred Fitzpiers, in his Lydgatian retreat to a country practice, contemplates marrying Grace Melbury and settling in Little Hintock, he asks himself: "Why should he go further into the world than where he was? The secret of happiness lay in limiting the aspirations; these men's thoughts were coterminous with the margin of the Hintock woodlands, and why should not his be likewise limited—a small practice among the people around him being the bound of his desires."[2] What might in an earlier novel have been the disenchanted revelation of the inevitability and virtue of limits is for Fitzpiers an untenable dream. Immediately after he does in fact marry Grace, he falls in love with the richer and more "modern" Mrs. Charmond. The men whose thoughts were "coterminous" with the woods are themselves a dying breed, and the volatile and unstable Fitzpiers, who simply cannot internalize the limits he almost chooses, though he is an anomaly at Hintock represents a majority of the culture at large. The strangely distant narrator knows this, although none of his characters does. Fitzpiers, to be sure, is too shallow to be regarded as Promethean; yet the very compromises he is forced to make at the end of the novel in returning to Grace diminish him, as Grace's return to him leaves us only with the dignity of Marty South, who has been able to remain true to her impossible ideal. The novel implies no growth in compromise, only loss of the little dignity Fitzpiers had in the authenticity of his passion.

Thus if Hardy endorses the notion that the "secret of happiness lay in limiting the aspiration," it does not mean that he found the idea attractive or even practicable. Happiness is not a normal or safe human condition. The characters who aspire absurdly and beyond the control of their own will have about them a quality of heroism that distinguishes them impressively from those less ambitious and more controlled, those who have not tested the limits of social constriction or aspired beyond the security of their station. Hardy's narrative voice keeps him aloofly distant from the passions it describes;[3] he remains almost archaeologically disengaged from the action, protected from it so thoroughly that he can afford to release within his narratives precisely those energies that earlier realists, in their compassionate focus on the details and surfaces of ordinary experience, kept submerged. The self-effacement of the "Everlasting Yea," which might be taken as the ideology of the Victorian realist's world, is not in Hardy a tough-minded acceptance of a limiting reality. Rather, it is an act of self-protection, felt in the narrator's own refusal to engage himself, and yet largely and tragically inaccessible to the actors in his dramas. It is unnatural in life, requiring extraordinary discipline of will and feeling, and probably unsustainable. Self-denial is itself a romantic dream, and its consequences can be as destructive.

The primary reality among Hardy's characters is their uncontrollable, irrational desire in an imperfect world. The large aspirations that mark the romantic hero, that are manifested in Victor Frankenstein with catastrophic and Tertius Lydgate with pathetic results are not, for Hardy, rare exceptions to the human norm. They can manifest themselves anywhere; they can be felt, in small, in Dick Dewy's love of Fancy Day, as well as in Giles Winterborne's love of Grace. Whereas realism gets much of its originating thrust from a comic and ironic view of romantic aspiration and, through parody or Thackerayan satire, denigrates it as hypocritical or silly, Hardy treats aspiration neither as an aberration nor as a falsification, but as representatively, critically, tragically human. The qualities that distinguish the human from the merely natural are intelligence and language and the capacity to imagine and desire beyond the limits of nature. The human is the only element in nature incompatible with it.

Essentially, then, Hardy saw a world that was at once continuous with yet in almost every major respect the reverse of the world projected with such moral rigor, sincerity, and toughmindedness by the Victorian realists. If his landscape, for example, excludes the Alpine peaks, for an almost loving but careful registration of the local scene, it does not exclude the intensities that normally accompany them. The violence of the natural world intrudes into the flattest landscapes; and the upland stretches of Egdon Heath, "a vast tract of unenclosed wild,"[4] the hill above Weydon-Priors where Henchard sells his wife, the height from which Jude spies the distant lights of Christminster—all these release uncontrollable energies that destroy with the force of an Alpine torrent. With the realist's particularity and with a movingly precise vision of the details and energies of the natural world, Hardy yet creates a universe that stands in almost parodic antithesis to such landscapes as those of Barchester or Loamshire, although they might be taken as literally almost identical.

It is antithetical, for one thing, in respect to the rules of civilized living, according to which Trollope so carefully organizes his world, and to the notion that civilization is both more interesting and more important than the more primitive worlds it has displaced.[5] Civilization, his narratives demonstrate, is an arbitrarily acquired and extremely thin veneer over what is quintessentially human. The human, moreover, is both "natural" and hostile to nature, is both material and ideal. The rules of society, which govern Trollope's novels and largely determine both the texture and values of characters' lives, do not, even in Trollope, adequately cover the variety and complexity of experience; but in Hardy, those rules are powerful forces in the imagination of his characters and utterly powerless to control their actual behavior, while irrelevant to the shape of the narrative. That is, they serve as deadly obstacles to what is most valuable and interesting about humans and their fictions—the strength of desire. Notoriously, it is social convention that dooms Tess's relation to Angel Clare; it is social convention that keeps Jude from fulfilling his early ambition. Yet those conventions, mere "ideas" by which society organizes itself, are powerless to keep Jude or Tess safe from the instincts that so often govern their behavior. The conventions in Hardy exist not as a general idea on which variations must be played but as a human fiction that is both necessary for society and destructive of its most interesting members. In effect, Hardy replaces Whately with Freud (and the Schopenhauer that lay behind Freud). The world does not correspond to human need, bringing individual and social together. But human need is divided and self-destructive, requiring both the protection of society and freedom from its restraints.

The antithesis implicit in Hardy's attitude to the rules manifests itself as well in his choice of subjects. There is, of course, a long tradition in realistic fiction of the comic use of peasants and rustics. Their lives are imagined as light echoes of the dominant narratives, which relate to less rustic, more literate protagonists. In Scott we find a world of rustics who bear with them the vitality and the authenticity of unself-consciously transmitted tradition and who frequently have a fictional life richer than that of the aristocratic heroes and heroines. In George Eliot, rustics often appear to comment shrewdly on the blindnesses of the protagonists and to invoke traditional wisdom with choric force, so as to impose a traditional pattern on the realist's potential disaster. In Hardy, however, although the tradition of both Scott and George Eliot is at work, the focus is distributed so that rustics and protagonists often blend into each other; rustics might well be protagonists. Clym Yeobright and Grace Melbury are only two who are educated beyond their class and are variously pulled back into it. To Trollope, a focus on a Dick Dewy or a Giles Winterbourne might have seemed misguided or wasteful. Where Trollope had argued that educated classes are on the whole morally and intellectually superior, and everywhere in his fiction implied the need for and the power of civilization to repress or outstrip savagery, Hardy opposed such a view, and novels of manners, of the drawing room and of the club:

> All persons who have thoughtfully compared class with class—and the wider their experience the more pronounced their opinion—are convinced that education has as yet but little broken or modified the waves of human impulse on which deeds and words depend. So that in the portraiture of scenes in any way emotional or climactic—the highest province of fiction— the peer and peasant stand on much the same level; the woman who makes the satin train and the woman who wears it. In the lapse of countless ages, no doubt, improved systems of moral education will considerably and appreciably elevate even the involuntary instincts of human nature; but at present culture has only affected the surface of those lives with which it has come in contact, bending down the passions of those predisposed to tur-

moil as by a silken thread only, which the first ebullition suffices to break. With regard to what may be termed the minor key of action and speech—the unemotional every-day doings of men—social refinement operates upon character in a way which is oftener than not prejudicial to vigorous portraiture, by making the exterior of their screen rather than their index, as with untutored mankind.[6]

On this account, realism, in its preoccupation with social rules and material surfaces, misses entirely the primary realities of human experience. Civilization is a veneer, and reality lies primarily in what realists would have thought of as extreme—in the very checkering they attempted to eschew: the emotional or climactic is the highest province of fiction.

This sort of emphasis leads away from the realist's concentration on character toward a more traditional (or romantic) emphasis on plot. Hardy's finding in tragedy a model for his narratives is a logical consequence of the new preoccupation with narrative structure. And in his own writing about fiction, he talks about the importance of structure with a seriousness exceeded only by George Eliot among the novelists who immediately preceded him. Symptomatically, as he looks back for models of satisfactorily structured novels, he singles out Scott's *Bride of Lammermoor*—"an almost perfect specimen of form." Thackeray's disapproval of that novel, as I earlier suggested, had to do with its very singularity among Scott's works. All of Hardy's critical and narrative instincts opposed Thackeray's casualness about narrative form. Like George Eliot, instead, he asks that the work of art have the structure of an "organism," and that everything in it be related to everything else.[7]

In some well-known notes on fiction Hardy laid out several propositions that help clarify how, in his peculiar relation to realism, he had moved to a more "modern" preoccupation with structure. He is realism's continuator and adversary:

> The real, if unavowed, purpose of fiction is to give pleasure by gratifying the love of the uncommon in human experience, mental or corporeal.
> This is done all the more perfectly in proportion as the reader is illuded to believe the personages true and real like himself.
> Solely to this latter end a work of fiction should be a precise transcript of ordinary life: but,
> The uncommon would be absent and the interest lost. Hence,
> The writer's problem is, how to strike the balance between the uncommon and the ordinary so as on the one hand to give interest, on the other to give reality.
> In working out this problem, human nature must never be made abnormal, which is introducing incredibility. The uncommonness must be in the events, not in the characters; and the writer's art lies in shaping that uncommonness while disguising its unlikelihood, if it be unlikely.[8]

The "uncommon," the "ordinary," "transcript," "illusion"—these are by now all familiar terms or concepts, but Hardy has somehow rearranged them. He argues for the risk of incredibility in plot in order to insure credibility in character. His actual practice seems to correspond to this argument, and *The Mayor of Casterbridge,* in a mere recital of its events, would seem absurd; yet from it Henchard emerges with overwhelming conviction. The love of the "uncommon" that Hardy attributes to his readers is, surely, his own love; and the "ordinary" world as he imagines it is a world of intensities and extremes. "Romanticism," he had written a few months earlier, "will exist in human nature as long as human nature itself exists."[9]

These notes indicate what is evident in the fictions, that as a self-conscious artist, Hardy was profoundly aware of the fact that art was—and ought to be—something other than reality. He seeks for organism and relevance in his fictions, for the symmetry of plot, for the imposition of consciousness upon experience. And in this respect, he is radically, at least in intention, at odds with all the realists who preceded him. He develops to an extreme their sense that experience and history may, in the long run, be without meaning or value. That sense allowed Thackeray to risk the near dissolution of many of his later narratives. It forced George Eliot to a new imagination of narrative. But for Hardy it is precisely the disorder of experience that requires the order of art. Value is human; it does not inhere in nature. If as Henry James and J. Hillis Miller have argued, the novelist's model is the historian, Hardy's model is self-consciously the artist. For, he says, "History is rather a stream than a tree. There is nothing organic in its shape, nothing systematic in its development. It flows on like a thunderstorm-rill by the road side; now a straw turns it this way, now a tiny barrier of sand that."[10] Hardy's is the world of Huxley's *Evolution and Ethics,* a world in which not following nature but building human structures against it is the way to survival. For Hardy, art is the place where structures can be created against the disorders and irrelevances of history. For art unabashedly projects consciousness upon raw experience, upon "crass casualty." Art, indeed, names that.

It is this special aesthetic quality that we find in all of his great novels; an unembarrassed symmetry of action and reaction imposed upon the inorganic streaming of experience. The novelist hides behind his language and peeks out into the wilderness, even the savagery, that contends in human nature with the constructed ideals of society. Hardy shares with Thackeray the realist's sense of how every climax becomes only a moment in a process; and thus of how the dream of a stable achievement, of closure, is misguided in all respects but that of death. "It is the on-going—i.e. the 'becoming' of the world that produces its sadness," says Hardy. "If the world stood still at a felicitous moment there would be no sadness in it."[11] Yet unlike Thackeray, who retreats into the guise of the sage old disenchanted figure whose narrative strategy is to deflate each climactic moment as it comes, Hardy moves even further from the action in his distinctively labored and distant voice and yet produces dramas of desire and will, focusing on moments of passion with tragic clarity and intensity.

Thus realism, as practiced by Trollope or advocated by the early George Eliot, seemed to Hardy merely conventional—as conventional, at least, as Austen perceived the gothic novel to be. "Representations" of reality were of necessity merely conventions of ways to imagine reality. The disparity between art (organic) and life (merely streaming) assured that Hardy's own carefully outlined structures were no less "true" than the large loose monsters of the other Victorians. In the curious progress of realism's self-contradictory impulses, Hardy can be taken as the perfect exemplar. His fiction almost defines itself as being what Trollope's and Thackeray's is not, and all in the name of a faithful and sincere registration of the way things are. The way things are had changed, so that Hardy might have subscribed to the credos of realism I quoted in the first chapter although he constantly violated its conventions. The world had been transformed, and what the "dull grey eyes," the "cold lentils" actually indicated could not be contained within the dominant modes of mid-century realism. Hardy was essentially concerned with the artist's responsibility to this new imagination of the world: "By a sincere school of Fiction we may understand a Fiction that expresses truly the views of life prevalent in its time, by means of a selected chain of action best suited for their exhibition. What are the prevalent views of life just now is a question upon which it is not necessary to enter further than to suggest that the most natural method of presenting them, the method most in accordance with the views themselves, seems to be by a procedure mainly impassive in its tone and tragic in its developments."[12] The special pleading here is obvious. Yet it is true that the dominant comic mode of the realist tradition, evident from Jane Austen to mid-century, was shifting even in Trollope, but certainly in George Eliot. Comic endings had become more questionable—not only in Thackeray's *Newcomes,* or in *Little Dorrit,* but even in such Trollopian comedies as *Mr. Scarborough's Family,* or in *Middlemarch;* and catastrophe became a possible conclusion—in *The Mill on the Floss,* or *Beauchamp's Career.* The "impassivity" Hardy advocates suggests something of the defensive maneuvering required of his narrators, whose voices imply the discovery that the limiting of aspirations is not a morally healthy repression of precivilized human energy, but directly contrary to the human condition. Such repression can not end in comic compromise, but only in violent explosions of unaccountable and catastrophic energy.

But advancing secularism and an exciting yet disruptive new science had in fact radically transformed "the view of life prevalent" in Hardy's time. George Eliot's and Conrad's response to this transformation seems, finally, even more radical than Hardy's. In every case, however, this transformation had vast consequences for fiction. It entailed the final dissolution of the kind of vision that allowed Whately to endorse Austen's realism by in effect endorsing reality, and that, in various ways, lay behind almost all Victorian realism to mid-century. Yet more important (since writers had already been undercutting traditional faith in the meaning and order of the world), the transformation would ultimately disrupt the process of realism by which it moved through parody to new imaginations of the real requiring yet newer parody.

Hardy's kind of tragic and shapely—"geometric," he would call it—fiction does not follow out the full disruptive consequences of the new world view. Instead, it rebounds almost parodically away from earlier conventions of realism, while sustaining much of its mood. He had a deep commitment to the conventions of art itself rather different in kind from that of the realists, for whom art required attention more to the implications for living than to the medium itself. Thus, with all his self-consciousness about the indifference of the universe, Hardy could never imagine an antiart which, in its own dissolutions of traditional forms, mimicked the dissolution of meaning in the universe. "Good fiction," he wrote, "may be defined as the kind of imaginative writing which lies nearest to the epic, dramatic, or narrative masterpieces of the past."[13] In addition, Hardy's realism is distinctly continuous with Wordsworth's. Experience must, in Hardy, be made meaningful, even if the "meaning" is that the world has none, or is inimical to human consciousness. Beyond the disastrous failures of a nature ever completing itself, never complete, of a world incompatible with human intelligence, there remains the power and dignity of the human itself. Such power can *make* the world relevant by imposing on it human intelligence.[14] Michael Henchard has more than a nominal connection to Wordsworth's Michael. In seeing through the veneer of civilization, Hardy finds a Wordsworthian universality even in the peculiarities of his peasants. As he noted in his diary, apparently in 1881: "Consider the Wordsworthian dictum (the more perfectly the natural object is reproduced, the more truly poetic the picture). This reproduction is achieved by seeing into the *heart of a thing* . . . , and is realism, in fact, though through being pursued by means of the imagination it is confounded with invention."[15] He could not drop at least this aspect of the realist's program although all his emphasis is on imagination, enthusiasm, passion. Realism defends him from the charge of mere invention. He is, rather, seeing with Ruskinian and Wordsworthian clarity.

But in Hardy, too, the ultimate severance of art from representation is already more than latent in his primary belief in the incompatibility of consciousness with the entirely material world from which it aberrantly emerged. As at last in *The Well-Beloved,* Hardy is continuously aware of the disparity between the human imagination of the real and the possibilities of the real itself. At its worst, this issues in what was often called Hardy's fashionable pessimism. But in the drama of the novels themselves, it points directly back to the sort of world implied in *Frankenstein,* one in which inexplicable destructive forces issued inevitably out of what might have seemed the most ideal conditions of civilization. The unnameable nonhuman reality burst forth, as he puts it, at "the first ebullition," over the impossibly tenuous restraints of civilization. In Hardy, the monster stalks freely and visibly again, bringing with him an art strikingly akin to that which the early great realist practitioners of realism, in their imagination of an uncheckered world of compromise and disenchantment, had laughed away through their parodies and satires.

2

The Mayor of Casterbridge is the novel that most precisely and power-fully focuses the relation of Hardy's new vision both to the realistic tradition out of which, and against which, it is imagined, and to the tradition of romance. It is a novel that belongs centrally in the nineteenth century, echoing with its naturalistic fidelity, with its preoccupation with "character," with its thematic concern about the relation of the individual to society, about the relation between past and present; yet it is also a novel that embodies a distinctly "modern" vision and that points forward, as Albert Guerard has noted, to the work of Conrad and the early modernists. Henchard, Guerard explains, traces a career remarkably similar to that of Conrad's Lord Jim, whose life is determined by a single instinctive act which he is doomed to redeem and repeat to the end.[16] But I consider Hardy's novel here, rather than at the end of this study, because "modern" as Hardy's fiction may seem to be, it does not follow out in its narrative method the full implications of its vision. Reversal is not a rejection of order. The Mayor of Casterbridge evidences in a moving and satisfying way Hardy's fundamental unwillingness to surrender to the disorder he sees. It is a final assertion of the possibility of human control, however monstrous, against the ultimate horror of a world inimical to intelligence, casually destructive, and inaccessi-ble to the very language by which humanity designates it. It risks the "vio-lence" Bersani attributes to narrativity in order to affirm the power of imagi-nation and the necessity for order.

In the preceding chapters, I have been concerned to examine the way realism moved toward an increasing multiplication and fragmentation of narrative as writers attempted to come to terms with their developing sense of the disorder of experience itself, and of the violence to reality done by dogma, ideals, and selfish desire. In Trollope and Thackeray, the contriv-ances of fictional ordering are postponed or diluted or, in subplots, qualified by alternatives. The large loose baggy monster had come to represent not so much an aesthetic slovenliness as one valid aesthetic consequence of the realistic vision, requiring us to see any narrative line as only one possibility. The rigorous shaping hand of the novelist, which in a different sort of art was to be hidden under the pressure of a Flaubertian aesthetic ideal, was for the Victorians to be restrained in the interest of the most honest possible registra-tion of reality. The artist, among the Victorians, might comment and judge, but not control.

The Mayor of Casterbridge is an aggressively manipulated narrative. It belongs, in this respect, to a narrative tradition governed not by the criterion of plausibility but by that of coherence of feeling. It is one of those remark-able Hardyesque achievements that manage to carry overwhelming conviction while, at every instance, inviting us to dismiss them as incredible. From the perspective of realism, this represents a falsifying tradition of romance; but in *The Mayor of Casterbridge* it is brought into uneasy but effective conjunction with the traditions of realism. The organizing pressure of feeling that gives to romance its distinctive form and makes both *Frankenstein* and *Wuthering Heights* so remarkably symmetrical has an interesting and honorable life among the Victorians. Even among them, where the three-decker novel predominated, and serial publication encouraged the very disorder the realist instinctively found authentic, there are fictions that focus intensely around a single consciousness and absorb the world into that consciousness's needs. Even *Northanger Abbey* is controlled by the desires (however long delayed and uncertainly understood) of the heroine. Catherine Morland, in her consumption of the world about her, bespeaks those monstrous energies that Austen, in creating her, was mocking. *Jane Eyre*, too, reflects the shaping of experience to personal need. And even *Great Expectations* is ultimately constructed so that almost everything in the world reflects Pip or refers to him.

These narratives, all directed—within the conventions of realism—to demonstrate the folly of great expectations and the moral disaster of imposing the self on experience, nevertheless blur the distinction between the self and other. The special strength of the narratives depends largely on the sense, beyond reason or the power of the mimetic method to record, that the protagonist's fate is somehow entirely created by the self. It is not at all simply wish fulfillment, not at all simply that Jane Eyre gets Rochester but, rather, that she gets the conditions in which she actually lives by virtue of qualities intrinsic to herself. The figure that keeps her from Rochester, "Bertha Mason," is an element of herself that she consciously restrains but cannot eliminate, so that the figure that gives her Rochester is also Bertha Mason, who literally purges Rochester of those qualities that make him unfit for Jane. The landscape of *Jane Eyre* is a romantic one in that it is the self projected, with all its irrationalities and inconsistencies. One can talk and must talk about a literal landscape and about other characters, but *Jane Eyre* is also most powerfully a novel of the self coming to terms with itself. Similarly, as Julian Moynahan brilliantly showed many years ago, the landscape of *Great Expectations* is Pip projected outward. The realist's lesson of disenchantment is there not simply a new recognition of the incompatibility of selfish aspiration with a contingent and varied universe, full of other selves, but a discovery of personal responsibility and, indeed, of personal power. Pip, in a sense, wills the destruction of his sister, of Miss Havisham, and almost of himself. Such novels, like *Frankenstein* gothically before them, reflect the power of consciousness even as they dramatize the powerlessness of the self apart from the community. Each of them projects some monster into the world as Maggie Tulliver evokes the flood, and Victor creates his hideous progeny.

In such novels, plot bears the burden of uncommonness, and in *The Mayor of Casterbridge*, Hardy is consistent with his own dictum that the unreality should be in plot rather than in "character." But plot is not merely—if it is also—a vehicle for the display of "character." It is the means through which Hardy imposes a structure on the world and animates it. One feels in the plot of *The Mayor of Casterbridge* a mysterious but irresistible power lying behind the beautifully observed quotidian and asserting itself against the will of the protagonist in such a way as to imply a dramatic if uneven contest. One feels it despite the simple and abstract assertion of Hardy's pessimism, as in the narrator's invocation of the "ingenious machinery contrived by the Gods for reducing human possibilities of amelioration to a minimum."[17] However much Hardy will imply or, as in later novels, overtly argue the indifference of the world to human concerns, the plot of *The Mayor of Casterbridge*, the many twists, the curious and convincing hostility of the elements, of the landscape itself, so resonant with life, imply a meaningful—if perverse—world. And if this "plot" is further complicated by a richly subtle sense of the way the "external" animosity is inherent in the human will itself, that insight does not diminish the force with which the structure of the novel resists the disorder and meaninglessness toward which, we have seen, realism has been moving. The effect is achieved particularly by Hardy's relish for the "uncommon," his insistence on facing up to the most extreme possibilities.

In the almost numbing sequence of catastrophes that befall Henchard, none is diminished or minimized. They exist not in an aura of nostalgia for intensities no longer available to the disenchanted narrator in the grey modern world, but as continuing realities that no wisdom can efface. Henchard, the "man of character" whose story the subtitle announces, is imagined as precisely the sort of character who would find the realist's disenchantment unendurable. His story is, in a way, about Victorian realism and possible alternatives. Henchard moves in a landscape of ancient ruins, cornfields, Egdon Heath, all governed by the inexorable repetitions and transformations of time, all threatening to absorb him: yet in this landscape Henchard asserts his specialness, refusing to acquiesce in or compromise with the forces that require that he diminish his claims and make his peace. But he outwits both society and nature by anticipating the worst they can do, and he leaves his "will" to assert his final contradictory power.

Against the extravagance of Henchard's plot, there is a realist's subplot—plausible, moderate, compromised. Farfrae is a character from a mid-Victorian novel whose moderate demands, quiet self-interest, refusal of excess, and emotional shallowness all operate within the text as a commentary on Henchard's way of being. Farfrae's amiable shallowness is first observed in his moving rendition of "It's hame, and it's hame, hame fain would I be, O hame, hame to my ain countree" (p. 43). This is followed by his announcement that he is going to America, and echoes with a developing realist preoccupation with dilettantism. Hardy seems to be taking up the tradition that had led Thackeray to focus on a protagonist like Pendennis, capable of surviving and of resisting the worst excesses of moral enthusiasm, by virtue of a fundamental shallowness; and in a voice reverberating with the awareness that the secret of happiness lay in the limiting of aspiration, he tests the mixed and compromised realist hero, Farfrae, against the overreacher, Henchard. When, at the end, Elizabeth-Jane attempts to enlist Farfrae in a search for the wandering Henchard, Farfrae has no objections: "Although Farfrae had never so passionately liked Henchard as Henchard had liked him, he had, on the other hand, never so passionately hated in the same direction as his former friend had done; and he was therefore not the least indisposed to assist Elizabeth-Jane in her laudable plan" (p. 285). It is part of the astonishing achievement of the novel that we feel in Farfrae's generosity less that is admirable than we would if, Henchard-like, he had been vengeful and adamant. Farfrae achieves the life of compromise and stands finally in the landscape of Casterbridge humanly diminished before Henchard's grand disasters. Henchard's story and Farfrae's comment almost parodically on each other. Henchard's reverses the comic pattern, which informed the earlier realistic fiction, and in its reversal averts the ultimate inconsequence of the middling life Farfrae enacts, the realist's casual disorder of experience and the inhuman indifference of Hardy's nature.

Ironically, Hardy's violation of the conventions of realism does not free his narrative for the creative unions of romance but leads to the very defeat from which, one might have thought, the rejection of realism would have protected it. Even here, Hardy plays with realism's conventions; for it was certainly a part—if an "impure" part—of the conventions of Victorian realism that manipulations of plot (Dickensian coincidences are only the extreme examples) enact for the protagonists the desires hindered by the particularities and complexities of experience. We have seen such enactment in *Northanger Abbey;* but Thackeray uses it as well, if almost cynically, and Trollope, too, with casual ease. The comic tradition of the novel relied very heavily on the coincidence, as it is used so conventionally and effectively in *Tom Jones.* But in the happy ending for Farfrae and Elizabeth-Jane, that tradition is implicitly criticized. If the realist must use coincidence to resolve narratives, the most "realistic" use of such coincidence, Hardy implies, is not comic conjunction but tragic disruption. Coincidence must become the chance that explodes the fantasy of happiness. If Elizabeth-Jane goes on to a life of "unbroken tranquility," she continues to wonder "at the persistence of the unforeseen" (p. 290). Everything in the novel points to the exceptional nature, not of disaster, but of that "tranquility"; what predominates in life is the "unforeseen," and injustice. Elizabeth-Jane, whose relation to the narrative is of major importance, must renounce the enthusiasm that made Henchard so much a man of character. In Elizabeth-Jane it is not shallowness, as it is with Farfrae, that makes for survival. Although she is one of the lucky ones, she *knows* she is lucky. And having had more passion to begin with, she knows the price of tranquility, as Farfrae does not.

Thus, despite Elizabeth-Jane's concluding voice, *The Mayor of Casterbridge* is almost a celebration of disaster. The disaster, or at least the willingness to confront it, is Henchard's dignity. He chooses his own disaster, down to his last moments when, with the possibility of a new beginning before him, we learn that "he had no desire." Henchard becomes an inverted romantic hero: he makes his own fate. The novel, while asserting man's contingent and compromised nature, imagines the possibility of something freer. It pushes beyond the "small solicitation of circumstance" to a celebration of demonic human energies that realism had, at least since Frankenstein, been struggling to repress.

3

Critics have long recognized that Henchard, in one way or another, *is* the world of *The Mayor of Casterbridge*. Like Frankenstein before him, he absorbs all external reality into his dream of the self. Technically, this means not only that every character and event in the novel relates directly to Henchard, but that the more intensely one examines the novel, the more evident it is that every character in it reflects aspects of his enormous selfhood. As Victor Frankenstein is his monster's double, but also Clerval's, his mother's, his brother's, Walton's,[18] so Henchard is the double of Farfrae and Elizabeth-Jane, Jopp and Abel Whittle, Newson and Lucetta. As Victor moves with erratic repetitiveness from act to reaction, from aspiration to repentance, so Henchard enacts his self-division and Hardy projects that division on the landscape of his narrative. It is all done with the recklessness of conventional plausibility that marks gothic conventions, and yet it achieves a new sort of plausibility. For the large techniques of romance are incorporated here into the texture of a realism that allows every monstrous quirk its credible place in a social, historical, and geographical context belonging importantly to the conventions of realism. The landscape of the self in this novel almost displaces the landscape of that hard, unaccommodating actual to the representation of which the realist has always been dedicated. But self and other exist here in a delicate balance, and it is probably more appropriate to say that in *The Mayor of Casterbridge* Hardy makes overt the continuing and inevitable presence of romance in all realistic fiction.

We may take the remarkable first scene, in which Henchard sells his wife, as a perfect example of the way Hardy's narrative embodies the tensions between the conventions of realism and that of romance in style and substance, and the way it daringly asserts the presence of the uncommon in the common. The whole sequence confronts directly the problem of inventing satisfying ways to cope with the limiting pressures of the realist's contingent world on large human energies and aspiration. Exploiting the conventions of realism to free itself from the conventional real, and at the risk both of alienating its readers by claiming kinship with great tragedy or mere sensationalism and of disrupting the life of its protagonists, Hardy's narrative implies both a new freedom of imagination and a new conception of human dignity. The freedom and the dignity are precisely in the willingness to take the risk—of uncommon art, of large hopes for renewal.

Strikingly, the human action begins in more than disenchantment, in utter fatigue with the Victorian realist's happy ending—marriage. By the time we meet the still young Henchard, he has been married for some time, and there is no romance in it. The ideal of the hearth, of the limited but satisfying life to which Dickens led his protagonists, in which Adam Bede resolves his career, has turned bitter. The married couple are not at home and content, but on the road and wearily out of touch with each other. We are here beyond the point to which George Eliot takes us when she begins *Middlemarch* with the fated marriage of Dorothea and Casaubon. For Hardy is not engaged in exploring the process by which marital ideals dissolve into sullen separateness and bitter disappointment. That is part of the progress of realism, to be sure. But Hardy begins with the given—with the assumption that marriage is bitterly disappointing and imprisoning. And that assumption, one might note, casts a suspicious shadow over the happy marriage between Farfrae and Elizabeth-Jane, with which the novel concludes.

Yet the scene is narrated with a realist's tender care for precision, an almost awkward quest for authenticity, which seduces us into trusting the narrator. Henchard, for example, is described as a man of "fine figure, swarthy, and stern in aspect; and he showed in profile a facial angle so slightly inclined as to be almost perpendicular" (p. 1). The language struggles to place the characters and define them against recognizable nonliterary categories, and implies that the narrator has a wide familiarity with the ways of agrarian laborers. He notes a typical "sullen silence," apparently bred of familiarity, between the man and the woman. He describes Henchard's "measured, springless walk," which distinguishes him as a "skilled country man" rather than as a "general laborer" (p. 1). Later, he describes the furmity tent with the particularity customary to the realist: "At the upper end stood a stove, containing a charcoal fire, over which hung a large three-legged crock, sufficiently polished round the rim to show that it was made of bell metal" (p. 4). The narrator's omniscience is restrained: without entering the minds of his characters he implies a wise familiarity with their ways of thought and feeling: "But there was more in that tent than met the cursory glance; and the man, with the instinct of a perverse character, scented it quickly" (p. 5). Later, we are told that the "conversation took a high turn, as it often does on such occasions" (p. 5). Everything implies a quiet, worldly-wise narration of a story growing out of and repeating a thousand such untold stories buried in history, and whose connections with life outside the fiction will be constantly suggested. Peasant wisdom and bluntness mix with the larger historically saddened intelligence of the narrator. Yet within moments we discover that these devices have been working to force our acceptance of Henchard's sale of Susan: "It has been done elsewhere," says Henchard, "and why not here?" (p. 9).

Just as the scene begins to burst the limits of the conventions of realism, and daringly requires comparison to the abrupt beginning of *King Lear,* so Henchard attempts to free himself from the limiting conditions of his life. Everything noted in the densely particular style suggests that he has been diminished by his context; the sullenness of his relation to a wife who has herself been ground down by "civilization" (p. 2); the "stale familiarity" (p. 2) of their relationship; the "dogged and cynical indifference" (p. 1) manifest in every movement and feature of the man. As we meet him plodding beside his wife, Henchard is (significantly) reading a ballad sheet, turning from the reality of his intimacy with her to a poet's dream of the uncommon. As he drinks, this partly defeated man is transformed, rising to "serenity," then becoming "jovial," then "argumentative," and finally "the qualities signified by the shape of his face, the occasional clench of his mouth, and the fiery spark of his dark eye, begin to tell in his conduct; he was overbearing—even brilliantly quarrelsome" (p. 5). The latent Henchard, released from the re- strictions of convention and responsibility, becomes realized. He asserts the sense of his own power and is longing to be free to exercise it: "I'd challenge England to beat me in the fodder business; and if I were a free man again, I'd be worth a thousand pound before I'd done 't" (p. 6).

In George Eliot, this boast would be deflated immediately, but here the larger wish becomes father to the fact, and the realistically created scene slides into romance in which Henchard is hero. Within a few pages, by a process we are not allowed to observe, Henchard has become mayor of Casterbridge. But he is clearly a man who, however firmly his will keeps him under control (as it keeps him from drinking for twenty-one years), acts outside the limits that confine ordinary people. He seems able to withstand the pressures that impinge on other lives, yet all of his life in reality curls around the monstrous secret of the sale of his wife. As Frankenstein hides from his monster, attempts to rejoin the community and conceal his great dream and his great mistake, so Henchard hides from the reality so vividly and abruptly rendered in the first scene. All of the novel grows—as all of *Frankenstein* grows—from the narrative of the inevitable reemergence of that hidden fact, that illicit thrust at freedom, into the community in which Henchard seeks to find his peace. And as with Frankenstein, but more richly and complexly, we find that the protagonist in the community is ultimately only reenacting his forbidden scene. In Casterbridge Henchard seeks with respectability to assert the absolute power of his self over a constricting and contingent world. The pressures he denied at the start avenge themselves on him with a completeness far beyond what the logic of his situation would require. But once set in a world carefully defined in the language of social analysis and historical tradition, once seen in the context of delicate financial and human transactions, Henchard must be destroyed. The man of large feeling and deep need—the hero of romance—cannot survive in the context of a carefully particularized society. Henchard is incapable of compromise. Neither success nor failure can be ordinary for him. And since the conven-

tions the novel adopts make failure the only possibility for the largely aspiring man, it must be an extraordinary failure. The novel concentrates on his
losses, juxtaposes his large ambitions to the moderate ones of Farfrae, and
conspires to keep him from the comforts of the real. Henchard is his fate; and
the narrative line transcends the limits of realism by cooperating with
Henchard's refusal to compromise. All coincidences conspire to make things
worse than the compromising conditions of realism would demand.

In retrospect, one feels, they are not quite coincidences, but Henchard
writ large. His domination of the book, uncharacteristic of Hardy's work as a
whole, forces us to see his hand—or spirit—everywhere. He evokes all the
characters whose coincidental appearances play so important a part in the
novel; and with each of these, at some point, he reverses roles. In the third
chapter, for example, we learn of Susan and Elizabeth-Jane's search for
Henchard, which brings them to Casterbridge and reopens his past; not long
before we heard of Henchard's search for them, itself significantly cut short
by "a certain shyness of revealing his conduct" (p. 15). Again, Henchard is
responsible for persuading Farfrae, who will end the novel as the new mayor
of Casterbridge, to remain in the town. Later, Lucetta, who had nursed him
in an illness, arrives in order to marry Henchard, and he must repay her
kindness and reverse their early relationship. The furmity woman comes to
town to expose him and, in the powerful scene in which she is brought to
trial before him, she argues: "he's no better than I, and has no right to sit
there in judgment upon me." Henchard agrees, "I'm no better than she" (pp.
174–75) Even Jopp, who is responsible for the information leading to the
skimmity ride, arrives in town just after Farfrae to take the job that
Henchard has offered to Farfrae; by the end, Henchard is living where Jopp
lives. Henchard creates the world which is to destroy him—even becomes
that world.

The remarkable force of the idea that, as Hardy quotes Novalis, "character is fate" (p. 98) is worked out with a minuteness that seems to translate
the whole world of the novel into a psychic landscape. Farfrae's dramatic
entrance into the novel, for example, corresponds precisely to the moment
when Henchard, defending himself against the demand that he replace the
bad wheat he has sold, says, "If anybody will tell me how to turn grown
wheat into wholesome wheat, I'll take it back with pleasure. But it can't be
done" (p. 31). Farfrae arrives and does it; and he stays because of Henchard's
overwhelming emotional demands on him: "It's providence!" Farfrae says,
"should anyone go against it?" (p. 55). Henchard makes "providence."

More important for a full sense of the daring of Hardy's achievement in
his challenge of realist conventions is the way he takes pains to call attention
to the creaking mechanics of his novel. It is as though, if we had not noticed
how remarkable, unlikely or chancy an event has been, Hardy wants to make
sure that we do not find it plausible or commonplace. When Farfrae turns
up, the narrator remarks, "He might possibly have passed without stopping
at all, or at most for half a minute to glance in at the scene, had not his advent

coincided with the discussion on corn and bread; in which event this history had never been enacted" (p. 32). Here Hardy turns what might very well have been taken as a donnée of the plot into a coincidence upon which the whole plot must turn. As the story unfolds, Henchard's impulsive energy can be seen to be responsible for every stage of his eventual self-obliteration. He too impulsively reveals his past to Farfrae; he too intensely punishes Abel Whittle; he too ambitiously tries to outdo Farfrae in setting up a fair for the holidays; he too hastily dismisses Farfrae and too angrily responds to Farfrae's determination to set up his own business; he cuts off the courtship between Farfrae and Elizabeth-Jane though, as the narrator remarks, "one would almost have supposed Henchard to have had policy to see that no better modus vivendi could be arrived at with Farfrae than by encouraging him to become his son-in-law" (p. 97). Later he too hastily buys corn and then far too hastily sells it. He opens Susan's letter about Elizabeth-Jane at precisely that moment when being recognized as Elizabeth-Jane's father, "the act he had prefigured for weeks with a thrill of pleasure," was to become "no less than a miserable insipidity. . . . His reinstation of her mother had been chiefly for the girl's sake, and the fruition of the whole scheme was such dust and ashes as this" (p. 110).

The novel even implies that it is Henchard's responsibility that Susan dies. After reading a letter from Lucetta, Henchard says, "Upon my heart and soul, if ever I should be left in a position to carry out that marriage with thee, I *ought* to do it—I *ought* to do it, indeed!" The narrator comments, "The contingency he had in mind was, of course, the death of Mrs. Henchard" (p. 101). And the narrative immediately records the death of Mrs. Henchard. It is this kind of thing—possibly to be described as simple coincidence, possibly to be explained in naturalistic terms—which finally gives to *The Mayor of Casterbridge* its distinctive shape and power. Every detail of the action seems to feed into Henchard's being, and every detail of the text requires that we accept it only if we are willing to accept the extravagant with the plausible, or as part of it.

George Eliot had tried, by subtle allusion and careful elaboration of plot, to make the ordinary reverberate with mythic force. But in Hardy, sometimes with, sometimes without mythic allusions, the plot itself makes the real mythic. Henchard, the tragic king, responsible both for his kingdom and the sin that blights its wheat and him, must move with ironic absoluteness to death. And the movement toward death is prefigured early. "Why the deuce did I come here!" Henchard asks himself as he finds himself in the place of public execution after he has discovered, because of his refusal to heed the instructions on the envelope, that Elizabeth-Jane is not his daughter (p. 109). "The momentum of his character knew no patience," the narrator later remarks (p. 164). That momentum moves him, past all possibility of compromise, to disaster. He is saved from suicide after the skimmity ride only by the magical appearance of his effigy in the water. When the furmity woman returns, Henchard has no instinct toward the deception which would keep his long-held secret quiet. By attempting to kill Farfrae he not only finally alienates the last man who can save him, but makes it impossible for Farfrae to believe him when he attempts to inform Farfrae of Lucetta's illness. Again, his relation to Farfrae is rather like Oedipus' relation to the careful Creon. Thus, since he carelessly gave Jopp Lucetta's letters he is responsible for Lucetta's death in two ways.

Finally, his last two self-assertive acts complete his self-annihilation. He breaks into the royal visit, demanding the recognition which he had lost and forcing another scuffle with Farfrae. And when Newson returns to claim Elizabeth-Jane, Henchard unhesitatingly (driven by those same impulses which led him to sell his wife) asserts that she is dead; his final act of deceit loses for him his last possibility of ordinary survival.

His last acts have about them the quality, not of a modern novel, but of a pagan, religious ritual of self-annihilation. He refuses to plead for himself to Elizabeth-Jane: "Among the many hindrances to such a pleading not the least was this, that he did not sufficiently value himself to lessen his sufferings by strenuous appeal or elaborate argument" (p. 283). Elizabeth-Jane discovers that "it was part of his nature to extenuate nothing, and I live on as one of his own worst accusers" (p. 285). She then goes out to look for Henchard. We find that, to the last, the power of his being draws people after him. Elizabeth-Jane and Farfrae seek him; Abel Whittle against Henchard's command, follows him, and aids him as he can. Henchard walks until he can walk no more and ends in a hovel (the whole scene deliberately and daringly constructed to recall King Lear and Edgar in the storm) by writing his will— and the will wills his total obliteration:

"MICHAEL HENCHARD'S WILL

"That Elizabeth-Jane Farfrae be not told of my death, or made to grieve on account
        of me.
"& that I be not bury'd in consecrated ground.
"& that no sexton be asked to toll the bell.
"& that nobody is wished to see my dead body.
"& that no murners walk behind me at my funeral.
"& no flours be planted on my grave.
"& that no man remember me.
"to this I put my name.
                                        MICHAEL HENCHARD." (P. 289)

The irony of "willing" his self-obliteration is powerful, complex, and inescapable. Even the putting of his name in upper-case letters becomes an important part of the effect. For Henchard's last written words are the name he is asking to obliterate—and boldly imprinted. The annihilation he asks is in excess of the possible, and so by a wonderful and moving irony, Henchard effects in death what he always fell short of in life—the dominance of his name. It is as though Henchard has stumbled onto the modernist criticism that reminds us of the peculiar status of language. It cannot quite name what it names; it speaks only of itself. It is a fact in the world, but not a representation of it. Henchard becomes here the absolute self of the fiction he created of his life and of the world. He ends, like the late-century writers who had, in effect, given up on the ideals of the Victorian writers speaking to their audiences and attempting to move the world. Since he cannot transform the ideal into the real, he transforms the real into the ideal.

In death, Henchard takes us as far as this novel can to the self-annihilating consequences of the contradictions and failures of the realist ideal. But in the last chapters, the narrator finally extends to Farfrae, that mixed sort of protagonist of realistic fiction, the kind of irony to which he could have been vulnerable throughout the novel. Everywhere, of course, Farfrae acts so as to represent a practical alternative to Henchard's egoist passion for the absolute. The final complex of alternatives and doublings comes when Henchard arrives at the wedding feast, like the ancient mariner, an uninvited guest with a monstrous, Frankensteinian tale he might tell. But he is mute, and hears instead Donald's voice "giving strong expression to a song of his dear native country that he loved so well as never to have revisited" (p. 281). And yet here is Henchard, actually "revisiting" his home, although he had intended to flee it forever. It is Henchard, not Farfrae, who sentimentally leaves the canary; and it is at this point that Farfrae is described as "not the least indisposed" to try to find Henchard, but largely because he has never cared enough either to hate or to love him. For a moment, that is, we can almost say that romance is parodying realism, that it is, through Hardy, having its revenge on an art that has attempted to drain all excess from experience and to subject human nature to the rules of common sense and the inevitable contingencies of ordinary life.

But the last word in the novel belongs to Elizabeth-Jane, a figure who does not fit easily into any of the patterns I have been suggesting apply to the novel, and one who seems rather at home in the world of realistic conventions that Henchard's narrative implicitly mocks. Elizabeth-Jane provides the only other perspective from which we see a large part of the experience, and despite her obvious littleness in relation to Henchard, she is a character more impressively drawn and more important than she is generally given credit for. Although she never surrenders to her impulses or to her needs, she is not, as I have already suggested, simply a Farfrae. If Farfrae, in supplanting Henchard in every detail of his life, in fact continues the life of the Henchard who is excessively sensitive to the demands of respectability, Elizabeth-Jane, herself entangled in respectability, becomes the most authentic commentator on Henchard's experience. Her heart remains always in hiding. It stirs momentarily for Henchard's grand misguided attempts at mastery. But in her quiet submission to the movements of the novel's narrative, she becomes an expression of the way in which "happiness was but the occasional episode in a general drama of pain" (p. 290). By accepting this view, staying protected within the limits of respectability and not rejoicing too much when good fortune comes, she survives to find "tranquility" and to forget the Henchard whose death brought her vision. She is the best sort of realistic audience to a tragic drama.

Her preoccupation with respectability indicates her acceptance of the limits society imposes on action and on dreams, but with her, clearly, the acceptance is an act of self-protection. There is something in Elizabeth-Jane of Hardy's own tentativeness, for while, in Henchard, Hardy ambitiously projects the passions of a large ego beyond the limits of conventional fiction, as, one imagines, he himself would have liked to do, the narrative voice in which he tells the story has something of Elizabeth-Jane's own reserve, and of the wisdom Elizabeth-Jane has achieved by the end of the novel. Henchard is Hardy's monstrous fantasy: but he must, like the monster, be destroyed. Thus, it is through Elizabeth-Jane that Hardy allows us to return to the conventions of realism with a new understanding of their importance and of their tenuousness. Elizabeth-Jane makes us aware that it is not possible any longer to imagine the world as fundamentally accessible to the commonsense structures and language of earlier realists, that behind the veneer of society and quiet movement of ordinary life, there lies the "unforeseen," the continuing pain, the irrational intensities of nature and human nature.

Elizabeth-Jane's ultimate vision is a consequence of the experience of disaster. It embodies the wish in art that Hardy seems to have feared to enact in life. The only way to overcome the "worst" that lies beneath all human experience is to confront it intensely. Ironically, what Elizabeth-Jane arrives at is, in effect, the ideology of realism. She has learned and she teaches "the secret . . . of making limited opportunities endurable; which she deemed to consist in the cunning enlargement, by a species of microscopic treatment, of those minute forms of satisfaction that offer themselves to everybody not in positive pain" (p. 290). We emerge from the world of *The Mayor of Caster-bridge*, in which the balances of fictional reality have all been reversed and in which, by the sheer force of narrative intensity, the conventions of realism are found wanting weighed against the monstrous energies of human nature, with a sense that the compromises of realism are after all essential. They do not, we see, adequately describe reality; they are modern disguises of realities that, ironically, belong to far more conventional literature; but they are conditions for our survival. Elizabeth-Jane does not allow herself to feel the pressure of Henchard's selfhood as we feel it in his bold concluding signature. Instead, she sensibly (and realistically) follows Henchard's literal instructions on the grounds "that the man who wrote them meant what he said" (p. 289). But in his life, he had rarely done what he "meant."

Realism survives in Hardy, not as a program for writing fiction, but as a discipline to be learned in the containment of the monstrous and the self-divided energies that make of mankind such an anomaly in a hostile universe.

Notes

1. *Daniel Deronda* (Harmondsworth, 1967), p. 876.

2. *The Woodlanders* (London, 1920), pp. 160–61.

3. J. Hillis Miller, *Thomas Hardy: Distance and Desire* (Cambridge, Mass., 1970), pp. xiii–xiv and passim.

4. *The Return of the Native* (London, 1920), p. 1.

5. The explicit discussion in Hardy of the cost of civilization is fairly common in the nonfiction. The most interesting instance is "The Dorsetshire Labourer," *Life and Art* (New York, 1925), pp. 20–47.

6. "The Profitable Reading of Fiction," *Life and Art*, p. 73.

7. Ibid., p. 69.

8. Florence Emily Hardy, *The Early Life of Thomas Hardy: 1840–1891* (London, 1928), pp. 193–94.

9. Ibid., p. 189.

10. Ibid., p. 225.

11. Ibid., p. 265.

12. "Candour in English Fiction," *Life and Art*, p. 76.

13. "The Profitable Reading of Fiction," p. 61.

14. See J. Hillis Miller's discussion of this problem in his Introduction to Hardy's *The Well-Beloved* (London, 1975).

15. Hardy, *Early Life*, p. 190.

16. (*Thomas Hardy* [Norfolk, Conn., 1964]) points out the connection between Henchard and *Lord Jim* (see esp. pp. 146 ff.). John Bayley (*An Essay on Hardy* [Cambridge, 1978]) also makes connections between Conrad and Hardy.

17. *The Mayor of Casterbridge* (Boston, 1962), p. 277.

18. See Knoepflmacher, "Thoughts on the Aggression of Daughters," pp. 88–119.

A Social Comedy? On Re-Reading *The Woodlanders*

John Bayley*

One of the pleasures of re-reading any great novelist is to see if and how perspective and proportion change. Developments and big scenes which impressed on first acquaintance may recede in later readings, and quite different impressions replace them. This is specially true of Hardy, in whose work the idea of "impression," like the idea of "passivity," is unusually important. And of none of his novels is it so true as in the case of *The Woodlanders*.

The reason is clear. As several critics have observed, *The Woodlanders* is a particularly rich mix-up of Hardyan modes and moods. In *Thomas Hardy and Women*, Penny Boumelha points out that "it draws on genres so widely

*Reprinted from *Thomas Hardy Annual No. 5*, ed. Norman Page (London: Macmillan, 1987). Reprinted with permission by Macmillan, London and Basingstoke, and by Humanities Press International, Inc., Atlantic Highlands, N.J.

disparate as to be at times incompatible."[1] That is true, though incompatibility is not something that usually worries Hardy much. His imagination, his narrative, the texture of his consciousness and his prose, all take it in their stride. None the less it is true that the switch from one genre and one mode of feeling to another is something that strikes one more strongly with each re-reading, changing the impression and seeming to shift the emphasis. In the earlier novels, most notably in *Far from the Madding Crowd*, the separate modes lived together, not so much in harmony with each other as in a happy state of natural indifference. Hardy himself seems neither to know nor to care that comic, pastoral, pathetic and tragic modes—to name only the most obvious ones—are all collectively at work, in spite of the fact that he was both self-conscious and ambitious in the matter of genre, not infrequently reminding the reader of his text's affinities with the traditions both of classic tragedy and of dramatic comedy. Yet the literary Hardy does not himself seem aware of the alter ego who unknowingly observes and conveys—the perceiver who pays no regard to the literary craftsman who invokes literary models. It struck me once, and I tried to express the point in a suitable metaphor, that Hardy's text "is like a landscape of which the constituent parts—cows, birds, trees, grass— pay no attention to one another."[2] And the author himself often gives the impression of being in the landscape, and behaving like one of its denizens.

The Woodlanders was originally planned, so Hardy says, with the idea of a follow-up to *Far from the Madding Crowd*; the scenario being laid aside in favour of *The Hand of Ethelberta*, which the author thought would represent a new departure, daringly removed from what might become a pastoral stereotype. At that stage in his writing career the mixture of modes in *The Woodlanders* would have seemed natural enough. But by the time he came to write *The Woodlanders*, as it now appears, Hardy had not only more sense of his position as a novelist but an intention of speaking his mind on marriage and on society in general, as was done in the French novels he had been reading. The novel therefore had not only to carry the usual Hardyan mixture of modes, but several extra ones as well, and not the sort that would tend to live together and pay no attention to their fellows. Hence the impression of disparateness and incompatibility; hence, too, the special interest in re-reading, and feeling each time a different impression of the whole.

No one, I should think, is troubled at a first reading by the mixture of modes in the novel, and by what Penny Boumelha calls "its interrogative awareness of the literary modes within which it is working." The woodland itself no doubt impresses us most, its ancientness and its darkness, which are both grim and reassuring in their suggestion of unchanging ways of men locked into the pattern of the seasons, of growth and decay. Wood and man are at one, like the darkness which meets the woodlanders "flatly on the threshold" as they open their cottage doors by night; and which, as Grace looks out from Giles Winterborne's hut at night, "seems to touch her pupils like a substance." The woodland suffers like man, lives and dies as he does in close and binding proximity to its own kind. Hardy's descriptions of the woodland—its greenness and blackness, its fungus and moss, its distortions of growth and its tangles of boughs wounded by rubbing each other—are compelling and instantly accepted: as is the case with the background of memorable novels we feel as if we had lived in the place all our lives. Indeed we accept implicitly, and at first reading, what we may subsequently recognize as a true analysis when we read it in David Lodge's Introduction to the novel[3]: that Hardy has placed side by side a traditionally pastoral view of the woodland country and its denizens, and a Darwinian view, contemporary in its time, of both wood and woodlanders as locked in the same struggle for survival, participants and victims in the same unyielding process. In fact both wood and village are slums, the wood in particular a cramped tenement in which few individual trees will get their chance to develop and grow.

Complementing each other as they do, these "impressions" are quite compatible. No one reading The Woodlanders for the first time would find the Darwinian and the pastoral wood incongruous with one another; rather the two seem natural aspects of Hardy's vision. In the same way the reader accepts the distinction between woodland life and polite society, and the way in which the story interweaves the two, with Grace as the passive prize or go-between in the middle. He is absorbed by the image of Marty South splitting gads by night in her cottage; by her and Winterborne planting the young pines together; or when she stands among the branches of a felled oak like a great bird, adroitly stripping off the bark into glove fingers with her simple tool made from a horse's leg-bone. Her image and Winterborne's personify woodland ways, like those of Gabriel Oak and Bathsheba in Far from the Madding Crowd, and at first reading the narrative seems balanced on the same axis between country pursuits and urban or worldly restlessness and guile, Sergeant Troy and Fitzpiers supplying the same sort of disruptive influence.

Episodes like Grace's skirt being clutched in the man-trap, and the foray of the maidens into the wood on St. John's Eve, seem variations on memorable moments in the earlier novel, like the sword exercise in the dell of ferns, and Bathsheba catching her dress in the dark wood on Sergeant Troy's spur. Grace's flight and sojourn in Winterborne's hut parallels Bathsheba's night in the wilderness after the drama of Fanny Robin's coffin and Troy's departure. But in the earlier novel these scenes are done with the poetry of absolute conviction. In The Woodlanders they seem more in the nature of ritual expedients. Or rather they come to seem so on re-reading.

This is not a weakness. Of all Hardy's novels The Woodlanders has the most curious kind of depth in it, a perspective of impressions that lengthens with each perusal. The most obvious explanation is that Hardy, like Grace, was in a divided state, divided between the kind of new, enquiring fiction he wanted to write, and the traditional kind which had been so successful and which had won him an admiring audience. But that is only the beginning of a more complex matter, involving, as we might expect, the element of daydream and fantasy which was the most powerful in Hardy's creative temper.

It is this element, more latent and indefinable here than in the other novels, which declares itself more openly with each re-reading.

The first impression is much more straightforward, the woodland itself more important than any of the characters, and personified in the figure of Winterborne, whose importance at first seems greater than that of the female characters. We are told at the beginning that in such an isolated woodland community "dramas of a grandeur and unity truly Sophoclean are enacted in the real, by virtue of the concentrated passions and closely-knit interdependence of the lives therein," though this may only happen "from time to time." But we may remember this promise on the last page of the novel, even if we have forgotten it in the meantime, when Marty South, as Sophoclean chorus, is uttering her requiem over the grave of Winterborne. Moving it is, deeply so, but to re-read the novel is to feel also how pre-determined it is. This at any rate, so Hardy seems to be assuring himself and the reader, is the note which will resolve any incompatibility in the genres which have come together more spontaneously, if more disconcertingly, in the second half of the novel. If it is given to Marty to have "touched sublimity at points," in the steadfast part of Antigone, Grace, a few pages back, has "slily" pointed out to her husband that in his efforts to win her back he has been quoting from *Measure for Measure:* "Love talks with better knowledge, and knowledge with dearer love." It is to that deeply unsatisfactory though in its own way no less touching world—the world in which Isabella asks no better man than the Angelo who has deserted and betrayed her—that Grace and her husband inevitably belong. It is a striking instance of the inspired literalism of Hardy's creative genius that he can invoke the two different worlds so openly, and bring them together to such effect.

None the less it seems to me that the *Measure for Measure* world of *The Woodlanders* does predominate over the Sophoclean one, which comes with re-reading to seem both more *voulu* and more subdued. It has none of the rugged inevitability which marks the end of *The Mayor of Casterbridge.* Rebekah Owen's account of what Hardy said about the end of *The Woodlanders* does not sound altogether convincing, and it is probable that Hardy was apt to talk at large about such matters as a means of protecting himself from criticism.[4] According to her account Hardy said he was not interested in Grace and found her "provoking." "If she would have done a really self-abandoned impassioned thing (gone off with Giles), he could have made a fine tragic ending to the book, but she was too commonplace and straitlaced, and he could not make her." That may be true up to a point, and it sounds like many novelists, Tolstoy included, who tell us that real characters must do what they want, and cannot be forced into convenient unreality by their creators. But if Grace did not go off with Giles it was not so much that she wasn't up to it as that Hardy knew the novel could not be ended in that way. Such a denouement would have been wholly out of keeping with Hardy's essentially unheroic temperament and cast of mind. Winterborne's chivalry to Grace requires no more than passivity. But, more important, the sort of "fearless" ending which Hardy was prepared to boast about, apparently, to his acquaintance, would in fact have broken that balance of the genres which gives its true personality to the novel. It is characteristic that he does not like that balance—he seems more consciously estranged from it than in any of his other novels—and yet he cannot do without it, any more than a landscape can do without its mutually indifferent constituent parts, its woods and fields and hedgerows, sheep and cows.

We may come to feel, though, that the genre effects in The Woodlanders are not so much incompatible as that they can give a disquieting impression of cancelling themselves out. The writer's separate impulses are confused; their competing attractions result in a form of paralysis, comparable to the paralysis which descends on the Melbury household when Grace is neither one thing nor another, neither a free agent nor a married woman. A part of Hardy, we can be sure, would have agreed with Winterborne's own deep feeling that the "adamantine barrier of marriage" cannot be dissolved by mere law; that such a thing, as Winterborne feels, "did violence to custom." Naturally there is no possibility in the novel of escape that way, just as there is no chance of Grace eloping with Winterborne, or Winterborne settling down with Marty. Hardy's fiction has its deeply embedded customs and expectations, as in country life. The word "adamantine," probably borrowed from Paradise Lost where the rebel angels are confined "in adamantine chains and penal fire," has a typical incongruity with the concept of doing violence to custom, which no doubt reflects Hardy's own feelings, and specifically his feelings about marriage. He might have wistfully longed to be a Miltonic or Shelleyan rebel, but he also knew it was not to be. Except in fantasy, where so much that is deepest in his fiction resides. The Woodlanders is full of intimations of emancipation—from class, from marriage, from male and female bondage—and yet these cannot be fulfilled, not just because of Mrs Grundy and the circulating libraries, but because creativity for Hardy was closely associated with passivity and defeat. The liberations of fantasy had more power for his secret self than fearless endings or bold social affirmations.

Much of Hardy's passivity does in fact proceed from the cancelling out of conflicting impulses. Though Hardy may not "like" Grace he is himself very closely associated with her and her situation, as he is in another way with that of Fitzpiers. And the refined defeatism of Winterborne is close to him too, one image of his "simple self that was," and of "one of those silent, unobtrusive beings who want little from others in the way of favour or condescension." This involuntary closeness to his characters is probably the real reason for the alienation from them which is evident in the novel, and particularly towards its end. Hardy plumps for Winterborne at the end, as the nearest thing to a tragic protagonist, but this isolates the image of the man and lends him the unreality of being seen only through the eyes of others. Winterborne is the only rustic in his work who is idealized by Hardy, and who exemplifies in individual form that mixture of modes which characterizes the novel, while its self-negating aspect shows itself more clearly in him. He is a romantic figure, with his brown face and eyes of cornflower blue; in the cyder season he might be "Autumn's very brother"; where Grace and Fitzpiers are associated with *Measure for Measure,* Winterborne's tutelary being is the doomed Chatterton, the "marvellous boy" who wrote the verses about autumn that Hardy quotes.

In another mode Winterborne exhibits what Hardy, in a scientific and elegiac parenthesis, calls "an intelligent intercourse with Nature." It is an incongruous phrase, in one sense, for a man who is simply a part of the remorseless and mechanistic process which makes the woodland, like the world, the epitome of an unfeeling struggle for survival. But though Hardy idealizes Winterborne he does not sentimentalize him. It is Marty's love which calls him "a good man," who "did good things." The man the novel's art presents has to get along as best he can, like the others in it. It is natural for the womanly love of Marty and Grace to sentimentalize him at the end, when they read a psalm over his body "in that rich, devotional voice peculiar to women on such occasions," and their tender voices fill the hut "with supplicatory murmurs." Hardy reminds us, though, that the Psalter of Giles which they borrow for the purpose had been kept at hand by him "for the convenience of whetting his penknife on its leather covers." The consciousnesses of men and women hardly meet each other, and Marty accepts this fatalistically. "The one thing he never spoke of to me was love; nor I to him." It is easy and natural for Grace in her distress to invent her great romantic love for Giles after he is dead, and the nature of this love, and her need for it, is shown by the novel with dispassionate sympathy.

What it shows more trenchantly, though, with each re-reading, is the social comedy which is the ultimate ground of the novel. It is, after all, more markedly an undercover novel than any other in Hardy's work; and the modes which, as Penny Boumelha suggests, interrogate one another in it, come to the tacit conclusion—or so we may have the impression at last—that sex and class, and all that they bring in the way of obsession and possession, can be seen in the end as a comedy that is grim, certainly, but not so grim as all that. There is an ironic affinity, never openly commented on, between the woodland, its way and those who live by it, and the idea of the social jungle, which is equally secretive, competitive, ruthless. Melbury, the man of the woods, is more socially obsessed than any other Hardy character; and he sacrifices his daughter, his savings, and his peace of mind to his social ambition. Giles is as conscious as he is, and our re-readings show him less in the light of a man of the woods, who can make trees grow as he plants them by stroking their young roots in the right direction, than as a man who is caught up in the unforgiving social process. His embarrassments in this field are remorselessly repeated. At his most sanguine moment he takes Grace to a simple tavern in Sherton which he has been familiar with for twenty years but in which she feels very uncomfortable—the tastes she has now acquired have "been imbibed so subtly that she hardly knew she possessed them till confronted by this contrast." It is a repeat of the unfortunate evening party he gave for Grace, in which a dead caterpillar appeared among the greens on her plate, and in which she gave an involuntary start and blink when old Robert Creedle inadvertently splashed her in the eye when ladling the broth. That splash and that involuntary blink stay in the reader's mind more than do the set-piece dramas and disillusionments contrived for Grace, and give her a touching social and personal reality. Like the other characters she is helpless in the grip of a social process, which determines her consciousness and responses more than she knows.

As they did Hardy's. There is a secret humour in *The Woodlanders* which underlies the social comedy and gives it a kind of innocent cynicism. Hardy knew well enough that he was in the same position as Grace, as in a sense he was in that of Fitzpiers, and of Winterborne too. He was close to all three, for like them he was conscious of living in two worlds, and by being so emotionally and intimately aware of both, unfitted for either. Fitzpiers has a name old in the county's annals, and though his family have decayed to nothing it is still held in almost superstitious respect, until he marries into Grace's family and finds that in the eyes of the woodlanders he has become almost one of themselves. It is a much more realistic variation on the romantic story of Tess's origins, in Hardy's next novel.

It is the social comedy at its core which keeps *The Woodlanders* realistic. As comedy heroine Grace is more instinctively realised than Tess, more convincing in herself, although Hardy devotes so much more fervour and fantasy to the later heroine. Clearly Hardy can't forgive Grace for not being more amenable to his fantasy: that again shows that she and her position are too much like those of his actual self. Hardy's fantasy has here to realise itself—and does—in the undercover play of social comedy. The more we read *The Woodlanders* the more we may feel it to be in essentials a rustic version of *The Hand of Ethelberta*, the novel which displaced it chronologically in Hardy's earlier development.

This would go with his alienation from the characters, and indeed from the novel itself, about which his diary implies that he felt indifference, and the wish just to get it finished. A natural enough sentiment in any novelist, yet it is clear that *The Woodlanders* would not lend itself to those moments and fantasies of *power,* which had become what Hardy's imagination chiefly sought and fed on where the novel was concerned. Not only is there nothing in the novel comparable, say, to the nocturnal ride of Tess and little Abraham, and the death of the horse Prince; there is nothing even so powerful and mesmeric as the Fanny Robin and Sergeant Troy theme in the novel that was perhaps to have preceded it—*Far from the Madding Crowd.* The characters of *The Woodlanders* do not even require much coincidence or the dark dealings of fate to set them on their ill-omened journeys. It is a novel purely of psychological relation, and though this gives it a particular interest and fascination it also makes its author very uneasy.

Hardy's as it were involuntary closeness to the characters means that he cannot fantasize about them in the full-blooded way he could wish, as he was to do with Tess, or with Sue, and Avice. What occurs is more of a regression to the world of *Desperate Remedies*, with Grace in the part of Cytherea and Felice Charmond in that of Miss Aldclyffe. Hintock House, like those in *Desperate Remedies* and *Two on a Tower*, seems based on his childhood acquaintance with the big house of Kingston Maurward and its owner, the lady who taught him and was so kind to him. To find the psychological centre of his novel regressing in this way must have been disturbing to him, especially at a time when he was not only anxious to become "bolder" in his treatment of fictional themes, but when the deterioration of his own marriage had made him brood over its unsatisfactory aspects as a social institution.

The involuntary dilemma resolves itself in a unique sort of social and economic comedy—indeed it might be said that economics take over the sort of role in *The Woodlanders* which is played in *Desperate Remedies* by the traditional ingredients of the thriller mystery. Cytherea in that novel is pursued by two men—"hero" and villain. Neither Winterborne nor Fitzpiers fits these parts, but while Grace plays the part of the passive heroine, "given" to whatever man can take her, the doctor and the woodlander are connected with her by the most complex socio-economic factors, all of which are of absorbing though covert interest to the author. If Winterborne can get Grace he allies himself to money and a rising class, and though the doctor would be marrying beneath him he would acquire a finished social product, perfectly presentable in upper-class life, as well as a sound economic asset.

These factors are drolly at odds with the simpler fictional pattern in the novel—the villain and hero pattern of *Desperate Remedies*—and it is this which produces Hardy's particular sort of social comedy, a comedy excessively laborious and overdone in *The Hand of Ethelberta*, but in *The Woodlanders* effectively underplayed and even moving. Grace plays the part of damsel in distress, but is as often, and more decisively, rescued by the villain as by the hero. Winterborne, who should get the girl in the end, fails and dies; and Fitzpiers as villain redeems himself, saves the heroine by means of a magical potion, and finally from the clutches of the sea-monster man-trap. The anti-typhoid remedy, with which Fitzpiers supplies Grace to ward off from her the same death as Winterborne's, is one of the most gratuitous pieces of mumbo-jumbo in Hardy, but it has the decisive effect of making her feel how clever, accomplished and attractive he is, sentiments which at this point in the novel she should feel only for the "hero." Moreover although Grace rescues herself from the man-trap, by her own agility and quickness of mind, it is witnessing the villain's genuine misery and grief at her loss, when he supposes she has been badly hurt, which decisively determines her becoming his own again. The villain has himself passed the kind of tests heroes pass, by rejecting Felice the false Florimel, with a little magic help from Marty, who reveals the secret of the false hair.

It is typical of Hardy's peculiar genius that all this reversal acts to have the opposite of any parodic or depreciatory effect. The hero becomes more moving for his failure, the villain the more interesting and convincing, the heroine more equivocal and more alive. It is impossible not to feel that, for all his protestations, this is the way Hardy's underlying powers of fantasy really wanted it to be. He can identify deeply with all three players: in their ambitions, or lack of them, their status, their dreams and desires. His most persistent and powerful fantasy; the erotic link with the social superior, which had been played out at a simple level in his unpublished first effort, *The Poor Man and the Lady,* and in the touching nouvelle *An Indiscretion in the Life of an Heiress,* here takes on its most subtle and multiform shape, more subtle in its way than when it achieves its grand apotheosis in *Tess of the D'Urbervilles.*

Intimate indications of the erotic theme make an early appearance. As Grace is driven home by Winterborne after finishing at a fashionable school she looks at the orchards he points out, and in which the different apple species were once familiar to her, but her inner eye is looking at "a broad lawn in the fashionable suburb of a fast city, the evergreen leaves shining in the evening sun, amid which bounding girls, gracefully clad in artistic arrangements of blue, brown, red, and white, were playing at games, with laughter and chat, in all the pride of life, the notes of piano and harp trembling in the air from the open windows adjoining." Hardy's curious style of subterraneous humour is much in evidence here. (Why should these high-class modern misses seemingly wear every colour except green? And how can a whole city be "fast," unless it be in contrast to the innocence of the bounding girls?) Entering Grace's mind and merging it in his own fantasy of femininity, he travels easily in his own fashion to her bedroom, which "wore at once a look more familiar than when she had left it, and yet a face estranged. The world of little things therein gazed at her in helpless stationariness, as if they had tried and been unable to make any progress without her presence." Relations between the fashionable suburb, with its school of bounding girls, and the home world of helpless little things, is at once droll and touching. More important, it mixes the intimacy of Hardyan fantasy with his down to earth sense of the reality of things. All the persons in *The Woodlanders* are touched with a new kind of smallness, not at all like that of French realism, though it may derive in part from Hardy's reading in the French novelists, but congenial to his never backward sense of the unfitness of things, which becomes all too dramatically explicit in *Tess* and *Jude.* In *The Woodlanders* it is still below the surface, in the sub-world of Hardy's consciousness.

To the creative power of that consciousness it is specially important here that the characters live in the novel between two worlds, unable to go forward or back. So, in his own creative life, did Hardy himself, and it explains both his proclaimed estrangement from the novel, and its heroine, and his subterraneous attachment to them. Grace's erotic attraction proceeds from her being part country and part town, from the felt life that comes from her division between worlds, as well as between genres. This is clear if we compare her with those two completely lifeless heroines, Fancy Day of *Under the Greenwood Tree* and Anne Garland of *The Trumpet Major,* both pre-formed products of a selected genre. At the same time the divisions in Grace are not so emphatically stylized as they are in Tess and in Sue Bridehead, who owe to them a pseudo-tragic status on which Hardy is rather too insistent. Indeed the two later heroines forfeit in some degree the attractions of divided genre because of the way Hardy frames them inside a pre-formed scenario of doom.

Grace is a survivor. And so is Fitzpiers. Hardy does not like survivors but he can do nothing about it. "He could not make her" be otherwise, as he may or may not have said to Rebekah Owen. A great part of the effectiveness of the novel comes from Hardy not being able to do anything about it, from his not pursuing what is in practice his own self-indulgent path, as he did in *A Pair of Blue Eyes* and *The Mayor of Casterbridge,* as he was to do more spectacularly in *Tess* and *Jude.* His love of disaster found itself balked in *The Woodlanders* with the result that the hero and heroine (as Grace and Fitzpiers ambiguously are) occupy a position midway between the genre figures in the earlier novels and the tragic state of Tess and Jude and Sue. The way a wry social comedy—*Measure for Measure* comedy if we like—asserts and carries through its powers to a rising finish, is revealed if we compare the end with that of *The Return of the Native,* where a drop in tension and a loss in the novel's inner selfhood takes place. Whatever its other qualities, that novel lacks comic sharpness, which in *The Woodlanders* gives so marked a feel to the ending, to the wry survival of hero and heroine in their by no means uninteresting new situation, and the stasis of the abandoned woodland and its dead champion.

Grace as survivor is exhibited significantly early in the novel, when Fitzpiers from his window watches the passers-by open the gate which has been freshly painted. Grace is the only one adroit and wary enough to perceive its condition and push it open by arming herself with a little stick. This slight incident connects her with the genre heroine who always just escapes the misfortunes which beset her. But her wedding itself significantly resembles that of Cytherea Graye to the villain Manston in *Desperate Remedies*, Hardy's paragraphing emphasizing the passive wait for something inevitable.

> . . . She awoke: the morning had come.
> Five hours later she was the wife of Fitzpiers.

Cytherea Graye is a heroine whose name itself suggests with ingenuous transparency a mixture of genres—the passive deaths and lives of the poet's Elegy, and the chastely beautiful Shakespearean heroine glimpsed by the voyeur. The poet Gray makes an incongruous appearance on the day of Grace's wedding, with Winterborne "sometimes seen" stretched indifferently under a tree in the vicinity, and Grace imagining the "purple light" of love, which she is conscious now of not particularly feeling. Uncertain and all but unconscious in *Desperate Remedies,* the comedy now is both subtle and unmistakable, the humour a vehicle of uninsistent truths. It is in its own way touchingly comic that Hardy, who sees Tess and Sue from a man's point of view as sexual beings, with sex attributed to them from outside, should be instinctively so much at one with a heroine like Grace or Cytherea. He felt at home with them, and thus (in the case of Grace) indifferent to them, rather than seeing them with any masculine fervency. Hardy, we can be sure, felt as doomed by his wedding as Grace was, and as uncertain of what had become of imagined passion. He was a congenital survivor himself, largely through the means of passivity, and his imagination correspondingly admired the grander notion of those self-driven to their doom—Eustacia and Henchard, Tess and Sue.

Hardy's involuntary closeness to Grace and Fitzpiers is thus at the heart of the novel's comedy. He is in league with Grace's combination of the passive and the adroit, seeing her as "she moved along, a vessel of emotion, going to empty herself on she knew not what." He is as much or more in league with Fitzpiers, whose first appearance, in Grammer Oliver's gossipings to Grace, is of a curious innocency and childishness. He seems to have confided in the old woman ("Ah, Grammer. . . . There's only me and not me in the whole world") as artlessly as Hardy might have done with his own mother. Like Hardy, Fitzpiers is "a deep perusing gentleman," and, as Grammer Oliver says, "a man of strange meditations." No other novel of Hardy's has so closely humorous a relation between the "me and not me"— "not me" being the woodland scene by which the poetry of the novel is engrossed, but to which it cannot belong. Grace's own position as, so to speak, both "me and not me" is not only one in which Hardy himself is closely involved, but is embodied in the novel's mixture of modes, a testimony to the mobility of consciousness which makes his fictions—and this one peculiarly—so restlessly alive, like Melbury's own movements, reflecting his sense of Grace's new-won superiorities. More than usually with Hardy, the different modes identify with social pressures and aspirations, and all that is both uneasy and seductive about them.

It has often been said that Mrs Charmond and the world she represents are unreal compared to the woodlanders and their life, because Hardy's imagination is not at home in her world. On the contrary; it seems to me that he conveys it with remarkable understanding and poignancy. Felice Charmond, like Grace herself, is a "self-made" woman, a woman, that is to say, not entirely at home in the "me" which circumstances, and her own enterprise and initiative, have conspired to construct. There is a real bond between the two, implicit in the way in which both look to Fitzpiers, the "superior" man, and cling to the reassurance of their social achievement which his attentions represent. There is no simple contrast in the novel, of a Gray's Elegy sort, between peaceful Hintock and restless world. Restlessness and aspiration seep, as it were, into every nook of the woodland, disturbing Winterborne and Marty

South as much as the others. Hardy's peculiar humour is instinct in the graphic scene of Marty splitting the gads: the most vivid account of cottage industry anywhere in Hardy's work. For all her skill—and though Winterborne calls it a trade, we believe her when she says she could learn it in two hours—there is no satisfaction in it for her. The blistered hand holding the billhook might have been as good at drawing or playing an instrument ("Hands, that the rod of empire might have swayed, Or waked to ecstasy the living lyre"), but the trite point from the Elegy is given real substance and feeling in the image of Marty brooding about her hair and her love, brooding in the same situation of restless fatigue as Felice Charmond herself, with whom the long locks of her chestnut hair intimately and secretly connect her.

The whole notion of mobility, which is so unexpectedly and disturbingly alive in *The Woodlanders,* does more than give a more deeply felt and impressioned picture of its characters than any genre picture could do. It also disturbs Hardy's determinism, his essentially rather comforting notion that everything in human nature and affairs goes on "like the hands of a clock" (one of Fitzpiers's occasional reflections as reported by Grammer). Maybe that was why he sometimes professed to be alienated from this novel, though there is other evidence that he felt in fact very close to it, and in it. Images of Grace as quite at home in the new world she has entered, even though it will always be partly the "not me," go incongruously with visions of Marty herself bounding about in the "fast city," clad in an artistic arrange-ment of blue, brown, red, or white, of carpets on farm labourers' stairs, and pianos in their sitting-rooms. To all these promises and possibilities, which his own life so fully exemplified, something in Hardy's make-up, and the reassurance which the sombreness of imaginative fiction represented to him, remained inimical. Did he resent Grace for being successful, at least poten-tially, where her touching predecessor Geraldine Allenville, the fantasy por-trait of *An Indiscretion in the Life of an Heiress,* was of course condemned to an abrupt but fated extinction, as Tess was to be? His master-fantasy, that of the Poor Man and the Lady, had so far involved the death of the lady—an Elfride or a Geraldine—before failure or disillusion of a more humdrum kind could come along. Grace as "poor girl" reversed the pattern, succeeding where the poor man had failed, though at the cost of becoming involved in a realistic pattern of uncertainties and infidelities.

Hardy himself, like Fitzpiers, had a roving eye and the capacity to feel tenderly towards several ladies at the same time. Furthermore, and paradoxi-cally, this is the only Hardy novel in which a husband and wife get along moderately well and affectionately together, engaging, both overtly and im-plicitly, in the sort of shifts, deceits, keeping up of appearances and salvaging of domestic pride, which are commonplaces of the routinely imperfect mar-ried state. Both by nature and from the growth of experience Grace seems set to become that least rewarding of all women to most novelists, and to Hardy in particular: the sort who get along by means of life's small comforts and compensations, in the midst of general and accepted unsatisfactoriness.

This is the state so resonantly hinted at in the discovery of Elizabeth-Jane at the end of *The Mayor of Casterbridge,* the state of "making limited opportunities endurable" by means of "those minute forms of satisfaction that offer themselves to every person not in positive pain."

The contrast involved is certainly the most important in Hardy's creative imagination. It produces that unusual sense of perspective in the novels which is also their sense of humour. On the one hand his fantasy, harmoniously allied with the traditions of the form, spun its web of drama and death, tragedy and suffering. On the other, he implicitly represents the small possibilities of life, its little ironies, but taken—in novels as in poems—in a not sardonic sense. The combination of the two in *The Woodlanders* is particularly marked, and the incongruity involved is sufficient to "disturb" the novel in a way that is unique in the works of his maturity. From his comments I suspect that it made him uncomfortable too, and he did not repeat the kind of situation that gave rise to it. In *Tess* and *Jude* the fantasy figures dominate, and tragedy is comfortably in control. It is characteristic of Hardy that in *The Woodlanders* he was himself personally most alienated from situations which in fact show us most clearly—for him all too clearly—how his art works.

With this in mind it is illuminating to compare the ending of *The Woodlanders* with that of *Jude the Obscure.* In both the same sort of compensatory mechanism seems at work, restoring the dignities and finalities of tragedy, the positiveness of pathos and love, but in fact there is a very significant difference. Arabella has the last word in *Jude,* declaring that Sue Bridehead has never found peace since she left Jude's arms, "and never will again till she's as he is now." This seems, indeed is, an appropriate comment on which to conclude, but the least observant reader can hardly help noticing that Sue certainly had no peace when she was in Jude's arms—Hardy saw to that and devoted considerable ingenuity to his task. It might be said to be a satisfactory irony that the two women whose words conclude the novel—Arabella and the widow Edlin—show a similar lack of understanding of what has been going on in it, one piously maintaining that Sue "said she had found peace" in returning to the schoolmaster Phillotson, the other sardonically denying that for her such peace can be had, except in death or with the true loved one. The trouble is that the two women inadvertently reveal that their author himself was in a sad state of muddle on the point. Hardy was deeply involved with Sue as a fantasy figure, as deeply as he had been with Tess. But there was no doubt that Tess loved Angel Clare, and Hardy showed it with all the tenderness he felt for the idea of her. Moreover he could and did kill her off, as he killed off most of his fantasy ladies, from Elfride and Geraldine onwards. She has the ingenious fantasy attribute that she keeps men, and kept Jude, in a state of perpetual amatory fever by "withholding" her self. Hardy imagines her as the incarnation of the voyeur's dream, the girl glimpsed but never attained, the charmer who never becomes a domestic possession.

However satisfactory to Hardy's day-dream, such an image of Sue presents a problem to the novelist's sense of reality. What was she like in herself?

And this problem Hardy never begins to solve: his ending merely calls attention to the lack of a solution. There are intimations that a "real" Sue, as opposed to Hardy's dream of her, might have got along somehow, however much trouble she caused herself and others; and that she might have settled in an imperfect marriage, either with Jude or Phillotson, to which time would have added the usual humdrum philosophical compensations. Or she might have evaded both of them and lived as the kind of ambiguous spinster not uncommon in any age and society. But Hardy is trapped, as he was not in *The Woodlanders,* in both a predetermined fantasy and a predetermined "tragical" situation. And the tragical element requires that Sue, like Cathy and Heathcliff, can have no peace outside Jude's arms, a view manifestly untenable in an intelligent reading of the novel.

The trouble is that the mode mixture is not working equably in *Jude,* as it worked in *The Woodlanders.* To quote Penny Boumelha again, the "interrogative awareness of the literary modes within which it is working . . . is crystallised in the figure of Grace . . . , the centre of its shifts in tone and point of view." Grace cannot be "a realist heroine," because "she migrates unsettlingly between pastoral survival, tragic protagonist, realist centre of consciousness, and melodramatic heroine." The narrator seems to know his way around the other characters, but, as Miss Boumelha shrewdly notes, in relation to Grace his tone becomes curiously "tentative and deferential." Hardy calls her "a conjectural creature who had little to do with the outlines presented to Sherton eyes," and says that "what people saw of her was . . . truth, mainly something that was not she."

This presents a great contrast with the modes in which Sue is seen, with their mixture of Hardy's personal fantasy, tragic pathos, and a strong attempt at realistic and objective definition. Sue, in fact, recedes into a muddle as a result of being treated in these ways; she is trapped among them as she is represented as being trapped among the conditions of life; yet it helps not at all that Hardy's formal treatment of her imitates the given facts of her story—very much the reverse. But the mode mixture in which Grace is portrayed is so yieldingly malleable that she escapes easily, living in the between-land of what I have called "she and not she." And with surely admirable results, for the whole tone of the book is that of living between worlds, and with ambiguous identity, to which Hardy's consciousness is itself deeply given. Because Grace is divided between two suitors, and thus two ways of life, it has been suggested by another critic that her significance lies in "providing Hardy with an opportunity to do a first sketch for Sue Bridehead."[5] But the resemblance of form and pattern is misleading, for no one less like Sue than Grace could possibly be imagined. Indeed her success is in the fact that she is so unlike, and in the reasons for it, reasons which even Miss Boumelha seems to think add up to a kind of failing or failure on Hardy's part. But Hardy's "failures," in this sense, are often more interesting, and more convincing deep down, than his more striking and notorious creations.

Sue is such a creation, and it is in the final words of her novel that we may perhaps discover how fundamentally unreal she is. The more often we read *The Woodlanders,* on the other hand, the more richly satisfying and convincing become Grace and her exit, and both are managed in terms of a peculiarly Hardyan kind of social comedy. The success may even be partly due to Hardy's own haste and cursoriness in working on and completing the novel, for such exigence often finds him at his peculiar best. Grace disappears into the monotonies of living; and Hardy's nearness to her is shown by nothing so much as Marty South's own words that close the novel, giving the reader an unexpected intimacy with Hardy's own feeling for himself as a "strange continuator" of "my simple self that was." Although Grace, as Marty thinks, has forgotten Winterborne at last, the valediction has a kind of bleak comfort that is wholly apt for her, as well as for Marty herself. It is the comfort of small things, which Marty invokes in remembrance, and which spread a commonplace benediction like the unperturbed cadence of a parson's voice. There is no question here of "love" being invoked, as in *Jude,* as a means of elevating the finale *tel quel,* for Marty's tenderness knows of Winterborne's nature ("the one thing he never spoke of to me was love; nor I to him"), and she is celebrating the days together and their small activities as any wife might do in looking back on any marriage, no matter how unsuccessful. Elegiac as they are, Marty's words confirm the sense of the novel as predominantly a comedy of small things, and very honest ones.

Notes

1. Penny Boumelha, *Thomas Hardy and Women: Sexual Ideology and Narrative Form* (Brighton: Harvester Press, 1982). This and subsequent quotations are taken from ch. V of Penny Boumelha's book.

2. John Bayley, *An Essay on Hardy* (Cambridge University Press, 1978; repr. 1979) p. 31.

3. David Lodge, Introduction to *The Woodlanders,* New Wessex Edition (London: Macmillan, 1975) pp. 13–22.

4. Quoted by Carl J. Weber, "Hardy and *The Woodlanders,*" *Review of English Studies,* xv (1939) 332.

5. Ian Gregor, *The Great Web: The Form of Hardy's Major Fiction* (London: Faber, 1974) p. 156.

Pure Tess: Hardy on Knowing a Woman

Kathleen Blake*

From the title page, the reader knows Hardy's heroine as Tess of the D'Urbervilles and as "A Pure Woman," in other words, as individual and as

*Reprinted by permission from *Studies in English Literature, 1500–1900* 22(1982): 689–705.

pure abstraction. The novel's title and subtitle introduce a dialectic of knowledge which is shown to generate both good and ill, Tess's charm and her tragedy. This dialectic shapes theme, imagery, and allusion, narrative structure, and dramatic interaction, and it also makes itself eloquently felt throughout in Hardy's own language about his heroine. It even permeates the language of critics responding to the novel. At stake are Hardy's ideas about knowledge of the beautiful and the beloved, and, as a novel about knowing a woman, *Tess* offers his finest exposition of these ideas.

Hardy's post-romantic historical moment as well as his own reading and temperament inducted him into the epistemological wars whose battle lines are laid out by Hume and Kant. Kant takes up arms against Hume's characterization of experience as a mere aggregate of perceptions and instead declares the power of the mind to legislate experience.[1] Hardy's fascination with eighteenth- and nineteenth-century philosophers of understanding and their notable literary heir, Shelley, has been pointed out by Tom Paulin in his study of the writer's poetry. This epistemological interest is well represented in a picture Hardy once drew; sketching a landscape where he had danced with a girl, he superimposed a pair of giant eyeglasses to depict the contingency of reality upon the focal powers of the observer's eyes.[2] And he says in *Tess* that "the world is only a psychological phenomenon, and what [things] seemed they were" (p. 108).[3]

Of abiding interest to Hardy is apprehension of the general in relation to the particular within the seeming that makes reality, and the way a woman is apprehended provides a measure of this dialectic which reveals its complexity. And so in *Tess* he explores the question: what happens when the object of knowledge is also the object of aesthetic response[4] and of love? He finds what happens full of delight and danger.

The novel's title names the particular and attaches it to the universal in the subtitle. Tess bears a proper name as a unique person, while she is universalized as a pure woman. In defending his controversial subtitle in the preface to the fifth and subsequent editions of the novel, Hardy suggests connotations of the word "pure" that critics had missed. He says, "They ignore the meaning of the word in Nature, together with all aesthetic claims upon it, not to mention the spiritual interpretation afforded by the finest side of their own Christianity" (p. viii). This whole statement is more provocative than clear, and I believe that the final reference to spirituality aims more at scoring a debater's point than anything else, in that it allows Hardy to capitalize by means of irony on a meaning overlooked by his Christian critics. Many such critics had balked at attributing purity to a fornicator, unwed mother, sometimes religious skeptic, a wife who rejoins her former lover, a murderess. Tess failed to impress them with ethical purity, judged according to religious doctrine, erotic morality, or the law of the land.[5] But, dissatisfied with commonplace understanding of his phrase, Hardy hints at wider, alternate meanings. In the case of this subtitle, signification does vary profoundly as a function of inflection. "A púre woman" does not equal "a pure wóman" (while "a púre woman" may go either way). The first proclaims Tess a woman of certain character; the second proclaims her a woman, as though placing her within a natural and aesthetic class, as though linking her appeal to a general concept of woman's place in nature's scheme. In suggesting the connotation of natural and aesthetic purity in his preface, Hardy moves the meaning toward a new realm, that of the archetypal, essential, ideal, generic.

Though Hardy hints at such factors in Tess's purity, I cannot claim that he usually uses the word "pure" with these connotations. His critics might have defended their interpretation by pointing to the author's habitual and quite ordinary presentation of purity as an erotic characteristic, as equivalent to maidenhood, the "pure and chaste" (p. 336). This meaning hovers behind Angel Clare's notion of the "spotless," "unsullied," that is, sexually "intact" state (pp. 337, 435). Alec D'Urberville shifts the meaning somewhat. As he sees it, Tess need not be physically intact to remain psychologically "unsmirched" by erotic experience (p. 411). Still, his meaning involves a notion of erotic morality. Indeed, J. T. Laird's study of the novel's development through manuscript and published versions reveals the easy interchangeability, for Hardy, of the words "chastity" and "purity." Hardy is undeniably concerned with the erotic issue in Tess's case. His revisions reveal such concern. For instance, in later versions he takes care to downplay the heroine's sensual responsiveness and culpability, while emphasizing Angel's attraction to her specifically virginal appeal.[6] Hardy makes Tess an ever purer woman, in this sense. Critics might have claimed justification for their moral, and more particularly erotic standard of assessment.

Very few have apprehended purity in any other way. Among these few, D. H. Lawrence calls Tess a self-establishing aristocrat and in that sense "pure-bred." J. Hillis Miller calls parenthetical attention to the word "pure" and allows us to see that, like Lawrence's phrase "pure-bred," certain phrases of Hardy's such as "pure inadvertence" and "purely the product of the writer's own mind" connote the entire, integral, and essential.[7] In the novel itself the most significant sample of such a meaning appears in Hardy's description of Tess as "a field-woman pure and simple" (p. 357). The passage strips her of individuality to make her a figure in the landscape, and it departs from ethical/erotic signification. The phrase itself does not propose that a field-woman is pure and simple; it proposes that she is a field-woman and nothing but a field-woman. It asserts very nearly the same thing as an early characterization of Tess: "she was a fine and picturesque country girl, and no more" (p. 14). In such a manner may the subtitle suggest the meaning—a woman and nothing but a woman, unspotted, unsullied, unsmirched by particularity—while the title specifies the particular woman by her own name. Tess presents the paradoxical spectacle of the "*almost* standard woman" (p. 114; emphasis mine). On the one hand, she is a being for whom "the universe itself only came into being . . . on the particular day in the particular year in which she was born" (p. 199). On the other hand, she is "a visionary essence of woman—a whole sex condensed into one typical form" (p. 167).

The novel's hero, Angel Clare, favors the latter, purist point of view. As we know, Hardy shaped Angel partly from his understanding of Shelley, as he did Jocelyn Pierston in *The Well-Beloved* (1897). It is worthwhile to look at Walter Bagehot's portrait of the poet since it made a strong early impression on Hardy[8] and may well have influenced his presentation of these Shelley-like heroes, setting him to contemplate the sort of purity in women desired by such men. Admiring Shelley, Bagehot also criticizes him as an idealist and simplifier in love, as in his other passions, so that his poetry expresses desire for all women in one rather than for any one woman. In his analysis of the Shelleyan experience of love for a single, unvarying figure under many apparitions, Bagehot seems to point Hardy toward the novelistic fantasia of *The Well-Beloved*, with its Shelleyan epigraph (from *Laon and Cythna*), "One shape of many names." This novel follows its hero's infatuations with serial copies of his single idea of the feminine. Bagehot finds such a passion intense at the expense of complexity or potential for development. He perhaps seeds Hardy's mind with a definition of purity and a line of thought leading to *Tess* and its subtitle when he calls the beloved of a Shelley poem "the pure object of the essential passion."[9] Here "pure" exempts the beloved not only from erotic but from *any* adulteration. As aesthetic and romantic object, she becomes generic for her gender.

2

"A field-man is a personality afield; a field-woman is a portion of the field; she has somehow lost her own margin, imbibed the essence of her surrounding, and assimilated herself with it" (p. 111). This is another way of calling her a field-woman pure and simple, and such a notion of purity enters into Hardy's fascination throughout *Tess* with loss of margin, that is, with diffusion of uniqueness in favor of generic status. Hardy examines the trade-off between gain and loss in this transaction. Thus he points out the field-woman's "charm" (p. 111), while the novel as a whole subjects the sources and consequences of such charm to a probing critique.

While a woman's release from personality to become a portion of the field, an "essence of woman," or "soul at large" (p. 167), is the most significant mode of marginlessness treated, there are a number of others contributing to the novel's theme. For example, alcohol breaks down margins and offers pleasing expansion beyond petty, everyday identity. The imbibers at Rolliver's Inn find that "their souls expanded beyond their skins, and spread their personalities warmly through the room" (p. 27). In the same way, the Saturday-night revelers of Tantridge reel home liberated from the confines of self into harmony with natural forces, "themselves and surrounding nature forming an organism of which all the parts harmoniously and joyously interpenetrated each other" (p. 81). In a lovely image, the moonlit, misty halos that waver round their unsteady heads, compounded of the light, the dewy air, and the fumes of their own breathing, spread these men and women abroad into the night. No longer Car Darch, Nancy, and their partners, they merge with the atmosphere, and nature "seemed harmoniously to mingle with the spirit of wine" (p. 84).

Nature, like wine, can gratify the soul by drawing it forth from its margin. Tess seeks out the hour between day and night whose balanced light lets loose the spirit and allows it to wander "an integral part of the scene" (p. 108). "Our souls can be made to go outside our bodies when we are alive," Tess says, and cultivates the feeling by gazing at the stars (p. 154). As dawn illumination makes Tess look like a "soul at large," and as a moonlit mist allows the Tantridge revelers to join with the night, other effects of light serve to blur the psychological edges. The dancers of Tantridge dim into the nebulosity of a warm atmosphere of candle-lit sweat and peat-dust. They merge with the natural scene amidst a sort of "vegeto-human-pollen," and become nature gods, figures of Pan whirling Syrinx, Lotis attempting to elude Priapus (p. 77).

Supporting the idea and imagery of marginlessness, a system of mythological allusions drawn from nature cults metamorphoses the particular into the general throughout the novel, as seen in the opening pageant of the Marlott club-walking. Here women of the village re-enact a timeless Cerealia. Their white dresses unify them into group identity and release them to some extent from the "real" into the "ideal" (p. 11). Much criticism has been devoted to such mythic patterning, as well as to the animal imagery that assimilates Tess to nature. In the same vein, Angel and Tess converge like two streams at Talbothay's Dairy, and the entire sequence is famous for its humano-natural convergences. The pair becomes by implication another generic "instalment" of young lovers like any other springtime "instalment of flowers, leaves, nightingales, thrushes, finches, and such ephemeral creatures" (p. 165).

In sex we see one of nature's strongest means of diffusing unique personality. Hence Hardy's strange narrative device of triplicating Tess in the other dairymaids who fall in love with Angel. According to "Nature's Law," "the differences which distinguished them as individuals were abstracted by this passion, and each was but portion of one organism called sex" (p. 187). It has distressed many readers, but Tess herself seems to be partly duplicated and replaced in Angel's heart by her surviving sister Liza Lu, in accordance with the abstracting law of love.

Nature's power of duplication, or triplication, figures elsewhere as temporal repetition. Hence the novel's preoccupation with history, especially in the form of D'Urberville family history. Like multiplication of those in love or loved, repetition of the doings of all who went before seems to erode autonomy, and Tess finds this loss of margin sad instead of welcome. Hardy makes repetition structural to his novel by introducing tales parallel to Tess's round Dairyman Crick's table, and many critics have stressed the ballad origin of her story.

Throughout the novel the marginless state takes different forms, both attractive and disturbing. In a landscape description on the final page marginlessness appears again. Here at the end Tess has symbolically lost her margin by suggested merging with the sister who takes her place at Angel's side. Just so, the landscape extends itself by means of a characteristically limit-dissolving light, and the pair gazes at "landscape beyond landscape, till the horizon was lost in the radiance of the sun hanging above it" (p. 507). This description of a boundless panorama oddly parallels a description of the mental viewpoint of the stranger Angel meets in Brazil, who persuades him to take the long view of Tess's moral breach: "to his cosmopolitan mind such deviations from the social norm, so immense to domesticity, were no more than are the irregularities of vale and mountain-chain to the whole terrestrial curve" (p. 434). And in a comparable description Tess herself reveals panoramic possibilities, a unity of infinite extension like a limitless landscape, for her eyes do not confine themselves in color to black, blue, gray, or violet, but present "rather all those shades together, and a hundred others—, . . . shade beyond shade—tint beyond tint" (p. 114).

Of course, I must reach a turn in my argument with these examples of marginless vistas, for no one can forget the counter-examples of vividly localized landscapes created by Hardy in *Tess*. He describes closely hilled-in and utterly distinct valleys. Blackmoor Vale is intrinsically different from the Vale of the Little Dairies. The two dairy valleys could not contrast more strikingly with the Chase and Flintcomb-Ash. Not even the train joins these separate locales, and Hardy insists that "every village has its idiosyncrasy, its constitution, often its own code of morality" (p. 75).

Just as Hardy closes in his boundless landscapes, so he indicates constraints on each of the previously mentioned marginless states. Without alcohol souls again contract within their skins. Nature sometimes refuses to intermingle and harmonize with the feelings and thus blur the line dividing scene and figure, as when Tess's arrival produces no impression at all on Blackmoor Vale. Only approximately mythic, the club-walking female votaries wear white gowns which a bright sun reveals to be of noticeably different shades and cuts, and in these women "ideal and real clashed slightly" (p. 11). Pans and Syrinxes resume ordinary personal identities as Car Darch, Nancy, and other Tantridge locals. Tess and Angel do not complete as standard an "instalment" of nature's springtime scenario as the birds and flowers do, for aberration marks their love. The generalizing power of sex does not carry the other dairymaids into actual equivalence with Tess, nor does Liza Lu adequately replace her, as many readers have felt. Tess only partly recapitulates stock family traits. She shares some of the fatalistic passivity of the D'Urbervilles and seems destined to repeat their violence, but she does not inherit her father's foolish vanity nor her mother's fecklessness and cheer. While Tess's history repeats traditional folklore materials, personal experience gives them very personal meaning—"What was comedy to [others] was tragedy to her" (p. 231).

Just one page after Hardy calls Tess a field-woman who merges with the field and yields her own margin, he forcefully reconfines her within herself.

With her baby and no husband, she occupies those fields as a "stranger and alien" (p. 112). Much of the book shows how far Tess diverges from the field-woman pure and simple.

A parallel exists between this individuation of Tess and another example of human individuation in the book, and in this parallel lies an important commentary. Hardy presents in his rustics a seemingly collective "Hodge," whose generic oneness disappears upon closer inspection. We soon realize that each "walked in his own individual way the road to dusty death" (p. 152). Explaining his convictions about Hodge in an article on "The Dorsetshire Labourer," Hardy observes of rustic laborers that "the artistic merit of their old condition is scarcely a reason why they should have continued in it. . . . It is too much to ask them to remain stagnant and old-fashioned for the pleasure of romantic spectators."[10] This suggests the "artistic" appeal of gener-alizations about Hodge, thus illuminating Hardy's reference to the "aes-thetic" dimension of purity in the preface to *Tess*. Placing such purity in a problematical light, the statement provides a critical gloss on the "charm" seen in the field-woman who loses her margin to form part of the field. The "Dorsetshire Labourer" passage judges such artistically agreeable class group-ing as the wrongful imposition of the spectator's eye, distorting in a way that does disservice to its object.

Thus Tess, like Hodge, may lack a certain charm when viewed as only an individual, but when viewed as someone released from the margins of indi-viduality into pure womanhood, she gains charm at a certain risk. That risk dominates the drama that unfolds between Tess and Angel Clare.

3

Certain statements by Hardy concerning perception serve to introduce his critique of Angel's attitude toward Tess. On the one hand, Hardy lacks misgivings about the truth-value of perception legislated by the categories of the perceiver's mind. As may be inferred from his declarations of the impres-sionistic nature of his own work, he surrenders without protest the possibil-ity of reliable mental access to things-in-themselves.[11] On the other hand, Hardy does have misgivings about the impact on the Tess or the Hodge mentally modified in the name of the artistic, aesthetic, charming, and in this way made subject to another's subjectivity. Thus a striking passage in *The Well-Beloved* describes the rolling together into one composite essence of all the bones of the drowned in Deadman's Bay and the single roar made by these surf-rolled bones in the listening ear. Yet the passage makes the roar a shriek, for those joined in death seem to call out to some good god to disunite them from their grisly idealist oneness (pp. 12–13).[12] No more than these dead men distressed by their loss of individuality in the minds of those who thrill to the composite music of their bones does Tess always relish or gain by being appreciated as a pure woman. Hardy examines the meeting point of epistemology, aesthetics, and love. He shows that knowledge of the beloved and the beautiful is liable to be specially compromised. He shows the special danger of appreciation, for it may dissipate the desire to know more.[13]

The problem is, Angel's infatuated taste makes him dispense with further knowledge. Appreciating Tess "ideally and fancifully" (p. 260), he "subdue[s] . . . the substance to the conception" and "drops the defects of the real" in favor of an ideal (pp. 313, 312). Finding Tess lovely and loving her, he considers corporeal absence almost more appealing than presence (p. 312). He regularly renders her a type in his mind: archetypal milkmaid, "virginal daughter of Nature" (p. 155), "daughter of the soil" (p. 162), representative of primitive consciousness untouched by modern doubt, and perfect sample for his contemplation of "contiguous womankind" (p. 155). It is true, he sometimes thinks he delights in her for her very self rather than, for instance, the things he has told his family she represents (p. 211). One occasion shows his capacity to imagine Tess's apprehension of the world from within her own center of self, and, another time, he tries to project her viewpoint as one different from his own as that of a man (pp. 198–99, 278). However, the crisis of their relationship reveals his habit of generalization when it comes to Tess and his commitment to her purity in the erotic sense *and* as a being so summed up by his conception of her that she must remain pure of any particular experience worth mentioning. Seeing Tess as essence and type, Angel cannot admit the relevance of experience for her, and so he refuses to hear her confession about her past affair with Alec. Once confronted by Tess's un-intactness, Angel's penchant for generalization intensifies, and he casts the fallen Tess as the typical peasant woman and representative of a decadent family, in contrast to the idealized "new-sprung child of nature" (p. 297) and example of "rustic innocence" (p. 304) he had expected. Significantly, he inveighs against "womankind in general" (p. 308). Angel typecasts Tess in terms of class, family, nature, and sex, but sexual typing exercises the most powerful sway. The novel stresses it by making the drama hinge on the issue of erotic purity, which is definitive for women but not for men—Angel's own un-intact state bothers him very little. His horror of Tess's un-intactness bespeaks his allegiance to the purity of the generic as such, as well as to the feminine principle of erotic purity that furnishes the dramatic test.

Tess usually resists imposition of generic classification upon her specificity. Even though she does sometimes enjoy release from self, as in contemplating nature, she is no addict of the marginless experience. (She doesn't drink, for one thing, and dislikes repeating stock traits, hereditary or folkloristic.) She resents being understood as "every woman" by Alec and responds angrily by exclaiming, "Did it never strike your mind that what every woman says some women may feel?" (p. 97). Just so, when Angel perceives her as a "soul at large" and calls her by the names of female deities as if she presented a "visionary essence," a "typical form" of woman, Tess wants none of it: " 'Call me Tess,' she would say askance" (p. 167). In successive revisions Hardy gives increasing point to this reply by making Tess speak it at first softly and simply but finally askance.[14] She wants to be loved for herself and not for the image superimposed on her. Sadly she realizes, "she you love is not my real self, but one in my image" (p. 273), and this same thought gives rise to a moment of self-pity for ill use (p. 294). She comes to judge Angel's condemnation as reflective of his fastidious mind more than her own fault (p. 296).

For her own part, she is slow to consider people in absolute terms. Certainly, Hardy allows for some typing by Tess of Angel, of a man by a woman. She idolizes him during their courtship, though "Angel Clare was far from all that she thought him" (p. 246). And she exposes a set notion of masculinity when she values Angel for *not* fulfilling it (p. 247). However, Hardy distinguishes between the attitudes of hero and heroine by calling Angel's love more insistently idealizing, while Tess's exhibits more "impassioned thoroughness" (p. 260). She even prefers not to reduce her enemy to a type. One might suppose that Alec's offenses against her, the diabolism of the scenes in which Hardy places him, and his own Satanic self-references would invite Tess to view him as the devil, but she refuses to do so: "I never said you were Satan, or thought it. I don't think of you in that way at all" (p. 445). Reluctant to be the pure woman, Tess is reluctant to regard even the man who drives her to murder as pure devil.

Tess is the greatest among a number of Hardy's works concerned with the loose fit between type and individual. For instance, the poem "The Milkmaid" treats the difference between the milkmaid's seeming embodiment of nature and her actual artificiality of spirit, and "The Beauty" treats the difference between the stock beauty of a woman's face and her personal sense of herself. Like Tess, the speaker in "The Pedigree" hates the thought that, while feeling "I am I," one only exemplifies hereditary traits. A similar thought dismays the dead in "Intra Sepulchrum." In life they considered themselves unique, but once in the grave they realize that, to others, they must have appeared to be quite commonly fashioned. Typing by sex draws Hardy's attention in a number of novels. Whether to explain Paula Power's timidity by her sex or by her temperament, for example, gives the hero pause in *A Laodicean* (1881; p. 303). Hardy's distrust of sexual generalizations appears as early as in *Far from the Madding Crowd* (1874) in a passage on Boldwood's habit of "deeming as essentials of the whole sex the accidents of the single one of their number he had ever closely beheld" (p. 258).[15] Hardy shows such distortion turning dangerous in *Tess of the D'Urbervilles*. In fact, he shows how dangerous it becomes just because it is so pleasant. Delighting to regard the particular Tess as an expression of the universal, Angel delays knowing better what pleases him so much, and the delay proves disastrous.

4

However, the novel incurs a danger comparable to the one it exposes. That is, many critics complain about Angel in terms roughly like mine in the last section,[16] but should we also be complaining about his creator? Hardy generalizes about Tess and women almost as incautiously as Angel does. After all, he is the one who calls Tess a field-woman pure and simple and maintains that such a woman loses her margin to form part of the landscape while a field-man remains a personality afield. And he is the one who calls such a woman charming. His imagery and allusions assimilate Tess to nature and nature myths as animal and goddess. As a case in point, Hardy and not Angel "apotheosizes" Tess as a "divine personage" in the famous baptism scene. He presents her to the view of her brothers and sisters, and the reader, by the light of a candle that "abstracted from her form and features the little blemishes which sunlight might have revealed," "transfiguring" her, rendering her regal and divine, purifying her into "a thing of immaculate beauty" (pp. 119–20). Of course, he does remind us that Tess's apotheosis involves seeing by a certain light quite as much as it involves Tess-in-herself. And Hardy may be said to de-apotheosize his heroine in the treatment immediately following. When he describes Tess's burial of the infant, homely little blemishes return. Tess garnishes the grave with a bunch of flowers in a container in no wise abstracted or transfigured, a "Keelwell's Marmalade" jar (p. 123). Throughout the novel Hardy alternates between idealizing and particularizing Tess. By alternating in this way while also calling attention to it, he may be said to exhibit while also examining the epistemological sources of her tragedy.

Yet in his own language Hardy can seem more intrepid than self-examining. He often generalizes about women surprisingly for a man who had pondered the fairness of it in earlier novels, who had analyzed the potential distortions in a comment on Boldwood and dramatized the real harm that could be done through the story of Angel and Tess. Without apparent self-consciousness Hardy refers in *Tess* to "the woman's instinct to hide," to "feminine loss of courage," to "feminine hope" that is obstinately recuperative, to the usual "feminine feelings of spite and rivalry" (pp. 250, 384, 311, 378). Sentences such as the following appear: "like the majority of women, she accepted the momentary presentment as if it were the inevitable"; "let the truth be told—women do as a rule live through such humiliations"; "she had gathered . . . sufficient of the incredulity of modern thought to despise flash enthusiasms; but, as a woman, she was somewhat appalled" (pp. 312, 135, 419). As phrases, "like the majority of women" and "women do as a rule" clearly generalize. The last-quoted sentence does so more subtly and equivocally. Does "as a woman, she was somewhat appalled" assign her feeling to her as a representative of her sex or as a particular individual who happens to be female? Imagine an apparently parallel sentence reading, "he had gathered sufficient of the incredulity of modern thought to despise flash enthusiasms; but, as a man, he was somewhat appalled." Parallelism is only apparent here, for "man" would signify either a particular individual who happens to be male or else a representative of the human race. The word "man" and the masculine pronoun are often said to function generically. But in standing for mankind as well as for a single man, they do not implicate masculinity. Unless strongly conditioned by context, these words do not act as gender generics since their ambiguous reference vitiates their power of specifically sexual generalization. But "woman" and "she" undergo no such vitiation.

Hardy gives signs of some awareness of the shaping or constraining force of language upon apprehension. For instance, he cites with interest Comte's statement concerning the difficulty of expressing new ideas in existing language, that is, the vehicle for existing conceptualization.[17] The conventional may be so conveniently expressed as to discourage more original response, which inspires Hardy's amusing characterization of Angel Clare's conventional brothers as men who express more than they observe (p. 205). Hardy's sensitivity to the power of labels appears in his dislike of the word and concept Hodge and in his bemusement over his own creation of a concept in creating (or re-creating from ancient usage) the word "Wessex." His seriousness about the need for new language to express new thoughts appears in the striking coinages and syntactical inventions of his poetry. And he indicates critical awareness of the sexual concepts built into language in this observation of Bathsheba's in *Far from the Madding Crowd*: "it is difficult for a woman to define her feelings in language which is chiefly made by men to express theirs" (p. 405).

Hardy does not entirely free himself from masculine language, but his generalizations about women grow less casual and copious as novel follows novel. Practically every folly of Bathsheba Everdene manages in the telling to reflect on her sex. On just one page, she "had too much womanliness to use her understanding to the best advantage," and "she loved Troy in the way that only self-reliant women love when they abandon their self-reliance" (p. 214). In contrast, Sergeant Troy is allowed to represent only himself by his sins. Even in *Far from the Madding Crowd* Hardy passes glancing judgment on the validity of typecasting by sex, but *Tess of the D'Urbervilles* really scrutinizes the sexual typing that plays havoc with a woman's life. In his verbal habits Hardy only partly separates himself from Angel's mental ones, while the irony of the overlap draws attention and actually extends the novel's interest as a commentary on the heroine as pure woman. It dramatizes the author's susceptibility to an outlook shown to be dangerous in the hero. I believe *Tess* must have prepared the way toward the more fully feminist *Jude the Obscure* (1896). This work still hazards generalizations about women; it speculates as to whether Sue Bridehead succumbs to womanly conventionality, or lack of courage, or irrationality. But the novel renders these generalizations so multiple and contradictory as to throw each other into question if not to cancel each other out.[18]

5

This is not to say that Hardy condemns generalization altogether. In his literary notebook he cites Herbert Spencer on biological classification. To group particular organisms into general groups is distortive, yet such grouping is useful and necessary "so long as the distorted form is not mistaken for the actual form . . . giving to the realities a regularity which does not exist."[19] In his essay on "The Profitable Reading of Fiction" Hardy disdains an art of merely photographic particularity and values creative transformation of the subject more than the subject itself. He shares Taine's approval of "imaginations which create and transform."[20] In fact, according to the preface to *The Dynasts* (1903), he relishes an essence-abstracting art such as mumming and aims at parallel effect by means of "dreamy conventional gestures" and an "automatic style." In any dramatization of *The Dynasts* "gauzes or screens to blur outlines might still further shut off the actual."[21] This hypothetical stage direction recalls various treatments of marginlessness in *Tess* and indicates Hardy's penchant for departicularization. Similarly, Florence Emily Hardy's biography records his speculations on a future fiction that would delineate visible essences and abstract thoughts, "the Realities to be the true realities of life, hitherto called abstractions. The old material realities to be placed behind the former, as shadowy accessories."[22] These opinions reveal a devotee of the ideal like Jocelyn Pierston and Angel Clare.

As a matter of fact, Hardy believes that two of the best things life has to offer, both love and art, depend on idealization.[23] Florence Emily Hardy cites a very interesting note of Hardy's about love: "It is the incompleteness that is loved. . . . This is what differentiates the real one from the imaginary. . . . A man sees the Diana or the Venus in his Beloved, but what he loves is the difference."[24] This formulates a dialectic of the general and the particular in the lover's understanding. The general may be said to initiate the experience rather than derive from it, since the type must be viewed in the woman for her departure from type as an individual to be known and loved. Hardy brings this formulation to life in his novel through the attraction of his hero, himself, and, by invitation, his reader toward Tess as the "almost standard woman." As the almost pure woman she commands love.

Such cognitive dynamics in love make it unstable and even treacherous, and Angel Clare's example might seem to recommend letting the standard go and relieving Tess of the painful consequences of only almost fulfilling it. But *The Well-Beloved* shows that not only is love lost but aesthetic response, too, in the loss of a standard. Its Shelleyan hero is finally cured of his mainly disastrous erotic idealism. The single, absolute image of the well-beloved meets extinction in the course of Pierston's symbolic illness, and afterwards he finds himself able to respond to a woman in her manifold particularity, frailties and all. He enters into her situation and viewpoint and takes an interest in her for herself as he has never done before. However, loss attends this gain, for he finds "I can no longer love" (p. 212). Besides that, he finds himself losing artistic inspiration as a sculptor. According to Hardy, then, response to loveliness as well as love itself depends on idealization, which may, in turn, prove over-dominant and destructive. This helps to clarify his prefatory comment on Tess as pure woman, aesthetically understood.

6

Whereas Hardy points out the charm as well as the clash that may be seen in the interplay of ideal and real, critics of the novel tend to focus on ideal *or* real. Actually, most express a preference for a real Tess and judge Hardy according to his failure or success in embodying her, while a number of them simultaneously betray their own attraction toward an ideal Tess in their language about her. Suspicious of Hardy's sexual generalizations, Ellen Moers condemns him for basing his novel on a cultural stereotype, an "all-purpose heroine," a "fantasy of almost pornographic dimensions." John Bayley takes a milder tone but also observes that a "male fantasy" plays a part in the creation of Tess. He credits Hardy with only involuntary insights into his heroine's subjectivity.[25] Taking the other side, Arnold Kettle and Dorothy Van Ghent praise Hardy for particularizing Tess. According to Kettle, he displays "mistrust of . . . all ways of thinking that give abstract ideals or principles . . . priority over the actual needs of specific human situations," and, according to Van Ghent, he shows artistic commitment to "the concrete body of experience," "body of particularized life," and "concrete circumstances of experience, real as touch."[26] Van Ghent contrasts interestingly to Bayley, for while he finds stereotype-shattering insights into Tess's uniqueness occasional and unintended, she considers abstracting, philosophical passages to be the intrusions.[27] The two agree, though, and exemplify much critical response in their predilection for a Tess made to seem real.

Irving Howe also appreciates the "real" Tess and he exonerates Hardy from a charge of molding his heroine to fit male preconceptions. Yet he himself indulges more freely in sexual generalizations than he is quite willing to admit Hardy does. After praising Tess's individuation by Hardy, Howe reminds us always to remember that "she is a woman." While claiming that Tess represents herself and not an idea, he all but counters the claim in the way he puts it: Hardy's purpose is "not to make her a goddess or a metaphor, it is to underscore her embattled womanliness." Here the critic, like the author on occasion, falls afoul of the generic implications of the word "woman."[28]

Comparable tension between statement and implication appears in Jean Brooks's chapter on *Tess.* In her view, Hardy finds idealizing perception such as Angel's the projection of a "lifeless image," distorting, betraying, and entirely "inadequate." As evidence that Hardy condemns depersonalization, she cites the two harvesting scenes. One assimilates Tess to the machine she services—she loses independence of action or will. One assimilates her to the natural scene—she loses her margin and becomes a portion of the field. Brooks follows Hardy in disapproving of the first mode of assimilation and finding charm in the second, but fails to point out that *both* dissolve the margin of distinct personality. Brooks's preference for personalization over depersonalization begins to look like preference for one sort of depersonalization over another. In fact, in celebrating Tess's uniqueness, Brooks's own language stresses the heroine's womanhood in a way that transforms the individual woman into an abstraction: she praises Tess's "vibrant humanity, her woman's power of suffering, renewal, and compassion."[29]

John Lucas and Rosalind Miles are two more critics who applaud Tess's effort to live as a fully real individual, while the conflicts found in the language they employ to express their view are especially striking. Lucas himself recognizes certain stereotypical and demeaning connotations of the phrase "a pure woman."[30] Still, he goes ahead to use this phrase. He admires Tess's striving not to be fixed by images of purity and womanhood, and actually points out the irony of the subtitle—it invokes one of the standardized identities men seek to pin on her. But in his admiration for Tess's individuality, he pins this identity on her himself: "Simply, Tess is a pure woman." Hard-beset by male-imposed labels, according to Lucas, she is determined to live "from some center, some awareness of herself as pure woman, purely a woman."[31] Similarly, according to Miles, while Hardy gives Tess representative status, he never loses sight of her personal uniqueness, "as a woman, and a woman living in that time and place." It is strange but not unusual that she should cite in admiration of an individualized Tess the passage that describes her as a figure forming part of the landscape, "a field-woman pure and simple."[32]

In covert re-introductions of gender generics into discussions of Tess even by those who declare Hardy's and their own respect for individuality, we see paradoxically dramatized the delight-giving, dangerous dialectic of knowledge that the novel is about. In fact, the subtitle of my own essay may seem correspondingly equivocal—because of the usage of the word "woman" in our language. But I mean to equivocate. "Hardy on Knowing a Woman" means "Hardy on Knowing a Woman as Individual and Sexual Abstraction." The way a woman is known reveals the complexity of knowing. That is, *Tess* invites but frustrates over-simplification. It is easy to say that Angel wrongs Tess by perceiving her not just as herself but as an essence and type of womanhood, harder to face the ultimate force of the fact that he also loves her because of it. So does Hardy. So do we, if he has his way. Object of desire and also aesthetic object as the preface hints, Tess as pure woman is beloved and beautiful, inspires love, inspires art by the same token that she suffers misapprehension and misuse. Finally she really does lose her margin, her life.

Notes

1. Immanuel Kant, *Prolegomena to Any Future Metaphysics*, rev. of Carus trans., intro. Louis White Beck (Indianapolis: Bobbs-Merrill, 1950), p. 57.

2. Tom Paulin, *Thomas Hardy, The Poetry of Perception* (Totowa, New Jersey: Rowman and Littlefield, 1975), p. 24.

3. *Tess of the D'Urbervilles* (1891). Library Edn. (London: Macmillan, 1949). For all of Hardy's novels I use the texts revised by him for the 1912 Macmillan Wessex edn. Page numbers are given in parentheses.

4. Kant's thinking provides a remarkable analog to Hardy's in that he locates "the faculty of thinking the particular as contained under the universal" in the judgment, which is also the seat of aesthetic response—see Kant, *Critique of Judgment*, trans. J. H. Bernard (New York: Hafner, 1951), p. 15.

5. See contemporary response to the novel in Laurence Lerner and John Holstrom, eds., *Thomas Hardy and His Readers* (New York: Barnes & Noble, 1968), pp. 58–102. See also Mary Jacobus, "Tess's Purity," *EIC* 26 (October 1976):318–38. Understanding purity in the usual ethical/erotic sense, Jacobus argues that Hardy increasingly "whitewashes" (p. 336) his heroine in his revisions, creating a Tess who seems the less self-responsible for being presented as immune to what happens to her and who therefore strikes us ultimately as more victimized than tragic.

6. J. T. Laird, *The Shaping of Tess of the D'Urbervilles* (Oxford: The Clarendon Press, 1975), pp. 129, 128, 171.

7. D. H. Lawrence, from *Study of Thomas Hardy* in *Phoenix* (1936) in *D. H. Lawrence, Selected Literary Criticism,* ed. Anthony Beal (New York: Viking, 1966), p. 197; J. Hillis Miller, "Fiction and Repetition: *Tess of the D'Urbervilles*," in *Forms of Modern British Fiction,* ed. Alan Warren Friedman (Austin and London: Univ. of Texas Press, 1975), pp. 67, 69.

8. Paulin, p. 17, notes the importance for Hardy of Bagehot's 1856 essay, "Percy Bysshe Shelley."

9. Walter Bagehot, "Percy Bysshe Shelley," in *Literary Studies,* 3 vols. (London and Toronto: J. M. Dent; New York: Dutton, 1911), 1:97.

10. From *Longman's Magazine* (July 1883):252–69, in *Thomas Hardy's Personal Writings,* ed. Harold Orel (London: Macmillan, 1967), p. 181. Hardy's interest in the Hodge question also appears in his poems "Drummer Hodge" and "The King's Experiment" from *Poems of the Past and the Present* (1901) in *Collected Poems of Thomas Hardy* (New York: Macmillan, 1946), pp. 83, 148–49.

11. For instance, "The Profitable Reading of Fiction," *Forum* (New York) (March 1888):57–70, in *Thomas Hardy's Personal Writings,* p. 119, states his preference for impressionism in art over photographic transcription. Though I use Kantian language here, I am aware that the fit is only approximate. Kant's categories imply universal frameworks of subjectivity, whereas Hardy attributes various viewpoints to various viewers, but linking Kant and Hardy is a notable lack of regret that we cannot know anything absolutely (as thing-in-itself).

12. *The Well-Beloved,* Wessex edn. (London: Macmillan, 1952).

13. It is worth noting that, for Kant, aesthetic judgment may involve cognition but adds nothing to it—see *Critique of Judgment*, p. 38. Hardy goes further in his critique here.

14. Laird, p. 56.

15. "The Milkmaid" from *Poems of the Past and the Present*, "The Beauty" and "Intra Sepulchrum" from *Late Lyrics and Earlier* (1922), "The Pedigree" from *Moments of Vision* (1917), in *Collected Poems*, pp. 143–44, 583–84, 647–48, 431–32; *Laodicean*, Library Edn. (London: Macmillan, 1951); *Far from the Madding Crowd*, Library Edn. (London: Macmillan, 1949).

16. For instance, Rosemary Sumner in *Thomas Hardy, Psychological Novelist* (London and Basingstoke: Macmillan, 1981), p. 139, is exceptional in her call for sympathy with Angel.

17. *The Literary Notes of Thomas Hardy,* ed. Lennart A. Björk (Göteborg: Acta Universitatis Gothoburgensis, 1974), p. 137—citing Auguste Comte, preface to vol. 4 of *System of Positive Polity.*

18. See my "Sue Bridehead, 'The Woman of the Feminist Movement,' " *SEL* 18 (Autumn 1978):720–21, 726.

19. *Literary Notes*, pp. 93–94—citing Spencer's *Principles of Biology.*

20. *Forum* (New York) (March 1888):57–70, in *Thomas Hardy's Personal Writings*, p. 119—citing H. A. Taine, *History of English Literature.*

21. "Preface" to *The Dynasts* (1903), in *Hardy's Personal Writings*, p. 43.

22. Florence Emily Hardy, *The Early Life of Thomas Hardy* (New York: Macmillan, 1928), p. 232—citing a notation of 4 March 1886.

23. Hardy resembles Kant in his belief in the mental legislation of experience through a priori principles (such as thinking the particular as contained under the universal, in Kant's terms). And, for both, such inevitable epistemological contingency may have its own value. For Kant, though we cannot ultimately apprehend noumena, we cannot rest satisfied with phenomena, and the limits of knowledge define the opportunities of faith, the realm of the "as if" discovered by the mind in discovering its own limits—see *Prolegomena*, pp. 103–106. Hardy's view bears comparison but differs in part. For him, love and the beautiful, more than metaphysics, thrive in the realm of the "as if." He is also more aware of the dangers that attend the attractions of this realm.

24. Florence Emily Hardy, p. 314—citing a notation of 28 October 1891 (the period of *Tess*).

25. Moers, "Tess as a Cultural Stereotype," from "Hardy Perennial," *New York Review of Books* (9 November 1967):31–33, in *Twentieth-Century Interpretations of* Tess of the D'Urbervilles, ed. Albert La Valley (Englewood Cliffs, New Jersey: Prentice-Hall, 1969), p. 100; Bayley, *An Essay on Hardy* (Cambridge: Cambridge Univ. Press, 1978), pp. 188, 190.

26. Arnold Kettle, "Introduction" to *Tess* (1966), and Dorothy Van Ghent, "On *Tess of the D'Urbervilles*," from *The English Novel* (1953), in *Twentieth-Century Interpretations of* Tess, pp. 21 (Kettle); 50, 53 (Van Ghent).

27. Van Ghent, p. 49.

28. Howe, *Thomas Hardy* (New York: Macmillan, 1967), pp. 109, 129–31.

29. Brooks, *Thomas Hardy, The Poetic Structure* (Ithaca, New York: Cornell Univ. Press, 1971), pp. 246, 249–50, 253.

30. *The Literature of Change, Studies in the Nineteenth-Century Provincial Novel* (Sussex: Harvester; New York: Barnes & Noble, 1977), p. 178—Lucas briefly associates the subtitle description with other conventional images of Tess as toy, child, virgin to be deflowered, and "standard woman."

31. Lucas, pp. 178–79.

32. Miles, "The Women of Wessex," *The Novels of Thomas Hardy*, ed. Anne Smith (London: Vision, 1979), p. 42.

Psychic Evolution: Darwinism and Initiation in *Tess of the d'Urbervilles*   Elliott B. Gose, Jr.*

The novels of Thomas Hardy have often been praised for their concern with the issues which the Victorian era was forced to face by developments in philosophy and science, and by social change. Although all of these concerns

*Reprinted from *Nineteenth-Century Fiction* 18, no. 3 (December 1963): 261–72. © 1963 by the Regents of the University of California. Reprinted by permission of the Regents of the University of California.

can be found in *Tess of the d'Urbervilles,* the most central to the book are Hardy's interpretation of two specialized developments in mid-Victorian thought, Darwinism and anthropology. The impact of the Darwinian controversy on Hardy is well known, but his interest in the new science of anthropology has not been much remarked. Commentators have, of course, frequently noted his interest in folklore and superstition, but usually as an indication of the cultural and intellectual conflict which was so important in making Hardy the kind of Victorian writer he was. Victorian England was characterized not only by conflicts but by attempts at synthesis; the concept of evolution, for instance, was not confined to the study of biology but spread to the humanities as well. Its most obvious application was in charting the history and culture of man; thus, most of Hardy's novels deal in some form with the problems of social evolution. He usually goes behind contemporary problems, however, to what is always a key relation to him, that of man to nature. Specifically, in *Tess* he brings together the evolutionary view of man as a product of nature with the anthropological findings about early man's attempt to control nature through primitive rituals.

On December 18, 1890, shortly after he finished writing *Tess,* Hardy made the following entry in his notebook:

> Mr. E. Clodd this morning gives an excellently neat answer to my question why the superstitions of a remote Asiatic and a Dorset labourer are the same: "The attitude of man," he says, "at corresponding levels of culture, before like phenomena, is pretty much the same, your Dorset peasants representing the persistence of the barbaric idea which confuses persons and things, and founds wide generalizations on the slenderest analogies."
>
> (This "barbaric idea which confuses persons and things" is, by the way, also common to the highest imaginative genius—that of the poet.)[1]

Mr. E. Clodd of the quotation was Edward Clodd, an anthropologist friend, and from references in *Tess* there can be no doubt that Hardy had been doing a fair amount of reading in anthropology. To begin demonstrating Hardy's use of it, we might look at a passage in the novel which indicates his interest in primitive rites.

> The house . . . was of recent erection—indeed almost new—and of the same rich colour that formed such a contrast with the evergreens of the lodge. Far behind the corner of the house—which rose like a geranium bloom against the subdued colours around—stretched the soft azure landscape of The Chase—a truly venerable tract of forest land, one of the few remaining woodlands in England of undoubted primæval date, wherein Druidical mistletoe was still found on aged oaks, and where enormous yew-trees, not planted by the hand of man, grew as they had grown when they were pollarded for bows. All this sylvan antiquity, however, though visible from The Slopes, was outside the immediate boundaries of the estate.[2]

Hardy's contrast between the newness, neatness, and tameness of The Slopes, and the antiquity and wildness of The Chase is intensified by the mention of the "Druidical mistletoe . . . still found on aged oaks." He is referring to Pliny's famous description of the central rite of the Druids, who

> esteem nothing more sacred than the mistletoe and the tree on which it grows, provided only that the tree is an oak. But apart from this they choose oak-woods for their sacred groves. . . . After due preparations have been made for a sacrifice and a feast under the tree, they hail it as the universal healer and bring to the spot two white bulls, whose horns have never been bound before. A priest clad in white robe climbs the tree and with a golden sickle cuts the mistletoe, which is caught in a white cloth. Then they sacrifice the victims, praying that God may make his own gift to prosper with those upon whom he has bestowed it. They believe that a potion prepared from mistletoe will make barren animals to bring forth.[3]

It is to The Chase that Alec takes Tess the night he seduces her. And Hardy reminds us of its character in that scene too. "Darkness and silence ruled everywhere around. Above them rose the primeval yews and oaks of The Chase." Slight though this allusion is, it serves as a clue linking the scene with the pattern of sacrificial images which are present in the most vivid scenes in the novel. Before going on to analyze them, however, we must look briefly at the images which forbode Tess' rape. One of these, Hardy specifically has Tess interpret as prefigurative, the pricking of her chin by a thorn on the red roses given her by Alec (chap. vi). Earlier, he has Alec smoke a red-tipped cigar in front of Tess, and then offer her a strawberry:

> He stood up and held it by the stem to her mouth.
> "No—no!" she said quickly, putting her fingers between his hand and her lips. "I would rather take it in my own hand."
> "Nonsense!" he insisted; and in a slight distress she parted her lips and took it in (chap. v).

Tess' passivity is emphasized heavily in the first two sections of the book and, as this incident indicates, is an important ingredient in her becoming Alec's victim. Although the victim of a ritual sacrifice and the aspirant in a ritual initiation can be easily distinguished by intellectual analysis, in this novel we shall find Hardy tying the two together in an emotionally convincing manner.

In 1887, three years before beginning *The Golden Bough,* James Frazer had published *Totemism,* an authoritative statement on a subject which Western man was just beginning to grasp. Although we have no proof that Hardy read the book, we may assume that by 1889 he would have known some of the rituals documented by Frazer, including a common form of totemic initiation, being "smeared with blood." The meaning of this ceremony, according to Frazer, is indicated "by the following custom. Among the Gonds, a non-Aryan race of Central India, the rajas, by intermarriage with Hindus, have lost much of their pure blood and are half Hindus; hence one of the ceremonies at their installation is 'the touching of their foreheads with a drop of blood drawn from the body of a pure aborigine of the tribe they belong to' " (pp. 42–43).

This custom of symbolic initiation among primitive tribes is imaginatively adapted by Hardy to form an important figurative pattern in the plot of *Tess*. It makes its appearance in the death of Prince, the incident earlier in the book which caused Tess to go to The Slopes. She had fallen asleep on a wagon she was driving to market with the result that her horse was run down by the mail cart.

> The pointed shaft of the cart had entered the breast of the unhappy Prince like a sword, and from the wound his life's blood was spouting in a stream, and falling with a hiss into the road.
> In her despair Tess sprang forward and put her hand upon the hole, with the only result that she became splashed from face to skirt with the crimson drops.[4]

The consequence of Tess' falling asleep is to deprive her father of his means of livelihood. Her guilt causes her to go to The Slopes where Alec, after telling her he has sent a new horse to her father, seduces her. Cause and effect on a symbolic level are also evident. Like the d'Urbervilles, Prince's name shows him to be of noble blood, though like them he is decrepit. The rendered image of his death by the "pointed shaft" is parallel with the covert image of Tess' rape by Alec.

As indicated by these two incidents and the description of the slaughter of rodents at harvest (chap. xiv), Hardy saw that man's relation to nature was based on certain harsh realities and inexorable cycles which would necessarily be reflected in primitive rituals. Yet looked at more closely, Hardy's characterization of Tess indicates that rape may be too strong a word for what happens in The Chase. In chapter xii we find out that, "temporarily blinded" by Alec's "ardent manners," Tess "had been stirred to confused surrender awhile." In other words Tess is not merely a victim of Alec's lust, nor of Hardy's view of nature's ironic and fateful law of cause and effect; despite her mother's bad advice and her own physical weariness, she is finally responsible for her own nature and development. Hardy emphasizes her no longer having a peasant mentality like her mother's, and her having lost contact with the real meaning of natural processes. In fact at the end of chap. xiii he rebukes her for the Victorian moral conscience with which her modern education has provided her.

Then in "Phase the Third" of the novel, Hardy puts her in a situation where her consciousness of being outside the social pale is in conflict with the unconscious "appetite for joy which pervades all creation, that tremendous force which sways humanity to its purpose" (chap. xxx). In making this and similar statements, Hardy is affirming a certain attitude toward nature, an attitude that puts a somewhat different emphasis on the relations among natural creatures than did Darwin's notion of the survival of the fittest. The two views are not, of course, incompatible as Hardy's term "appetite" indicates, and I shall show presently how Darwin's concept is connected with the initiation ritual we have noted in *Tess*. But first I would like to distinguish between Darwin's theory of natural selection and the older theory of evolution. Where Darwin's theory emphasizes competition for survival, the other asserts the connection of all life and leaves room for the concept of cooperation. Hardy was aware of both, but he saw man's progress as being tied to evolution. Of several notebook entries on this subject, I pick the most relevant. "The discovery of the law of evolution, which revealed that all organic creatures are of one family, shifted the center of altruism from humanity to the whole conscious world collectively."[5] In the light of such a belief we can appreciate Tess' reaction to the burial of Prince. "The children cried anew. All except Tess. Her face was dry and pale, as though she regarded herself in the light of a murderess" (chap. iv). We might also notice how the idea of initiation becomes associated with the idea of evolution at this point. Both beliefs connect the individual who accepts them with the past and determine his future actions. Noting Tess' emotional adherence to both, we may draw some interesting conclusions about her nature. Her reaction to suffering can be seen as a weakness because it leaves her vulnerable, but it can also be seen as a strength because it makes her aware as she had not been before. As we noted, Hardy felt that " 'the barbaric idea which confuses persons and things' is . . . also common to the highest imaginative genius—that of the poet." Tess' retrogression to anthropomorphism may thus be seen as a step forward in Hardy's conception of what I would like to call psychic evolution.

The conception of psychic evolution is evident from many hints in Hardy's writing, but especially from a comment he wrote the year before he finished *Tess*. "A 'sensation-novel' is possible in which the sensationalism is not casualty, but evolution; not physical but psychical. . . . [In the latter] the casualty or adventure is held to be of no intrinsic interest, but the effect upon the faculties is the important matter to be depicted" (*Early Life*, p. 268). *Tess* is obviously such a "sensation-novel." Reading it, we must forget the sensationalism and melodrama (Hardy felt that "it is not improbabilities of incident but improbabilities of character that matter," *Early Life*, p. 231). But once we have seen what Hardy intends us to focus on, we can sympathize with Tess' struggle to advance on the scale of psychic evolution and we can appreciate the insight Hardy showed in connecting the psychical and the physical, in rendering the struggles of mind through evolutionary and ritualistic images. Although he tends to make a dichotomy between mind and body, he always ties them together, always makes us aware that Tess cannot separate her spiritual rapture from her position in the environment. Perhaps the scene where this is brought home most strikingly is the one in which she moves through the garden listening to Angel's flute. Despite the exaltation she feels from the music, her body is being stained by "sticky blights which, though snow-white on the apple-tree trunks, made madder stains on her skin" (chap. xix).

The scene in the garden may be taken as one of many omens that Tess' effort to achieve psychic evolution will finally be unsuccessful. Although Hardy favored evolution with its sympathy and cooperation, he did not forget natural selection with its competitive lack of compassion. Man's aggressive nature must be reckoned with, as we have seen in Alec's seduction of Tess. A variation on this active-submissive relation is given much later in the novel when Alec makes another bid for Tess on the platform of the threshing machine at Flintcoomb Ash. In response to his suggestion

> She passionately swung the glove by the gauntlet directly in his face. It was heavy and thick as a warrior's, and it struck him flat on the mouth. Fancy might have regarded the act as the recrudescence of a trick in which her armed progenitors were not unpractised. Alec fiercely started up from his reclining position. A scarlet oozing appeared where her blow had alighted, and in a moment the blood began dropping from his mouth upon the straw. . . .
> "Now, punish me!" she said, turning up her eyes to him with the hopeless defiance of the sparrow's gaze before its captor twists its neck. "Whip me, crush me; you need not mind those people under the rick! I shall not cry out. Once victim, always victim—that's the law!" . . . He stepped across to her side and held her by the shoulders, so that she shook under his grasp. "Remember, my lady, I was your master once! I will be your master again. If you are any man's wife you are mine!"[6]

Although Tess says that once victim, always victim is the law (of nature), she has actually taken the first step toward denying the dominance Alec gained when he sealed their relation with her blood. When she finally kills him, she draws all his blood, and Hardy has her say afterwards, "I feared long ago, when I struck him on the mouth with my glove, that I might do it some day for the trap he set for me in my simple youth." The image depicts man's aggressive nature, for the trap was to catch a bird, as is clear both from an earlier comment of Hardy's that she "had been caught during her days of immaturity like a bird in a springe," and from one of her accusations against Alec: "O, you have torn my life all to pieces . . . made me a victim, a caged wretch."[7] It is evident, therefore, that despite Hardy's hatred of cruelty and his hope that in man cooperation based on evolutionary kinship would overcome competition based on natural selection, he recognized the strong hold of the more brutal means of maintaining relations.

In *Tess* Darwinian self-assertion manifests itself in an aggressive-submissive pattern which has its locus in the relations of Alec and Tess but is generalized to include society past and contemporary. In his commentary on the seduction scene earlier, Hardy includes a hint that retribution for past misconduct by Tess' ancestors might be involved. He immediately repudiates such visiting of "the sins of the fathers upon the children" (chap. xi) on philosophic grounds, but the connection of the aristocracy with aggression is based symbolically throughout the novel, as in her striking Alec with the warrior's glove. Another important use of it is in the legend of the d'Urberville coach, which is mentioned twice, but never fully explained. The first time, Angel tells her about it. "A certain d'Urberville of the sixteenth or seventeenth century committed a dreadful crime in his family coach and since that time members of the family see or hear the old coach whenever—But I'll tell you another day—it is rather gloomy" (chap. xxxiii). Later, Alec adds a little more: "One of the family is said to have abducted some beautiful woman, who tried to escape from the coach in which he was carrying her off, and in the struggle he killed her—or she killed him—I forget which" (chap. li). Taking the relation between Alec and Tess as a modern repetition of this legend, we can see that the moral of it will be that the victim can turn on her aggressor. That is certainly the outcome in Tess' life. The connection of the coach with the problem is evident: the legend is mentioned in the first place because Tess was bothered by the sight of the coach she and Angel were to use on their wedding night.

> A close carriage was ordered from a roadside inn, a vehicle which had been kept there ever since the old days of post-chaise travelling. It had stout wheel-spokes, and a heavy felloes, a great curved bed, immense straps and springs, and a pole like a battering-ram. The postilion was a venerable "boy" of sixty—a martyr to rheumatic gout, the result of excessive exposure in youth, counteracted by strong liquors—who had stood at the inn-doors doing nothing for the whole five-and-twenty years that elapsed since he had no longer been required to ride professionally, as if expecting the old times to come back again. He had a permanent running wound on the outside of his right leg, originated by the constant bruising of aristocratic carriage-poles during the many years that he had been in regular employ at the King's Arms, Casterbridge (chap. xxxiii).

Just as Prince is the victim of the battering ram of the mail coach, and Tess is of Alec, so the postilion is of the "aristocratic carriage-poles." The development of this "boy" has been arrested at that point in the past when he was forced to submit to aristocratic dominance to be used as an object instead of a person. We might almost say that the postilion has undergone a ceremony of blood initiation which commits him for life, whether or not conditions change afterward and his position becomes anomalous. In a similar way, Tess in her youth has also been initiated by her blood bath from the victim Prince. Both she and the "boy" have become victims bound always to submit in the presence of an aggressor. As victims they belong to an almost sub-human order, one closely tied to brute nature. But Tess has the possibility of changing her state by marrying Angel. He himself realizes the symbolic import of their wedding, that after it Tess will no longer be a peasant, forced to submit to the toils of manual labour. He even decorates the bridal chamber appropriately: Tess looks at "the tester of white dimity; something was hanging beneath it, and she lifted the candle to see what it was. A bough of mistletoe. Angel had put it there; she knew that in an instant. This was the explanation of that mysterious parcel . . . whose contents he would not explain to her, saying that time would soon show her the purpose thereof" (chap. xxxv). But the marriage is never consummated, and the blood seal of Alec, given under the mistletoe in the darkness of The Chase, is consequently never revoked.

After leaving Angel, Tess undergoes a reversal of psychic evolution. Having lost her chance of breaking free of Alec's seal, of becoming a fuller individual guided by Angel's high spiritual nature, she reverts first to the peasant level with her family, and then below that to the animal level after she leaves them. "There was something of the habitude of the wild animal in the unreflecting instinct with which she rambled on—disconnecting herself by littles from her eventful past at every step, obliterating her identity." This reversion to instinct is imaged also in her reenactment of the circumstances leading up to her earlier despoilment.[8] In The Chase Alec had "made a sort of couch or nest for her in the deep moss of dead leaves." This time "her haunted soul" causes Tess to enter an upland plantation where "she scraped together the dead leaves till she had formed them into a large heap, making a sort of nest in the middle. Into this Tess crept." She moves herself back up to the human level after one of the most striking incidents in the book. She hears strange sounds and when daylight comes

> Under the trees several pheasants lay about, their rich plumage dabbled with blood; some were dead, some feebly twitching a wing, some staring up at the sky, some pulsating quickly, some contorted, some stretched out—all of them writhing in agony, except the fortunate ones whose tortures had ended during the night by the inability of nature to bear more. . . .
>
> "Poor darlings—to suppose myself the most miserable being on earth in the sight o' such misery as yours!" she exclaimed, her tears running down as she killed the birds tenderly. "And not a twinge of bodily pain about me! I be not mangled, and I be not bleeding, and I have two hands to feed and clothe me" (chap. xli).

As her dialect indicates, Tess reacts as a peasant here, but this again leaves her a potential victim. Despite her rejection of Alec on the machine, she has to give in to him finally when her father dies, and her family is left homeless. As we might expect, her life with him, while materially good, is sensual, soulless. When Angel meets her again at the "pleasure city" of Sandbourne, he has "a vague consciousness of one thing, though it was not clear to him till later; that his original Tess had spiritually ceased to recognize the body before him as hers—allowing it to drift, like a corpse upon the current, in a direction dissociated from its living will" (chap. lv). He should be completely conscious of what has happened, however. For the climax of his belated conversion had been his realization that "the beauty or ugliness of a character lay not only in its achievements, but in its aims and impulses; its true history lay, not among things done, but among things willed" (chap. xlix). Alec has subdued her pride and will, immersed them in luxury, but upon her meeting Angel again, that will comes to life. She stabs Alec to sever finally the blood bond between them. The image describing his fate is very similar to that used in the scene with Prince, whose death was almost directly responsible for putting her under Alec's domination. "The wound was small, but the point of the blade had touched the heart of the victim." Murdering him is the only way left to her, and to do it she has to regress as far down the human scale as Alec had in The Chase, back that is to the pagan Druids. Angel feels "amazement at the strength of her affection for himself, and at the strangeness of its quality, which had apparently extinguished her moral sense altogether" (chap. lvii). And the last important scene in the novel is given a background appropriate to Tess' state: "At an indefinite height overhead something made the black sky blacker, which had the semblance of a vast architrave beneath and between; the surfaces echoed their soft rustle; but they seemed to be still out of doors. The place was roofless." They have reached the Druid's Stonehenge, and when Tess asks if it is a "heathen temple," Angel replies, "Yes. Older than the centuries; older than the d'Urbervilles." By chance or instinct she falls asleep on the Stone of Sacrifice. "Her breathing now was quick and small, like that of a lesser creature than a woman. . . . Soon the light was strong, and a ray shone upon her unconscious form, peering under her eyelids and waking her" (chap. lviii). She is taken away by the representatives of society, who have surrounded her while she slept.

A combination of social pressure, mischance, and willfulness have put Tess in a position where she can gain temporary happiness only by discarding civilized self-restraint. As a result of her blood sacrifice of Alec, her own death has become inevitable. Although Tess was obeying the kinship-through-evolution code when she put the pheasants out of their misery, in brutally freeing herself from a brute relationship, she moved down the scale of psychic evolution to the primitive level. Seen, therefore, in the perspective of the patterns Hardy has constructed, her death is called for by the dark law of man's earliest relation to nature as much as by any unenlightened social law. And set in the elemental grandeur of Stonehenge, it would have been a fitting primitive sacrifice.

Early in the novel Hardy had speculated whether "at the acme and summit of the human progress [human relations] will be corrected by a finer intuition, a closer interaction of the social machinery than that which now jolts us around and along; but such completeness is not to be prophesied, or even conceived as possible" (chap. v). This analysis, adequate enough as a statement of the central problems in *Jude the Obscure*, refers to only a part of what actually goes on in *Tess of the d'Urbervilles*. Through his feeling for man's place in the evolutionary scale of progress and regress, and his insight into the ritual necessities of man's relation to nature, Hardy makes Tess appealing not as a victim of society but as a human being caught in the ebb and flow of history, environment, and self.

Notes

1. Florence Hardy, *The Early Life of Thomas Hardy* (London, 1928), pp. 301–302. Clodd's contention was a truism by 1891, being in fact the necessary premise for comparative anthropology. Hardy's observation had precedent too. In *Primitive Culture* (first ed. 1871), Edward Tylor, the father of English anthropology, frequently made the point. See for instance the end of chap. viii: "A poet of our own day has still much in common with the minds of uncultured tribes in the mythologic stage of thought."

2. Since there are so many editions of *Tess* available, I will make my citations by chapter. This passage is from chapter v.

3. Quoted by Frazer in chapter lxv of his one volume abridgment of *The Golden Bough*. Also quoted by Bullfinch in *The Age of Fable* (1855).

4. Chapter v. This scene is analyzed both by Dorothy Van Ghent in *The English Novel: Form and Function* (New York, 1953), and by Arnold Kettle, *An Introduction to the English Novel*, Vol. II (London, 1953).

5. Florence Hardy, *The Later Years of Thomas Hardy* (London, 1930), p. 138. Although Hardy wrote this particular version of his belief in 1909, he had written a similar one the year before he began *Tess* (*Early Life*, p. 294). And he is completely straightforward in *Tess* itself, referring to the cruelty of the pheasant hunters, "at once so unmannerly and so unchivalrous towards their weaker fellows in Nature's teeming family" (chap. xli).

6. Chap. xlvii. After she descends from the machine, Alec says to her, in an image reminiscent of primitive sacrifice, "How the little limbs tremble! You are weak as a bled calf, you know you are."

7. Chap. lvi. Ellipsis Hardy's. This is an early version of the passage, available in the Modern Library hardcover edition of *Tess*. The revised version is much less illuminating: "O, you have torn my life all to pieces . . . made me be what I prayed you in pity not to make me be again!"

8. This parallel is noted by John Holloway in his article "Hardy's Major Fiction" in *From Jane Austen to Joseph Conrad*, ed. Rathburn and Steinmann (Minneapolis, 1958). Holloway also comments on the Darwinian motifs in *Tess*.

"The Spirit Unappeased and Peregrine": *Jude the Obscure*   Philip M. Weinstein*

"It is a city of light," he said to himself.
"The tree of knowledge grows there," he added a few steps further on.
"It is a place that teachers of men spring from and go to."
"It is what you may call a castle, manned by scholarship and religion."
After this figure he was silent a long while, till he added:
"It would just suit me." (49–50)

Alone and in a setting which fails wholly to corroborate his utterance, Jude sounds a characteristic note of the novel. He would be where he is not,

*Reprinted from *The Semantics of Desire: Changing Models of Identity from Dickens to Joyce*, 125–45. © 1984 by Princeton University Press. Reprinted with permission of Princeton University Press.

and he has only words to express this desire. More than Hardy's other novels, *Jude the Obscure* stresses the importance and the impotence of words, the huge arena between actuality and ideality which they fill. Jude's Christminster is a place less visualized than conceptualized, a mirage of words—"the tree of knowledge . . . what you may call a castle manned by scholarship and religion." He imagines it as existing spatially "out there" while Hardy reveals it, through Jude's words, as a fabric of "figures," woven from "in here." When Jude resolves, in one transcendent apotheosis, to house his spirit in its ideal home, he ignores the extensive gap between actual and ideal, the instrumental steps necessary if one would try to journey from the one realm to the other. On a scale unique in Hardy's work, this novel insists on the hopelessness of making that journey, and on the fraudulence of its imagined end. The novel spreads before its hero, not the transcendental home of the spirit, but innumerable halfway houses that betray the spirit even as they promise it material abode.

"There was no law of transmutation" (55), Jude learns in his painstaking study of the classical languages.[1] No key exists that will magically ease his transformation from artisan to savant, transposing the languages of learning to the grammar of his native discourse. Between Jude and knowledge there lie the certainty of years of study, the risk of faulty pedagogic methods, the obstacle of immovable class prejudice. Jude remains childlike in his approach to these barriers. Seeking unconditional union with the ideal itself, he hardly hesitates over the means for this achievement: "What was most required by citizens? Food, clothing, and shelter. An income from any work in preparing the first would be too meagre; for making the second he felt a distaste; the preparation of the third requisite he inclined to. They built in a city; therefore he would learn to build" (59).

In his mind's eye he is already there. His clichés as to a profession have no specific reference. The actual conditions of his approach, like the actual conditions of Christminster, are scarcely considered. Jude moves absentmindedly through the material of his life—its contingent days and places—enamored of the immaterial absolute, bruising himself on the fleshed-out conditional. He seeks, outside himself, a perfect receptacle for his immaculate spirit. He finds, outside himself, no such receptacle but instead a bewildering array of strictly human approximations: not pure but adulterate, not ideal but embodied, not transcendentally given but mediated and ambiguous. The landscape of *Jude the Obscure,* unlike that of *Tess of the d'Urbervilles,* is overwhelmingly cultural. The landmarks within it comprise the range of human institutions and conventions by which the journeying spirit finds itself stymied rather than fulfilled: a landscape of signifiers emptied of those meanings they promise. If the basic unit of *Tess* is the blood, the basic unit of *Jude* is the word. (In *Jude* wounds are expressed through talk, not blood.) If the world of *Tess* is mainly the horizontal one of natural immersion, the world of *Jude* is the vertical one of cultural aspiration, counterfeit, and failure.

Jude is Hardy's most insistent seeker—his characteristic posture is dedication—and he inhabits a novel crammed with advertisement, with signifying artifacts that promise to fulfill the seeker's desire, to connect him with his goal. At the simplest level of false advertisement there are Arabella's dimple and false hair, Vilbert's quack medicine, the adulterated beer whose impurities Arabella (but not Jude) detects. At the next level, not deceptive in themselves but slippery in their relation to the seeker, are the icons of Greek and Biblical culture—the statues of Venus and Apollo, the Latin cross and the Ten Commandments—which misleadingly propose a realizable harmony between acolyte and symbolized values.[2] More diffuse are the secular institutions of education and profession, of marriage and divorce. Designed to bestow communal structure and purpose upon inchoate human desire, these institutions remain oblique to the movement of Jude's and Sue's actual lives. In their role as the culture's licensed forms for individual thought and feeling, they act as false beacons, beyond following, beyond ignoring. As Robert Heilman suggests, they are inextricably woven into the fabric of the characters' consciousness.[3]

Misleading connectives, promising to deliver the spirit of its burden or connect it with its goal, punctuate the novel. Jude and Sue tirelessly write each other letters, seeking to express their deep selves and to make contact with the other. The letters are more eloquent than speech. By ignoring the disconcerting presence of an interlocutor, they succeed, if not in telling the truth, at least in making a narrative of their lives.

The fundamental category of a misleading mediator, a connective that fails to make good on its promise, is language itself. *Jude the Obscure* uses discourse in a thoroughly modern way, unique in Hardy's novels; the words a character uses appear less as the transparent bearer of private spirit than as the opaque, already motivated property of a public culture; the words have already been coopted.[4] What may be most obscure about Jude Fawley and Sue Bridehead is that, at the center of their being, they are mute. The language they have access to—and it pours out of them helplessly, it is the blood of their spirit—is often an incoherent amalgam of the commonplaces of their culture, more faithful to the psychic stresses of a Swinburne or Newman, a J. S. Mill or Matthew Arnold (whom they are echoing) than to their own inarticulate need.

A. Alvarez is right when he claims that "the essential subject of the novel is not Oxford, or marriage, or even frustration. It is loneliness" (421). Jude and Sue's abundant speech only accentuates their separateness. Alvarez (and J. I. M. Stewart makes the same point) notes that "no character ever properly seems to connect with another in talk" (420), but this aspect of the novel—which is endemic in Hardy's art—seems to me not a flaw in *Jude the Obscure*. For once Hardy has constructed a novel which accommodates the awkward silence at the core of his vision. The characters are there, given in their completeness, before they are empowered with speech. Speech is, as it were, a late accomplishment of the species, more capable of releasing chorus-like platitudes than of articulating individual need. The spoken words proliferate in *Jude the Obscure* like cartoon utterances, cascading like soap-bubbles from the already finished figures who remain mute beside their utterance.

Whether such effects of verbal alienation are intentional or not, the novel certainly renders the conditional thinness, the ardent abstractedness of Jude's dedication to western culture. He has its words, but they never sound quite like his own. J. I. M. Stewart writes: "We are nowhere made to *feel* what brought him his Greek and Latin; he is seen in virtually no concrete situation relevant to it. . . . Again, the extended passage in which Jude is represented as wandering about Christminster and hearing the ghostly *ipsissima verba* of departed Oxford men . . . is a poor and even embarrass-ing substitute for something not really created in the book" (189).[5] "No concrete situation . . . something not really created": that is less the novel's problem than its elusive achievement. Indeed, it is not surprising that this facet of Hardy's art should be more pronounced in *Jude the Obscure* than in his other novels. Only here is the protagonists' discourse insistently intellec-tual; elsewhere they do not proclaim their insertion within this or that larger cultural tradition. Insofar as the insertion is itself suspect—revealing the protagonists' isolation rather than their belonging—then the abstractness of the urged positions, the precarious purchase of the speaker upon his own utterance, is itself germane.[6] Jude's relation to his sought-after culture *is* ghostly and abstract rather than fleshed-out and instrumental; it is right that he should enter the city at night, hearing its medley of disembodied voices. Jude's great moments at Christminster are equally verbal—his two orations rehearsing "the Articles of his Belief, in the Latin tongue" (141) and grap-pling with the "difficult question" (335) of his intellectual career—and on these occasions Hardy stresses the only facet of Christminster available to Jude: its words.

Jude is so enamored of these words that he tends to speak them as a substitute for his own, and even the "autobiographical" sketch he gives of himself in that last oration is ringed round with ironies. It is a speech "from the heart" delivered to a coarse and unreceptive audience rather than to the university hearers he craves, and it is not the truth of Jude but the "story" of Jude, the fiction he must shape to deliver himself at all:

> It takes two or three generations to do what I tried to do in one; and my impulses—affections—vices perhaps they should be called—were too strong not to hamper a man without advantages. . . . I was, perhaps, after all, a paltry victim to the spirit of mental and social restlessness, that makes so many unhappy in these days! . . . And what I appear, a sick and poor man, is not the worst of me. I am in a chaos of principles—groping in the dark—acting by instinct and not after example. . . . (336)

In each of its twists (the speech begins on a cheerful note but turns bitter and self-indicting as it goes on), Jude's oration exaggerates and distorts his nature. Successively presenting himself as too impatient, too impulsive, too passionate, too restless, in "a chaos of principles," Jude's words miss the naive sweetness and hesitancy, the gently yearning idealism, the desire to respond coupled with the baffled resentment of failure, that most deeply characterize his way of encountering experience.[7] Jude is no Prometheus, no peer of Huxley or Spencer; nor is he an impulsive man, raging in the dark. Rather, he is a mild and civil man, confused by the words and promises of others and by the flux of possibilities within himself, a man who really seeks, in Lawrence's fine phrase, "not a store of learning, nor the vanity of educa- tion . . . [but] to find conscious expression for that which he held in his blood" ("The Study of Thomas Hardy," 210). Had he discovered that the richness he yearned for lay inchoate in his own blood, he might have suc- ceeded in forging an authentic voice.

As it is, both Jude and Sue rely upon one external voice after another to make sense of their confusing experience. At their nadir, Father Time's murder of himself and the two younger children, they engage in a desperate game of quotations, seeking to alleviate their misery by finding a previously articulated ground for what would otherwise seem unbearably groundless:

> "No," said Jude. "It was in his nature to do it. The doctor says there are such boys springing up amongst us. . . ."
>
> She sobbed again. "O, O my babies! They had done no harm! Why should they have been taken away, and not I!"
>
> There was another stillness—broken at last by two persons in conver- sation somewhere without.
>
> "They are talking about us, no doubt!" moaned Sue. " 'We are made a spectacle unto the world, and to angels, and to men!' . . . There is some- thing external to us which says, 'You shan't!' First it said, 'You shan't learn!' Then it said, 'You shan't labour!' Now it says, 'You shan't love!' . . . I talked to the child as one should only talk to people of mature age. I said the world was against us, that it was better to be out of life than in it at this price; and he took it literally. . . . We went about loving each other too much—indulging ourselves to utter selfishness with each other! We said— do you remember?—that we would make a virtue of joy. I said it was Nature's intention. . . . It is best, perhaps, that they should be gone. . . ."
>
> "Yes," replied Jude. "Some say that the elders should rejoice when their children die in infancy."
>
> "But they don't know! . . . I am driven out of my mind by things! What ought to be done!" She stared at Jude, and tightly held his hand.
>
> "Nothing can be done," he replied. "Things are as they are, and will be brought to their destined issue."
>
> She paused. "Yes! Who said that?" she asked heavily.
>
> "It comes in the chorus of the *Agamemnon*. It has been in my mind continually since this happened." (346–48)

These three pages allude to a veritable chorus of voices. Jude and Sue inhabit a world of verbal echoes; they automatically refer the inexplicable events of their lives to the swarm of formulae cluttering their heads. Sue's consciousness is like a larder stocked with nothing but phrases. She has so persuaded herself that the key to the children's disaster lies in something she said or failed to say that she (and Jude with her) misses one of the primary causes silently visible to every reader: the paucity of wordless physical affection has scarred Father Time as deeply as any utterance. It is typical of Sue and Jude to overlook such an incarnate cause, as they despairingly cast about among their treasury of remembered sayings for an intellectual formulation that will fit the case. None does fit the case, and at a certain point the accumulation of allusions takes on a tinge of absurdity. The event is so overexplained as to become unexplained. The pointed weight of allusive wisdom suddenly turns arbitrary and weightless—a bandying of words.[8]

It takes the insight of someone like Nietzsche (a thinker whom Hardy cursorily repudiated) to identify the verbal malaise here.[9] Jude and Sue have not impressed upon their discourse the form of their own embodied spirit. They have not mastered the words they utter, making them their own, for Jude and Sue remain trapped within a linguistic world-view which holds that truth is external, universally applicable, and has already been uttered. The purpose of education in such a world-view—and this is the education that Jude seeks—is to acquaint the student with this already articulated body of truths. Nietzsche knows, by contrast, that what passes for a culture's truths are its willed assertions, its claims rather than its discoveries: "Whatever exists, having somehow come into being, is again and again reinterpreted to new ends, taken over, transformed and redirected by some power superior to it; all events in the organic world are a subduing, a *becoming master*, and all subduing and becoming master involves a fresh interpretation, an adaptation through which any previous "meaning" and "purpose" are necessarily obscured or even obliterated" (*On the Genealogy of Morals*, 513).

It may now be possible to identify one of the peculiar tensions in *Jude the Obscure*. It is the tension between the morally elusive facts of embodied life, as Hardy presents them, and the static assumptions of discourse, as Sue and Jude reveal them. On the one hand—in the realm of behavior—we find the ever-changing, morally opaque play of power and penetration; and on the other—in the realm of discourse—we find the naive expectation of a fully appropriate moral paradigm, one that accounts for all contingencies, as promised by the formulae of the Greek and Judeo-Christian traditions. This tension exists in one form or another throughout Hardy's novels, for his vision of behavior is far more sophisticated than his or his protagonists' assumptions about the ways in which their culture's discourse organizes and evaluates experience.

Another way of putting it is to say that Hardy sees the dynamics of behavior with a moral flexibility approaching Nietzschean candor, but that—unlike Nietzsche—he has not extended his perception of life as an interplay of powers into a perception of language as an interplay of powers as well. He stops short of Nietzsche's claim that discourse is not the transparent reflection of a pre-existent and static reality waiting to be named by the words, but rather the mediated expression of a thrusting will to make sense of experience. Discourse is actually as non-transcendental, as unsanctioned and contingent, as the experience that it is meant to organize: a dilemma that Hardy seems more to reveal than to acknowledge. Put most simply, since all discourse is inflected by will, Jude and Sue will either inflect their terms so as to express their own experience or parrot the terms that express someone else's experience. Thus, to return to Nietzsche's verb, Jude and Sue do not *master* the meaning of Father Time's act because they do not personally will that knowledge into consciousness and language with sufficient intensity. Borrowers rather than makers of discourse, they do not generate, from their own anguish, the native phrasing that will put them in touch with their own inchoate experience. Their dependence on prefabricated formulae marks their evasion of (to paraphrase Lawrence) that which they hold unseeing in their own blood. Through borrowed discourse they remain obscure to their own necessities, looking passively without for explanations that lie unformulated within. As Howells remarked in 1895, "All the characters, indeed, have the appealing quality of human beings really doing what they must while seeming to do what they will" (379).

"What they must" do is dramatized by Hardy, if not conceptualized by Jude and Sue. Arabella's effect upon Jude rarely extends as far upward as his consciousness. He receives "a dumb announcement of affinity *in posse*," and he responds instinctively, "in commonplace obedience to conjunctive orders from headquarters, unconsciously received" (63). "In short, as if materially, a compelling arm of extraordinary muscular power seized hold of him— something which had nothing in common with the spirits and influences that had moved him hitherto" (67–68). This "muscular power" of Arabella is as unquestionable as it is unexplained, and Hardy shows us how her unwelcome suasion affects Jude's speech even as it bypasses his consciousness. He is not the man openly to air resentment against her (or against anyone), so it must emerge in the disowned duplicity of his language:

> "Of course I never dreamt six months ago, or even three, of marrying. It is a complete smashing up of my plans—I mean my plans before I knew you, my dear. But what are they, after all! Dreams about books, and degrees, and impossible fellowships, and all that. Certainly we'll marry: we must!" (80)
>> "Do be quiet, Arabella, and have a little pity on the creature!"
>> "Hold up the pail to catch the blood, and don't talk" . . .
>> "It is a hateful business!" said he.
>> "Pigs must be killed." . . .
>> "Thank God!" Jude said. "He's dead."
>> "What's God got to do with such a messy job as a pig-killing, I should like to know!" she said scornfully. "Poor folks must live."
>> "I know, I know," said he. "I don't scold you." (88)[10]

There is something amiss—literally, something missing—in these speeches, as though Jude's consciousness could not tolerate the tension in his feelings. "I mean my plans before I knew you, my dear" is a feeble lie to Arabella and to himself, and "I don't scold you" is the age-old formulation used to avoid acknowledgment of scolding. Jude is avoiding his own emotional confusions; his language achieves clarity at the expense of candor. Nietzsche refers to this behavior as a particular species of lying: "wishing *not* to see something that one does see; wishing not to see something *as* one sees it. . . . The most common lie is that with which one lies to oneself" (*Twilight of the Idols*, 640).[11]

Jude's discourse with Sue displays as well these pockets of disingenuousness:

> "Of course I may have exaggerated your happiness—one never knows," he continued blandly.
> "Don't think that, Jude, for a moment, even though you may have said it to sting me! . . . If you think I am not happy because he's too old for me, you are wrong."
> "I don't think anything against him—to you, dear." (207)

When he takes her hand a little later, she draws it away. He then retorts that his gesture is innocent and cousinly, whereupon she repents but insists on apprising Phillotson that he has held it:

> "O—of course, if you think it necessary. But as it means nothing it may be bothering him needlessly."
> "Well—are you sure you mean it only as my cousin?"
> "Absolutely sure. I have no feelings of love left in me."
> "That's news. How has it come to be?"
> I've seen Arabella."
> She winced at the hit; then said curiously, "When did you see her?"
> "When I was at Christminster."
> "So she's come back; and you never told me! I suppose you will live with her now?"
> "Of course—just as you live with your husband." (228–29)

She winced at the hit: Hardy underlines the strategic skirmishing within their intimacy. The point is not that Jude is sinister but that he maintains his obscurity; he will not acknowledge the cutting edge of his own voice. These two lovers like to speak of their love as something too sublime for earth, but there is considerable malice lurking in their discourse, and the scene in which he coerces her to marry him by using the threat of a return to Arabella can only be called extortion. Jude's behavior is steeped in the exigencies of his embodied feelings, but his language reflects those exigencies only on condition that it need not acknowledge them. If this be true of Jude, so much the more does it apply to Sue.

I shall say little about Sue since she has already received exhaustive critical commentary. She bears on my argument, however, because it is through her portrayal that Hardy most asserts and then undermines the reader's confidence in a common standard of values capable of articulation. "The 'freedom' she has been at such pains to assert," Ian Gregor notes, "and which . . . would seem to have provided an unequivocal point of vantage . . . [begins to be] seen as something much more ambivalent, a nervous self-enclosure, the swift conceptualizing, safeguarding the self against the invasions of experience. Sue's scrutiny is keen, but it is judiciously angled" (215). Sue's verbal assertions are gradually revealed as fully vulnerable to the contortions of her instinctual life. She is uncontrollably capricious, addicted to a coquetry that (in Robert Heilman's words) "is, in the end, the external drama of inner divisions, of divergent impulses each of which is strong enough to determine action at any time, but not at all times or even with any regularity" (313). She is incurably at war with her own body, and her final behavior amply bears out Freud's contention that the sting of conscience is fueled by aggression turned inward. [12]

Hardy reveals in Sue perhaps his most audacious perceptions about the human aspiration for clarity of purpose and a life devoted to realizing the spirit within. Hardy shows not only that her asserted values have no transcendental basis (they are stained and mediated by the very fact of her being embodied), he shows her bodily grounding to be—itself as well—something opaque and indeterminate, a source of further confusion rather than clarifying authority. She confesses to Jude that "I am called Mrs Richard Phillotson, living a calm wedded life with my counterpart of that name. But I am not really Mrs Richard Phillotson, but a woman tossed about, all alone, with aberrant passions, and unaccountable antipathies" (223). Not really Mrs Richard Phillotson, and not in any clarifying way a woman at all. Jude's great-aunt's friend notes the elusiveness of Sue's natural identity: "She was not exactly a tomboy, you know; but she could do things that only boys do, as a rule" (133).

By way of contrast with such elusiveness, the profound solidity of *Tess of the d'Urbervilles* derives from its hold on sexual identity as something absolute. Sexual identity appears there as an ultimate ground of amoral meaning, lying beneath the relative and collapsible ones of moral assertion. The world of *Jude the Obscure* has become unmoored from this natural certitude. In the portrait of Sue Bridehead Hardy suggests that, to the unappeased spirit in search of articulate paradigms, nothing—not even the body's native stresses—can be reliably categorized. Life is a something foreign to the classificatory demands made by the spirit. In its utterances, its values, and even its bodily grounding, life is a phenomenon of stain, illogic, and obscurity.

Within this context Arabella and Father Time come into focus as the polar opposites of the novel. Arabella lives in the contingent. She is as canny about daily survival and as ignorant of ultimate purposes as Jude is learned in cosmic platitudes and inept in local procedures. She has no goal but knows unerringly the way. She measures accurately the appropriate method for killing a pig just as, during Jude's final illness, she "critically gauges[s] his ebbing life" (407). The stains and deformations of time are unthinkingly accepted by Arabella. Pious and pagan utterances flow forth from her, with equal appositeness, either genuinely attuned to her desire or asserted with conscious hypocrisy. She is true to herself because she recognizes no standard beyond her embodied nature that she could betray. In her very fickleness she places and measures the obscure deceits of others, their attempt to square their incarnate existence with those immaculate values to which it is alien. She is exactly as well adjusted to the meaningless conditions of life as Father Time is incapable of coping with them.

That solemn child is the ultimate doomed Platonist in Hardy's world. Absorbing somewhere in his consciousness the full ravage wrought by time upon value, he has frozen his perception of the world into a posture of unforgivable stasis. He lives in a perpetuated, last-judgment landscape, all things appearing to him in their form of final exhaustion. Accepting time's ravage, he repudiates utterly the mercy and promise of its moment-by-moment process. On the train he passively regards "his companions as if he saw their whole rounded lives rather than their immediate figures" (290). Unlike his mother, whose rough humanity resides in her openness toward process rather than meaning, Father Time has fixed upon an absurd meaning at the expense of process. He "seemed to have begun with the generals of life, and never to have concerned himself with the particulars" (291). His optic can only envisage life as a gathered and complete insult inflicted on himself and others. He is an extreme instance of that mentality that Nietzsche calls "Socratism": "Wherever Socratism turns its searching eyes it sees lack of insight and the power of illusion; and from this lack it infers the essential perversity and reprehensibility of what exists. Basing himself on this point, Socrates conceives it to be his duty to correct existence" (*The Birth of Tragedy*, 87). Father Time corrects existence too. He cancels his role within it.

I began by noting Jude's characteristic desire to be where he is not, a desire that reflects, according to J. Hillis Miller, "the experience of an 'emotional void' within, a distance of oneself from oneself" (xii). Miller claims that this absence in Hardy's characters is at last recognized as inalterable, and that they end by seeking the only release conceivable, that of death. More important to my reading of Hardy is the impact of an "emotional void" upon behavior itself: the pockets of dream-like passivity, of mental absence, that lie submerged within his protagonists' most earnest aspirations, waiting to wreck them. Jude and Clym are only the most reflective instances of a range of characters—Troy, Wildeve, Fitzpiers, Henchard among them—whose project, whatever energetic flourish it may begin with, contains a debilitating emptiness within. Their projects fail because all projects, once embarked on, either fail to meet the conditions of daily life or—meeting them—produce ennui and then disabling fatigue. These characters have sufficient energy to scorn the available, not to create alternatives; and this is so, one finally gathers, because their imagination is stocked with nothing but unrealities. The desirable is keyed to a mental vocabulary that simply negates whatever in Hardy's world can be actually experienced. Thus Hardy dramatizes characters whose consciousness of what they want and why they want it remains continuously out of phase with the vagaries of their incarnate behavior. They have no terms for finding out what they are actually doing, and no way of actually doing what they want. Indeed, they seem, in some central part of their being, to be spirits stunned to find themselves placed on earth and embodied in flesh. This gap between the consciousness of essential being and the opacity of contingent existence they express through a lurking and inexpungeable passivity. At critical moments they blank out.

Jude, for example, first slides back into his married routine with Arabella with an eery complicity. She tells him she can get a day off; he finds the notion "particularly uncongenial," yet says, "Of course, if you'd like to, you can." She tells him the train they can take, and he responds, "As you like." She gathers her luggage, "and they went on to the railway, and made the half-hour's journey to Aldbrickham, where they entered a third-rate inn near the station in time for a late supper" (200–201). They pass the night together. Where, one wants to know, is Jude during this transaction? Bodily, of course, with Arabella, and the effortless complicity of his physical behavior seems dependent on a corresponding mental absence. Jude's spirit has, for the moment, slipped out. Hardy provides no notation of a conflicted state of mind.

Such "absences" mark Jude's spiritual career as well. His campaign displays such a blundering and absentminded sense of purpose that no reader can be surprised by its failure. When, for instance, a casual acquaintance at Marygreen avers that "Such places [as Christminster] be not for such as you," Jude's long-sustained undertaking immediately falters: "It was decidedly necessary to consider facts a little more closely than he had done of late. . . . 'I ought to have thought of this before,' he said, as he journeyed back. 'It would have been better never to have embarked in the scheme at all than to do it without seeing clearly where I am going, or what I am aiming at' " (135). Again, one wonders, where has his consciousness been during these previous years of "preparation"? Why is he so unaware of himself as a conditional creature? When under stress he is incapable of looking about him and charting the most intelligent course; instead he leaps into the transcendent and allusive ideal. Consider his behavior when being pressed to remarry Arabella:

> "I don't remember it," said Jude doggedly. "There's only one woman—but I won't mention her in this Capharnaum!"
>
> Arabella looked towards her father. "Now, Mr. Fawley, be honourable," said Donn. "You and my daughter have been living here together these three or four days, quite on the understanding that you were going to marry her. . . . As a point of honour you must do it now."

"Don't say anything against my honour!" enjoined Jude hotly, standing up. "I'd marry the W—of Babylon rather than do anything dishonour-
able! No reflection on you, my dear. It is a mere rhetorical figure—what
they call in the books, hyperbole."

"Keep your fingers for your debts to friends who shelter you," said
Donn.

"If I am bound in honour to marry her—as I suppose I am—though
how I came to be here with her I know no more than a dead man—marry
her I will, so help me God! I have never behaved dishonourably to a
woman or to any living thing. I am not a man who wants to save himself at
the expense of the weaker among us!"

"There—never mind him, deary," said she, putting her cheek against
Jude's. "Come up and wash your face, and just put yourself tidy, and off
we'll go. Make it up with father." (387)

The scene is remarkable, and Hardy has no other novel in which one
can imagine it. We see strikingly how Jude's allusive words create his "absence" from his coming fate. His mind rises into the empyrean, with
Capharnaum, the Whore of Babylon, rhetorical figures, the theme of honor;
it will not register the meaning of the specific act he is about to commit.
Indeed, he *would* marry the Whore of Babylon because, somehow, his sense
of himself remains idealized—permanently astray from, immune to, the
sordid physical situations in which he finds himself. One hears a sense of
verbally engendered immunity in his bland twaddle about "mere rhetorical
figures," and Hardy nicely places Jude's tone of smug caprice, by having
Donn retort: "Keep your figures for your debts. . . ." Donn and his daughter
are content to humor Jude's proliferation of weightless abstract identities ("I
have never . . . I am not . . ."). The more he breezily defines his unfettered
spirit, the more easily they exploit his befuddled and conditional body.

What we see in such behavior is absence, and absence increasingly
marks Jude's career.[14] He defines himself at first by what he will do, at last by
what he has not done. He cherishes at first expectations of what is to be, at
last memories of what has not happened. His return to Christminster indicates a final surrender of his attempt—at best half-hearted—to realize himself, to make an authentic home for his unsponsored and unreleased spirit.
Thereafter he is given over to the "Remembrance Games." He lives wholly,
now, in the schizoid space between failed expectation and ignored actuality,
his mind focused on poignant scenarios (more fictive than true) with Sue and
Christminster, his body abandoned to approaching death. His last gesture is
characteristically verbal—he dies in words—and as usual he is quoting someone else. I think it is crucial to see that he is not Job; he is not an innocent
and successful man, massively undone by an unholy pact between God and
the devil. Rather, he is obscurely complicit in his own downfall, though it be
his peculiar fate never to identify that complicity, never to find the words
that will tell him who he is in all his incarnate perplexity. His death scene
only gains poignance through its verbal indeterminacy, and it is the apex of

Hardy's art that, four pages later, he can create a dialogue between Arabella and the Widow Edlin that matches Jude's death speech in resonance:

> "Did he forgive her!"
> "Not as I know."
> "Well—poor little thing, 'tis to be believed she's found forgiveness somewhere! She said she had found peace!"
> "She may swear that on her knees to the holy cross upon her necklace till she's hoarse, but it won't be true!" said Arabella. "She's never found peace since she left his arms, and never will again till she's as he is now!"
> (413)

Words at their best reveal the inadequacy of other words, and Hardy puts this last speech with unchallengeable authority in the mouth of Arabella. Rooted in the earth and stained in every way by it, strengthened as much as stained, Arabella places Sue's verbal and emotional evasions before us. Beyond this, though, Arabella's words bear the mark of subjective limitation that is the fate of words in this novel. Behind the verbalized truth that "she's never found peace since she left his arms," there lies, in the silence created by her speech, a truth that is darker yet: that, condemned to a body whose stresses she could neither disown nor make her own, Sue Bridehead found no peace in Jude's arms either. She found no peace anywhere. In this most unsettling of Hardy's novels the obscure spirit is compelled to move, in Eliot's words, "unappeased and peregrine,"[15] able to achieve nowhere—not in thought or feeling, not in the discourse of culture or the ground of nature—a form for its embodiment.

Notes

1. Ian Gregor comments suggestively on this phrase in his excellent study of Hardy (*The Great Web* [London: Faber and Faber, 1974], 210).

2. The most pathetic instances of icons that express the gap, rather than connection, between worshipper and sacred image are the models—first of wood and then of cake—that Jude constructs of Christminster.

3. "Hardy's Sue Bridehead," *NCF* 20(1966):307–23; Heilman's astute analysis considers convention in the novel only indirectly, insofar as Sue's failure to transcend the clichés of her period reveals the extent to which personal identity itself is socially composed.

4. Janet Burstein shows persuasively that in *Jude*, unlike many of the earlier novels, there is no mythic return. The past in all its facets is inaccessible, not least because its language is no longer applicable to the conditions of modern life: "Instead of nurturing human relationships by illuminating personal insights that may be generally valid, language in a postmythic world seems chiefly to reflect the disparity between individual and general or conventional perceptions" ("The Journey Beyond Myth in *Jude the Obscure*," *Texas Studies in Language and Literature* 15(1973):505).

5. Critics like Stewart, Alvarez, Irving Howe, and Ian Gregor have helped me most in my reading of *Jude the Obscure*, because they confront directly the novel's recurrent linguistic awkwardness. None of them argues that the dislocation of discourse is part of Hardy's purpose.

Nevertheless, in their uneasiness they take the reader further into the novel than those critics who speak of Jude as an unproblematic, Promethean, or Job-like hero.

6. John Bayley makes a similar point in his fascinating *Essay on Hardy,* which I came upon while completing my own study: "His [Hardy's] autodidacticism, his acquired learning, helped to disorientate him, as it helps to give that characteristic instability to his prose. There is a sharp contrast in it between the physical perceptions, which are always his own, and the opinions and ideas which seldom are: it is indeed a part of his honesty to advertise their coming from somewhere else" ([Cambridge: Cambridge Univ. Press, 1978], 17).

7. Some such rationale is needed to place a passage like the following: "You know what a weak fellow I am. My two Arch Enemies you know—my weakness for womankind and my impulse to strong liquor. Don't abandon me to them, Sue, to save your own soul only! They have been kept entirely at a distance since you became my guardian-angel!" (361)

This is plausibly how Jude would characterize himself but certainly not—in its capitalized simplicities—an accurate portrait. Eliot's Sweeney says, "I gotta use words when I talk to you," and Jude's words are likewise condemned to come from a cultural stockpile and therefore to remain at a distance from the private dilemma they would describe. Though he pursues a different argument, Jerome H. Buckley also notes the inaccuracy of Jude's self-portrait: "Jude is neither the drunkard nor the amorist; he is betrayed by ordinary appetites and feelings, by his own temperament, and perhaps most of all by the disparity between flesh and spirit in the world itself, the distance between the real and the ideal" (*Season of Youth: The Bildungsroman from Dickens to Golding* [Cambridge, Mass.: Harvard Univ. Press, 1974], 175).

8. In its exploration of the space between formless actuality and substanceless allusion, *Jude the Obscure* is, surprisingly, a precursor of *Ulysses.* Few writers prior to Joyce reveal better than Hardy does (even if unwittingly) the potential arbitrariness of allusive reference, the failure of external verbal contexts to provide alignment for internal embodied dilemmas.

9. Hardy's few references to Nietzsche are dismissive: "To model our conduct on Nature's apparent conduct, as Nietzsche would have taught, can only bring disaster to humanity": so wrote Hardy to *The Academy and Literature* in 1902 (quoted in Florence E. Hardy, *Life of Thomas Hardy* [London: Macmillan, 1962], 315). In 1914 he mentioned Nietzsche again, writing to the *Manchester Guardian* that "[Nietzsche] used to seem to me (I have not looked into him for years) an incoherent rhapsodist who jumps from Macchiavelli to Isaiah as the mood seizes him, whom it is impossible to take seriously as a mentor" (quoted in William R. Rutland, *Thomas Hardy: A Study of his Writings and their Background* [Oxford: Blackwell, 1938], 48).

10. It is worth juxtaposing the notorious pig-killing scene in *Jude the Obscure* against a vastly different treatment of the same material in *A Pair of Blue Eyes:*

> Robert Lickpan, the pig-killer, here seemed called upon to enter the lists of conversation.
>
> "Yes, they've got their particular naturs good-now," he remarked initially. "Many's the rum-tempered pig I've knowed."
>
> "I don't doubt it, Master Lickpan." Martin's answer expressed that his convictions, no less than good manners, demanded the reply.
>
> "Yes," continued the pig-killer, as one accustomed to be heard. "One that I knowed was deaf and dumb, and we couldn't make out what was the matter wi' the pig. 'A would eat well enough when 'a seed the trough, but when his back was turned, you might a-rattled the bucket all day, the poor soul never heard 'ee. Ye could play tricks upon him behind his back, and 'a wouldn't find it out no quicker than poor deaf Grammer Bates. But 'a fatted well, and I never seed a pig open better when 'a was killed, and 'a was very tender eating, very; as pretty a bit of meat as ever you see; you could suck that meat through a quill.
>
> "And another I knowed," resumed the killer, after quickly letting a pint of ale run down his throat of its own accord, and setting down the cup with mathematical exactness upon the spot from which he had raised it—"another went out of his mind."

"How very mournful!" murmured Mrs. Worm.

"Ay, poor thing, 'a did! As clean out of his mind as the cleverest Christian could go. In early life 'a was very melancholy, and never seemed a hopeful pig by no means. 'Twas Andrew Stainer's pig—that's whose pig 'twas."

"I can mind the pig well enough," attested John Smith.

"And a pretty little porker 'a was. And you all know Farmer Buckle's sort? Every jack o' em suffer from the rheumatism to this day, owing to a damp sty they lived in when they were striplings, as 'twere." . . . (New Wessex Edition [London: Macmillan, 1975], 236–37).

The passage is of course whimsical and bucolic, but its legendary porkers are artistically superior to their sentimental counterpart in *Jude,* if only because the latter's "eloquently keen reproach of a creature recognizing at last the treachery of those who had seemed his only friends" (54) is incredible. The pigs in *A Pair of Blue Eyes* are also incredible, but they are not drawn so as to require belief: their interest is openly humorous rather than unpersuasively realistic.

11. See also Richard Benvenuto's argument that Jude's human dignity resides in his capacity to tell such lies to himself and thus continue to value objects that he knows to be tarnished: Arabella, Sue, Christminster ("Modes of Perception: The Will to Live in *Jude the Obscure,*" *Studies in the Novel* 2 (1970): 31–41).

12. Freud's fullest discussion of conscience (in *Civilisation and its Discontents*) provides an unimprovable gloss on Sue Bridehead:

His [the individual's] aggressiveness is introjected, internalized; it is, in point of fact, sent back to where it came from—that is, it is directed towards his own ego. There it is taken over by a portion of the ego, which sets itself over against the rest of the ego as super-ego, and which now, in the form of "conscience," is ready to put into action against the ego the same harsh aggressiveness that the ego would have liked to satisfy upon other, extraneous individuals. The tension between the harsh super-ego and the ego that is subjected to it, is called by us the sense of guilt; it expresses itself as a need for punishment. . . . As long as things go well with a man, his conscience is lenient and lets the ego do all sorts of things; but when misfortune befalls him, he searches his soul, acknowledges his sinfulness, heightens the demands of his conscience, imposes abstinences on himself and punishes himself with penances" (*The Standard Edition of the Complete Psychological Works of Sigmund Freud* [London: The Hogarth Press, 1953–74], 21:123–26).

13. Hardy's use of plot is at moments like this so overtly clumsy that one wonders if he is not verging upon intentional absurdity—an intentional repudiation of the salient lines of a strong plot. For instance, when Jude attempts to commit suicide and the ice ignobly refuses to permit his romantic gesture, we are not far from Beckett's impotent Molloy, helplessly setting about, when he has a spare moment, to open his veins, and never succeeding.

14. The treatment of Jude and Sue's children, unnamed and of no importance while alive, obsessively and injuriously mourned when dead, reveals the same theme of absence.

15. The relevant lines are from "Little Gidding," II:

> But as the passage now presents no hindrance
> To the spirit unappeased and peregrine
> Between two worlds become much like each other,
> So I find words I never thought to speak
> In streets I never thought I should revisit
> When I left my body on a distant shore.

Hardy's Comic Tragedy:
Jude the Obscure

Ronald P. Draper*

In *Unsent Letters,* a series of semifictional, semibiographical letters, Malcolm Bradbury reflects on his time as a young man in the Nottingham of the 1950s, where the youthful avant-garde of the day cadged drinks in the milk bars "and, sitting on park benches, wrote their novels, all of which began: 'The agony continues, unabated.' "[1] These were, surely, the spiritual heirs of Hardy's long-suffering and much-protesting Jude Fawley. However, Bradbury's inarticulately angry young men had less excuse than Hardy's articulate stonemason; and it has to be admitted that, great though its charms may be, Nottingham does not quite possess the air of hoary antiquity combined with romantic idealization that makes the Christminster (alias Oxford) of *Jude the Obscure* such a potent symbol of history and convention fused into the same fatally attractive environment.

Christminster is inhabited by people and by ghosts. The ghosts are literary figures whose writings have so shaped the image of the place for Jude that it becomes an elusive fabrication of intertextuality, represented by the anthology with which chapter 1 of part 2 ("At Christminster") concludes—its farrago of "memorable words" from Arnold, Sir Robert Peel, Gibbon, Browning, Newman, Keble, Addison, and Bishop Ken sounding in his ears as he falls asleep on his first night there. The people are workingmen and -women whom Jude later comes to see as the real citizens: "These struggling men and women before him were the reality of Christminster, though they knew little of Christ or Minster."[2] But if this statement seems to imply that a kind of progress is made from literary illusion to sociological enlightenment, that impression is misleading. Jude never actually banishes the ghosts altogether. Alternation between dream and reality becomes the pendulum on which his nature swings, and which likewise provides the pattern of the novel's plot. "The agony" in this proleptic novel "continues, unabated" because of this permanent condition of instability, which in itself is a manifestation of the psychology of the avant-garde. Thus another hard-won insight of Jude's is that he and Sue were in advance of their day: "The time was not ripe for us!" he says, toward the end of their catastrophic partnership. "Our ideas were fifty years too soon to be any good to us" (419). To be part of the avant-garde is to dream a dream of a better world, but also to bump up constantly against the unreformed, and almost, it seems, unregenerate, nature of the real world, so that, as Jude goes on to say, the resistance inevitably encountered by advanced ideas brings "reaction" (which he attributes to Sue) and "recklessness and ruin" (which he sees as the consequence for himself).

*This essay was written specifically for this volume and is published here for the first time by permission of the author.

Such words suggest a somewhat ambiguous attitude toward avant-gardism: and if I have begun by treating what many readers regard as the most tragic of Hardy's novels in a somewhat comic manner it is because it seems to me a moot point whether *Jude the Obscure* should be designated as comedy or tragedy. Perhaps it did to Hardy, too, for when the novel was serialized in *Harper's New Monthly Magazine* (prior to publication in book form), the first installment appeared under the title "The Simpletons" and the second under the changed title of "Hearts Insurgent" (see "Note on the Text," 438). This ambiguity continues in the character of the work as we have it in the published version, where Hardy opts for the more neutral title *Jude the Obscure*. Thus from one point of view Jude can be seen as a heroic figure struggling to realize a noble ambition to become an enlightened scholar, who is defeated by the inert, selfish condition of the society in which he has the misfortune to find himself, while from another he appears as a foolishly inveterate idealist who seems quite incapable of learning from experience. His career is a remarkable series of seesaws, deliberately intended, it would seem from one of the letters to Edmund Gosse that are included in the *Life*, to illustrate a contrast:

> The "grimy"features of the story go to show the contrast between the ideal life a man wished to lead, and the squalid real life he was fated to lead. The throwing of the pizzle, at the supreme moment of his [Jude's] young dream, is to sharply initiate this contrast. But I must have lamentably failed, as I feel I have, if this requires explanation and is not self-evident. The idea was meant to run all through the novel. It is, in fact, to be discovered in *everybody*'s life, though it lies less on the surface perhaps than it does in my poor puppet's.[3]

In the actual presentation of this particular scene (part 1, chapter 6) the contrast between ideal and real is more like Fielding than Greek tragedy, with Arabella as a very plausible Molly Seagrim. In this connection Hardy himself, reacting to some adverse reviews, says: "As to the 'coarse' scenes with Arabella, the battle in the schoolroom, etc., the newspaper critics might, I thought, have sneered at them for their Fieldingism rather than for their Zolaism," and he adds that he has "felt akin locally to Fielding, so many of his scenes having been laid down this way [he writes from Max Gate, near Dorchester], and his home near" (*Life*, 273). Furthermore, Jude's self-communings not only have the exaggerated air of a man in cloud-cuckoo land, but also come near to being comically blasphemous: "Yes, Christminster shall be my Alma Mater; and I'll be her beloved son, in whom she shall be well pleased" (58). What follows may be the gods' revenge on hubris, but, if so, it comes in the form of a rapid descent from the sublime to the ridiculous, which is more like Augustan bathos: "On a sudden something smacked him sharply in the ear, and he became aware that a soft cold substance had been flung at him, and had fallen at his feet"—a something which he immediately recognizes as "the characteristic part of a barrow-pig."

Nor is this the first time that such a thing happens to Jude. How seriously Hardy intended his phrase *my poor puppet* (in the extract from the *Life*
quoted above) I am not sure, but it has a certain appropriateness. One of the
first scenes in the novel has young Jude failing in his task of defending
Farmer Troutham's corn and luxuriating in the sense that a "magic thread of
fellow-feeling united his own life" with that of the birds, only to become all at
once "conscious of a smart blow upon his buttocks, followed by a loud clack,
which announced to his surprised senses that the clacker [with which he
should have been scaring off the birds] had been the instrument of offence
used" (35). It is much the same when Jude's earnest attempt to con the Greek
New Testament (signaled to the reader with deliberate pomp by isolating its
title in the text in capitalized Greek lettering) is abruptly displaced by the
sex instinct aroused in him by Arabella, which "seemed to care little for his
reason and his will, nothing for his so-called elevated intentions, and moved
him along, as a violent schoolmaster a schoolboy he has seized by the collar"
(64).

There are touches of this comic exaggeration in the presentation of Sue
as well. Aunt Drusilla, for example, illustrates Sue's naughtiness as a young
girl with a tale of how she walked into a pond with her petticoats pulled up
above her knees, saying: "Move on, aunty! This is no sight for modest eyes!"
(130). This preludes her teasing perversity as a woman who provokes her
lovers, but denies them satisfaction. The extraordinary psychology underlying such coy behavior has excited much excellent critical comment (including Robert B. Heilman's celebrated article, and Rosemary Sumner's and
Rosemary Morgan's more recent books),[4] and Hardy himself elaborates on it
with the care of one fascinated. In the preface to the 1912 edition of *Jude* he
cites—with evident gratification—the opinion of a German reviewer who
told him "that Sue Bridehead, the heroine, was the first delineation in fiction
of the woman who was coming into notice in her thousands every year—the
woman of the feminist movement—the slight, pale 'bachelor' girl—the intellectualized, emancipated bundle of nerves that modern conditions were
producing, mainly in cities as yet; who does not recognize the necessity for
most of her sex to follow marriage as a profession, and boast themselves as
superior people because they are licensed to be loved on the premises." Yet
in places, at least, the narrator of the novel finds her a subject for ironic
banter rather than sociological comment—as when he observes that "Sue's
logic was extraordinarily compounded, and seemed to maintain that before a
thing was done it might be right to do, but that being done it became wrong;
or, in other words, that things which were right in theory were wrong in
practice" (239).

The Hardy of such wry little satires-of-circumstance poems as "Ah, Are
You Digging on My Grave?" and "The Curate's Kindness" is also present in
Jude the Obscure. For example, the story of Jude and the composer of "The
Foot of the Cross" might well have been turned into verse; and though the
pun with which the composer dismisses music ("But music is a poor staff to

lean on") may not be a very good one, there is something ludicrous about the eagerness with which he produces his wine list as a practical, commercial alternative. The difference, however, between Hardy the poet in this vein and Hardy the novelist is that the novelist widens the listener's or reader's response. There is a significant change in the musician's manner when he discovers that Jude is a poor man rather than a prosperous potential buyer, and the effect of the disclosure on Jude is to make him abandon his hope of finding a mentor capable of giving his miseries a sympathetic hearing. The reader takes in these reactions; they modify the undoubted sense of the comic in the episode; and in the still-wider context of Jude's career the comedy dissolves into that recurrent pattern of illusion and disillusion which makes Jude more a representative of the vanity of human wishes—a Johnsonian figure driven on to pursue the beckoning ideal, but doomed perpetually to disappointment.

The comedy, then, may be regarded as something embittered by the prevailing tone of disenchantment. This does not take us far enough, however. There is a more frustratingly tragic power at work. The comically external force that repeatedly makes its violent impact on Jude is the other side of a tragic force that seems arbitrarily to take over the novel and produce a plot "almost geometrically constructed." This is a phrase, yet again, taken from one of the letters to Gosse (10 November 1895; *Life*, 271). These letters show Hardy fully conscious of what he is doing—though sometimes admitting, sometimes denying, premeditation. The one dated 20 November 1895 is perhaps the most specific: "Of course the book is all contrasts—or was meant to be in its original conception. Alas, what a miserable accomplishment it is, when I compare it with what I meant to make it!—e.g. Sue and her heathen gods against Jude's reading the Greek testament; Christminster academical, Christminster in the slums; Jude the saint, Jude the sinner; Sue the Pagan, Sue the saint; marriage, no marriage; &c., &c." (*Life*, 272–73).

These are contrasts which are not only juxtapositions, like the descent from dream to pizzle, or Jude's dying recitation from the Book of Job interrupted by cheering from the spectators at the Remembrance games, but also reversals in the fates of the two central figures, so contrived that they appear forever mismatched. The teasing character of Sue seen against this background becomes the expression of an ironic power that is itself perverse. The result is an enormous elaboration of the X-pattern that Hardy had already employed in *The Return of the Native* where Clym Yeobright and Eustacia Vye encounter each other when they are set on opposite courses—he to return to his native heath, she to do all she can to escape it. In *Jude the Obscure* the principals change intellectual places to their mutual frustration: Sue begins as the sceptic and disbeliever, Arnoldian Hellenist and opponent of convention, respectability and puritanical duty, but after the deaths of her children she undergoes a nervous collapse that is followed by reaction toward the conformity she had previously despised ("Sue the Pagan, Sue the saint"). Jude, Gothic rather than Hellenic both in his ideals and in his trade as stonemason, begins as devotee of Christminster; modulates to highly orthodox Christianity, during which phase he hopes to become a priest ("Jude the saint"); and then—partly as a result of his disillusioning encounters with reality, but even more, and with intense irony, as a result of his absorption of Sue's liberalism—swings round to more modern ideas, becoming a skeptic and finally a complete opponent of the conventional establishment of his day ("Jude the sinner").

The "marriage, no marriage" part of this design is still more strikingly "geometric" in execution: First Jude is married *to* the intellectually incompatible Arabella, and Sue *to* the sexually incompatible Phillotson; then Sue is divorced *from* Phillotson, and Jude *from* Arabella, to form a liaison with each other that is "no marriage," yet spiritually a perfect one (in terms of the plot, this is the junction of their X); and finally Sue, under the influence of her masochistic reversion to orthodoxy, is married again *to* Phillotson, and Jude, under the influence of his weakness for drink, is married again *to* Arabella. Though the pattern sometimes strains the reader's credulity, it powerfully reinforces the sense generated throughout the novel that man's, and woman's, aspirations are mockingly out of tune with the actual shape of their lives.

There are also hints in the novel (supported again by one of Hardy's comments to Gosse on "a doom or curse of hereditary temperament" [*Life*, 271]) that the destiny that misshapes the lives of Jude and Sue might be linked with inherited tendencies. Aunt Drusilla warns them that the family has a bad history of wedlock, and on the eve of their abortive attempt at marrying—largely for the sake of little Time—their wedding "guest," Mrs. Edlin, tells them an ill-omened tale of marriage breakup that leads to the boy's comically solemn warning: "If I was you, mother, I wouldn't marry father!" (301). Sue likewise reacts to Mrs. Edlin's "horrid" story with the comment "It makes me feel as if a tragic doom overhung our family, as it did the house of Atreus" (302)—though as Sue is somewhat prone to exaggeration, this makes only a qualified effect; and Jude's rejoinder, "Or the house of Jeroboam," followed by "said the quondam theologian," lessens rather than strengthens its force. Thus if heredity is an issue, it lacks the seriousness of a centrally tragic idea. It is at best just a minor contribution to the sense that the celestial cards are stacked against Jude and Sue.

Sue's "tragic doom" is, in fact, a phrase that sounds a little out of tune with the curious music of *Jude the Obscure*. Dark and gloomy notes are recurrent, and the reader is given the impression that even when things appear to be going right for Jude and Sue, they won't stay that way for long. To heighten that effect, Hardy has a habit of undercutting even the limited intervals of happiness in their lives, as when the carefree excursion made by Jude and Sue to the Great Wessex Agricultural Show is rounded off with a characteristic memento mori from little Time: "I should like the flowers very very much, if I didn't keep on thinking they'd be all withered in a few days!" (316). Nevertheless, to borrow Lawrence's phrase (in the *Study of Thomas*

Hardy), there is nothing "necessarily tragic" in Hardy's tragedy. In a well-known pronouncement on Tolstoy's Anna Karenina and Hardy's Eustacia, Tess, and Sue, Lawrence asserts that these heroines "were not at war with God, only with Society. Yet they were all cowed by the mere judgment of man upon them, and all the while by their own souls they were right." As an observation this can be extended beyond these particular women; and, indeed Lawrence himself generalizes it to make it the distinctive "weakness of modern tragedy." What destroys Hardy's protagonists, despite their frequent tendency to complain against some hostile force that they seem to regard as inherent in nature, is their inability to adjust to the world in which they live. There is perhaps a level beyond this at which Hardy himself questions the rationality of a creation that permits of such mismatching between individual and the world, and this may ultimately be a justification for the rhetoric of fate; but on a more immediate level of perception his characters are frequently seen to be the authors of their own undoing by the process of engaging in what Lawrence calls "a war with Society" rather than the ultimate powers of the universe.

This is certainly the case with Sue and Jude. They are characters who in some respects may be regarded as neo-Ibsenites, seeking to live by a new individualistic code that puts them at odds with the insistent demands for conformity made on them by their Victorian world, and that keeps them in a state of perpetual tension with society. Sue ultimately collapses under the strain this struggle entails, and becomes a sort of "tragic" figure in her perverse capitulation to convention. But her status as tragic protagonist is ambivalent: She may be seen either as a neurotic woman, vainly justifying her weakness by a set of spuriously advanced ideas, or as a genuinely heroic "new woman," too isolated as yet to survive the hostility that her convictions attract. Hardy, it seems, chooses not to resolve this ambiguity; though he does offer the suggestion that she is a special type—a type likely to become more numerous in the future—for whom special conditions ought to be devised.

Jude, for his part, seems to grow in stature and become increasingly independent of the world's opinion, but he is ultimately defeated by the effects of Sue's collapse, which he, not quite unwittingly, helps to bring about by his obsession with Christminster. When the latter-day Sue develops extreme orthodox notions about the indissolubility of marriage, he partly realizes that Christminster—for which in this context one can surely read "the Oxford Movement"—is precisely the place that has fostered them; but he does not seem to remember that it was he, after all, who brought her back there against her better judgment. (If he is not quite the proverbial dog needlessly returning to his own vomit, he is rather like the venturer on a second marriage whose action, according to Dr. Johnson, represents "the triumph of hope over experience.")

Such causes and effects belong to what Lawrence defines as the "smaller system of morality, the one grasped and formulated by the human consciousness" as distinct from "the terrific action of unfathomed nature" that is the background against which Hardy's tragic action is set in most of his novels. To argue, however, as Lawrence does, that this "smaller system" is also a diminished system incapable of generating a true tragic effect is to ignore the fact that tragedy, especially in the novel, is itself a matter of "the human consciousness." There is no tragedy unless the characters' minds are influenced. Even the traditional tragedy that Lawrence finds in Shakespeare and the Greeks presupposes an ethos that is subscribed to by the audience, or is seen as powerful in its effect on the minds of the characters on stage, or, as frequently happens, is shared by both. The tragic reverberations are especially powerful when the latter condition obtains (i.e., when an ethos commands the assent of both characters and audience). An outstanding example is Sophocles's *Antigone*. The Greek audience was not only aware of Antigone's motive for insisting on the burial of her brother's corpse, but in all probability also accepted the idea of burial as a universal duty imposed by the laws of life. What she believed, and the way she acted on her belief, was seen not as a private and personal quirk, but as a sacred duty backed by divine authority. But, as the Hegelian interpretation of the play demonstrates, there is another view, inherent in the text, whether or not it was Sophocles's intended "meaning," which sees the burial as the source of two potentially equal compulsions—that which operates on Creon as well as that which operates on Antigone. Creon feels compelled to forbid the burial because the brother had rebelled against the state. He is motivated by a sense of public, political duty that is every bit as strong as Antigone's private, religious duty. Once this point is perceived, the audience's response becomes a matter of balanced sympathies rather than absolute identification with one ethical mode, and with this balance creeps in the possibility of doubt. Creon may be seen as insecure in his tyranny, but Antigone may also be seen as extreme in her devotion. The modern condition of intellectual uncertainty is born, and the interpretation of the "tragedy" becomes dependent on how the characters' actions are related to their convictions.

Jude the Obscure is a tragedy in which this process is still-further advanced, and, indeed, much further advanced than in any of Hardy's own preceding work. The characters' underlying insecurities are brought nearer the surface, and the audience—now converted into the more reflective novel reader—is invited to judge them against a background that is presented as still more insecure. Education becomes a major, and necessarily ambiguous, force acting upon the minds of the central characters to detach them from communal values. The "terrific action of unfathomed nature," which, as D. H. Lawrence rightly observes, plays such an important part in the Wessex novels, recedes in significance as the territory of *Jude* extends beyond the Dorset (or "South Wessex") heartland to "Mid," "Upper," and "North Wessex" and as its peripatetic characters migrate from Marygreen to Alfredston, Christminster, Aldbrickham, Kennetbridge, Stoke Barehills, Melchester, and Shaston with a restless movement even greater than that of Tess Durbyfield's wanderings.

Christminster, the recurrent focus of Jude's odyssey, is itself a major center of education, functioning as the nodal point of his illusions, while simultaneously offering the strongest contrast, and the greatest resistance, to them. To Jude's old acquaintance, John, it is merely a place of "auld crumbling buildings, half church, half almshouse, and not much going on at that" (132), but to Jude himself it is "a unique centre of thought and religion—the intellectual and spiritual granary of this country," its apparent inactivity being only "the stillness of infinite motion—the sleep of the spinning-top." This exchange takes place in part 2, chapter 6. But in the same chapter, only a few pages later, Christminster, as reflected in the person of the Master of Biblioll—sole respondent to Jude's pathetic letters begging for intellectual assistance—becomes neither of these things, but simply an expression of the established social structure. The august academic's reply to Jude is couched in terms that embody the received wisdom of conformity: "judging from your description of yourself as a working-man, I venture to think that you will have a much better chance of success in life by remaining in your own sphere and sticking to your trade than by adopting any other course" (136–37). The restlessness of his spirit, nourished, if inadequately, by his autodidact culture, urges Jude into motion, while society would have him be static. This stability, as seen by the self-educated Jude, is, however, merely another form of illusion. Within another two paragraphs he stands at the Fourways, a crossing point of thronging activity in the center of the city, and senses that here is "a book of humanity infinitely more palpitating, varied, and compendious than the gown life" (137). Its range is wider, both geographically and historically ("men had stood and talked of Napoleon, the loss of America, the execution of King Charles, the burning of the Martyrs, the Crusades, the Norman Conquest, possibly of the arrival of Caesar"), and it includes the vital movement of the sexes as well ("loving, hating, coupling, parting"). And as he perceives this living, changing nature of the city, Jude also perceives the further irony that those who formally represent the processes of education, the students and teachers of Christminster university, "were not Christminster in a local sense at all." The Arnoldian stability of this fictionalized Oxford is itself an illusion; the reality is not academic, but popular, and partakes of the changing, fluctuating consciousness of men and women.

It is one of the many ironies of this novel that Jude, the young man "on the move," should, initially at least, hitch his wagon to such a motionless and dully glowing star as static "Christminster academical": and a still greater irony that when he is more truly enlightened by the intelligence of Sue, his education should crucify him on the cross of her insecure relapse into Christminster conservatism. To become a modern, individualized consciousness is to court this kind of disaster, since it is a process that necessarily involves uprooting and isolation. Jude and Sue's nomadic life dramatizes their separation from the conformist world of their day. In one very obvious way it is their refusal to abide by the conventions of marriage that leads to Jude's loss of employment with Biles and Willis and to the gossip that subsequently drives him and his family away from Aldbrickham. By Lawrentian standards, this is a trivial basis for tragedy, something Jude and Sue ought to have been capable of rising above. It is not, however, as cause and effect that this social ostracism makes its chief impact on the reader, but as outward sign and symbol of the exposed and vulnerable state to which Jude and Sue are reduced. As "free spirits" they are at the mercy of their own mental fluctuations, alienated from the unthinking support of an "objective" social structure by the very freethinking nature of their own thoughtfulness.

That this liberated couple should ultimately move back to Christminster—the place of all places that, as Sue intuitively realizes, they ought to avoid—is difficult to account for. But, again, explanation at the level of cause and effect is relatively unimportant. What Christminster represents for Jude is an overriding compulsion to find his home in an ideal community of learning—a "university" town in the true sense of the word, where he could find a proper role by virtue of his innate worth and dedication. The yearning for such a Platonic society in which he might fulfil his aspirations is so great that it draws him despite the repeatedly discouraging lessons of experience. And, paradoxically, for Sue as well (despite her initial reluctance), Christminster becomes a transcendent goal, embodying for her, however, that conformity which exercises its emotional hold over her and dictates her conduct in defiance of her emancipated reason. Her rejection of traditional institutions and the traditional role of woman in the earlier parts of the novel may have its intellectual justification (there is little evidence to suggest that Hardy is adopting an antifeminist stance), but her coquettish behavior and her teasing perversity reveal how shallowly these "advanced" ideas have taken root in her personality. Her intellectualism is a willful, hothouse growth, not a mature development; it is brittle and always vulnerable to an emotional crisis. One of her rare moments of true insight is when, having caught sight of her divorced husband, Phillotson, in the streets of Christminster, she feels "a curious dread of him; an awe, or terror, of conventions I don't believe in," which comes over her "like a sort of creeping paralysis" (348). For her, as for Jude, the journey to Christminster becomes a savage pilgrimage, with absurd and fantastic moments, testifying to the inner compulsions of modern pilgrims of the intellect.

Still, nothing in an artistically mature Hardy novel is as straightforward as that. The recurrence of such themes as rootlessness and peripatetic wandering in *Jude the Obscure* cannot automatically be equated with the tragicomically insecure. Arabella, it must be remembered, is just as much of a wanderer as either Jude or Sue—if not more so, since her uprooting from the countryside takes her not only to the same urban centers of Aldbrickham and Christminster as Jude and Sue, but also to London, the metropolitan antithesis of Wessex, and even as far away as Australia. Yet she remains firmly in control of herself. She, too, is unconventional, not least in her method of wooing, and quite unembarrassed by traditional sentiments of motherhood. The difference is that she knows herself emotionally, and is clever enough to satisfy her instincts within the appearances demanded by a conventional society. If Sue is the New, and insecure, Eve, representative of the vulnerability of the immature avant-garde, Arabella is the Old Eve, secure in her power to get what she wants by consciously manipulating conventions that have no unconscious hold over her. Sue and Arabella can also be seen as the embodiments of the Spirit and the Flesh respectively, which, failing to cohere in the same woman, split Jude so that he becomes dangerously divided against himself—exposed to destructive oscillations between intelligence and sexuality, heroic self-denial and abysmal drunkenness. But neither Sue nor Arabella is a mere morality figure. Each is a convincingly realized character in herself—often, indeed, more acutely observed and plausibly portrayed than Jude. Jude often seems like a projection of Hardy's own triple preoccupation with class, convention, and learning; but Sue and Arabella seem to be created from knowledge of actual women (Sue, in particular, undoubtedly owes something to Tryphena Sparks). They may still be a man's portrayal of woman, and the work of a man who is himself the product of Victorian values, even though rebelling against them. But Arabella in particular is a character who stands outside the ideals that Hardy derived from other men, such as Shelley and John Stuart Mill; and her downright earthiness brings the novel into contact with a world that is neither etherealized by intelligence nor frustrated by convention. In a comedy she might well be the heroine by virtue of her capacity to adjust to reality; in this tragedy, which so often verges on comedy, she embodies a female will that is reasonably good-natured when getting its own way, but untrammeled by conscience or guilt when dealing with opposition. She is ruthless and cunning in the ways of the world, so that she can use the sensitivity of others to her own advantage. Jude is thus putty in her hands precisely because he is unworldly and lacks her instinct for self-preservation.

It is also an element in the tragedy of Sue and Jude that they cannot live, as Arabella can, by instinct. Sue's original marriage to Phillotson is effected almost in violation of her physical feelings, as she admits when Aunt Drusilla says that he is one of those men "that no woman of any niceness can stomach" (210). Sue's own sexual appetite is not very strong—it operates negatively by making her unable to sleep with Phillotson, rather than positively in response to the virility of Jude. Jude, on the other hand, is a healthy sexual animal (in that respect, Arabella is his true partner), but his sexuality is so contravened by his conscious aspirations that it often seems to become merely a trap for him to fall into when blinded by his extravagantly high-minded notions. The animal in him takes revenge for being so neglected in the interest of the spiritual; and his thirst for drink functions in much the same way. Arabella, by contrast, manages to accommodate her instinct very successfully. Sue's dread of losing spontaneity by marriage—the formal process by which a woman is "licensed to be loved on the premises" (278)—is quite alien to Arabella, who is, ironically, both more calculating and more relaxed than Sue ever manages to be. Deceitful and exploitative as she is,

Arabella can live spontaneously within the appearance of conformity (even though in one phase of her life she is actually guilty of the crime of bigamy), while Sue resists the chains of society only to live perpetually on edge and in a state of self-conscious anxiety.

It is thus impossible to pin down the tragic effect in *Jude the Obscure* to one version of tragedy. Its very modernity consists in this—that its episodes can seem both harrowing and ludicrous, and that its two main characters can seem to be both self-consciously perverse and the victims of a hypocritical, uncomprehending society. If there is a central, unifying theme it is probably to be found in the maladjustment associated with the struggle toward liberation and modernity that makes tragically social misfits of Jude and Sue. Education, in its widest sense, plays a major part in this: Christminster deludes the hero and Melchester oppresses the heroine.

Yet far from being a diatribe against the evils of education, *Jude the Obscure* is, on the contrary, a passionate plea on its behalf. In his 1912 preface Hardy expressed a wry sympathy with the disgusted "American man of letters" who bought a copy of the novel because the reviewers told him it was a scandalous work, only (to his disappointment) to find it "a religious and ethical treatise." Jude's dream of self-improvement is his undoing, and Sue's inability to bring her emotions into accord with her advanced opinions is fatal to the happiness of both of them; but there is no moral to be drawn that would support the status quo ante. Neither the Master of Biblioll's advice nor Jude's dying repetition of the words from *Job*, "Let the day perish wherein I was born," receives the author's endorsement or is expected to gain the reader's approval. Unlike, say, the ending of *King Lear*—where there is a complete sense of exhaustion and Kent's words on Lear, "He hates him / That would upon the rack of this tough world / Stretch him out longer" (V.iii.313–15), command universal agreement—the ending of *Jude* is one of unresigned laceration. The cries from the Commemoration sounding so discordantly against Jude's biblical incantation still carry the burden of discontent with the Christminster that is, as opposed to the Christminster that ought to be— the Christminster of Jude's imagination; and this is a burden that has accompanied Jude throughout his career. Similarly, Arabella's final words on Sue, "She's never found peace since she left his arms, and never will again till she's as he is now!" (428), operate to subvert the pious note of peace on which Mrs. Edlin would end Sue's story. The pulse of protest still throbbing under these words reminds the reader of that refusal to conform which gave Sue her vitality and charm in spite of all, while in Jude's black chorus there still survives an energy of dissatisfaction that focuses on the gap between the ideal and the real in Christminster.

It is this continuing impatience that especially distinguishes *Jude the Obscure* from traditional tragedy. There are hints that things might already be changing for the better so that a future poor scholar with the aspirations of Jude might not be left to rot in such embittered obscurity, and to this extent Jude's case might be felt as a provisional one only. But from within the circumstances in which he found himself, Jude has been shown struggling to affirm the creativity of the spirit, despite the inertness of established institutions. He has acted, albeit often quixotically and sometimes foolishly, in accordance with the novel's epigraph, "the letter killeth." So has Sue, until the point where her inner contradictions have suffocated her will. Although neither protagonist is given a traditionally tragic ending, in the form of Hamlet's "the readiness is all" or Antigone's splendidly convinced defiance (indeed, it may be that Hardy deliberately parodies such endings in Sue's hollow resignation and Jude's final curse), the temper of the novel itself continues to deride the barrenness of conformity. The restlessness on which the novel concludes complicates its tone and perhaps aborts its tragic status; but such an ending keeps it nonetheless appropriately true to the instability that it has fostered throughout. And what certainly survives is the sense that Jude and Sue in their heyday were, after their fashion, sincere seekers for truth, and that, whatever the rights and wrongs, the folly and wisdom, of their actual accomplishments, they did make a heroic attempt to live not by the letter but by the spirit. The result is, generically speaking, a hybrid—a wild "Polonial" novel, tragical-comical-historical-antipastoral-satirical, and even parodic—but nonetheless compelling and absorbing for all that.

Notes

1. Malcolm Bradbury, *Unsent Letters* (London: Deutsch, 1988), 96.

2. Thomas Hardy, *Jude the Obscure*, ed. Terry Eagleton, New Wessex Edition (London: Macmillan, 1974), 137; hereafter cited in the text.

3. Florence Emily Hardy, *The Life of Thomas Hardy, 1840–1928* (London: Macmillan, 1962, 1972), 272; hereafter cited in the text, identified by "*Life*").

4. Robert E. Heilman, "Hardy's Sue Bridehead," *Nineteenth-Century Fiction* 20 (1966): 307–23; Rosemary Sumner, *Thomas Hardy: Psychological Novelist* (London: Macmillan, 1981); Rosemary Morgan, *Women and Sexuality in the Novels of Thomas Hardy* (New York: Routledge, Chapman & Hall, 1988).

INDEX